BREAK FREE OF THE

HOW TO

RPARENTING TRAP

RAISE

AND PREPARE YOUR

AN ADULT

KID FOR SUCCESS

JULIE LYTHCOTT-HAIMS

"THE RIGHT BOOK AT THE RIGHT TIME."
—Daniel H. Pink, *New York Times* bestselling author of *Drive* and *A Whole New Mind*

Additional Praise for *How to Raise an Adult*

"The best parenting advice . . . Our children are engaged in the serious work of becoming an adult. With this book, Lythcott-Haims provides the missing user manual." —*Chicago Tribune*

"This book is the antidote to helicopter parenting. Lythcott-Haims's research, combined with a decade of experience as a Stanford dean, makes for some important insights into the state of parenting in America today." —*San Francisco Chronicle*

"Run, don't walk, to your nearest bookstore and get this book! It's Malcolm Gladwell meets Paul Tough meets Madeline Levine in a fresh, timely take on raising excellent adults from former Stanford freshmen admissions dean and parent Julie Lythcott-Haims. Never preachy, and oh-so-relatable, Lythcott-Haims is spot-on with her approach to parenting, overparenting, and preparing your children for the adult world." —*Speaking of Apraxia*

"*How to Raise an Adult* is a total no-brainer to read if you have a kid in college, about to go to college, has ever gone to college, or will ever go to college. Seriously, if you are a parent with college in your future, current, or past—stop reading this blog post and go and find this book. . . . A gift to all of us who are educators, and to all of us who are parents." —*Inside Higher Ed*

"[*How to Raise an Adult*] may just be the *Black Hawk Down* of helicopter parenting. Lythcott-Haims . . . Stanford's former dean of freshmen and undergraduate advising, has seen varieties of extreme parental interference suggesting not just a lack of common sense, but a lack of wisdom and healthy boundaries . . . When parents laugh and enjoy the moment but also teach the satisfaction of hard work, when they listen closely but also give their children space to become who they are, they wind up with kids who know how to work hard, solve problems, and savor the moment, too. In other words, get a life, and your child just might do the same someday." —*The New York Times Book Review*

"[*How to Raise an Adult*] is refreshing in many ways, and as parents ourselves, we highly recommend it." —*The News & Observer*

"Julie Lythcott-Haims is a national treasure. She is a psychologist, sociologist, and anthropologist rolled into one, recording the attitudes and rituals of twenty-first-century smart kids who can't tie their shoelaces—and of their anxious, hovering parents. Reminding us that we are charged with transforming children into adults capable of meeting the challenges of life head-on, Lythcott-Haims dispenses compassion and a good kick in the pants in equal and appropriate measure. A must-read for every parent who senses that there is a healthier and saner way to raise our children."
—Madeline Levine,
author of the *New York Times* bestsellers
The Price of Privilege and *Teach Your Children Well*

"In her easy-to-read prose . . . the author does a superb job of laying out the facts . . . Her advice is sound and obviously much needed . . . if parents want to raise productive adults." —*Kirkus Reviews*

"Have the good intentions of American parents gone awry? In this timely and bracing work, Julie Lythcott-Haims chronicles the many dangers of overparenting—from thwarting children's growth to hurting their job prospects to damaging parents' own well-being. Then she charts a smart, compassionate alternative approach that treats kids as wildflowers to be nourished rather than bonsai trees to be cultivated. For parents who want to foster hearty self-reliance instead of hollow self-esteem, *How to Raise an Adult* is the right book at the right time." —Daniel H. Pink,
author of the *New York Times* bestsellers
Drive and *A Whole New Mind*

"I've loved this book from the moment I saw the title. Julie Lythcott-Haims understands that the goal of parenting should be to raise autonomous adults, not have name-brand college admissions to brag about. Her double perspective—as a mother of teenagers and a former longtime freshman dean at Stanford—makes her uniquely equipped to show parents how to do exactly that. Wise, honest, compassionate, and deeply informed, *How to Raise an Adult* ought to be at the top of everybody's stack of parenting books." —William Deresiewicz, author of the *New York Times* bestseller *Excellent Sheep: The Miseducation of the American Elite and the Way to a Meaningful Life*

"A convincing vision of overprotected, overparented, overscheduled kids . . . After presenting the problem in detail (through interviews with college admissions officers, educators, parents, and others), she offers a number of viable solutions . . . This vigorous text will give parents the backup needed to make essential changes."

—*Publishers Weekly*

"Lythcott-Haims has written an accessible book about a serious problem in current U.S. society that is having major and long-lasting consequences."
—*PyscCRITIQUES*

"Some of the suggestions [in *How to Raise an Adult*] . . . are great advice that we can heed as grandparents. And it's not too late to incorporate some of her ideas for our adult children." —*AARP.org*

"Lythcott-Haims wrote this intriguing read with empathy and insight, offering multiple strategies for bringing up healthier children who can thrive as adults." —*Stanford Magazine*

"As a psychologist, sociologist, anthropologist, and mother rolled into one, Lythcott-Haims skillfully reminds us that we are charged with transforming children into adults capable of meeting the challenges of life head-on, with self-reliance and confidence." —*Wellbeing Magazine*

"While empathizing with the parental hopes and, especially, fears that lead to overhelping, Lythcott-Haims offers practical alternative strategies that underline the importance of allowing children to make their own mistakes and develop the resilience, resourcefulness, and inner determination necessary for success." —*Tips on Life & Love from Simon & Schuster*

"While the book aims to show us how to better raise adults, Lythcott-Haims also shows how this will make us better adults. . . . The timing of Lythcott-Haims wonderful book could not be better. The pendulum has swung away from helicopter parenting . . . and parents are looking for the guidance and insight in finding a better way. Lythcott-Haims offers readers just that." —*Grown and Flown*

"These aren't the usual self-help tips endlessly recycled in parenting bestsellers. Think of them as encouragement for people who, finding themselves surrounded by frantically whirring helicopter parents, need affirmation and guidance as they look for a better way. . . . The world may not need more Ivy League graduates. It does, however, need all the functional adults it can get." —*The Christian Century*

"*How to Raise an Adult* is a bit of a manifesto, and I mean that in the best way." —*BookPage*

"This is such a terrific book. So incredibly timely. Parents will love it and devour it because it's such a concern . . . instead of thinking about raising children, we need to be thinking about raising adults."
—*CBS This Morning*

"Lythcott-Haims breaks down the source of helicopter parenting habits, and uses studies and stories to illustrate the developmental, emotional, and psychological toll that overparenting can take on children. She also gives parents some constructive tips for stepping back and allowing the next generation of leaders to become fully formed adults."
—*Melissa Harris-Perry* (MSNBC)

"Julie Lythcott-Haims, I hope *my* child has a dean, teacher, others like you out there. . . . Thank you for spreading this really important and powerful message." —*Fox & Friends*

"Reveals some terrifying truths." —*The Telegraph* (UK)

"At last, a parenting book I can get behind." —*The Independent* (UK)

BREAK FREE OF THE

HOW TO

OVERPARENTING TRAP

RAISE

AND PREPARE YOUR

AN ADULT

KID FOR SUCCESS

JULIE LYTHCOTT-HAIMS

 ST. MARTIN'S GRIFFIN 𝔐 NEW YORK

www.stmartins.com

The names and identifying characteristics of some persons described in this book have been changed.

Designed by Kelly S. Too

The Library of Congress has cataloged the Henry Holt edition as follows:

Lythcott-Haims, Julie.
  How to raise an adult : break free of the overparenting trap and prepare your kid for success / Julie Lythcott-Haims.—First edition.
    p. cm.
  Includes bibliographical references and index.
  ISBN 978-1-62779-177-9 (hardcover)
  ISBN 978-1-62779-178-6 (e-book)
  1. Parenting.   2. Parental overprotection.   3. Parent and child.   I. Title.
  HQ755.8.L97 2015
  306.874—dc23

                                                                    2014044394

ISBN 978-1-250-09363-9 (trade paperback)

First published by Henry Holt, an imprint of Henry Holt and Company, LLC

First St. Martin's Griffin Edition: August 2016

10   9   8   7   6   5   4   3   2   1

To Dan, who always

~ and ~

To Sawyer and Avery, the soon-to-be adults we're raising.

CONTENTS

PART 3: **ANOTHER WAY**

PART 4: **DARING TO PARENT DIFFERENTLY**

INTRODUCTION

Caminante, no hay camino, se hace camino al andar.
(Traveler, there is no path. The path is made by walking.)[1]

—Antonio Machado (1875–1939)

This is a book about parents who are overinvolved in the lives of their kids. It looks at the love and fear behind our overinvolvement. It looks at the harm we cause when we do too much. And it looks at how we might achieve better long-term ends—and help our kids achieve even greater success— by parenting differently.

I love my kids as fiercely as any parent does, and I know that love is the foundation for all we do as parents. But in my years researching this book I've learned that many of our behaviors also stem from fears; perhaps chief among them is the fear that our kids won't be successful out in the world. Of course it's natural for parents to want their kids to succeed, but based on research, interviews with more than a hundred people, and my own personal experiences, I've come to the conclusion that we define success too narrowly. And what's worse, this narrow, misguided definition of success has led us to harm a generation of young adults—our children.

I came to know, care, and worry about young adults over the course of my ten years as freshman dean at Stanford University. I loved that work and found it a sheer privilege to be alongside other people's eighteen- to twenty-two-year-old sons and daughters as they began to unfold into the adults they would become. My students made me laugh and they made me cry, and I rooted for them no matter what. This book is not an indictment of them or of their generation, people born after 1980—known as Millennials.

Their parents, though—*we parents, I'll say, for I, too, am one of them*—are another story.

I want to put all of my cards on the table. I'm not just a former dean at Stanford, I'm a graduate from Stanford and Harvard Law School as well. I'm writing this book not because of those opportunities, or despite them, but informed by it all, keeping in mind at every turn that my privilege and experience can be both a help and a hindrance in this analysis. And as I've said, I'm also a parent. My husband and I have two teenagers—a son and a daughter who are two years apart—and we are raising our kids in Palo Alto, in the heart of Silicon Valley, as energetic a hive of overparenting as you are likely to find on the planet. Whereas once upon a time I was a dean at a highly selective university tut-tutting the behaviors of overinvolved parents, in the years I've spent thinking about this topic I've slowly come to appreciate that I'm not much different from the parents I once rather breezily chastised. In many ways, I am the problem parent I'm writing about.

FATHER (AND MOTHER) KNOWS BEST

In the earliest moments our love is our umbilicus, our heartbeat, our body, and then our arms, our kiss, our breast. We bring them home to a sheltering roof and we delight weeks later when they make their first intentional eye contact with us. We nurture early babbles into first words and applaud as they gain strength to roll over, to sit up, to crawl. We scan the horizon of the twenty-first century and see an increasingly interconnected and competitive world that at times seems familiar and at times utterly not. We gaze down at our precious little ones with a promise to do all we can to help them make their way into the long life that lies ahead. There is no amount of direction on our part that will teach them to stand or walk before they are ready. But we are eager for their progress.

We see almost instantly that they are their own person, but we also want them to start where we left off, to stand on our shoulders, to benefit from all we know and can provide. We expose them to experiences, ideas, people, and places that will help them learn and grow. We want them to reach and be stretched by the kind of rigor and opportunity that will maximize their potential and their chances. We know what it takes to succeed in today's world and we're quite eager to protect and direct them, and be there for them at every turn, whatever it takes.

Many of us remember a time when, in comparison, parents were rather uninvolved in childhood. When a parent (usually a mom) would throw the door open on weekday afternoons and tell us, "Go out and play and be home for dinner." Our parents had no idea where we were or exactly what we were doing. There were no cell phones for keeping in touch or GPS devices for tracking. Off we went into the wilderness of our block, our neighborhood, our town, our vacant lots, our parks, our woods, our malls. Or sometimes, we just snuck a book and sat on the back steps. Childhood doesn't look that way today and many young parents don't relate to childhood ever having been that way.

FATHER AND MOTHER HAVE CHANGED

When, why, and how did parenting and childhood change? Even a cursory hunt yields a bounty of shifts. A number of important ones take place in the mid-1980s.

In 1983, one shift arose from the increased awareness of child abductions. The tragic 1981 abduction and murder of a young child named Adam Walsh became the made-for-television movie *Adam*, which was seen by a near record-setting 38 million people.[2] The faces of missing children began staring out at us over breakfast from the back of milk cartons soon after.[3] Walsh's father, John Walsh, went on to lobby Congress to create the National Center for Missing and Exploited Children in 1984, and to found the television show *America's Most Wanted*, which aired on Fox beginning in 1988. Our incessant fear of strangers was born.

Another shift—the idea that our children aren't doing enough schoolwork—arrived with the publication of *A Nation at Risk*[4] in 1983, which argued that American kids weren't competing well against their peers globally. Since then, federal policies like No Child Left Behind and Race to the Top have fomented an achievement culture that emphasizes rote memorization and teaching to the test against the backdrop of increased competition from students in Singapore, China, and South Korea, where such teaching practices are the norm. American kids *and* parents soon began struggling under the weight of more homework and began doing whatever it takes to survive school, as was illuminated in the 2003 book *"Doing School": How We Are Creating a Generation of Stressed Out, Materialistic, and Miseducated Students* written by Stanford School of Education lecturer Dr. Denise Pope,[5] and the 2010 film *Race to Nowhere*.[6]

A third shift came with the onset of the self-esteem movement—a philosophy that gained popularity in the United States in the 1980s that said we could help kids succeed in life if we valued their personhood rather than their outcomes.[7] In her 2013 best-selling book *The Smartest Kids in the World: And How They Got That Way*, Amanda Ripley cites the self-esteem movement as a uniquely American phenomenon.[8]

And a fourth shift was the creation of the playdate, circa 1984.[9] The playdate emerged as a practical scheduling tool at a time when mothers were entering the workforce in record numbers. The combination of more parents working and the increased reliance on day care meant fewer kids were going home after school, and it was harder to find either a location or a time for play. Once parents started scheduling play, they then began observing play, which led to involving themselves in play. Once a critical mass of parents began being involved in kids' play, leaving kids home alone became taboo, as did allowing kids to play unsupervised. Day care for younger kids turned into organized after-school activities for older kids. Meanwhile, concerns at the turn of that decade over injury and lawsuits prompted a complete overhaul of public playgrounds nationwide.[10] The very nature of play—which is a foundational element in the life of a developing child—began to change.

Observing such shifts among other things, in 1990, child development researchers Foster Cline and Jim Fay coined the term "helicopter parent" to refer to a parent who hovers over a child in a way that runs counter to the parent's responsibility to raise a child to independence.[11] Focused on giving advice to parents of young children, Cline and Fay had their finger on the pulse of important changes that took place in American parenting in the prior decade, and which are commonplace today, twenty-five years later. That means the oldest members of the helicoptered generation turned thirty circa 2010. They are also those known as "Generation Y" or "Millennials."

In the late 1990s, the first of the Millennial generation began going off to college, and my colleagues and I at Stanford began to notice a new phenomenon—parents on the college campus, virtually and literally. Each subsequent year would bring an increase in the number of parents who did things like seek opportunities, make decisions, and problem solve for their sons and daughters—things that college-aged students used to be able to do for themselves. This was not only happening at Stanford, mind you; it was happening at four-year colleges and universities all over the country, as conversations with colleagues nationwide confirmed. Meanwhile my husband and I were raising our two little kids, and without fully realizing it we were doing a good deal of helicoptering in our own home.

THE BIG BOOM

Members of the baby boom generation, born between 1946 and 1964, were the first to earn the label "helicopter parent." Their children are the older wave of the "Millennial" generation I'm concerned about. Baby boomers' grandparents believed "children are to be seen but not heard," and their parents' standard retort was "because I said so." In contrast and perhaps in response, as teenagers and young adults the baby boomers championed free thinking and the rights of the individual, questioned authority, and reshaped or outright overturned many fundamental paradigms and mores of American society.

Of course, boomers weren't the first parents in history to hover over their kids like helicopters—in 1899 General Douglas MacArthur's mother apparently moved to West Point with him and lived in a suite at Craney's Hotel overlooking the Academy, where she could watch him by telescope to see if he was studying.[12] But when the baby boom generation—at 76 million members the largest generation in American history until their own children were born—starts a trend, whether in fashion, technology, or parenting, it quickly reaches a tipping point. So perhaps it should then be no surprise that when Boomers became parents they managed to change the very nature of parenting in the United States.

Based on their own values and experiences, and in the context of those various societal factors taking place in the 1980s discussed above, Boomers took a more involved role in the lives of their children. Whereas Boomers' parents had been emotionally distant, Boomers were emotionally present in their kids' lives, often becoming one of their kids' closest friends. Whereas Boomers' parents were hands-off, Boomers tried to control and ensure outcomes for their own kids and became their strongest advocates. Whereas Boomers' parents adhered to hierarchy, structure, and authority, Boomers questioned these things with a vengeance and ushered in massive societal changes such as the sexual revolution, two income–earning households, a steep rise in divorce rates, and the perhaps not unrelated mind-set of spending "quality time, not quantity time," with kids (that is, it's not how much time we spend that matters, it's how we spend the time).[13] As parents, Boomers, ever accustomed to expressing their opinions, being heard, and getting their way, wanted to "be there" for their kids, whatever it took, still challenging the system, but now on behalf of their kids, often supplanting themselves as a buffer between their kids and the system and its authority figures. Even when their child is grown.

Looking at only the short-term results, a very involved style of parenting offers short-term gains in the forms of safety, opportunities attained, and outcomes secured. As with General MacArthur—who graduated first in his class at West Point—a very involved parenting approach seems, in some significant ways, to "work." Seeing evidence that this was so, by the 2000s this very-involved style of parenting became less like the exception and more like the rule. My generation, Generation X (born between 1965 and 1980), followed the Boomers' suit when we became parents, as did the Millennial generation (born between 1980 and 2000) as they became parents. The baby boomers are now grandparents, but, as with much they've contributed to American society, for good or for ill, their influence on parenting could be with us long after they are gone.

TO WHAT END?

A heightened level of parental involvement in the lives of kids obviously stems from love—unquestionably a good thing. But by the time I stepped down as dean at Stanford in 2012 I had interacted not only with a tremendous number of parents but with students who seemed increasingly reliant upon their parents in ways that felt, simply, *off*. I began to worry that college "kids" (as college students had become known) were somehow not quite formed fully as humans. They seemed to be scanning the sidelines for Mom or Dad. Under-constructed. Existentially impotent.

Tremendous good can be said about the baby boomers—they were drafted into and questioned the Vietnam War, lay their bodies on the line in the monumental civil rights and civil liberties struggles of their day, and fueled the greatest economic growth our nation has ever seen. But did Boomers' egos become interlaced with the accomplishments of their children to such an extent that they felt their own success was compromised if their children fell short of expectations?[14] And did some of these parents go so far in the direction of their own wants and needs that they eclipsed their own kids' chances to develop a critical psychological trait called "self-efficacy"—that is, what eminent psychologist Albert Bandura identifies as "the belief in one's capabilities to organize and execute the courses of action required to manage prospective situations"?[15] There's a deeply embedded irony here: Maybe those champions of self-actualization, the Boomers, did *so much* for their kids that their kids have been robbed of a chance to develop a belief in their own *selves.*

Did the safety-conscious, academic achievement-focused, self-esteem-promoting, checklisted childhood that has been commonplace since the mid-1980s and in many communities has become the norm, rob kids of the chance to develop into healthy adults? What will become of young adults who look accomplished on paper but seem to have a hard time making their way in the world without the constant involvement of their parents? How will the real world feel to a young person who has grown used to problems being solved for them and accustomed to praise at every turn? Is it too late for them to develop a hunger to be in charge of their own lives? Will they at some point stop referring to themselves as kids and dare to claim the "adult" label for themselves? If not, then what will become of a society populated by such "adults"? These were the questions that began to gnaw at me and that prompted me to write this book.

These questions were on my mind not just at work but as I made my way in my community of Palo Alto, where the evidence of overparenting was all around me—even in my own home. Too many of us do some combination of overdirecting, overprotecting, or over-involving ourselves in our kids' lives. We treat our kids like rare and precious botanical specimens and provide a deliberate, measured amount of care and feeding while running interference on all that might toughen and weather them. But humans need some degree of weathering in order to survive the larger challenges life will throw our way. Without experiencing the rougher spots of life, our kids become exquisite, like orchids, yet are incapable, sometimes terribly incapable, of thriving in the real world on their own. Why did parenting change from preparing our kids *for* life to protecting them *from* life, which means they're not prepared to live life on their own? And why do these problems I'm writing about seem rooted in the middle and upper middle classes? After all, parents care deeply about doing a good job and if we're fortunate enough to be middle- or upper-middle-class, we have the means—the time and disposable income—on our side to help us parent well. So, have we lost our sense of what parenting well actually entails?

And what of our own lives as parents? (*"What life?"* is a reasonable response.) We're frazzled. Worried. Empty. Our neighborhoods are photoworthy, our food and wine are carefully paired, but with childhood feeling more and more like an achievement arms race, can we call what we and our children are living a "good life"? I think not. Our job is to monitor our kids' academic tasks and progress, schedule and supervise their activities, shuttle them everywhere, and offer an outpouring of praise along the way. Our kids' accomplishments are the measure of our own success and worth; that college bumper sticker on the rear of our car can be as much about our own sense of accomplishment as our kids'.

In the spring of 2013 I attended a board meeting for an organization that provides financial support to Palo Alto's public schools. In casual conversation afterward as the parents were taking one last piece of coffee cake and heading out into their day, a woman who knows of my work pulled me aside. "When did childhood get so *stressful*?" she pleaded with a far-away look. I put my hand on her shoulder as tears slowly filled her eyes. Another mother overheard and came toward us, nodding her head. Then she leaned in, asking me, "Do you *know* how many moms in our community are medicated for anxiety?" I didn't know the answer to either question. But a growing number of conversations like this with moms like these became another reason to write this book.

The dean in me may have been concerned about the development and prospects of young adults who had been overparented—and I think I've made better choices as a parent thanks to spending so much time with other people's young adults. But the parent in me has struggled with the same fears and pressures every other parent faces, and, again, I understand that the systemic problem of overparenting is rooted in our worries about the world and about how our children will be successful in it without us. Still, we're doing harm. For our kids' sakes, and also for our own, we need to stop parenting from fear and bring a more healthy—a more wisely loving— approach back into our communities, schools, and homes. Through research woven together with real-life observations and commonsense advice, this book will show us how to raise our kids to become adults—and how to gather the courage to do so.

PART 1

WHAT WE'RE
DOING NOW

1

KEEPING THEM SAFE AND SOUND

THIS IS HOW IT STARTS

Childhood is the most researched phase of life, and parenting occupies sizeable shelf space in any decent bookstore. The takeaway for any parents who are paying attention (and we're *all* paying attention) is that it is our job to keep kids safe and sound. It is basic. It is biological.

Among the photos in my son Sawyer's baby book, there's one of him at seven months of age in which he stares out at the camera, unsmiling. The camera captured only a little baby lying at a slant atop a slide, but I recall that my strong hands were holding him in place just beyond the camera's eye.

It was Sawyer's first trip to the park, his first trip down a slide, and as I look at the picture I can still hear myself and my husband both chirping, "It's all right, baby, we're right here." From the look on my son's face, we hadn't managed to be convincing.

When I see the photo I recall the dread that filled me that day as my baby lay perched at the top of that small slide. It couldn't have been more than four feet off the ground, and my husband and I were on either side, but still I worried. Would Sawyer be afraid as he traveled that short distance? Would he get to the bottom, plop out onto the rubbery ground, and maybe bonk his head? Would he have an unpleasant experience we might— *should*—have prevented?

Over the years when I've sat nestled on the couch with Sawyer looking at the images of his earliest childhood, I've characterized the fear in his eyes as his. But these many years later I wonder if my baby was just mirroring what he saw in his dad's eyes and my own. How does a parent travel from that place of wanting to utterly protect an infant to the place of letting them go out into the waiting world?

PREVENTING ACCIDENTS

In a world of abundance and advanced technology, we feel capable of ensuring that no child will get hurt in any way and have faith in our ability to exert control. Toward that end we've made the world much safer, more predictable, and kinder for kids. It starts when our babies are in utero where every facet of pregnancy is monitored. Once born, our children enter homes completely safeguarded for their protection.

We've also made the world beyond our home as safe as possible for kids. Between 1978 and 1985 every state enacted laws requiring children to be in car seats, and mandatory seat belt laws soon followed.[1] These laws sounded the death knell for cherished freedoms—like the "way, way back" of the family station wagon—but the goal of saving kids' lives was by far the greater concern. At the same time, the American National Standards Institute approved the first-ever bicycle helmet standard and by 1994 more than a third of the U.S. population was covered by a bicycle helmet law. Efforts to safeguard children also led to increased use of helmets and pads for things like roller skating, ice skating, and skateboarding. Without question, these laws and practices saved lives.

We parents took things a step farther, though, personally functioning as bumpers and guardrails between our kids and the world, as if our kids will be totally safe as long as we are present. I was thinking about this the other day when I saw a parent and child crossing the street together—it could have been any city or town. The mother walked confidently. Her son, a kid of about eight years, was a step behind wearing earbuds and staring at his cell phone. The mother looked left and right and left again, and then she and her kid proceeded through the intersection. The kid never once looked up. Soon after, I read about a product called MiniBrake for kids' bikes that lets a parent operate a brake on the child's rear tire via remote control if the kid nears a busy street.

School is the critical first locus of opportunity for our kids' intellectual development, but just getting them to and from the place leads to safety concerns. We resolve this by being alongside them as much as logistics allow.

When our kids are little many of us escort them to school to make sure they're safe, and often we carry their stuff to lighten their load. I chuckled recently at the sight of a dad with a tiny, bright pink backpack strapped across his broad shoulders as he biked the three blocks home from the local elementary school behind his daughter, who couldn't have been more than seven or eight. It was adorable. But that afternoon, and on many more afternoons before and since, I've wondered, *When is a kid old enough to carry her own stuff?* And *What degree of independence is right for an elementary school kid?* Seeing parents so proximally close to elementary schools in my town, I wanted to investigate how far-reaching this trend might be.

I spoke with a mom named Lora in an Ohio suburb who told me of a mother who escorts her third grader onto the school bus every day. And yes, the kid is healthy and able-bodied. She told of a father who bikes the mile-long trip to and from school right behind his daughter; he sounded just like the dad with the pink backpack in my town, except his kid is a sixth grader. Even when school is within walking distance and although carbon emissions are a mounting concern, many of us drive our kids. Often, we don't stop escorting at the school doors.

I spoke with a family friend named Ellen Nodelman, who since 1969 has graced the halls of Rockland Country Day School, a private, pre-K through twelfth grade school located across the Hudson River from Manhattan, in the town of Congers, New York. Ellen began on the faculty in the English department at RCDS, then continued teaching and serving as academic dean and college guidance counselor. Over her forty-plus years in those roles, she was eyewitness to the rising phenomena of parents at and beyond the school gate.

Half of the kids at RCDS take school buses, "and a good half of the kids who *could* take the bus are driven by a parent," says Nodelman. Rather than just drop kids off, parents of younger students will sometimes come inside the school with their kid, and some want to come right into the classroom with them. "We try to keep them from coming beyond the main lobby. If they could do what they wanted they would spend the whole day in class with them." She adds, "We've had some ask."

———

Then there's the cell phone—a recent enough development in the lives of parents and child communication so as not to have *caused* helicopter parenting, but that certainly facilitates the ability to helicopter if the tendency is there. Researchers call it "the world's longest umbilical cord."[2]

Take, for example, the mother of a Beverly Hills high schooler who insisted her son text her hourly on his way to and from a beach outing with friends. It was the drive, not the boogie boarding in the Pacific Ocean, that scared her. Or the Stanford parent who contacted the university to say he thought his daughter was missing because he hadn't heard from her in over a day. Or the parent of an American college student on a study abroad program in New Zealand who called the program director terribly worried that her son hadn't answered his phone since returning from a hiking trip in the mountains (she knew he was back on campus because she tracks him by GPS).

Parental vigilance and technology buffer the world for our children, but we won't always be there to be on the lookout for them. Raising a kid to independent adulthood is our biological imperative and an awareness of the self in one's surroundings is an important life skill for a kid to develop. When we're tempted to let our presence be what protects them, we need to ask, *To what end? How do we prevent and protect while teaching kids the skills they need? How do we teach them to do it on their own?*

THE OVERBLOWN FEAR OF "STRANGER DANGER"

Many of these safety precautions—regulations, gear, parents helping kids cross streets and brake their bikes and travel to school—aim to protect kids from *accidents,* but we're also very concerned about humans who might *intend* to harm our kids. Toward that end, we teach children never to talk to strangers; supervise them in any outdoor play that still exists; accompany them almost everywhere; and keep them right by our side in the grocery aisles. Decades-old childhood rituals have been impacted. Take Halloween, for example. Kids used to scamper through neighborhoods gleefully gobbling up candy offered by neighbors and strangers. But today in my community children as old as twelve or thirteen are escorted by parents who hover at driveway's end and who will check each and every piece of candy for a razor blade or needle before the child is permitted to gorge themselves silly (which really isn't allowed anymore, either).

You might think these precautions are well founded, when in fact almost all reports of razor blades and needles in Halloween candy have been debunked as hoax or prank.[3] And the overriding concern about stranger abduction is also based on rare incidents. Evidence suggests that the initial airing of the 1983 movie *Adam*—about the 1981 abduction and murder of a child—was the catalyst for the fear of stranger abduction that is commonplace in America today.[4] In the early 1980s, child safety advocates falsely claimed that hundreds of thousands of children were disappearing every year, by lumping together runaways and kids "kidnapped" by noncustodial parents with the very few cases of stranger abduction that were actually taking place. Today our smartphones and 24/7 Internet access amp up the frenzy, alerting us at a moment's notice when anything bad has happened to a child, anywhere in the world. Our fears continue to be fueled by the media, whose ratings go up when they tell scary stories. Parents all over the country have told me matter-of-factly, or wistfully, that kids just can't walk alone anymore. Why? "Because of pedophiles." We *perceive* that our nation is a more dangerous place, yet the data show that the rates of child abduction are no higher, and by many measures are lower, than ever before.[5]

The U.S. Justice Department published its first study on "missing, abducted, runaway, and thrownaway" children (NISMART-1) in 1990, and its second, and most recent, study in 2002 (NISMART-2). NISMART-2 showed that an estimated 797,500 children were reported missing in that one year, and of that number, just 115 children were the victims of the most serious, long-term nonfamily abductions called "stereotypical kidnappings" (40 percent of whom were killed). While NISMART-2 was conducted some time ago, we can have confidence that the number of "stereotypical kidnappings" today is now no worse and likely lower, because FBI statistics show the number of missing persons of all ages went down 31 percent between 1997 and 2011, "and the numbers of homicides, sexual assaults, and almost all other crimes against children have been dropping, too."[6]

Let's put these data into context. In 2014, the U.S. population was approximately 318 million, and 74 million of those were children. If 115 of those were victims of stereotypical kidnappings, and 40 percent of them were killed, that is an infinitesimal number. Children abducted by strangers represent .01 percent of all missing children.[7] The other 99.99 percent of children reported missing have been erroneously thought by caregivers to be missing, taken by family members, have run away, or have been thrown away (meaning their families do not want them to return). It is a cruel myth that more and more children are going missing and that most missing children have been abducted by strangers.

Of course, serious harm coming to any child is an unspeakable trag-edy, and real child predators are out there even though very few commit stranger-to-stranger crimes. But why do we base our daily decisions about our children's comings and goings on a one-in-a-million chance that our kid could be killed by a stranger, when, as the *Palm Beach Post* reported in 2006, in any given year a child is more likely to be killed in an equestrian accident (1 in 297,000), as a result of youth football (1 in 78,260), or as a passenger in a car (1 in 17,625)?[8] Taking the long view, we need to teach our kids street smarts, like the importance of walking with a friend instead of alone, and how to discern bad strangers from the overwhelming majority of good ones. If we prevent our children from learning how to navigate the world beyond our front yard, it will only come back to haunt them later on when they feel frightened, bewildered, lost, or confused out on the streets.

Look, I've felt these fears, too. Even though I'm familiar with these data and as a result, theoretically, should know better, I've succumbed to the myth of stranger danger. I remember the first time Sawyer walked home alone from a friend's house through our low-crime, upper-middle-class neighborhood. He must have been about ten, it was twilight, and the walk was ten minutes at most. Even knowing what I know about our fears being way overblown, even knowing what I know about the importance of devel-oping independence in our kids, I felt my heart beating in my throat and had to work very hard to focus my mind on other things as the minutes ticked by until my boy was safe at home.

Terrible things happen everywhere in the world. But terrible things have always happened and they are statistically less likely to happen today than in previous decades. Yet we hear about bad things wherever they've hap-pened and mere moments after they occur. Our evolutionary fight/flight responses are triggered but we never have the experience of fighting back or running away from the stressor, so we stay on heightened alert.

Evolutionary biologist Robert Sapolsky is an expert on human stress. In *Why Zebras Don't Get Ulcers: A Guide to Stress, Stress-Related Diseases, and Coping*,[9] now in its third edition, he explains how a fear of the bad things that *might* happen can cause us harm.

> When we activate the stress-response out of fear of something that turns out to be real, we congratulate ourselves that this cognitive skill allows us to mobilize our defenses early. And these anticipatory defenses can be quite protective, in that a lot of what the stress-response is about is

preparative. But when we get into a physiological uproar and activate the stress-response for no reason at all, or over something we cannot do anything about, we call it things like "anxiety," "neurosis," "paranoia," or "needless hostility."

Thus, the stress-response can be mobilized not only in response to physical or psychological insults, but also in expectation of them. It is this generality of the stress-response that is the most surprising—a physiological system activated not only by all sorts of physical disasters but just thinking about them as well.[10]

Basically, the 24/7/365/worldwide news cycle is a recent development in human existence and we haven't evolved to cope with it yet. There *is* such a thing as too much information.

CRIMINALIZING COMMON CONDUCT

Even if we aren't personally fearful, we are socializing ourselves to feel negligent unless we are on constant alert for predators. A child alone outside is such an uncommon sight that when we do see unattended children we fear something is wrong. Has the child wandered off from the attending adult? Or worse, is the child unsupervised? The police or child protective services might get called.

A South Carolina woman named Debra Harrell was jailed in 2014 for child abandonment after allowing her nine-year-old daughter to play at the park while Harrell worked her shift at McDonald's. Harrell was released on bond a day later and soon regained custody of her child, who had been placed in Social Services; but, as of this writing, her Department of Social Services case is still ongoing with a court date pending.[11]

Writer Kim Brooks was arrested for leaving her four-year-old son alone in the car for five minutes on a cool day, and then had to hire a lawyer to defend herself from a charge of "contributing to the delinquency of a minor,"[12] which, if proven, could have resulted in her kids being taken away from her. A person some would call a Good Samaritan had been in the parking lot and recorded a video of Brooks's child alone, then contacted the police.

But were the strangers who saw Brooks's son and Harrell's daughter acting as Good Samaritans or as fearmongering safety vigilantes? No harm came to Harrell's daughter or Brooks's son; the *potential* for harm is what constituted the mothers' criminal offenses. These are just two of the over a dozen recent published cases in which parents (almost always mothers) have faced criminal charges for behavior that was not only commonplace a generation ago but is arguably a necessity today, in the sense that kids can't literally accompany parents at all times. Kids are *twenty* times more likely to be killed by relatives than strangers[13]—but vigilante fearmongerers acting as Bad Samaritans are ready to indict a mother just trying to do her best under trying circumstances, a mother whose kid has suffered no *actual* harm. These vigilantes are a real threat to worry about. And their numbers may be sizeable.

"Free-range kids" crusader Lenore Skenazy is trying to take on these vigilantes. In the back of her book *Free-Range Kids*[14] is a practical tool for parents who encourage their kids to be outside, unaccompanied: It's a perforated form that can be filled out and placed in any kid's backpack or even safety-pinned to their shirt. The form reads, "I am not lost. I'm a Free-Range Kid" and goes on to explain the rationale.[15] It sounds absurd. Dystopian. But it's also a practical, proactive counter-response to those who would fear we're thoughtlessly letting our kids play alone outside. Of course, that perforated form pinned to our kid's T-shirt might give a neighbor a chuckle and some measure of reassurance; the police, on the other hand, may nevertheless condemn us for violating the as-yet-unwritten code of when it is perfectly appropriate versus illegal to let our children play or roam freely.

Danielle and Alexander "Sasha" Meitiv of Maryland are "Free Range Kids" adherents, and regularly allow their ten year old to take his six-year-old sister to and from the neighborhood park, the public library, or the local 7-Eleven without either parent.[16] One day in early January 2015, two different neighbors called the police to report that the children were walking alone. The police quickly arrived and escorted the kids home in a police cruiser, and the officer had rather unkind words for the parents and asked the kids what they would have done if they'd been grabbed by a "creep." Child Protective Services soon asked the Meitivs to sign on to a "safety plan," but Sasha refused to sign anything before his attorney could review it. At this, the CPS worker told him, "If you don't sign, we will take your kids right away," and then the CPS worker called the police. Ironically, the Meitivs' two children normally carry one of Skenazy's "Free Range Kids" forms around with them, but didn't have it on them on the day they and their parents were apprehended. Would it have made a difference? Likely not. The state—through its police force and child protective services office—currently speaks with a far louder voice than Skenazy or her followers.

Middle-class parents like Kim Brooks and like the Meitivs may have the money and disposable time to handle the vagaries of the legal process, child-protective services visits, and fines. But poor and working-class parents like Harrell—who makes $8 an hour and had her daughter play in the park while she worked precisely *because* she could not afford day care or summer camp—confront this irresolvable conflict on a regular basis. There is an encroachment by police into our liberties that feels frightening,[17] and perhaps a sinister anti-women-in-the-workplace mind-set at work here, whether implicit or explicit I don't know. What I do know as sure as if I'd endured it myself is that the psychological toll taken on Brooks, Harrell, and the Meitivs is incalculable.

And what of the children who see their parents' judgment questioned in this very public and scary way? What of the children removed off to foster care—which in some circumstances is a harrowing tale of its own—while their parents battle the legal system? What are children to think of this?

A woman named Amanda was a member of my team at Stanford and coordinated the research efforts for this book. She is the mother of two young boys, raising them with her husband in the rural outskirts of Silicon Valley. Her older son, Roland, at four years old, is very much into trying out things and exercising his independence. Normally, Amanda is more than happy to let Roland try doing things for himself, like loading the washer and dryer or helping with meal prep.

Recently, Roland has repeatedly been asking if he could be left by himself, either at home or in the car, to avoid being dragged along on quick errands. Amanda believes he is more than capable of waiting patiently and safely occupying himself for a brief span of time without the constant observation of a parent or other responsible adult. However, knowing how often "neglectful" mothers have been making the news lately, Amanda had to explain to her son that strangers and the police would not like this and could get them into trouble.

Roland laughed out loud and said that he wouldn't be doing anything bad, and so he shouldn't get "busted." Amanda explained to her son that it was the other way around, that strangers and the police would think that it was *she*, the parent, who was doing something wrong by leaving a child alone, thinking that he wouldn't be safe without an adult always watching him. Roland replied incredulously, "Why don't people know that I can behave and can be safe all by myself and I am just fine?"

Perhaps little Roland had been listening to National Public Radio, which in summer 2014 reported that in Japan it's not uncommon for kids as young as seven and even four to ride the subway alone.[18] In the same breath the reporter stated that in the United States "somebody would call Child Protective Services." Our definition of neglect has stretched to prevent parents from determining when their children are ready for even a modest amount of autonomy, and sacrifices developmentally appropriate skill building to fears of the unknown. While we might write off the Japanese as crazy, our American insistence on children being observed and accompanied at all times makes us look like the crazy ones. Ironically—and quite cruelly (if you pause a moment to think about it)—the *unexamined* harm these days is that our kids grow up *believing* that an evil stranger, a fellow shopper in the grocery store, or worse, a neighbor offering candy at Halloween wants to do them harm or that their own parent is putting them in harm's way.

FENDING OFF THE FEARS OF FRIENDS

When I began to come to terms with my inclination to overprotect my son Sawyer and daughter Avery (who is two years his junior), and looked ahead to the college years and imagined the degree of self-reliance I would hope they'd have by then, I began focusing on how to provide more opportunities for independence during childhood. I began trying to put independence in their way, so to speak.

I've been doing it for a few years now. Here is a recent example. One night when Avery was in seventh grade, she told me that she and a friend were going to meet at their school that night to decorate the locker of another friend whose birthday was the next day. She was telling me this as we were doing the dinner dishes. I was perfectly comfortable letting her bike to the school despite it being night; the school is 0.3 miles from our house and we live in a very safe suburb. In fact, I'll go so far as to say I *wanted* her to do it because I want her to build her independence. But the friend's mother was very uncomfortable with Avery biking alone in the dark and offered to drive her there and back. Avery texted her friend, "No thx, I'm happy biking." After more pushback Avery texted, "My mom WANTS me to bike." But fear won out; the friend was already being driven and they could just as easily swing by our house. We'd look like some crazy renegade outlaws if we declined. There I stood wiping my hands on a dish towel wondering how I grow my kid when the fears of people around me will hold her back. I also worried a tiny bit what these parents must think of me.

When I met with a small gathering of parents in northern Virginia, a mother named Jane expressed a similar concern. [19] "You feel like a violent, crazy rebel. There's a perception that there are greater dangers when, in fact, it is safer now." Jane was comfortable letting her eleven-year-old daughter walk home alone from a Girl Scout meeting at night, but the meeting host wouldn't allow it. "But she's a girl," friends later said to Jane. "How can she walk alone?" Jane is interested in teaching her daughter how to be smart in the world and not a victim. She says she wants her daughter to learn to put on her " 'Don't take no shit' face."

When Avery started taking the commuter train to San Francisco for a camp the summer before eighth grade, I knew I needed to teach her about that face. And I did. We rode the hour-long route together for three days, and then she rode it on her own. As with Sawyer walking home alone from a friend's house for the first time, my heart was beating a hasty exit from my chest when I picked her up the first day she'd ridden the train alone. But from the look of confidence on her face, she'd matured a year in a day.

Yes, even those like Jane and me who are looking for opportunities to push our kids toward independence have latent fears. "I admire the Free Range Kids lady (Lenore Skenazy)," Jane told me. "But no one wants to be the parent who was so laid back that they end up on the news that night because something terrible happened." I agree; it's hard to navigate this cultural minefield. We're talking about big fears and the overreaching control that follows, but what we've really got to ask ourselves is *How much freedom does a developing human need?*

MISSING OPPORTUNITIES FOR GROWTH

One telltale indicator of this shift in attitudes about keeping our kids safe and sound is our view of babysitting. When I was a child of about nine or ten (late elementary school/middle school) I began babysitting children in my neighborhood in northern Virginia. Mothers hired me for daytime duty—in some communities it was called being a "mother's helper"—and I'd look after the child(ren) for a few hours, make a snack, entertain them, put them down for naps, and answer the phone and door. By age twelve, I was babysitting for one family regularly on weekend nights and earning minimum wage. Today, the National SAFE KIDS Campaign recommends that no child under the age of twelve be left at home alone and certainly not with responsibility for caring for younger children.[20] Fourteen states now have regulations on the books stating the minimum age allowed for leaving kids home alone, varying between age six (Kansas) and fourteen (Illinois), and the median is age ten.[21] While there are no state regulations about the minimum age for babysitting, the rule of thumb in many places is fourteen to sixteen years of age. (And yet, quite incongruously, thirty states allow sixteen-year-olds to marry without a parent's consent; in the remainder the minimum age is seventeen or eighteen.)

When you add the concerns about letting kids stay home alone to the concerns about letting them be out of the house alone, the amount of freedom enjoyed by American kids today shrinks to a fraction of what it was for their parents, and a fraction of a fraction of what it was for their grandparents. We seem interested in preparing our kids to live within a one-mile radius from us for the rest of their lives and uninterested in the life skills that only develop from increasing independence.

Even the Girl Scouts of America—those green-vested merchants of mints—has let safety concerns erode the opportunity to build independence. Their official handbook now states that some degree of adult involvement in cookie sales is required for girls as old as eighteen.[22] While I've never seen a girl that old supervised while selling cookies, I've seen plenty of middle school–aged girls sit passively, smiling, while the parents handle inventory and payment. Don't worry—the girls still earn a badge! But, I wonder, for what?

PROTECTING THEIR FEELINGS

And speaking of badges: Millennials have been called the "Everyone Gets a Trophy" generation for good reason. In what seems a misguided attempt to protect kids from hurt feelings, parents have made sure kids are rewarded for every little effort. Since the 1980s, American children have been recognized with badges, certificates, ribbons, and trophies for *participation*—as if just showing up is an achievement in and of itself and needs to be marked in parchment, plastic, or tin.

We heap praise on children for anything and everything. From toddlers hearing an exuberant "Perfect!" for a stick figure drawing, to children hearing a loud "Good job, buddy!" at the baseball diamond just for swings and misses, we applaud kids no matter how unimpressive the effort ("Good job, you put your shoes on") or how backhanded the compliment ("Good job, you didn't hit Billy").[23] Should kids get some kind of award or reward no matter now plain their achievement? Is this merely a way of showing unconditional love? Some think so.[24] Others say this leads to a false sense of what it takes to excel, and a belief in entitlement to recognition and promotion that will dog them in the workplace years later.

Amanda Ripley, author of the 2013 book *The Smartest Kids in the World*, which looks at how American students compare academically to kids around the world, homes in on the trophy-for-everyone movement, also known as "the self-esteem movement," as an inhibitor of academic progress and a contributor to America's poor ranking on international standardized tests.[25] In the 1980s, "American parents and teachers had been bombarded by claims that children's self-esteem need to be protected from competition (and reality) in order for them to succeed." The result, as psychologist Hara Estroff Marano, describes it in her cri de coeur against what she calls "invasive parenting," is a "nation of wimps."[26]

OVERUSING THE "BULLY" LABEL

Sometimes kids *are* bullies. When my godson was an eighth grader, a bunch of high school kids bullied him on Facebook for being gay. It was brutal. When bullying happens, kids need parents and other advocates to help them disentangle themselves from it and recover.

But as Susan Porter wrote in *Bully Nation*,[27] in a lot of situations we parents label something a bullying incident when it's a normal passage through child development and socialization (though unfortunate, and very hard to watch). In a culture where any child who makes someone else's child feel unhappy can be labeled a bully, the accusations parents levy against other people's children occupy a large place in the mind and heart of any school leader today. Porter encourages parents and educators to avoid the bully label and instead help children develop the resilience needed to handle the harsh social challenges of life.

Olaf "Ole" Jorgenson is head of school at Almaden Country School, a private preschool through eighth grade school located just down the road from me in San Jose, California. Ole has been a teacher and administrator in both public and private school settings for more than twenty-five years, in Seattle, California, Hawaii, and Mesa Unified, the largest school district in Arizona, as well as schools in Asia, Europe, and Latin America.

"Bullying is a problem in schools everywhere," Ole tells me.[28] "It has always been a problem and probably always will be. But *true* bullying—intentionally disempowering or isolating individuals and systematically demeaning and hurting them over a period of time—has not increased. It is no more common now than it was when I began my career twenty-five years ago." He continues, "The accusations parents make today about children as 'bullies' are often inhumane and sometimes just incomprehensible. Intelligent people who raise and love their own children vilify or even *criminalize* the behavior of other children, down to the elementary and even preschool grades. It's alarming and deeply saddening." Ole has a kind voice, and I can hear his concern over the phone. "People who work with kids know that relational aggression is developmentally appropriate. Yes, it's hurtful and mean-spirited and our parental instinct is to protect our children from harm. But kids need to learn how to get over being maligned. When you label another child a bully, particularly a *little* child, you're imposing intentions that child simply isn't developmentally capable of."

Ole says it's important to get a handle on this epidemic of the perception of bullying not just for the sake of the accused but for the child who has been hurt. "When you intervene on behalf of your child, your child becomes the victim. You're expressing the message 'You're incapable, you're not sturdy enough to resolve this yourself, you need me to come in and take care of this for you.'" You are, in essence, disempowering your child.

Ole gives me a few examples. "I was on playground duty, standing over by the foursquare courts. A second-grade boy came sprinting over to me holding his ball, and burst into tears. A girl followed closely behind him, looking mortified. I got down on my knee, stroked his shoulder, and asked the boy what was going on. 'She bullied me! She bullied me!' the boy cried. 'She said the ball was out but it was in. I saw it! It was in!'" The sadness in Ole's voice is palpable as he relays this story. "Where did a seven-year-old kid get this language?" he asks aloud. Ole used the foursquare situation to teach the kids the concept of a "do over." But, clearly, bully/victim labeling has permeated even our children's consciousness.

And parental misunderstanding of this terminology has become both comedic and sad, as another of Ole's anecdotes shows: "On the third day of school a couple of years ago, parents in a family new to our school demanded to meet with me because they were concerned about 'serious bullying' in our preschool. I was alarmed and immediately invited them in to talk. Bullying in *preschool*? I had my notebook out and was leaning forward in my chair, listening. Turns out their child had been bonked in the head with a plastic shovel in the sand play area. Was I aware of this? they wanted to know. The answer was no. Later I would learn that the teacher had observed the incident, came over immediately, and had separate con-versations with both children involved. She then brought the two children together so the aggressor could apologize, and sent them off running, observing them playing together happily for the rest of recess. In other words, it was resolved appropriately. But these parents sitting in my office wanted action taken. They wanted the other child (whom they continually called 'the bully') moved to a different class, with disciplinary consequences. They even suggested that maybe the 'bad' kid should be suspended or expelled. The children were *preschoolers* learning to work stuff out in the sandbox, with an adult's guidance. What do I say to these people?" Ole asked rhetorically. "Where do I even start?" He did find the words for these particular parents. But the problem persists in schools everywhere.

PLAYING IT SAFE—ON THE PLAYGROUND

Playgrounds seem to threaten the perfect storm—accidents, abductions, mean kids—so if you visit one today you're likely to find plenty of parents there to prevent all of these harms. We Americans are also prone to narrating and praising play, as Pamela Druckerman wrote about in *Bringing Up Bébé* in which she compared American parenting to French. In France, autonomous and independent play is highly valued, so the adults are much more likely to sit passively or chat among themselves on the sidelines.[29] In the United States the constant stimulation of our narration and praise can be exhausting for both parents and kids, and can make play less fun, according to Druckerman.

When writer Suzanne Lucas moved from Philadelphia to Switzerland with her two young kids, the difference in playground behavior was eye-popping. The first time she took her five-year-old to a Swiss playground, Lucas was overwhelmed by the equipment, which included zip-lines for sailing from tree to tree, and boards, nails, and hammers for building tree houses. Lucas stayed right beneath her daughter the whole time, "totally stressed out" to see her playing with all of this terribly dangerous stuff. Then she looked around and saw that she was the only parent at the playground. "It wasn't that the other parents were sitting on a bench reading a book," Lucas told me. "I was the ONLY parent at the playground."[30]

American parents and caregivers are actively involved in play—up at the swings, under the monkey bars, or next to the slide, as my husband and I were with Sawyer, with hands at the ready to catch a fall or prevent a scrape. Psychologist Wendy Mogel writes of the important life lessons that come from trial and error, in *The Blessing of a Skinned Knee*,[31] but twenty-first-century American parents seem to have equated "good" or "successful" parenting with ensuring our kids never experience even minor, short-term pain.

Parents aside, the playground structures themselves in the United States have become so safe and devoid of even the remotest possibility for imaginative play that many kids find them downright boring. Asphalt and gravel have given way to rubber and synthetic flooring designed to cushion falls; wooden structures have given way to colorful plastic; almost everywhere, anything that could trap a head or pinch a finger has been replaced. Hanna Rosin's 2014 *Atlantic* article "The Overprotected Kid" made this point by giving us a glimpse of a contrast, a modern-day playground in North Wales, United Kingdom, that looks more like a city dump than a place for kids, though kids have a tremendous amount of fun there.[32] Rosin's article spread like wildfire through social media, as readers faced a close-up view of how playgrounds—and by extension fun, and perhaps childhood itself—have changed. "New playgrounds are safe, and that's why nobody uses them," wails the headline of another recent article.[33] Play today is likely to be in the great indoors instead, around a digital device of some kind.[34] Meanwhile in 2012, an article in the highly respected journal *Pediatrics* reported that childhood obesity is quickly eclipsing childhood injury as a leading cause of morbidity, a change the *Pediatrics* article attributed in part to safety concerns overriding meaningful playground play.[35]

STUDYING ABROAD—WITH PARENTS

Tim Barton is the director of student services for the College of Global Studies at Arcadia University located in Glenside, Pennsylvania, on the outskirts of Philadelphia. Arcadia sends three thousand American students abroad each year—some of these students attend Arcadia full-time, but the vast majority come from an assortment of over three hundred American colleges and universities. I spoke to Tim one day near the end of the spring semester in 2014.[36]

The majority of students who go abroad with Arcadia have a positive experience. Still, there are plenty of parents who have expectations and anxieties as their kid ventures out into the world, and it's Tim who gets an earful when they're unhappy or worried. I ask Tim what's typical.

He tells a story of a female student who was headed for study abroad in London. On the morning of the student's scheduled arrival Tim got a call at 5:00 a.m. his time, 10:00 a.m. London time, from the student's father, who hadn't yet heard from his daughter. "You need to tell me if my daughter is okay!" the father yelled. "I need to know!" Tim immediately got online and tracked the young woman's flight. "Sir," Tim said, "she's probably not gotten through immigration or customs yet. My staff is there but they are collecting one hundred students. It's not possible for them to identify your daughter individually just yet." The father was irate. "This is unacceptable," he told Tim, yelling. "You're running a flimflam organization." Then the father hung up on Tim.

Tim—not yet out of bed—contacted his London staff to let them know of the father's concern and to ask them to call back when they'd made contact with the daughter. Some time between when Tim was getting dressed and having breakfast, the father called him back, this time with a tone of sheepish relief. "She's there. She's okay," said the father with an audible exhale. "She updated her Facebook status, and I saw it."

The father shared a laugh with Tim about now knowing how he rated vis-à-vis his daughter's friends, and soon the call was over. But inside Tim was thinking, "Do you realize an hour ago you were threatening me? Do you realize you said very inappropriate and rude things to me?" The father had offered no apology, but Tim gets it. "Parents just want to do what is best for their son or daughter," he says. "They're not mean people, not jerks. They're afraid. My job is to help them understand what's going on."

If you think about it, we worry when we don't hear from our kids only because it is now possible to be in constant touch. Merely ten to fifteen years ago it was impossible to check up on kids like this. Before cell phones, when kids went to the beach, it was impossible for them to call home; before cell phones, kids called their parents once a week at most from college (from the payphone in the dorm hallway, and only when long-distance rates were cheapest); before cell phones, kids went off to study abroad and sent *letters* and made the occasional phone call home. Just because we *can* be in constant contact, does it mean we *should*? Is it good?

Remember the boundless freedom of a college road trip to an away football game, a beach for spring break, or to see an indie band playing in the middle of nowhere? It was characterized by too many friends in too small a vehicle, doing rock-paper-scissors to see who would drive, with plenty of music, and whatever food and drink we could scrounge. The summer after my sophomore year of college, I drove from Washington, D.C., to Wisconsin and back—via Tennessee—in one weekend, just to attend an annual backyard party called Hammerfest run by a gorgeous boy. (That may be the very definition of "lovestruck.")

These adventures still happen today, but for many college students their parent comes along for the ride via cell phone. Can a kid still call it an adventure if their cell phone logs a parent's unanswered texts and calls, and if the kid knows they'd better check in with us lest we be terrified? *Thank God for Facebook—even if they're ignoring our mounting pleas for attention, we can at least see a status update and know they're safe and sound.*

Yes, we wince even when *imagining* harm coming to our kids, and it's our job as parents to keep our children safe. But we should open our eyes to the many ways in which hypervigilance keeps them penned in from the more liberated life they deserve to live and that in turn would prepare them for adulthood.

2

PROVIDING OPPORTUNITY

THE CHECKLISTED CHILDHOOD

When I think back on all that my partner Dan and I have tried to do for our kids, I see that our first effort to provide the best opportunities began with the desire for a particular nursery school.

As undergraduates at Stanford in the 1980s we learned of Bing Nursery School—a storied institution on the edge of the Stanford campus, which serves as laboratory for the psychology faculty (who conducted the famous "marshmallow test") and as the first educational stepping-stone for 450 lucky two- to five-year-old children each year. By my late twenties Dan and I had been married a few years and were ready to start a family. So, after finishing up my work at Stanford one day, I stopped by Bing to pick up an application. However, conceiving a child proved to be harder than our health teachers had threatened in high school, and our dreams gave way to months of reproductive disappointment and doubt. In June of 1999, after a small amount of medical help, as is common for so many of us these days (which may actually contribute to the vigilance many of us bring to parenting), our son, Sawyer, was born. Two days after bringing him home from the hospital, I found the Bing application, filled it out, and told Dan we needed to go turn it in. Immediately. It must have taken us ten minutes to get Sawyer properly strapped into the infant carrier, and another ten minutes to get the carrier properly strapped into the car. We tried to time our trip so Sawyer wouldn't need to nurse somewhere along the way. I was moving rather gingerly, having had a C-section. But we wanted our child to have a shot at Bing, and we feared we might be hurting our—*his*—chances if we delayed submitting the application by even a few weeks. Maybe we'd seem uncommitted. We felt we couldn't take that chance. Off we went, forgetting the diaper bag. . . .

Two years later, Sawyer was admitted to Bing's "Two's Room"—the precious experience for two-year-olds that precedes the regular nursery school experience for three- to five-year-olds. He spent a few hours three mornings a week in a play-based environment that felt charming, precious, and idyllic. Truth be told, I think Dan and I felt rather charming, precious, and ideal, too, just getting to be members of the storied Bing community. We beamed from behind the one-way glass along with the other chosen parents as we watched our progeny stack blocks, work puzzles, play dress-up, and paint. It was a magical place and a glorious start for any child.

By Sawyer's third birthday I was beginning my role as Stanford's freshman dean and Sawyer had moved up to one of three larger nursery school classrooms. By his fourth birthday, his sister, Avery, was beginning her own experience in the Two's Room. Avery went on to follow Sawyer through Bing, and off into the Palo Alto Unified School District—ostensibly the best public schools in the area and among the best in California and the nation. We felt we were successfully doing what we could to provide a strong educational foundation for our kids.

Now, however, I see the situation slightly differently: Bing is a truly terrific nursery school and it turned out to be a great fit for our two kids. But maybe another nursery school would have worked just as well and maybe it wasn't necessary to risk my post-op stitches and the stability of our newborn's early days to get that application in the very week he was born.

Dan and I may have been among the more comically ambitious new parents but we were not alone in our urgent hope to provide good prospects for our children. Even when a kid is barely a twinkle in her parents' eyes, parents these days believe (with good reason) that a college degree will be essential if that child hopes to succeed in today's economic marketplace. And from very early on—again, out of love as well as fear—parents arrange for each child to have as many enriching experiences as possible, so that the kid will be able to compete in middle school and high school and then get into a "good" college (much more on this later). This checklist of enrichment activities—including school activities but also outside of school—kicks in early.

By the time our kids get to elementary school, the in-school checklisted childhood begins to kick into full gear. We know their schedules and their teachers' names. We e-mail teachers and keep track of assignments. We watch them do homework and check it for errors. Once upon a time, parents saw their child's grades on a quarter or semester basis; today, parents access online portals where grades are uploaded weekly if not daily. An Atlanta mom told me she learned her son had failed a test before he'd even gotten home from school that day—and before he himself knew.

Once our kids are old enough to have curricular options, we tell them what to study. We arrange tutoring to rectify less than great grades and seek out additional academic enrichment. We determine which extracurricular activities done now will be valuable in maximizing our child's chances at Ivy League academies later on, and schedule those. We decide what sport they'll specialize in and get them the kind of practice and coaching that gives them a chance at an elite team. We explore which summer camps best augment their school experiences. We research which public service opportunity to embrace. We drive them to every one of these activities. Boredom never happens. It isn't on the schedule. And we should know, because we're on top of it all. Being on top of it all has become what *we* do.

THE SPORTS AUTHORITY

Nowhere is this more true than in organized sports, where we worry that if we're not vigilant our kid will miss out on playing time, a starting spot, the better coaches, the elite squad, and a chance at a college scholarship. In many communities we'll even "redshirt" our kindergartener—a term taken from NCAA rules that limit a college athlete to four years of eligibility but that allow a student to play in the fifth year (when they are likely to be stronger and larger) if they sit out their entire freshman year.

In the kindergarten context, "redshirting" refers to the practice of keeping otherwise academically and developmentally ready child back one additional year to give them an advantage in sports. It means that kids who turned five in spring or summer might be held back so as to start kindergarten at well over six years of age. Although parents who want to redshirt their kid and administrators who allow it may not have thought through the implications of bringing puberty into elementary school, there's no question that being more physically developed than your peers portends greater success on the playing field. Malcolm Gladwell illustrates this point in his book *Outliers: The Story of Success* with the example of professional hockey, which is disproportionately played by men born in January through March of any given year; basically they were bigger when the time came to enroll in pee-wee hockey, and being bigger as a four- or five-year-old meant being better, and over the years all of the subsequent incremental goodies associated with being better came their way.[1]

Whereas kids used to play a mix of sports, many of us now want our kids to *specialize* in a sport at an early age. The upside of early specialization is the chance to excel to a degree that will attract the attention of a college recruiter—which might yield an advantage in college admission and a scholarship. The downside is that kids' bodies can end up overdeveloped in some areas and underdeveloped in others, leading to injury.

Seeing this downside, in 2000 the American Academy of Pediatrics issued a policy statement discouraging the practice of kids specializing in a single sport prior to adolescence. More recently, an ongoing clinical study by Loyola University Health System has been looking at over twelve hundred children playing a variety of sports who came into the clinic either for physicals or for treatment of injury. In 2011 the researchers found that athletes who were injured "had a significantly higher average score on a sports specialization scale than athletes who weren't injured."[2] Long hours spent pursuing one sport year-round means that sports injuries previously only seen in professional athletes are now on the rise in childhood.[3]

My daughter, Avery, now thirteen, has danced for the past ten years, and I've seen the leg and foot injuries that arise among the most intense dancers and heard of similar types of injuries as well as back problems with gymnasts. The number of kids requiring surgery for severe injury from pitching (said to be the most dynamic motion in sports) has skyrocketed, by some estimates occurring sixteen times more often today than thirty years ago.[4] And the number of young children visiting the ER for concussions— whether from football, hockey, soccer, baseball, basketball, gymnastics, or cheerleading—has doubled in the past decade.[5] Maybe a bad back, ankle, knee, or pitching arm won't set you back too much in life, but a concussion can lead to permanent brain injury and even death.[6]

We're not just ensuring our kids play and perhaps specialize in sports; we're also amping up what it means to be a spectator. A generation ago parents would only attend the really big games—if that. Now we're at every game regardless of its importance, and often on the sidelines at every *practice*, rain or shine. As vice president of the United States, Al Gore was the nation's quintessential example of the good father (or mother) by making a point of never missing his son's games.[7] For we regular folk, leaving the office early or arranging to be back from a business trip just in time to get to our kid's game has become proxy for having our priorities intact. It's the new face of the 1980s "quality time" mantra.

Not only do we show up for games *no matter what*, we're very visible and vocal, perhaps to impress upon our kids that we *care*, or because everyone else is doing it and we don't want to appear uncommitted, or perhaps to try to exert some control over outcomes. We cheer like hell, and we'll also step in to question the coach, umpire, or referee. Kids' sports are one arena in which parents often fail so badly as role models that our behavior requires apology.[8] Dr. Tim Walden (not his real name), superintendent of a small, suburban school district in Massachusetts, is a seasoned high school administrator and occasional coach for his daughters' softball teams. In both roles he deals with parents who seem to believe that they have a final say in what their kid is going to be doing in school or on the field. Tim says with a deep sigh that on the part of many parents, there's now "an erosion of trust, or a lack of understanding of the construct of an authority figure." Due to the sensitivity of the topics he will discuss in this book, he asked to be anonymous.

This lack of respect for school administrators and coaches stands in stark contrast to parental attitudes a generation ago. Billy Fitzgerald coached baseball and basketball at Isidore Newman School in New Orleans from 1975 to 2014. His tactics won championships in both sports as well as the reverence of his players—NFL quarterback Peyton Manning being one of them. When former players came together in 2003 to renovate the Newman gym and name it after Coach Fitz, "the money poured in" not only from the former players but from their parents, who reminisced that "Fitz did all the hard work."[9]

But in that same year of the planned renovation and dedication, Coach Fitz's current crop of baseball parents felt anything but reverence toward him. The team had won the state championship in their division but went on to accomplish few goals over the summer, and after the final summer game Coach Fitz had delivered a sobering speech to his team, naming the flaws he saw in each kid. The kids went home and told their parents about it, and many of the players' fathers complained to the school headmaster about Coach Fitz. Soon, efforts to get rid of Coach Fitz were under way. The irony about kids' sports today is that we want our kids to have opportunities for challenge, rigor, and growth without their feelings getting hurt.

"The past was no longer on speaking terms with the present," wrote one of Coach Fitz's former players, Michael Lewis, a writer for the *New York Times*.[10] Coach Fitz was summoned to the headmaster's office and told to modify his behavior. He did so, and remained at the school for ten years after the summer of his sobering speech. He retired in 2014 from the school whose gym does indeed bear his name.

OUR CHECKLIST, THEIR LIFE

From early extracurricular activities to homework to sports, we tirelessly examine and revise our kids' checklist of experiences, certain that if we— *they*—just do one more thing, it might be enough to win them the big prize: admission to a highly selective college. High school guidance counselors— usually called college counselors at private and independent schools—know better than anyone that parents have become a highly involved force in the college admission process. A counselor's job is to know a kid's accomplishments and interests, size up their potential, and help a kid come up with a list of colleges to which to apply, including "safeties" on the one hand and "stretches" or "reaches" on the other. With parents' opinions and expectations very much in play, counselors have to perform a delicate balancing act between advising and supporting a student and responding to the concerns and opinions of the parents. When tension arises in the form of a kid and parent disagreeing about which schools should be on the list, counselors sometimes act as a buffer, if not a shield, between kids and parents. The guidance profession tends to attract people who are good at this kind of thing.

Amy Young is one of these diplomatically adept folk. She is director of college counseling at Avenues: The World School, a brand-new private school in the heart of New York City with administrators and teachers culled from elite New England and New York prep schools. Avenues was so new when I met with Amy in the spring of 2014 that she hadn't yet had a class of seniors. But Amy has been in the business for a while—most recently at Riverdale Country School, an elite private school in New York City—and she knows that when the time comes, the set of schools to which her students are admitted will have an enormous impact on public perception of Avenues. She is, of course, concerned about the school's reputation, but she's even more concerned about protecting her students from the fallout that can come when parents are displeased with admission options and results.[11]

It's particularly hard for Amy when she's looking at the list of safeties and stretches with a student and his or her parents, and the student says, "I'm perfectly fine with these college options; I just want to go where I'll be happy," but the parents disagree with the schools on the list. That's where Amy's job is to stand with and for the kid. "I'm trying to preserve their college application process as a growth experience. Trying to preserve their ability to make their own choices and feel good about them. Trying to help them cope with the fear that they're disappointing the people around them." At Stanford, I saw the other end of this process, when parents are still trying to control decision making at the college level. When parents trample on their child's desires, the kid might accede, wither, or grow defiant.

Three thousand miles west of Amy at Avenues is Tom Jacoubowsky, assistant principal for guidance at Henry M. Gunn High School, one of two public high schools in Palo Alto and the school my kid, Sawyer, attends, and Avery will attend. Gunn is a public school with approximately nineteen hundred students. The guidance caseload at Gunn is 270 to 1—a much more favorable ratio than the California average of over 400 to 1, but above the 150-to-1 ratio at many elite public schools around the country, and well above the ratio of most private schools such as Avenues. Yet while Tom and his team have five to ten times the caseload of someone like Amy at Avenues, they also have all the pressures of guiding the sons and daughters of Silicon Valley glitterati and Stanford faculty. I met with Tom to talk about this book in November 2013, shortly after Sawyer had started his freshman year at Gunn.[12]

Tom says what goes into a college application—what literally gets written in there—has changed dramatically since he was a teenager growing up near Palo Alto. For example, part-time work used to be a big part of a Palo Alto teenager's life. Nowadays, not so much. Tom says, "Kids don't work anymore and if they do work they don't arrange the work they do—their parents arrange things like internships for them. And they do it just to get into college." Like all good college or guidance counselors, Tom encourages his students to write about who they are and what matters to them. It can be hard for a kid to write anything meaningful about an activity if the primary "why" behind it is that their parents manufactured it or urged it on them in order to increase their chances for college admission. "The college admission deans say they don't want this done-just-for-college stuff, but those kids continue to get admitted, so . . ." Tom looks up at me with a shrug, then a smile.

In May 2014, I spoke with yet another of these gifted guidance counselors, Catharine Jacobsen, senior college counselor at Lakeside School in Seattle, a highly selective private school for grades 5–12 famous for being Bill Gates's alma mater as well as the school to which many Microsoft execs send their kids.[13] Despite the stress innate in her work, Catharine comes across as cheerful, confident, and reassuring. She is also a mother of two, so she very much gets the parents' perspective.

Catharine has been at Lakeside since 1992. "I have this intrinsic belief that kids are very capable, and know what they want and how to ask for it as long as there are reasonably friendly and responsive parents available, who are not insisting on their own agenda," she said. Then she told me about a recent conversation she'd had with parents of one of her high school students. The parents were trying to come up with suitable summer activities and classes for their son and Catharine sensed they were looking for opportunities with "ingredients" or "labels" that would impress a college admissions officer. "They were assessing their son as they would assess a potential employee at Microsoft," she said. During this and other conversations with parents, Catharine tries to educate parents and kids about the holistic nature of the college admission process—meaning that admissions officers try to assess the whole person based on a review of all information presented. She also tries to convey what can seem missing in a college applicant who has excelled with "ingredients" procured by someone else and bears "labels" of someone else's making.

Friends often ask me for advice on getting their kid into an elite college. If they're married or in a committed partnership I joke, *stay together*. It relieves some of the tension inherent in the conversation but it's also based on fact; reviewing the forms of my incoming freshmen at Stanford in any given year, 70 to 80 percent of them seemed to come from two-parent homes. My quip about staying together is also a way for me to signal that the loving relationships we model for our kids play a huge role in our kids' upbringing, sense of self, and ultimate success.

Of course, this is not what people are asking me. They're asking about a particular project, trip, experience, or internship they're evaluating for their kid. And in my community, which is full of well-educated, high-achieving, highly connected people, parents have access to—or can manufacture—some pretty amazing things. I tell them what matters most is that the activity be in furtherance of their kids' *actual*—buzzword "authentic"—interests, that it be a deepening of something the kid is already curious about, or is something new but related to interests the kid already has.

I tell everyone who asks that admissions deans may *seem* to be interested in what you've racked up by way of accomplishments, but what they really want to dig into and find is a sense of who you *are*. What matters to you? What are you curious about? What makes you tick? What do you like to think about? Once the admissions team knows from grades and scores that you've got the intellectual ability to do the work on their campus, they will want a sense of the traits and characteristics you'll bring to the classroom and college community. So I tell my friends that there's a bit of danger in having your kids do this and that just for college admission; your kid will have a hard time writing meaningfully about the experience, and if it was a super-fancy thing it can look less like evidence of who *they* are and more like evidence of who *you* are, that is, your affluence and influence. These are hard conversations to have, particularly with people accustomed to using their money, influence, and power to achieve outcomes for themselves and their kids. I tell this to my friends even though, as Tom Jacoubowsky noted, the kids with the A+ checklists of activities on their college applications *are* often accepted by their top-choice schools because I believe it's best for kids.

What do college admissions officers really want? Sidonia ("Sid") Dalby is an admission officer at Smith College, an elite private liberal arts women's college in Northampton, Massachusetts, which sits nestled in a little valley along with four other preeminent colleges: Amherst, Hampshire, Mount Holyoke, and University of Massachusetts at Amherst. Sid has been in the admissions business for three decades, and she took some time out of her busy day during the admissions season in April 2014 to chat with me.[14] I wanted to know what she sees in applicants and what she thinks about what she sees.

"I've seen a cultural shift," Sid told me. "Family time isn't always spent relaxing and lolling around. Depending on the family, free time can be structured, scheduled, and organized." Sid gleaned this from Smith's supplemental essay question "What is the best gift you gave or received?" to which a common answer was "time spent with grandparents." "Applicants write pieces that say 'he took me fishing,' 'she taught me to bake bread from the old country,' or 'she showed me a locket that has been in the family for three generations.' Simple family time spent with someone who loved them unconditionally is clearly a well-valued gift. It was noteworthy to me that high-achieving applicants chose to write about *that*," Sid reports. "And beautifully so." Maybe the students are craving that, Sid wonders aloud. I can see that the invented internships and opportunities Tom Jacoubowsky, Catharine Jacobsen, and I have seen don't matter so much to Sid.

So what do we make, then, of the evidence that the system is game-able; all of us know a "manufactured" kid who "made it" into a great school. Maybe the point is that making it into a particular school isn't an end in and of itself—that admission resulting from a great deal of manufacture says nothing about whether you'll make it once there, or in life, or feel good about yourself.

(MIS)SHAPING THE WAY THEY DREAM

In April 2014 former Yale English professor William ("Bill") Deresiewicz spoke to a crowd at Stanford about whether students at elite colleges are really just "excellent sheep." His book by the same name would come out a few months later.[15] In the Q&A after Deresiewicz spoke, a Stanford undergraduate named Chi Ling Chan made a statement in which she asked rhetorically, "What is shaping the way we dream?"[16] The elegant simplicity of her question stayed with me—haunted me, really—into the night and the following day. I didn't know her but I wanted to find her and learn more about her perspective. Through the magic of Facebook we met and soon spoke on the phone.[17]

Chi Ling is from Singapore and rose to the top of its very stressful school environment. "When parents or teachers ask us at age five or six, 'What do you want to be when you grow up?' our answer is contingent in large part on what we are exposed to by the people around us and from storybooks." She continued, "A friend from New York said that when he was asked this question in elementary school, classmates would say, 'I want to be an investment banker.' What kid would say that unless they have a parent in that profession?" As she asked this rhetorical question I was enjoying simply listening to her, and I found myself thinking, "I hope my daughter Avery will be this thoughtful and eloquent when she grows up."

"Yes we dream of our *selves*, of what we will become," Chi Ling told me, "but it's the environment that tells us what is *possible*. I don't think our dreams are limitless; they are bounded by the society we live in and its conception of what is respectable and good."

When I ended the call with Chi Ling, my mind flashed to a story I'd heard about parents in Ohio who picked out where their sixth-grade daughter would go to college and what she was going to major in. "Whaddya know," the woman relaying the story had quipped to me on the phone. "Six years later, that's where the daughter is going and that's what she's going to major in. They're trying to keep their kid from making mistakes, to ensure success from an adult standpoint."

Those parents are shaping the way their daughter dreams.

A Stanford undergraduate named Kayla relayed to me another story about this kind of parenting.[18] Kayla's story came from her study abroad experience at Stanford's campus in Santiago, Chile.

"We were halfway through our study abroad quarter in Santiago and my classmate Jenna's mom, Trish, was going to be visiting for her fiftieth birthday. Trish brought along her friend Isabelle and the two of them visited all of the classic Santiago tourist attractions. They offered to take Jenna and four of us friends to dinner at a very classy restaurant in their five-star hotel, and that's when I met Isabelle. Isabelle and Trish were excited to meet us and were very warm and welcoming. They kept mentioning how mature and sophisticated we seemed and they made sure to pass around the wine list, which I took to be an attempt at connecting with us on an equal level.

"Isabelle is a middle-aged mother living in San Francisco. She has three kids, aged four, eight, and eleven. Based on her Tory Burch flats and rather impressive wedding ring, not to mention a quick vacation to Santiago in the middle of the year, it appeared she came from an affluent household. Her husband, we would learn, works in venture capital.

"Isabelle and Trish had a lot of questions about what our study abroad program had been like so far. They were genuinely curious about Santiago culture and our experience. But after the bread was brought to the table Isabelle launched right into a line of direct questions, such as 'So, how do you think you got into Stanford, Kayla?' Her eyes were trained on me. I was caught a little off guard because a moment before we had been discussing saving room for the Chilean dessert known as tres leches cake. The shift in tone was palpable; all of a sudden it felt like the purpose of the dinner was to interview us rather than have a nice get-together. I've been asked this question before, but still don't really know the answer, so I went with, 'I got really lucky, I guess.' Isabelle chuckled, but that was not the end. "No really. What was it? Did you just have an insane GPA? Were you just constantly doing extracurricular activities? What was it?' Genuinely not knowing, I responded, 'I think I really wanted it. I put a lot of effort into my schoolwork and my essays because I wanted to go to a school like Stanford. And I think it was a great fit.'

"For the remainder of the evening Isabelle grilled my friends and me about how we got into Stanford and what we think was our 'special factor.' At one point Isabelle got up to go to the bathroom and Trish took the conversation in a different direction. But when Isabelle returned she redirected the conversation to the topic of Stanford admission. It was as if she had been given this once-in-a-lifetime opportunity to pick apart the minds of Stanford students, which she felt was vital for the success of her own children.

"The most striking aspect of the evening was how she kept saying her sons weren't good enough. She'd say, 'My kid's not that special, he doesn't have that "x" factor.' I could sense that my friends were increasingly uncomfortable as Isabelle described her kids this way, as was I. Each of us had been through the hoops as kids and we know it's hard enough without someone telling you at every turn that you're not good enough, or what you're doing isn't good enough, or that if it's fun then it doesn't matter for college. That night, I felt so sorry for Isabelle's kids.

"Soon Isabelle started asking what parents could do to increase the chances for admission to Stanford, and what did ours do? Each of us described in our own way how our parents were supportive but relatively hands off throughout high school, and that they told us to calm down and to relax in high school much more often than they applied pressure. Isabelle looked at us like we weren't human. Or like we weren't telling the truth.

"I tried to ask Isabelle what her children *like* doing and she responded, 'Well, one likes tae kwon do but he'll never be the best at that and it certainly won't get him into college.' She also started complaining about how she could not keep up with the prices of tutoring and after-school academic enrichment for her middle schooler.

"After a long back-and-forth between our attempt to give Isabelle some perspective on the role of parents and Isabelle's corresponding frustrated disbelief, I felt we made little progress. My friends and I felt some sort of responsibility to help Isabelle's children out, and also put her at ease. We had zero effect. Isabelle still seemed to think we'd gotten into Stanford because we were superhuman and her children weren't, so she was going to have to do everything in her power to overcome their deficiencies.

"We mentioned having friends from high school who ended up at different universities and who felt that they fit those environments really well. Isabelle wouldn't have it. There was a clear stratification of elite universities in Isabelle's mind and 'fit' was irrelevant. Isabelle wouldn't settle for less than Stanford. Not for her eight-year-old son."

Hearing this from Kayla, my mind turned back to Chi Ling. Even though Chi Ling was not speaking about her own parents or parenting, I took from her musings an important warning for us parents. We speak of dreams as boundless, limitless realms. But in reality often we create parameters, conditions, and limits within which our kids are permitted to dream—with a checklisted childhood as the path to achievement.

I have to admit that I have not been immune from trying to manage which activities and opportunities my children "chose" to pursue. In the fall of 2005, I was three years into my role as Stanford's freshman dean and our daughter, Avery, was four. On the first day of Stanford freshman orientation, we offered a dinner for parents, and I made a big speech about trusting their kid to make good choices and about letting their offspring forge their own paths. The next day was a Wednesday, my day to pick up Avery from Bing Nursery School, and as she and I were getting ready to head out, one of her teachers led me over to a table with a dozen small white canvases, each covered in watercolor. With unmistakable praise the teacher explained that Avery's watercolors made use of the entire canvas, which apparently is rather unusual for a four-year-old. I smiled and nodded and I tried to look interested, but inside I remember thinking, "Yeah, yeah, yeah, but it's not going to get her into Stanford." As dean I was getting quite good at telling other parents not to overdirect their kids' lives, but as a parent, I was having a hard time following my own advice.

HOW DREAMS WORK

For twenty-eight years, Phil Gardner has directed the Collegiate Employment Research Institute at Michigan State University, and in recent years he's seen a great deal of change when it comes to patterns and trends in the hiring of college graduates. According to Phil, "What is pervasive now is that parents are making decisions about what academic majors to pursue. If parents are choosing the major, if the student is not *enthused* about their major, it sets the kid up very poorly to transition out of college. When seeking a job all they can basically say to a prospective employer is, 'Mom and

Dad want me to do this.' These students are unhappy. And it is beginning to show."[19]

Of course, we should dream big and inspire our kids to do the same, and encourage and support them to the best of our means and ability. There's nothing inherently wrong with a checklist of things to be accomplished in order to set ourselves up well for the next thing in life; to be successful we have to set goals and work hard to reach them.

But if we've taught our kids that there is one predetermined checklist for their lives, we may be constructing a path that is more about us than them. And a path that isn't about them may be a path to nowhere. We have dreams for them, but musn't shape the way they dream.

3

BEING THERE FOR THEM

I've been a school administrator since 1998, and have had to call a lot of parents with bad news. I might say "Your kid has been cutting class; we found him on Route 1 at the Burger King. As a result, here is the consequence." In 1998, most of the time I could call home and get a supportive response like, "That's bad. We want to work with the school to make this right." But nowadays when I call home, I hear the parent go through a process of questioning my authority and my judgment. "Why are you doing this, Dr. Walden? Surely you're wrong."[1]

—Dr. Tim Walden, superintendent,
small suburban school district, Massachusetts

To fulfill our primary responsibilities as parents—keeping our kids safe and sound and making sure they get the right opportunities—according to our contemporary standards of safety and of opportunity, we parents have to run a lot of interference. All the time. And if we're fortunate enough to be middle or upper middle class, we have the time and money to be quite involved.

With the ultimate goal in mind of our kids being successful in an increasingly competitive world, we bring a "no mistakes" mentality to our kids' childhoods, and we do our part by accompanying them and controlling as many outcomes as we can. In many instances, although we know this is *their* childhood and *their* life, we fear they simply won't be as successful without our involvement. The good news is, we're more than happy to be there for them. "Being there" has become a core part of our efforts, mind-set, and sense of accomplishment as parents.

This means that where parents used to say good-bye when a child left the house for the day and trust in the capacity of the adults the child would encounter along the way—that teachers would teach well, that principals would run schools effectively, that referees would make good calls—today we don't place much stock in the systems and authority figures governing the lives of kids. So we've created a role for ourselves, a position that's partly personal assistant and partly like the role high-end publicists play in the lives of some Hollywood stars: observer, handler, and, often, go-between. We are a highly involved and sometimes formidable third party in all interactions that involve our children and other adults, always *there*, present physically or by cell phone, hovering, acting as our kids' eyes and ears, poised to anticipate problems, provide paperwork or materials, and intervene when questions need to be asked or answered. We don't trust systems or authorities. We don't trust our kids to be able to work out their own problems. Put simply, we don't trust anyone.

GOING TO BAT FOR THEM

With child's play now taking place right under our noses, we speak up for little Jane when little Johnny snatches her toy, or we rush to apologize for or defend little Johnny when he's met with the scornful eyes of the parents of Jane. We supervise recess in elementary school to make sure everyone is getting along and no one is excluded. We involve ourselves to such an extent that it's as if we are the ones heartbroken over the snatched toy, the teasing, or not getting our turn on the tire swing.

Today's grandparents see our behavior as overprotective and, at times, even absurd. I heard a woman named Donne Davis saying just that on my local NPR station one day, so I tracked her down. Davis founded a Bay Area social network for grandmothers called the GaGa Sisterhood. She tells me, "Moms seem so overinvolved in solving problems for their children instead of letting the kids learn to work it out. Whatever happens between the kids becomes a drama between the moms. Grandmothers might want to step in and say something, but if we say too much, our own kids might restrict our access to our grandkids."[2] She's right. I've seen this kind of intergenerational coup d'état brewing in my very own home (although I wouldn't have dreamed of restricting access: I depended upon my mother for child care!).

Look, today's grandmothers were raised in completely different times. And they weren't exactly watchful as parents. In fact between their smoke-

and drink-filled pregnancies, leaving us home alone while they were at work or out "finding themselves," and record-setting divorce and remarriage rates, many of us who were born in the '60s and '70s fended for ourselves to an extent that today might be called neglect. In fact, maybe we overparent in part as a *reaction* to our parents' laissez-faire approach and are justifiably skeptical about their opinions on child rearing. Still, I find myself sympathetic to what Donne Davis is saying—particularly about the drama we bring upon ourselves and into our kids' lives by arguing with other parents, and about how, when we step in to smooth things over, kids don't learn to do for themselves. In their groundbreaking 2009 book *Nurture-Shock: New Thinking About Children*, a manifesto about how recent strategies for raising children are backfiring, Po Bronson and Ashley Merryman refer to these things kids don't learn to do for themselves as the "unintended consequences" of our helpful intentions.[3]

THE CONCIERGE PARENT

We're not just clearing our kid's path of its obstacles, we're proactively taking precautions by being our kid's eyes and ears. And brains. Whether or not our kid is one of the 5.9 million with attention-deficit/hyperactivity disorder, we've all become the ones who pay attention on his or her behalf. We pay attention to cars at street crossings, to teachers at orientation, and to coaches at the start of the season. We snap to attention while our kid stands there bored or absorbed in a video game, a smartphone, or, if we're lucky, a book. At back-to-school nights we crowd our large bodies into the small desks, paying attention to what "we" need to know in order for our kid to be successful in the fifth grade.

As if *we* are the ones trying to get into college.

Many of us have fond memories of sleepaway camp. Wherever we may have gone, in whatever era, the food was likely to have been lousy, but the experience was likely to have been great. Part of its value was we got to be on our own—not *literally* alone, but outside of our so-called comfort zone and under the careful or not so careful watch of our teenaged counselors. I wondered if the sleepover camp experience was impacted by parental overinvolvement, so I went for a look.

Young Life Christian ministries brings tens of thousands of American teenagers into their residential camps each summer. Young Life is an evangelical outreach ministry; 85 percent of the kids that come to camp are non-Christian kids. The camps offer kids a chance to learn and grow, and have great fun, if kids immerse themselves in it. As with any immersive experience, it's hard to immerse if you're tied to the folks back home by cell phone. So at Young Life they expressly prohibit campers from bringing cell phones to the weeklong sleepaway camps. When the buses full of new campers are about to pull into camp, a counselor announces it's time to turn over cell phones and they'll be returned on the drive home in a week.

Young Life vice president of camping Steve Thompson says parents can violate both the letter and spirit of the rule. "Despite our clear statement of policy in advance, some parents send two cell phones with the kids so the kid can turn in one phone when asked, and then can sneak out and communicate with mom or dad on the second, hidden, phone."[4] Thompson attributes this to a parent's lack of trust in the basic systems and authority figures running our country, be they in schooling, government, or religious institutions. Apparently, even when sending kids to a camp rooted in religious ethics and values, parents feel lies are acceptable and rules can be broken in service to the larger goal of constant contact between parents and kids.

Boarding school—ostensibly a place devoid of parents—is no different. Parents call the dorm staff to ask them to make soup for their sick child, order pizza during finals week out of fear that their child isn't getting enough to eat, and fly to the school to pack up their kid's belongings when school lets out for the summer. Nowadays parents who can afford it sometimes opt to buy or rent a place nearby the school, *just because you never know what they might need*. Tyler Tingley, former head of school at both Phillips Exeter in Massachusetts and The Blake School in Minnesota, and now chief academic officer at Avenues in New York City, told me, "A growing phenomenon at Exeter was that parents would enroll their child as a boarder but six months later we'd discover that Mom or Dad had rented an apartment nearby. They had complicated reasons about doing it to be 'a good parent' to which I would reply, 'The experience of living independently is a great feature of boarding schools. You develop independence by learning how to do your own laundry.'"[5] And speaking of laundry, I know firsthand that parents come to college campuses to do it for their kids. It's not a rumor, and it's not a Stanford thing. It happens on campuses everywhere.

The United States Military Academy (a.k.a. West Point) has educated some of our nation's most promising young adults for over two hundred years. Located in upstate New York on the west bank of the Hudson River, about a ninety-minute drive from New York City, West Point's mission is "to educate, train and inspire the Corps of Cadets so that each graduate is a commissioned leader of character committed to the values of Duty, Honor, Country and prepared for a career of professional excellence and service to the nation as an officer in the United States Army." Since they've readied young adults for service to the nation and to be put directly in harm's way almost since the founding of our country, I wondered about their perspective on how the role of parents in the lives of college students and young adults has changed.

Colonel Leon Robert (pronounced Ro-BEAR) became a professor and head of the Department of Chemistry and Life Science at West Point after serving in Afghanistan. In keeping with protocol, he makes clear to me that he is speaking about his personal, anecdotal observations, and not on behalf of the Department of Defense or the U.S. Army.[6] "Graduates exit West Point with the rank of second lieutenants in the United States Army," Colonel Robert tells me. "The great majority are great men and women doing the right thing. But there are a creeping number who have parents that overmanage them, such as by driving them to their first assignment." I'm rather surprised, and try to picture it. "That's totally inappropriate," he continues. "You don't need your mother to show up at the front gate of Fort Bragg with you, or help you find an apartment. You're twenty-one, twenty-two, twenty-three years old. You need to deal with the landlord yourself. That's part of learning to act as an adult. Our graduates are mature leaders of character well prepared to lead America's sons and daughters and with all the right tools to be successful at the tasks the army will require of them. However, there are a small percentage of parents that will not, or cannot, 'let go' and continue to hover over their adult children."

West Point is in good company. The following are real-life examples of parents "being there" for their precollegiate and collegiate children.[7]

1. *David and Sue are from New England. Their daughter Emma, a high school senior, was accepted at a prestigious public university in the East and had just failed one of her final high school courses (and not for a "good" reason, like a serious illness). Worrying that the dean of admissions might impose some kind*

of consequence on their child up to or including rescinding admission, David and Sue write to the admissions dean to explain their daughter's situation.

2. *Rajiv and Parul are from the Washington, D.C., area. Their son Arjun was one of my incoming freshmen at Stanford a few years back. On the second day of orientation the three of them came to see me. Parul began the conversation by stating, "Arjun is interested in doing research in chemical engineering and we'd like to discuss those options with you." "Arjun," I replied, "That's great. Tell me about your experience with research, so I can help you think about the best way to get involved at Stanford." Arjun looked over at his dad, who told me the rather impressive story of Arjun's experience with research to date.*

3. *Jacqueline is from Los Angeles. Her daughter Jamie is a college sophomore at a large state school. Jacqueline could always be counted on to make sure Jamie met her deadlines in high school and even today Jamie still never misses a deadline; Jacqueline calls Jamie every day both to wake her up and to remind her of her upcoming assignments and test dates.*

4. *Bruce is from Chicago. His son Nicholas is a college junior at a private college in the Big Ten. Bruce is a finance executive in Chicago whose phone often buzzes multiple times a day with texts from Nicholas. Having flown into JFK for a summer internship, Nicholas took the subway to the heart of Manhattan near his summer sublet and exited the subway at a major intersection bustling with noisy taxis, cars, and people walking to and fro. Nicholas did not know quite where he was, or the direction of the apartment, so he texted his dad in Chicago for help. Bruce was delighted to get Nicholas's text and excused himself from a meeting with his colleagues in order to help Nicholas out.*

5. *Jan and Dulé are from Northern California. Their son August is a senior at an elite school in the Northwest. Writing was a struggle for August throughout his childhood, and either Jan or Dulé would lend a hand through the years by reviewing and editing his written work. It's easy for them to continue to help August while he is in college; he sends his parents draft papers electronically and they make their edits directly onto the Word document.*

6. *Chuck is from Seattle. His daughter Ann is entering graduate school at Teachers College at Columbia University. Chuck attends orientation with Ann and*

raises his hand with a question about the soundness of the data in a professor's presentation.

I have no doubt that these parents just want to help, or are fearful of the what-ifs that could result if they didn't involve themselves. Nor do I doubt that each of the young adults in the vignettes above feel grateful and relieved—perhaps even rescued—by their parents' help and involvement. *But, when should a person be expected to do these things for themselves?* Once the young adult enters the work world, perhaps?

The nonprofit organization Teach For America (TFA) was founded in 1989 to address inequity in K–12 education by placing recent college graduates as public school teachers in low-income communities for two-year teaching stints. In 2013, TFA was the second-largest employer of new U.S. college graduates (Enterprise Rent-A-Car ranked first, Verizon was third), and TFA's incoming cohort of fifty-nine hundred young men and women came from over eight hundred different colleges and universities all over the nation. From her perch as general counsel of TFA, Tracy-Elizabeth Clay has begun to encounter parents of TFA corps members who are very involved in helping their son or daughter segue into the world of work.

Parents call the main office and say, "Hi, my child is going to be part of your corps. I'm incredibly excited and proud. I'm in town now, looking for apartments for them. Do you guys have a list of apartment houses you recommend?" Tracy-Elizabeth's colleagues respond no; this is something TFA corps members have always been able to figure out for themselves.[8]

BEYOND THE CONCIERGE PARENT—THE ENFORCER

If we didn't manage to be successfully proactive, and something bad happened that we can't smooth over on our own, we're likely to consider taking up the matter with the authority figures involved. Dr. Tim Walden, the small suburban school district superintendent in Massachusetts, whom we met earlier, encountered a set of parents whose middle schooler didn't get picked for student council, and these parents wouldn't take no for an answer.[9] To them the school was very exclusionary because it put some requirements in place for student council eligibility, like grades and teacher recommendations, and their child wasn't the strongest student and had some disciplinary infractions. They escalated their concern from the student council adviser, past the principal, up to Dr. Walden, the superintendent.

"You want to listen to people and be democratic. But . . ." Dr. Walden sighed to me over the phone; clearly, some parents are pushing past the point of reason.

Back at West Point, then-Chief of Staff Colonel Gus Stafford—also speaking personally rather than for the Department of Defense or the army—talked me through the tremendous uptick in parental involvement at West Point, and the implied erosion of trust.[10] Being chief of staff means Colonel Stafford runs the staff, the budget, policy, and manpower, as he puts it. He is a graduate of West Point and is married to a former air force nurse, so he's steeped in military culture. He was formal with me, but also charming and forthcoming.

"We're a strange place," he says. "We have strange rules. For example, we have the Collapse Plan. It means that if you are a plebe—a freshman— and your roommate is going to be gone for the weekend, you are not allowed to stay in the room by yourself. You have to pack your stuff up and sleep with another set of roommates for the weekend." He says this policy is in place for all kinds of reasons, including protecting kids from sexual assault and protecting kids who are depressed. As a former college dean this all sounds really good to me, but apparently West Point's parents aren't as sanguine about the policy as I am.

"Mom and Dad will hear Johnny's got to move to a different room, and they'll call the tactical officer," Colonel Stafford tells me. "They'll ask 'why' and when they get the response about our policy they'll say, 'Are you afraid Johnny's going to commit suicide?' and 'Tell me about your record of sexual assaults.'" Want to make a military officer say "OMG"? This is how you do it. Parents second-guessing their decisions gets old for military leaders really fast.

As cadets get older they get to do a Military Individual Advanced Development activity (a.k.a. MIAD). The student picks a skill they want to develop, but there are different qualifications for each and sometimes a cadet will be "below the red line" for that activity, meaning not eligible. "Johnny may want to go to airborne school," Colonel Stafford tells me, "but his grades and military development put him below the red line. Johnny is upset. So Johnny tells Mom and Dad. Dad calls up and asks the tactical officer, 'I want to know why you're disadvantaging my son.'" This sounds just like Dr. Walden's rejected-from-student-council-parents, but it's the U.S. Army.

Colonel Stafford makes it clear that second-guessing of Academy policy and programs is not productive—that is, the TAC is not going to give into

Dad—and why. "Let's say the TAC gives in to Johnny's dad. Then Johnny tells his friend Bob, 'I got it switched when my dad called.'" It's the proverbial slippery slope, or the open floodgate, or whatever metaphor you want to use—and West Point isn't about to let it happen.

Parents are valued partners at West Point, Colonel Stafford tells me. Their trust in the institution and their goodwill toward it impact West Point's reputation and standing in local communities and in the nation at large. And parents can provide helpful support for a developing young adult. But sometimes a parent doesn't know where to draw the line, including parents who want to understand every component and aspect of the program. "That's okay," Colonel Stafford tells me, "but not required. The person who needs to understand the program is the young man or woman going through it." The parents may not completely trust the West Point authorities, nor their child, nor the world, and want to "be there" for their kids to try to ensure desired outcomes. For now, at least, even if a parent steps out of bounds, West Point holds the line.

As does the Peace Corps. For over fifty years the Peace Corps has been sending young American adults abroad for two-year stints to do some good in the world and grow a heck of a lot personally. Contact from concerned parents, once an anomaly, is now more commonplace.

Kate Raftery was the Peace Corps' country director for the eastern Caribbean and Peru in the 2000s, in addition to holding posts off and on at the Peace Corps for decades. Sometimes a Peace Corps volunteer just wasn't working out, and as a country director, Kate would have to make the decision to send that person home. "I've gotten more than one call from parents saying, 'You're ruining my child's life. They wanted to do two years and now you're sending them home.' I'd say, 'I believe when you speak to your son or daughter when they get home you'll see it's not something where on Friday I called them in and on Sunday I sent them home. It has been months of conversations and some efforts to try to help them improve. This is a conversation you need to have with your loved one, not with me. I'm interacting with your child as an adult. I'd encourage you to do the same.'"[11]

OUR CHILDREN, OUR SELVES

Parents who have always "been there" for their kid can find it next to impossible to stop when the kid grows up and goes out into the world. After all, the stakes in the real world are so much higher than they were in childhood, so if we've always "been there" it seems rather cruel to stop when they're grown and when their actions matter more than ever. Some parents actually *can't* stop; "being there" has become hardwired into us. It's not just how we parent anymore; it's who we *are*. And our children, though chronologically grown, are now quite dependent on us, and seem to need us more than ever to still "be there."

But truth be told, sometimes we like to "be there" for our kids because their need—whether real, perceived, or manufactured—gives our lives purpose and meaning. A dad named Jonathan living in the high-stress, high-achievement community of McLean, Virginia, sees parents there as defining themselves by who their children are, what they need, and what they accomplish. "Children are dependent on parents for everything, but parents have put themselves in that role because they feel their value and self-worth are tied up in that relationship."[12] We want to foster a closeness but we can end up manufacturing and then enabling a need.

We no longer know where to draw the line. San Jose educator Ole Jorgenson, who spoke earlier about the overuse of the "bully" label, sees parents showing up in school activities simply to watch and enjoy their kid's experience unfolding, but having difficulty separating from their children when doing so would be better for the kids. For example, Ole's middle school students travel on overnight field trips—to Yosemite, Catalina Island, and Washington, D.C.—and he's noticed a trend developing in which parents arrange travel parallel with their kids' school trips. They stay in hotels near the places their children are visiting, not as trip chaperones, but to be nearby their kids "just in case." It is not so much problematic for Ole as it is developmentally unhealthy for the kids. "It sends the message to preadolescents that they aren't ready for the independence they crave and need at that age."[13] It's the kind of thing that makes you cock your head to the side and say, "Huh?" I experienced similar moments as a college dean, such as when parents showed up for the rituals and traditions that serve the crucial purpose of folding a student into the college community.

Take Stanford's annual Band Run, for example—a late-night activity on the first day of orientation where the infamous Stanford Band runs through campus pied piper–style, picking up students at each freshman dorm along the way. By the time the run is over, the entire freshman class plus a bunch of upperclassmen are corralled in the Inner Quad learning to jump in the right places in the school's fight song "All Right Now." There on the sidelines in a golf cart in case anyone got injured, in recent years I saw parents trying to look inconspicuous as they stood against lampposts or tree trunks, watching, or trying to keep up with the fun unfolding by running along.

West Point has its own rituals and traditions that fold a cadet into the "long gray line," which is how the community of West Point alumni describes themselves. Colonel Stafford tells me that in the almost thirty years since he joined the long gray line many things have changed, like the twelve-mile road march back to West Point that marks the triumphant end of cadet basic training each summer.[14] "It's hard," he tells me. "They're carrying a thirty- to forty-pound pack on their backs, plus their helmet, weapon, and other gear. When the cadets finally get back to West Point, they have a personal sense of pride. Of 'I did it.' What's different today is we have some parents who say, 'I'm going to walk back with Johnny or Susie. We're going to all walk back together. We're going to be one with his experience.'"

I can hear the colonel's voice settle into a sigh. He has kids of his own. He knows how the world has changed. He respects parents. "I can understand the love, the commitment, and the support," he tells me. "But unwittingly they diminish the experience and the accomplishment of the individual who might have done it all on their own." I know he's right. I feel it in my gut, see it in my house, saw it on my campus.

Are we "being there" for them on school trips, the Stanford Band Run, and the long march back to West Point just in case the what-ifs of life eventuate, however unlikely that may be? Are we trying to relive our childhood? Or are we so singularly devoted to our children that our life feels utterly thin, lifeless, and without joy, when our children are not there for us to watch, coach, help, or dote on? Is observing their activities and experiences what gives our lives its greatest meaning?

In 2013 writer Michael Gerson confessed this existential intertwinedness in a *Washington Post* op-ed written on the eve of his son's departure for college. Of his son, Gerson wrote, "He is experiencing the adjustments that come with beginnings. His life is starting for real. I have begun the long letting go. Put another way: He has a wonderful future in which my part naturally diminishes. I have no possible future that is better without him close."[15]

You can't help but feel Gerson's anguish as you read his piece. But was Gerson only confessing, or was he in part boasting of his devotedness as a parent? Has sidling right up alongside our kid and making them the center of our world become a measure of how much we love them? If so, is it our love we're wearing on our sleeve, or our neediness? *Do we have an obligation to shield this raw need from our kids?*

The school trips, the Stanford Band Run, and the march back to West Point are all for the students. There is no need for the parents to "be there" for their offspring. Are kids having the authentic experience if Mom and Dad are there to experience it with them? Can we repress our own need to be there in favor of the delight they take in telling it to us later, or in not telling us at all? Can we be assured we've fostered a good connection with our kids without having to "be there" all the time?

4

SUCCUMBING TO THE
COLLEGE ADMISSIONS ARMS RACE

Once our kids are in middle school, on any given afternoon in any given semester, we fear—and it may be true—that if our kid gets a B, or doesn't make it onto the elite sport team, or in some other way fails to check off every item in the checklisted childhood, they won't get into the type of college we have in mind for them (and what we have in mind for them is some function of where we went, our belief about which colleges offer the "best" education, our sense of which college graduates have the "best" job opportunities, or our desire to have the most bragging rights over coffee or cocktails with friends, and so on). We then feel we must do as much as or slightly more than the next parents seem to be doing in order to facilitate the desired college outcome for our kids. So even when our gut is telling us *don't do that*—such as when we face an ethical conundrum about whether or not to do our kids' homework for them outright, or when we're simply exhausted from all of the scheduling, driving, and staying on top of things—our greater fear is what might go wrong if we fail to involve ourselves.

The college admissions arms race mind-set goes something like this: "If I let my kid write this paper on his own, he might not do well and may even do poorly, and yes I hope he'll learn from that and do better next time. But he'll be competing with a classroom full of other children, many of whose parents will have heavily edited or written their kid's papers. *My* kid might learn but *their* kid will get the better grade and be put into the honors program where they'll be exposed to greater things. *Their* kid will get into the college I want for *my* kid."

If we could go through life with a picture of our infants learning to walk plastered Google Glass–style in front of our eyes at all times, we'd have the reminder we need that kids learn and grow precisely by trying new things, being allowed to fail, picking themselves up, and trying again. But the holy grail of college admission—admission to highly selective colleges, that is, with its apparent refusal to acknowledge that stumbles and falls are what make the brilliant among us fallible *and* the fallible among us brilliant— seems to completely cloud our thinking.

Jane, whose daughter attends the very rigorous magnet public school Thomas Jefferson High School in northern Virginia, told me, "I would have thought my daughter would have more independence than she does. I would love for her to be making her own breakfast and packing her own lunches and doing her own laundry. But her life is so intense right now. If I want her to get any sleep at all, I'm going to try to do the things that help her. She doesn't need a mom; she needs an assistant to keep the pieces of her life together."[1] Jane's daughter travels ninety minutes by school bus to and from TJ, as the school is known. Between that travel, homework, school itself, meals, and sleep, there simply is no more time for Jane's daughter to do anything except the tasks that will affect her high school transcript.

There are a severely limited number of slots at these colleges we want our kids to attend, and an overabundance of people who want them. Hence the arms race. Why we're only interested in a small number of schools, what's wrong with that analysis, and what we can do about it will come in later chapters of this book. For now I want to shine a light on the extreme lengths to which we might go to ensure that our kids complete every item in the checklisted childhood and have a perfect and polished record to show for it.

TAKING A SHOT AT HOMEWORK

We see from admission results that the most selective colleges admit students with all As or darn near close to it. So, by hook or by crook we try to make sure those grades are gotten.

Some parents take the prophylactic measure of urging their kids to take easier courses. In her well-to-do Manhattan neighborhood, a mom named Laura tells me, "When a teacher is known not to give As, parents tell their kid to drop the class. Parents tell their kid to take the easier class so they'll get an A." This seems to be exactly the opposite of anything a mom or dad would have read in a parenting book. It's also likely to backfire as a strategy for elite college admission, since admissions deans asked whether they prefer to see the A grade on the transcript or the most challenging course taken, reply to our consternation, "BOTH!"

Regardless of what level coursework our kids undertake, when kids are doing their homework, we can't help but help. There are relatively benign ways to help—asking how much homework they have and checking up to see if they've done it, sitting with them while they do it, or offering suggestions when they struggle. Then there's the heavy-handed intervention of our rewriting or correcting—or of simply doing the assignment for them. If you're doing your child's homework from time to time, you are not alone.

We're worried about the quality of our kid's work, but in many communities the *quantity* of homework is an even more pressing concern. In 2014, Stanford lecturer Denise Pope, author and cofounder of the nonprofit Challenge Success, published results of a homework study that used a sample of 4,317 students from ten high-performing high schools in upper-middle-class California communities, where median household income exceeded $90,000 and 93 percent of the students went on either to two-year or four-year college. Students in the study averaged 3.1 hours of homework each night. (*Only* 3.1 hours, you may be wondering? Many of us have seen the upper end of those results.)

A student at Phillips Academy Andover in Massachusetts (known as Andover) told me he spent five hours every night on homework during his junior year. A Palo Alto High School freshman told me her biology teacher bragged on the first day of school that his course would prepare her for college-level science, with a nightly homework load to fit that bill. My son, Sawyer, regularly did three hours of homework a night during his freshman year of high school, and, on some nights, upward of five. When the homework load seems completely unmanageable on its own, let alone alongside the other things kids want and need to do—like extracurricular activities, eating dinner, having some downtime, and getting the nine hours of sleep pediatricians say is necessary for teenagers—what's a parent to do?

In 2012 a Stanford professor and parent of three told me about a time when he took homework matters into his own hands. We were attending a meeting of Stanford's admissions and financial aid policy committee and the topic of the amount of stress and strain high school kids experience was a discussion item. The professor leaned over to me and told me that one night it was well past bedtime and each of his three kids—all Palo Alto public schoolers—had a mountain of homework still to be done. His solution? He told his elementary schooler to go to bed, told his middle schooler to do the elementary kid's homework, told his high schooler to do the homework for his middle schooler, and he himself, the professor, did the homework for the high schooler. Sure, it's problematic. But why criticize this short-term repair when the system itself is so broken?

Teachers know we're doing our kids' homework and try to devise ways to stop us. During a group interview I conducted for this book with parents in Fairfax County, Virginia, one of the nation's top school districts, I spoke with a parent named Holley who is also an instructional aide. "Teachers want the children to do their writing in class because they know if they send a writing assignment home it does not come back as the student's own work."[2] This isn't just an issue of ethics, Holley tells me. Homework is meant to show teachers the level of a kid's understanding in the subject area; when parents do the homework teachers have no idea where the kids *are*.

Ellen Nodelman, my friend who taught English at Rockland Country Day School in New York, saw parental involvement in schoolwork skyrocket in the last fifteen to twenty of her forty-plus years at the school. "Parents are now vigilant over every homework assignment, and a whole lot of parents are doing their kid's homework for them. They do it under the guise of helping their kids, but the kids feel helpless. If parents aren't doing the homework but they're running out and hiring tutors to help kids with their homework, it's the same thing. It fosters a sense of dependence and helplessness in kids; they come to feel they just can't do it on their own."[3] *Yeah, yeah, yeah, but the homework is often hard, time-consuming (and the student needs time for other important activities), and the homework is often graded. How a student does on homework can affect his or her GPA. And Stanford won't take less than perfect. Besides—and here's where the arms race begins—all the other parents are helping their kids.*

GRABBING THE GLUE GUN

School projects are the type of homework that end up on display for everyone to see. They become a kind of in-your-face demonstration of just how far we'll go to ensure that our kids succeed.

Every California fourth grader learns about the Spanish missions in social studies class; how in the late eighteenth to early nineteenth centuries the Spanish colonized the territory now known as California by marching north from Mexico and building large adobe structures known as missions along the way. The culmination of this unit is an assignment called "the mission project," where kids are to make a three-dimensional replica of one of these adobe and red-tile-roofed structures.

As with any similar school project, the mission project is intended to assess a kid's knowledge of the subject and his or her creativity and precision in executing the assignment. Kids will use anything to make these large structures; some use Lego bricks to frame the mission. Others use pasta. I even saw one kid who baked a cake with white icing for the adobe bricks, red icing for the red-tiled roof, and the telltale Catholic cross made of candles. And as with any similar school project these days, the mission project has become an opportunity for parents to demonstrate just how skilled they are at being children—in this case, fourth graders.

When I went to see Sawyer's and Avery's mission projects, at least half were designed to such a degree of architectural or engineering precision that they could only have been made by parents. I'd raise my eyebrows and flair my nostrils at my husband (a designer, who, admirably, had restrained himself from becoming involved in our kids' projects), pointing my finger at *that project*. Each year I wondered who these parents thought they were fooling, and hoped teachers would be explicit about parental involvement being completely inappropriate, and then back that up with a ding to the kid's grade if the parent crossed the line. But it turns out it's very hard for all but the most seasoned of teachers to stand up to a well-heeled parent wielding a glue gun.

Hillary Coustan lives just north of Chicago, in Evanston, Illinois, the home of Northwestern University. She is a lawyer and adjunct law professor at Loyola and Northwestern, and is a graduate of Exeter, University of Michigan, and Stanford Law School. She is also the mother of two young sons. Hillary is smart, thoughtful, and frank. I talked to her on the phone one day about her experience with elementary school projects. Even though her kids are quite young, she was already familiar with parental overinvolvement.[4]

When her son Eli was four, he was in a local program for youngsters that culminated in the children making a presentation on a sea creature. "The point was to go through the motions of doing the project and talk about it in front of a crowd of people who love you," Hillary told me. Eli was assigned a shark. "I wanted to help him come up with a project he could do himself and feel proud of doing, something that didn't require me doing everything for him." At this age Eli's fine motor skills weren't very developed so he could not draw. But he could cut. Hillary decided to draw the front and back of a shark and have Eli cut it out, color it, staple it, and stuff it with newspaper.

A few days later it was time for the presentations. Among this group of fifteen or so kids—all four or five years old—a good number arrived with rather impressive work featuring trifold poster boards, shellacked photographs, and research and analysis that were beautifully typewritten. And then there was Eli, standing proudly with his little stuffed shark. There was some audience tittering throughout the presentations that night—some perhaps directed toward poor underperforming Eli, others toward the obvious fact that some parents had done their kid's project. Little Eli was unfazed. To this day, that stuffed shark occupies a prominent position on Eli's bedroom door.

In kindergarten, Eli wanted to participate in his school science fair. As with the shark project, Hillary wanted him to take on a project he could actually do himself. Eli understood and liked the idea of friction, so they went with it. He found some little toy cars to put at the top of a ramp, and a bunch of different materials he could use to make a road at the bottom of the ramp—a bath towel, tinfoil, and wood. He understood that the point was to test how far the cars would go as they encountered the different surfaces. But how will he do the data? Hillary wondered. Eli didn't know what an average was, she reminded me—he was in kindergarten. So Hillary suggested to him that he color a bar graph showing the different distances the cars had traveled. And that's what Eli did.

When Eli and his parents got to the science fair, the young elementary school kid next to Eli had an elaborate volcano that showed how different chemicals erupt differently, with the chemical names written in their scientific notation. The kid's dad was furiously fixing things while the kid just stood there. When people came by to observe the volcano project, the kid had nothing to say about it.

The next year Hillary signed on to be one of the science fair organizers. She hoped to make it a more robust opportunity for kids to discuss their projects, ideas, and conclusions, and really play the role of scientist, as opposed to an evening where the kids stand around mingling next to their trifold presentation boards. So she and her fellow organizers brought in outside scientists to judge the fair.

The science fair was held at night and was open to parents and the public. The judges came the morning after and walked around to see each project and spent a good deal of time engaging each young scientist in grade level-appropriate conversation; the kids responded, or didn't, depending on how familiar they were with their own project. The school made it explicit that no parents were allowed to come to the judging session. One component of the judges' rubric—made known to parents and students when the science fair was first announced—was whether the work was clearly the student's own.

FINGER ON THE BUTTON

Parents arguing with teachers about academic outcomes is the stuff of Internet meme and cartoon. We use technology as both our spy and our weapon.

Most school districts use some kind of student information software that includes a parent portal where parents can log on and see their student's attendance record, grades, and so on. I've never checked up on my kids' records online—this is one of those arenas where I want to reduce my involvement, not increase it, and where I expect my son and daughter to inform me of what's going on as needed, just as I informed my parents back in the day (or didn't; I realize that's one of the risks). To be frank, I just can't deal with that additional information—either logistically in terms of finding the time to log on, or emotionally in terms of figuring out what I'm supposed to *do* with all that data about my kids. I'm told that I'm an outlier, though, and that many parents not only log on but do so regularly.

Earlier I mentioned an Atlanta mom who'd told me that hours after her son took an exam she went online and learned he'd failed it; her kid wasn't even home from school yet and hadn't been notified himself. She lit into him by text, to which he responded, "Mom I thought I did well. I don't know what happened. I have to focus on this other class now." By the time this mother was talking to me several months later, she was worried not about the failed exam but about how the parent portal was messing with her relationship with her son.

At Jane Lathrop Stanford Middle School (JLS), one of three public middle schools in Palo Alto, many parents check up on their kids' grades quite frequently. Sharon Ofek is principal at JLS, where she balances a parent's need to know *now* with a teacher's need to keep teaching. For example, when JLS parents learn from the parent portal that their kid hasn't been turning in homework and now has a zero, they might e-mail the teacher saying, "You should have told me my child wasn't turning in work. Now I want you to tell me every time."[5] To the parent this is a benign request, but if a teacher has to e-mail all the parents whose kids haven't turned in homework each day, the teacher would spend a lot more time on parents and a lot less time on students. "That seemingly unobtrusive request becomes really challenging, particularly for teachers who see a couple hundred kids in a given week. How do we shift responsibility for learning to the student?" asks Ofek.

A nasty child custody battle in Tim Walden's school district in Massachusetts revealed just how substantial the volume of e-mail correspondence schools receive from parents had become. As superintendent, Dr. Walden received a subpoena from a boy's father for all e-mails related to the boy; the father hoped to use the content of some of his ex-wife's e-mails against her. Instead the subpoena revealed a different fact pattern: in the aggregate over the boy's freshman and sophomore years the father had e-mailed teachers and administrative staff over two hundred times. Ironically the mother had sent only about ten e-mails.[6] Technology has changed many things but the school day is still only six or seven hours long. How do teachers and administrators even begin to handle the enormous work increase caused by interactions with parents?

SCHOOLS IN THE CROSSFIRE

Parent involvement in the minutiae of teaching and grading children "impacts the *practice* of education," says Dr. Walden. He's worked in a few districts and in most, teachers used an electronic grade book in which daily homework, quiz, and exam results are entered. Some districts chose to use portal features that give parents access to the electronic grade book entries for their child. When schools opt to give parents such access, it provides fuel for parents who feel a need to know everything about their child at all times. Then, if a teacher alters the grade book during the course of the term, it can cause parents great concern. They e-mail or call asking, "Why did you do this assessment? Why did you change this? How come this hasn't been corrected or assessed yet?" This kind of constant second-guessing day in, day out, week in, week out, can wear some teachers down.

"We walk a tightrope," said Dr. Walden. "I believe we *should* be transparent—that a teacher's assessment should be fair, valid, credible, and to a certain degree we should deprivatize our practice. On the other side of the coin, teachers need academic freedom and flexibility—if we want them to differentiate to meet kids' needs, kids' strengths, and so on, not everything needs to be under a microscope."

Dr. Walden has seen schools achieve a balance when they put tight parameters around the use of the online grade books, and communicate those parameters to parents, for example, "This is how frequently it's going to be updated. This is how you'll be notified," and so on. Without tight parameters, schools end up putting too much time and effort into responding to a subset of parents, which then takes away from the attention they can give to all the other kids and to other parents. These controls make a teacher's life more sane, too. "For some of our teachers," Dr. Walden tells me with a withered voice, "parental access to their grade books makes them feel rather paranoid."

Schools that do not provide strong, clear boundaries between pedagogy and parents can suffer serious consequences (which means, of course, that student learning suffers). At a small independent school near New York City a decade ago, the headmaster felt it was better to appease parents than continue to uphold academic integrity. His solution? He encouraged his faculty to give kids As and Bs, and let the chips fall where they may. Parents were happier. The school environment was much more relaxed. Before anyone caught on, the headmaster had been fired for unrelated reasons. When the new leadership team discovered that there was a huge disconnect between student GPAs and SAT scores, the former headmaster's grading "policy," such as it was, was reversed and things got back on track. He had been misguided, but with a horde of well-heeled parents breathing down his neck, I imagine he felt tremendous relief when he decided to cut and run.

STRATEGIC DEFENSE INITIATIVES

Sometimes the arms race for elite college admission makes parents employ covert tactics. In academically competitive communities in particular, parents may feel it's best to lie to other parents about what we—*our kids*—are doing, particularly when it comes to extra enrichment. "Oh, Johnny's not working out with a strength coach," we say, when in reality Johnny sees a strength coach twice a week and is more likely to get on the elite team as a result. "Oh, Jenny's not doing much after school," we say, when in reality she's in a super-secret robotics club organized by a genius dad that gives kids a better shot at getting on the highly renowned robotics club at school. The best resources can seem scarce and we want to keep a good thing secret so as to secure a competitive advantage for Johnny and Jenny when it comes to applying to college.

Parents can also be quite defensive when our kid does something bad—steals or damages property, physically hurts someone, or puts themselves or others in danger. Sure, privately we might want to wring their necks with our own hands, but our mama and papa bear protective instincts come on strong when it seems our kids are backed into a corner. Sometimes we find the wherewithal to take a really deep breath and do the right thing—hear the facts, talk with the parties involved, sit down with our child and have a conversation about values, actions, and consequences, and then implement those consequences. But sometimes, fearing that the incident will go on their "permanent record," which we want to prevent at all costs, we come out swinging while our kid stands either meekly or smugly just off to the side. *We can't let this incident keep him out of college.*

Alcohol and drugs are often at the center of the problems kids get themselves into. Many school districts take a tough-love, 24/7 approach to underage drinking and drug use, meaning that if the police catch a student drinking or doing drugs, there will be school consequences such as loss of eligibility for sports or extracurriculars, even if the event did not occur within the context of the school year.

Before becoming a superintendent, Dr. Walden was a principal in a different Massachusetts district, one that engaged in a raging debate about whether to adopt the 24/7 philosophy. "Kids very actively involved in sports, student council, and honor roll would do something completely over the top, like get so drunk at a party they had to be hospitalized. When we implemented the consequences, like losing a sport for a portion of the season or being stripped of their captaincy, I would have parents come to the school with an attorney to fight the decision."[7] Ultimately Dr. Walden's school board declined to adopt the 24/7 philosophy, stating that it was too invasive. But part of the rationale was that board members knew full well that there were children in the community who were big-time partiers, whose parents would mount a legal defense—or offense—to combat any type of consequence resulting from their child being caught drunk or stoned.

Kids—particularly adolescent boys—often make poor choices as a normal part of their development as humans; they've got an impulse to do the bad or crazy thing but their prefrontal cortex is still developing, which means they can't yet appreciate the danger involved and so can't use what we would call "good judgment." While we're wide-eyed with fear over the risk they took, regardless of whether it led to a bad outcome, they're thinking, "Um, it seemed like a good idea at the time." Enforcing consequences for our own kids is essential. It's the only way they learn *not* to do those things.

If instead we hire a lawyer to defend our kid's bad behavior, we might achieve some kind of short-term "win" and feel reassured that the incident has not derailed their chances of admission to the "right" colleges. But when the teachable moments go untaught, what our kids get in exchange is the moral or ethical shortcomings that come from getting away with stuff.

ON THE FRONT LINES FOR THEM

Many college faculty reject the premise that students come out of Advanced Placement (AP) courses having learned what they would have learned in the "equivalent" college course. Faculty in such departments won't give the student college "units" or "credits" toward the major for these courses, nor will they allow the student to "place into" a higher course at the college. For example, Stanford's English, history, psychology, and biology departments have not accepted AP credit at least as far back as the 2006–2007 school year (the earliest year for which records are publicly available) and quite likely longer. And 2006–2007 was also the last year in which Stanford's economics faculty accepted AP credit for micro- or macroeconomics.

Regardless of their value as a substitute for college work, however, students load up on these courses because often they come with the best teachers, and because such courses are favored by college admission deans looking for students to have taken the most challenging courses available in high school. And, due to their higher degree of rigor, these classes offer more weight in the GPA (typically increasing a grade by an entire point, making a B look like an A). Therefore, in high school, nowhere are the academic stakes higher—and nowhere is the school transcript arms race more ferociously fought—than in AP and other advanced courses such as International Baccalaureate (IB) and honors classes.

So perhaps it shouldn't surprise us to learn that anecdotally, school officials say the greatest disparities between the quality of work done at home versus in class—that is, the most frequent and egregious evidence that parents are doing homework for their kids—occurs in honors, AP, or IB classes. Homework quality versus in-class work varies most greatly in classes like these because *the stakes are so high*—and many of us are doing our kids' homework for them. When our kids face the greatest academic hurdles in high school, some of us won't risk the possibility that they'll fall or flail. How? We stand in their place and face the challenge for them.

Schools try to prevent students from passing off third-party work as their own—plagiarism—by having them submit papers via websites like turnitin.com, which will scan the submitted material and report whether it duplicates someone else's published work. But software programs that uncover plagiarism are powerless when it comes to parents. (And the very notion that a parent is a "third party" when it comes to the child is a hard concept for overinvolved parents to grasp.)

Beth Gagnon regularly sees parents having a hard time drawing this line.[8] She has a marriage, family, and child therapy practice in New Hampshire, just outside the Boston area, a practice that is full of parents who are doing their best to help their kids cross off the items on their checklist. When parents admit to Beth that they wrote the essay when their kid was applying to a private high school, Beth uses humor to try to get parents to think about whether this impulse to stand in for their kids can or should ever end. Remember, these parents are coming to Beth for therapy—for solutions to their problems. Her standard routine goes something like this:

> Beth: "How is your kid going to function in college if you've done all this for them? How are they even going to get *into* college?"
> Parent: "I'll write that for them, too!"
> Beth: "Where does that end? Because I'm pretty sure the RA in the dorm is going to kick you out. You're not exactly age appropriate."

Presumably some laughter ensues, and if things go Beth's way, a little introspection, and then maybe a reality check and a commitment to work on that. But no matter how effective Beth is within the therapy session, her clients go back out into the real world with its relentless pressure on parents to do whatever it takes.

Many college admissions officers want to admit students who have demonstrated a genuine interest in their school. With kids being busy, shy, or just not interested, this is an area rife for parental involvement—or impersonation. In 2013, Ira Glass, host of Chicago Public Media's nationally broadcast radio program *This American Life*, interviewed Rick Clark, director of undergraduate admissions at Georgia Institute of Technology (a.k.a. Georgia Tech). Rick told Ira that he and his team regularly get e-mails and phone calls from parents *pretending* to be their own kids. It can be an e-mail from a boy thanking the school for his recent visit, sent from the mom's e-mail address. Or an e-mail using words like "awesome" and "cool," which is language Rick and his team almost never see from a high school student. Or a phone call from a mother acting as if she is her teenage daughter, who slips up about fifteen minutes into the call by saying, "What if she, I mean, I, wanted to list more than that number of activities on my application?"[9]

BRINGING IN REINFORCEMENTS

We probably couldn't pay someone to do our kids' homework without our internal ethical barometer going haywire, but we can hire people to help our kids get through high school with as much accomplishment and polish to show for it as possible. Kids can be tutored in virtually any (and in some cases every) subject—not just to remedy C, D, and F grades but to turn Bs into As and A minuses into A pluses. Kids whose families can afford it may prepare for the SAT for years, including enrolling in expensive test prep courses and making multiple attempts at taking the test in order to boost scores. I heard of a man who was offered more than $100,000 to tutor a high school kid through the AP, SAT, and all SAT subject tests.

If our kid attends public school—where college counselors routinely face a load of 150 to 400 students in contrast to their counterparts at private schools who face a load a fraction of that size—we might feel the urge to hire a "private admissions consultant" to give our kids' college applications the attention they deserve. These private consultants consult one on one and also offer things like essay-writing boot camp weekends. Parents of kids at private high schools hire these consultants, too. Some consultants offer an ethically dubious guarantee that they have "pull" at certain selective colleges. In 2013, 26 percent of college applicants reported having utilized such a person, three times the rate of kids who sought such services just ten years prior.[10]

In the summer of 2014, a Silicon Valley woman posted an ad on Stanford's job boards seeking a student who could mentor her fourteen-year-old son, whom she described as having "a high IQ and various talents, no special needs, and the ability to talk about complex subjects at adult levels." The job would entail working weekday afternoons with this young man "to make sure he exercises, organizes his folders, plans ahead, and talks through the normal teenage issues . . . and to help him improve his understanding of responsibility, consequences, and resourcefulness." The mom sought candidates who have achieved at least a 3.5 GPA in college, and offered $25 to $35 an hour for the work (the higher end for someone in or through grad school or with teaching/coaching experience).

Of course I don't know the particular reasons this parent feels the need to provide such mentoring for her kid, but it's reasonable to presume it has something to do with preparedness for college and perhaps for later life. The question I have is why is childhood itself not enough of a preparation? Why do our kids need special handlers? What is this great future for which we are so ardently preparing them? What would happen if this kid was left to his own—seemingly rather accomplished—devices? Even feeling as I do about these matters, a small part of me panics just reading this woman's ad. *Look what this parent is providing for her kid. Should I be trying to do the same?*

And *that* frightened feeling is at the parental heart of this academic arms race. A New Yorker explained the panic as he sees it. "We live in a time where we feel scarcity. We're no longer living the American dream. If *your* kid gets that job or that college spot, it's not there for *my* kid. In that environment parents will go to any length to make sure their kid can get into that Ivy League school."

Yes, there are too few spots at Stanford, MIT, and other Ivy League–type schools. But as I'll discuss in later chapters, scarcity does not portend a limited future for a student who does *not* get into those schools. President Obama drew attention to this fact in 2014 while touring colleges with his older daughter, Malia. "We tell her, 'Don't assume that there are ten schools that you have to go to, and if you didn't go to those ten, that somehow things are going to be terrible. There are a lot of schools out there.'"[11] Of course, it's easy for the president of the United States to take the long view about his daughter's future security, but his was reasonable advice in what is, for the rest of us, an unreasonable situation.

MARCHING WITH THEM INTO BATTLE

As is the case with other forms of twenty-first-century overparenting, stocking academic weaponry for our kid doesn't end when the child graduates from high school. Kids whose parents battled the college admission process for them become kids whose parents fight their battles in college. Stanford and colleges in every rankings tier around the country have seen parents show up to do the actual schoolwork of being a college student; they select the courses they feel will lead to their kid's success, choose their kid's majors, edit their kid's papers, call faculty to question grades, and bring lawyers to defend behavioral accusations. Working alongside college students as parents began increasingly to insinuate themselves in academic life, at times I found myself thinking, *Who's going to college here, anyway?*

Once a kid is in college, the next front in the battle is grad school and/or the job market. If our kids are accustomed to receiving our help, they will want—and need—it more than ever when the time for the job hunt comes.

In 2014, the economy was finally beginning to recover from the Great Recession that began in the 2008–2009 academic year. In terms of landing full-time paying work, the recession hit Millennials harder than any other generation.[12] Twenty- to twenty-four-year-olds with a college education had suffered the greatest percentage increase in unemployment rates.[13] This years-long slow start into the job market doesn't hurt only in the short run; people graduating college in a recession economy see their overall long-term earnings diminished by 10 percent—across their lifetime.[14] In addition, this particular generation of young people is graduating with more student loan debt than any previous generation. And they are searching for paid work in an era when employers offer not paid work but unpaid internships, and they are competing for jobs with others among the largest pool of college degree holders ever: The number of Americans aged twenty-five to twenty-nine who hold bachelor's degrees increased only 3 percent in the twenty years from 1975 to 1995 (21.9 percent to 24.7 percent), but from 1995 to 2012 that number jumped almost 10 percent (24.7 percent to 33.5 percent).[15] Millennials are also the first generation in the modern era to have lower levels of wealth and personal income than their two immediate predecessor generations (Gen Xers and Boomers) had at the same stage of their life cycles.[16] Put simply, the picture is not rosy. Many of us read these

headlines and think, *How can we send our kids out into THAT?* So we go
for the short-term win by hand-holding them, unaware of the long-term
cost, that is, *Are they ever going to be able to do anything for themselves?*

The Collegiate Employment Research Institute (CERI) at Michigan State
University surveys the national labor market focusing on what's going on
in the early career segment, and how employers can achieve more successful transitions from college to work. According to Phil Gardner, the director of CERI, parents didn't become seriously involved in their children's
work lives until the early 2000s recession fueled by the dot-com bust and
the 9/11 attacks.[17]

But by the mid-2000s, Gardner had heard a number of sensational
media reports about parental involvement in college students' job hunts and
in the workplace. Being a researcher, he wanted to move from anecdote to
data. So in 2006–2007, CERI's annual survey of employers included questions about the extent of parental involvement in recruiting and hiring
efforts and the activities parents are likely to engage in.[18] A total of 725
employers responded. (Keep in mind that this survey was conducted during
a growth economy before the Great Recession hit, and before the practice
of prolific texting/calling between parents and children, both of which have
been said to have exponentially increased parental overinvolvement in the
lives of young adults.)

Of the 725 employers, 23 percent reported seeing parents "sometimes"
to "very often" when hiring a college senior. Small companies hardly ever
encountered parents, but one third of large companies (defined as those
employing more than thirty-seven hundred people) witnessed parent
involvement. (This distinction may be the result of large companies being
more likely to participate in campus recruitment and job fairs, both of
which are rife with parental involvement.)

Through the CERI survey, Gardner sought to gauge the frequency of a
variety of types of parental involvement in the recruitment and hiring of
college students. The survey showed parents were: obtaining information
on the company (40 percent), submitting a résumé on behalf of a student
(31 percent), advocating that their son/daughter obtain a position or salary increase (26 percent), attending a career fair (17 percent), complaining
if the company does not hire son/daughter (15 percent), making interview arrangements (12 percent), negotiating salary and benefits (9 percent),
advocating for promotion/salary increase (6 percent), and attending the
interview (4 percent).

Mothers were more likely to do the front-end work of collecting company information and arranging interviews or company visits, while fathers were more likely to appear during negotiations and when the son or daughter was being disciplined. According to the CERI survey report, "One employer had advice for parents submitting résumés: 'Please tell your student that you have submitted a resume to a company. We have called a student from our resume pool only to find out they did not know anything about our company and were not interested in a position with us.'"[19]

"Some parents are helpful in good ways," says Gardner. "They explore job opportunities, encourage their kids, and provide emotional and sometimes temporary financial support, but *they don't do it for them.* You would not have seen parents ten to twenty years ago become involved in negotiations on starting offers and conditions of employment. But you do now." Employers report to Phil that parents who are overinvolved in recruitment and hiring don't quit—they continue in "Act Three" (the workplace) where they do work assignments for their kids. "We've interviewed some parents who said, 'Maybe we made a mistake because our kids are now in their thirties and they still want us to do their job search.'"

The lesson here is that even though we parents may one day be eager to exit the arms race—realizing, if belatedly, that our adult children ought to be able to handle things—we will have a hard time exiting the field. Our kids—accustomed to our involvement on all fronts—won't have the wherewithal to handle things if we go.

5

TO WHAT END?

Can we, for a moment, flash back to the benign neglect of the late 1970s and '80s? To children helping themselves to three slices of cake, or ingesting secondhand smoke, or carrying cocktails to adults who were ever so slightly slurring their words. To those evenings when they were not noticed; they were loved, just not monitored. And, as I remember it, those warm summer nights of not being focused on were liberating. In the long sticky hours of boredom, in the lonely, unsupervised, unstructured time, something blooms; it was in those margins that we became ourselves.[1]

—Katie Roiphe, *In Praise of Messy Lives*

Until rather recently an American childhood was filled with a wonderful set of freedoms. Kids not only survived, but grew up and thrived, and led our nation to become the greatest economic power the world has known. School mattered a great deal, and kids worked hard, even very, very hard, but school wasn't the only thing. Kids were free to roam their world and explore what became of interest to them. Sport was for sport. Play was play. These pursuits all contributed to kids' cognitive, psychological, and social development, and most of it happened out of the earshot of adults. If you're a Gen Xer like Katie Roiphe (quoted above), you know this. If you're a Millennial, this may sound like history or fiction.

Like Roiphe, at times I, too, long for childhood to be exactly as I remember it, and I feel quite a measure of sadness that our kids are raised within the structures of our fears and expectations rather than with those remembered freedoms. I long for my kids to experience the childhood of the past, sensing that they—we, all of us—might be all the better for such freedoms, even though my daily choices often contravene that desire. I wonder if that other childhood might still exist in pockets of this country—in places where life is less like a treadmill and more like a free run, less like a destination and more like a journey—and whether for the rest of us it is retrievable, recoverable, like retro fashion or furniture. When we let our hair down and let loose our most authentic selves, what is it that we really value? I think often that our kids' childhoods are as much about *us* as they are about *them*.

One day in 2008 as I made my way through the Stanford campus, I came upon a mother and daughter looking lost so I asked if I could help. "Yes," the mother replied. "We're looking for the Electrical Engineering building." "Ah. It's down this way and over there," I explained, pointing. Always eager to engage with a potential new student, I then tried to engage the daughter in dialogue without much success, while the mother continued to chat with me about her daughter's academic plans. When we were through, the daughter offered a small nervous wave of thanks or departure, and we parted.

In the course of our exchange, I learned the younger woman was not a teenage visitor but a college graduate in her mid-twenties interested in doing a PhD. And her mother was doing *all* the talking.

In a 2014 opinion piece, *New York Times* contributor Jon Grinspan compared parenting today to parenting of yesteryear and asked whether today's manner of overparenting articulates values we can be proud of as Americans. "There is a side of contemporary American culture—fearful, litigious, controlling—that we do not brag about but that we reveal in our child rearing, and that runs contrary to our self-image as an open, optimistic nation."[2] What we *do* brag about is our kids' perfectness even as simultaneously we evince so little *actual* faith in their ability to do the work of living life on their own, *the way every prior generation of humans somehow has.* Instead of a belief in them, we have great faith that *our* skills, plans, and dreams are the right tools for constructing *their* lives.

"There are two things children should get from their parents: roots and wings," said German writer, poet, and philosopher Johann Wolfgang von Goethe. It's time to start examining what it means to give our kid wings. It's time to imagine what we hope they'll be able to be and do when they've grown, left the nest, and gone wherever the wind takes them. It's time to ask whether parents and children can love one another forever but lead separate lives, and what can be gained when that happens.

It's rather wonderful that a mother had the time and inclination to accompany her grown daughter to visit grad programs. It's even more wonderful that the daughter welcomes the mother's participation. Avery was about seven when I observed this mother-daughter pair, and as I continued on toward my meeting, I found myself wondering what role I would be playing in Avery's life when she was in her mid-twenties. I can imagine wanting to be there for her exciting adventures—maybe to help, but more just to admire my lovely girl as she makes her way through the world.

Still, another part of me took a pause. I would want Avery to be able to trek to a grad program all by herself—to call me about it with great breathless enthusiasm in her voice, sure, but to experience the trip, its details, its challenges, and its joys on her own. As the mother and daughter turned the corner toward the Engineering Quad, I wondered whether that kind of separation is even realistic anymore, after childhoods that feature the omnipresence of parents well into the years of adulthood.

Thinking back on the thousands of young people I've known from Stanford and my community, and keeping those two I'm trying to raise very much in mind, I see that we want everything to be good and comfortable for our children. But that isn't the reality of the world we're preparing them for. They don't learn to make choices or to construct possibility from the vacuum of boredom. They don't learn responsibility or accountability for their own behaviors. They don't get the chance to stumble or build resilience. They feel supremely accomplished for things they really haven't achieved on their own or, in the alternative, believe they are incapable of accomplishing things without us. And there's no buffer from the stress. There's no freedom. No play. Hell-bent on removing all risks of life and on catapulting them into the college with the right brand name, we've robbed our kids of the chance to construct and know their own *selves*. You might say we've mortgaged their childhood in exchange for the future we imagine for them—a debt that can never be repaid.

PART 2

WHY WE MUST STOP

OVERPARENTING

6

OUR KIDS LACK BASIC LIFE SKILLS

In his 1999 book, *Raising Adults: Getting Kids Ready for the Real World*, sociologist and longtime church-based youth worker Jim Hancock points out that if we think we're raising *children*, then what we'll have at the end is just that—children; instead, he urges that our task is to raise *adults*.[1] It sounds obvious, but I've come to ask myself whether I or anyone for that matter knows what "being an adult in the world" actually means anymore, or how a child develops into that person.

Legally, we define "adult" in all kinds of ways, from being old enough to: marry without parental consent (age sixteen in a majority of states); fight and die for your country (age eighteen); and drink alcohol (age twenty-one). But on a developmental level, what does it mean to behave and think as an adult?

For decades the standard sociological definition of adulthood neatly mapped onto societal norms: completing high school, leaving home, becoming financially independent, marrying, and having children. In 1960, 77 percent of women and 65 percent of men had achieved all five milestones by age thirty, whereas in 2000 just half of thirty-year-old women and one third of their male peers had done so.[2]

These traditionally defined milestones are clearly outdated; marriage is no longer the prerequisite for a woman's financial security, and children no longer inevitably result from sex. One can reach adulthood neither marrying nor having children, or having done one, but not the other. These milestones are also heteronormative—gays and lesbians form meaningful committed partnerships and raise children, yet are still legally barred from the institution of marriage in many states. If we're measuring "adulthood" by milestones to which young people no longer aspire, we're not going to get very far. We need a definition more relevant for our times and might find it by asking young people themselves.

In a 2007 study published in the *Journal of Family Psychology*,[3] researchers asked eighteen- to twenty-five-year-olds which criteria they felt were most indicative of adulthood. Their criteria were, in order of importance: (1) accepting responsibility for the consequences of your actions; (2) establishing a relationship with parents as an equal adult; (3) being financially independent from parents; and (4) deciding on beliefs/values independently of parents/other influences. The researchers then asked these young adults, "Do you think that you have reached adulthood?" and only 16 percent said yes. Parents of these respondents were also surveyed as to whether their eighteen- to twenty-five-year-olds had reached adulthood, and both mothers and fathers overwhelmingly agreed with their children. Based on my observations of close to twenty thousand eighteen- to twenty-two-year-olds in my time as dean, I concur, and I find it problematic.

At the beginning of one recent fall quarter at Stanford, this happened: After a freshman had been on campus for a few days, the boxes he had shipped from home via UPS arrived on the sidewalk outside his dorm. But the young man left them sitting there; they were big and heavy—each a two-person job—and he didn't know how to get them to his room. As the student would later explain to the resident fellow—the faculty member living in his dorm who ended up marshaling some kind of assistance thanks to a call from the boy's mother—he didn't know how to ask anyone for help with the boxes.

This is a parenting failure. Kids don't acquire life skills by magic at the stroke of midnight on their eighteenth birthday. Childhood is meant to be the training ground. Parents can assist—not by always being there to do it or to tell them how to do it via cell phone—but by getting out of the way and letting kids figure things out for themselves.

Beth Gagnon, the psychotherapist in New Hampshire just outside of the Boston area, agrees. Her private practice is full of parents anxious about their kids and who are overhelping in response.

"We have moms literally driving their kids to school every day 'because it's icy out there,'" she told me. With the frustration in her voice palpable, I shudder to think what Beth would make of us doing the same in the gorgeous California sunshine. "Kids are supposed to acquire and complete certain developmental tasks at certain ages," she begins. "Even though many parents are highly educated and intelligent, they don't have a good concept of what is developmentally appropriate for kids."[4]

Beth Gagnon is so concerned about parents interfering with kids' development of life skills that she presents a workshop for parents of new middle schoolers. She'll say, "Nobody needs to raise their hand, but if you're still cutting your kid's meat at twelve, you need to stop." She adds, "I've had parents e-mail me saying 'Thank you for that workshop; I've just had my son cut his own meat.'"

Getting to school on their own, asking a stranger to hold a door or help with a box, and cutting their own meat are examples of the everyday things grown humans need to do for themselves. They also need to be prepared for when things go wrong.

Consider two scenarios where a grown person needs to have the wherewithal to *cope*, which is itself a life skill: (1) when we're away from home and get sick, and (2) when our car breaks down. Sure, we may hope our grown kids never experience such things, but since we're powerless to prevent them from happening, are we instead preparing our kids for them?

We are not.

Susan is an emergency room physician at a hospital located in the heart of Washington, D.C., and nineteen-year-old college girls are her "least favorite patients." Susan is kind and loving, and also a mother of two and stepmother to a third child, all of whom are under eighteen, so I'm a bit surprised by the bite in her voice. "For the most part college students are generally a healthy group of people, and at home their parents have taken care of them. Students will come into the ER with an upper respiratory infection and you would think the world has ended. They get very upset if you don't give them antibiotics and don't admit them, even though they just have a cold and need to drink fluids and lie down for a couple of days."[5] Susan goes on to describe college girls slumped in a puddle of tears on the cold linoleum emergency room floor pouring their great misfortune into their cell phone, presumably into the ears of friends and family. "They have no coping skills at all," says Susan.

I'd be mortified if Sawyer or Avery behaved this way in the ER at nineteen years of age. Sure the ER is scary, unfamiliar, and often an infuriating bureaucracy. But when you're there, you fare best when you can advocate for yourself. Flash forward a few years beyond college and our kids could have kids of their *own*. They need to be able to pull themselves together and to have the wherewithal to conduct themselves responsibly, confidently, and respectfully in the world.

Meanwhile, if you ever plan to travel by car, breaking down at the side of the road is a reality of life. Todd Burger is CEO of AAA Mountain West, which covers Alaska, Montana, and Wyoming, and he's going a bit crazy from the neediness of Millennial drivers. "Kids today have no preparedness," he tells me. Todd hails from Montana and owns a ranch where he's raising his own teenagers. There's a ruggedness in his tone of voice and a weariness as he talks about the life skills lacking in most young adults he interacts with these days.

AAA's mission is to provide *emergency* road service, not full-service solutions. That means they'll put on a spare tire, jump your battery, or tow you somewhere, but won't provide the full, long-term solution to your automotive problems. However, full-service-on-the-go is what young drivers want. "It's a know-nothing, fix-it-rapidly-for-me-because-my-parents-are-paying-for-this kind of mentality. What we notice most is they don't trust us; we're standing there and they pull out their phone to ask Facebook friends for help with their car. We don't know what to do with them. We really don't."[6]

I've talked to parents all over the country who say with dawning astonishment, things like: "My kid is a high school senior and doesn't know how to ride the Metro"; "If I took my teenagers to the city and said, 'Find your way home,' they would burst into tears"; "My kid never learned to cook because she had to do homework every night"; "My biggest fear is my daughter is going to college in a year and a half and I don't know how she'll get up in the morning." The parent uttering that last comment added that she told her daughter, "You need to make yourself breakfast." When the daughter asked why, the parent responded, "I need to know that you know how."

There's my point. *We need to know they know how.*

But how do we get there from here?

No one can *give* another person life skills. Each of us has to acquire them by doing the work of life. On our own. When we haven't prepared our children—and *ourselves*—for the inevitable day when they'll have to fend for themselves, it will be a rude awakening for us both. Yes, amid the tight structure of things to do that seem to be necessary to ensure success for our kids, it's hard to see how we have space and time to offer life skills lessons. But we must. When our kids—still often very much *children* though past the age of legal majority—move off to college or the working world, do we really want them to end up bewildered on a sunny sidewalk not knowing how to get their UPS boxes indoors, where their only recourse is to call us, knowing we'll figure it out for them? Is this solution sustainable?

A DIFFERENT KIND OF CHECKLIST

If we want our kids to have a shot at making it in the world as eighteen-year-olds, without the umbilical cord of the cell phone being their go-to solution in all manner of things, they're going to need a set of basic life skills. Based upon my observations as dean, and the advice of parents and educators around the country, here are some examples of practical things they'll need to know how to do before they go to college—*and* here are the crutches that are currently hindering them from standing up on their own two feet:

1. **An eighteen-year-old must be able to talk to strangers**—faculty, deans, advisers, landlords, store clerks, human resource managers, coworkers, bank tellers, health care providers, bus drivers, mechanics—in the real world.

   The crutch: We teach kids not to talk to strangers instead of teaching the more nuanced skill of how to discern the few bad strangers from the mostly good ones. Thus, kids end up not knowing how to approach strangers—respectfully and with eye contact—for the help, guidance, and direction they will need out in the world.

2. **An eighteen-year-old must be able to find his way around** a campus, the town in which her summer internship is located, or the city where he is working or studying abroad.

   The crutch: We drive or accompany our children everywhere, even when a bus, their bicycle, or their own feet could get them there; thus, kids don't know the route for getting from here to there, how to cope with transportation options and snafus, when and how to fill the car with gas, or how to make and execute transportation plans.

3. **An eighteen-year-old must be able to manage his assignments, work-load, and deadlines.**

The crutch: We remind kids when their homework is due and when to do it—sometimes helping them do it, sometimes doing it for them; thus, kids don't know how to prioritize tasks, manage workload, or meet deadlines, without regular reminders.

4. **An eighteen-year-old must be able to contribute to the running of a household.**

The crutch: We don't ask them to help much around the house because the checklisted childhood leaves little time in the day for anything aside from academic and extracurricular work; thus, kids don't know how to look after their own needs, respect the needs of others, or do their fair share for the good of the whole.

5. **An eighteen-year-old must be able to handle interpersonal problems.**

The crutch: We step in to solve misunderstandings and soothe hurt feelings for them; thus, kids don't know how to cope with and resolve conflicts without our intervention.

6. **An eighteen-year-old must be able to cope with ups and downs of** courses and workloads, college-level work, competition, tough teachers, bosses, and others.

The crutch: We step in when things get hard, finish the task, extend the deadline, and talk to the adults; thus, kids don't know that in the normal course of life things won't always go their way, and that they'll be okay regardless.

7. **An eighteen-year-old must be able to earn and manage money.**

The crutch: They don't hold part-time jobs; they receive money from us for whatever they want or need; thus, kids don't develop a sense of responsibility for completing job tasks, accountability to a boss who doesn't inherently love them, or an appreciation for the cost of things and how to manage money.

8. **An eighteen-year-old must be able to take risks.**

The crutch: We've laid out their entire path for them and have avoided all pitfalls or prevented all stumbles for them; thus, kids don't develop the wise understanding that success comes only after trying and failing and trying again (a.k.a. "grit") or the thick skin (a.k.a. "resilience") that comes from coping when things have gone wrong.

Remember: our kids must be able to do all of these things without resorting to calling a parent on the phone. If they're calling us to ask how, they do not have the life skill.

THE ORPHAN AS ROLE MODEL

I became a university dean because I'm interested in supporting humans in growing to become who they're meant to become, unfettered by circumstance or other people's expectations. I expected that the kids who would most need my help would be first-generation college students or low-income kids, and these populations certainly benefited from the mentorship and support that a dean could provide. But it was my solidly middle- or upper-middle-class students who had the most bewildered looks on their faces, looks that turned to relief when Mom or Dad handled the situation, whatever it was. These parents seemed involved in their college students' lives in ways that held their kids back instead of propelling them forward. So I was engrossed by the provocative 2012 piece in the *Chronicle of Higher Education*, "Don't Pick Up: Why Kids Need to Separate from Their Parents," by English professor Terry Castle, in which Castle offered the orphan as a role model for youth suffering from overparenting.[7]

Terry Castle has taught English literature to Stanford undergraduates for more than thirty years. She wrote the *Chronicle* article after she became baffled by the then-new phenomenon of college students communicating constantly with their parents before and after class, and just as baffled by her students' desire for such frequent communication. She took as her platform a dominant theme in English literature—the orphan as protagonist, known in academic circles as "the orphan trope." (Think Jane Eyre, Oliver Twist, Pippi Longstocking, and Harry Potter.) She argued that maybe these fictional orphans could teach us real folk a thing or two. After all, fictional orphans live lives of self-direction, breathtaking adventure, hard-won perseverance, and satisfying accomplishment, without a parent's help—or, as Castle suggests, maybe precisely *because* parents are absent.

This idea isn't just theory extracted from the made-up lives of characters in novels; NPR recently pointed to current leaders—Presidents Barack Obama and Bill Clinton, Justice Sonia Sotomayor, and New York mayor Bill de Blasio—who each lost a parent in childhood and rose to the upmost heights of their profession.[8] For these "eminent orphans," as Malcolm Gladwell calls them, losing a parent was "a spur, a propellant that sends them catapulting into life."[9]

"For better or worse," Castle writes, "the ferocious, liberating notion embedded in the early novel is that parents are there to be fooled and defied . . . that even the most venerated traditions exist to be broken with; that creative power is rightly vested in the individual rather than groups, in the young rather than the old; that thought is free. The assertion of individual rights ineluctably begins, symbolically and every other way, with the primal rebellion of the child against parent."[10] When I think of childhood in America today, I don't see anything remotely like this "primal rebellion" of which Castle writes. My students didn't seem to be "assert[ing their] individual rights"; instead they seemed to exist in a sort of placid, docile state, on pause awaiting further direction from a parent.

According to a 2009 Pew Research survey, today's parents report having fewer serious arguments with their children in their late teens and early twenties than they recall having with their own parents when they were that age. Only one in ten parents with children ages sixteen to twenty-four say they "often" have major disagreements with their kids. Among adults ages thirty and older, twice as many (19 percent) say they often had major arguments with their folks when they were young.[11] Yet, Castle wrote, "What the Life of the Orphan teaches—has taught me at least—is that it is indeed the self-conscious abrogation of one's inheritance, the 'making strange' of received ideas, the cultivation of a willingness to defy, debunk, or just plain old disappoint one's parents, that is the absolute precondition, now more than ever, for intellectual and emotional freedom."

In my milieu—my town, my kids' schools, even in my own house—I wonder where and how kids have that chance to develop intellectual and emotional freedom since parents are living childhood right alongside children, doing childhood for them, present so as to ensure that childhood is safe, scheduled, and going according to plan. And yes, everyone seems to be getting along pretty darn well. Our kids like us. Heck, they *more than* like us.

In a nationwide study of undergraduates in 2009, the students overwhelmingly cited their parents when asked who they consider heroes (54 percent), with God and Jesus a very distant second (8 percent).[12] "The reasons for choosing parents dealt principally with the sacrifices they had made, the opportunities and encouragements they gave their children, and their accomplishments in the world."[13] The same survey given in 1993 found that only 29 percent of students saw their parents as heroes, and various public figures in government, entertainment, and athletics, as well as teachers and professors—all cited as heroes in 1993—have virtually fallen off today's list.

Look, parents and adult children sharing frequent, "Hi, how are you, I love you," conversations is a tender and precious thing. Who wouldn't want that? And the cell phone doesn't *cause* overparenting. I was writing and speaking about overparenting well before most parents knew how to text. But in the aggregate, over the hours, days, weeks, and months of a school term, I saw students turning to parents constantly, as the first place to check in, as first resource, first recourse, as an impulse or reflex as natural as taking a breath of air.

If anything, today's childhood feels dystopian, like some futuristic story where parents' overprotection, overdirection, and hand-holding have been taken to their (il)logical conclusion. A successful entrepreneur dad confessed to me that his own life is the perfect example that risk taking leads to success, yet he can't stop himself from charting his kid's entire path for him and smoothing the bumps along the way. The 1972 novel *The Stepford Wives*—an allegory featuring feminist women turned into docile and submissive wives—comes to mind.[14] Are we raising Stepford Children?

Castle's piece concludes, "My own view remains predictably twisty, fraught, and disloyal. Parents, in my opinion, have to be finessed, thought around, even as we love them: They are so colossally wrong about so many important things. And even when they are not, paradoxically, even when they are 100 percent right, the imperative remains the same: To live an 'adult' life, a meaningful life, it is necessary, I would argue, to engage in a kind of symbolic self-orphaning."

Castle is neither psychologist nor anthropologist. She's an English professor, not an expert on child rearing. And of course, I am not taking literally her praise of the life of children who must fend for themselves. There is no question that parents need to be involved in the lives of children and that parental neglect, abandonment, or abuse is a serious and far more acute problem than the overparenting that concerns me. But Castle brings insight from fictional worlds where children thrive not despite their scrappy upbringing but because of it, to help us think about how kids might grow from being completely dependent upon us to become independent adults.

One of the key life skills our children must develop, after all, is the ability to live without us.

7

THEY'VE BEEN
PSYCHOLOGICALLY HARMED

In 2013 the news was filled with worrisome statistics about the mental health crisis on college campuses, particularly the number of students medicated for depression. Charlie Gofen, the retired chairman of the board at The Latin School of Chicago, a private school serving about eleven hundred students, e-mailed the statistics off to a colleague at another school and asked, "Do you think parents at your school would rather their kid be depressed at Yale or happy at University of Arizona?" The colleague quickly replied, "My guess is 75 percent of the parents would rather see their kids depressed at Yale. They figure that the kid can straighten the emotional stuff out in his/her 20's, but no one can go back and get the Yale undergrad degree."[1]

Our intentions are sound—more than sound: We love our kids fiercely and want only the very best for them. Yet, having succumbed to a combination of safety fears, a college admissions arms race, and perhaps our own needy ego, our sense of what is "best" for our kids is completely out of whack. We don't want our kids to bonk their head or have hurt feelings, but we're willing to take real chances with their mental health?

Here are the statistics to which Charlie Gofen was likely alluding:

In a 2013 survey of college counseling center directors,[2] 95 percent said the number of students with significant psychological problems is a growing concern on their campus, 70 percent said that the number of students on their campus with severe psychological problems has increased in the past year, and they reported that 24.5 percent of their student clients were taking psychotropic drugs. (Drugs that alter chemical levels in the brain to impact mood and behavior, the most commonly used of which are anti-psychotics, antidepressants, ADHD drugs, antianxiety medications, and mood stabilizers.)

An earlier, 2012, version of the same survey reported a 16 percent increase in visits to student mental health centers since 2000. Also since 2000, serious mental health concerns like depression and anxiety have dis-placed relationship concerns as the primary reason college students seek mental health services on campus.

In 2013 the American College Health Association surveyed close to one hundred thousand college students from 153 different campuses about their health.[3] When asked about their experiences, at some point over the past twelve months:

- 84.3 percent felt overwhelmed by all they had to do
- 79.1 percent felt exhausted (not from physical activity)
- 60.5 percent felt very sad
- 57.0 percent felt very lonely
- 51.3 percent felt overwhelming anxiety
- 46.5 percent felt things were hopeless
- 38.3 percent felt overwhelming anger
- 31.8 percent felt so depressed that it was difficult to function
- 8.0 percent seriously considered suicide
- 6.5 percent intentionally cut or otherwise injured themselves

The 153 schools surveyed included campuses in all fifty states, small liberal arts colleges and large research universities, religious institutions and nonreligious, from the small- to medium-sized to the very the large. The mental health crisis is not a Yale (or Stanford or Harvard) problem; these poor mental health outcomes are occuring in kids everywhere. The increase in mental health problems among college students may reflect the lengths to which we push kids toward academic achievement, but since they are happening to kids who end up at hundreds of schools in every tier, they appear to stem not from what it takes to get into the most elite schools but from some facet of American childhood itself.

OVERPARENTING AND MENTAL HEALTH

You're right to be thinking *Yes, but do we know whether overparenting causes this rise in mental health problems?* The answer is that we don't have studies proving causation, but a number of recent studies show *correlation*.

A study published in 2006 by UCLA clinical child psychologist and assistant professor of psychiatry and education, James Wood, found that parents who tend to take over tasks that children either are or could be performing independently limit the child's ability to experience "mastery," leading to greater rates of separation anxiety in their children.[4]

A 2010 study explicitly about "helicopter parenting" from the University of Texas at Austin[5] began by acknowledging the dearth of research in the field to date and the importance of moving from anecdote to empirical evidence. UT researchers Patricia Somers and Jim Settle interviewed 190 academic and student affairs professionals at colleges and universities around the country who consistently estimated the prevalence of helicopter parents on their campus at between 40 and 60 percent. Somers and Settle sought to differentiate the helpful parental behaviors from the harmful types. "Positive results accrue when the hovering is age appropriate; when parents and student engage in a dialogue; when the student is empowered to act; and when parents intercede only if the student needs additional help." They called this "Positive Parental Engagement." In contrast, "negative" helicopter parents are "inappropriately (and at times surreptitiously) enmeshed in their children's lives and relationships."

Also in 2010, psychology professor Neil Montgomery of Keene State College in New Hampshire surveyed three hundred college freshmen nationwide and found that students with helicopter parents were less open to new ideas and actions and more vulnerable, anxious, and self-conscious. "In students who were given responsibility and not constantly monitored by their parents— so-called 'free rangers'—the effects were reversed," Montgomery said.[6]

A 2011 study by Terri LeMoyne and Tom Buchanan at the University of Tennessee at Chattanooga looking at more than three hundred students found that a student with "hovering" or "helicopter" parents is more likely to be medicated for anxiety and/or depression.[7] They conducted the study because of what they were seeing in their classrooms. "We began to experience some really good students that were very capable, excellent at turning in their assignments . . . but when it came to independent decisions, if you didn't give them concrete directions, it seemed they were uneasy at times."

A 2012 study of 438 college students reported in the *Journal of Adolescence* found "initial evidence for this form of intrusive parenting being linked to problematic development in emerging adulthood . . . by limiting opportunities for emerging adults to practice and develop important skills needed for becoming self-reliant adults."[8] A 2013 study of 297 college students reported in the *Journal of Child and Family Studies* found that college students with helicopter parents reported significantly higher levels of depression and less satisfaction in life, and attributed this diminishment in well-being to a violation of the students' "basic psychological needs for autonomy and competence."[9] And a 2014 study from researchers at the University of Colorado–Boulder is the first to correlate a highly structured childhood with less executive function capabilities.[10] (Executive function is our ability to determine which goal-directed actions to carry out and when, and is a skill set lacking in many kids with ADD/ADHD.) "The more time that children spent in less-structured activities, the better their self-directed executive functioning. The opposite was true of structured activities, which predicted poorer self-directed executive functioning."

A researcher at the Beit T'Shuvah treatment and recovery center for addicts in Los Angeles recently conducted a study that found that the rates of depression and anxiety among affluent teens and young adults (such as those in Beit T'Shuvah's community) correspond to the rates of depression and anxiety suffered by incarcerated juveniles.[11] Director Harriet Rossetto explains these results this way: "If from the time you're born all your options are dictated for you and all your decisions are made for you, and then you're cast out into the world to go to college, it's like a country under colonial rule that falls apart when it gains its independence. They get to college and have no idea why they're there or what they ought to be doing there. They're lost. They're in such a painful place, and they seek to anesthetize that with drugs or other harmful activities like alcohol, gambling, or mutilation. Things that express their emptiness and sense of desperation. Often they become addicts simply because they don't know what else to do."[12]

THE LIFE SKILLS DEFICIT AND MENTAL HEALTH PROBLEMS

When parents have tended to do the stuff of life for kids—the waking up, the transporting, the reminding about deadlines and obligations, the bill paying, the question asking, the decision making, the responsibility taking, the talking to strangers, and the confronting of authorities, kids may be in for quite a shock when parents turn them loose in the world of college or work. They will experience setbacks, which will feel to them like failure. And, in a cruel twist of irony, they then won't be able to cope with that failure very well, because they haven't had much practice at failure, either.

When a seemingly perfectly healthy but overparented kid gets to college and has trouble coping with the various new situations they might encounter—a roommate who has a different sense of "clean," a professor who wants a revision to the paper but won't say specifically what is "wrong," a friend who isn't being so friendly anymore, a choice between doing a summer seminar or service project but not both—they can have real difficulty knowing how to handle the disagreement, the uncertainty, the hurt feelings, or the decision-making process. This inability to cope—to sit with some discomfort, think about options, talk it through with someone, make a decision—can become a problem unto itself.

Dr. Karen Able (not her real name) sees these kids in her practice as a staff psychologist at the Counseling and Psychological Services (CAPS) center at a large public university in the Midwest, where approximately 90 percent of the students live on campus or commute from just a few miles away. She has asked to be anonymous because of the sensitive nature of her work.[13]

Based on her clinical experience Able says, "Overinvolved parenting is taking a serious toll on the psychological well-being of college students who can't negotiate a balance between consulting with parents and independent decision making."

She explains how her sessions with students unfold. "At first they feel that if they need help, they should immediately contact a parent. Psychologically speaking, we know they don't really need help, that if they could persevere through the discomfort of not knowing what to do, they would essentially be practicing that skill, and will at some point learn to do it for themselves. I work with students to practice the critical thinking, confidence, and independence skills they don't yet have. But if they end up calling or texting a parent instead, they aren't practicing these skills in the ways I'd like them to, which means they still haven't acquired these skills."

Neither Karen Able nor I is suggesting that grown kids should never call their parents. The devil is in the details of the conversation. If they call with a problem or a decision to be made, do we tell them what to do? Or do we listen thoughtfully, ask some questions based on our own sense of the situation, then say, "Okay. So how do you think you're going to handle that?" Able adds that social media and texting exacerbate the tendency for students to turn first to parents instead of turning within, and for parents to immediately respond. "It all happens so quickly, it doesn't give the student an opportunity to figure out for themselves what should happen."

Lurking beneath the problem of whatever thing needs to be handled is the student's inability to differentiate the self from the parent. For some young adults, this sense of self can be developed. For others, the inability to differentiate can lead to more serious mental health concerns.

"When children aren't given the space to struggle through things on their own, they don't learn to problem solve very well. They don't learn to be confident in their own abilities, and it can affect their self-esteem. The other problem with never having to struggle is that you never experience failure and can develop an overwhelming fear of failure and of disappointing others. Both the low self-confidence and the fear of failure can lead to depression or anxiety," Able said.

Getting this glimpse behind the scenes into what could unfold for our kids when they're out of our sight can make us parents feel like we're in a straitjacket. What else are we supposed to do? If we're not there for our kids when they are away from home and bewildered, confused, frightened, or hurting, then who will be?

Here's the point—and this is so much more important than I realized until rather recently when the data started coming in: The research shows that figuring out for themselves is a critical element to a person's mental health. Your kids have to be there for *themselves*. That's a harder truth to swallow when your kid is in the midst of a problem or worse, a crisis, but taking the long view, it's the best medicine for them.

THE THREE OVERPARENTING STYLES THAT DO PSYCHOLOGICAL HARM

Psychologist and author Dr. Madeline Levine has a practice in Marin County, California, a region just north of the Golden Gate Bridge known for its beauty, proximity to wine country, and wealth. Levine rose to nationwide prominence for her *New York Times* best-selling books *The Price of Privilege* and *Teach Your Children Well*, which detail the stress and strain young people in middle- and upper-middle-class communities are under. She travels around the country at the invitation of PTAs, school boards, and community centers, telling parents everywhere to calm down and pull back.[14] As Levine tells it, the greatest harm lurking in the lives of our kids is not the rare occurrence of the perverted stranger on the street but the declining mental health and wellness of children whose parents do too much for them.

Levine has spoken on this topic before tens of thousands of parents in hundreds of communities in recent years, and on a chilly night in January 2014 I was one of them. She's been a friend of mine since I joined the board of Challenge Success, an organization she cofounded with Denise Pope to focus on the stress kids face. So I went mostly to welcome her to our community and to show support for her talk, titled "Parenting for Authentic Success." But I also went with this book in mind, interested to see how parents would respond to her research about the harms of overhelping.

The talk[15] was held at Henry M. Gunn High School, one of the top public high schools in the nation, and also the school my son, Sawyer, attends, with my daughter, Avery, soon to follow. So I was there not only as a friend of the speaker and as an author interested in the speaker's topic, but as a parent. My husband came, too, as did several hundred other parents. Dr. Levine warmed us up with a segment on parent perception, which went something like this:

"There's a popular, potent story right now that says success is a straight line from the right school to the right college to the right internship to the right grad school to your chosen profession."

"Raise your hand if this is the path that you took." About 5 percent of the hands went up.

"That's right," she said. "In any group of people only 1–10 percent have taken a straight trajectory. The much more common route is circuitous."

"But kids don't know this story," Levine continued. "You look like a genius to your kids. They don't know you struggled and failed; it's the biggest secret we keep from our kids. Our kids need to hear the everyday challenges that we have. We ought to share what our trajectory was, particularly when that includes failure." The parents tittered nervously as they faced the incongruity between their experience and their attitude. Levine had her work cut out for her. She talked for about an hour, followed by a substantial time for questions and answers.

The arc of Levine's message was that we should support our kids in being who they are by providing the opportunities that fit the kid as opposed to trying to make our kid fit our notion of who the kid ought to be—and to embrace the benefits of trial and error. It's a comforting message for me, and, I sense, for many in the room.

She then shared her research on the three ways we might be overparenting and unwittingly causing psychological harm:

1. when we do for our kids what they can *already* do for themselves;
2. when we do for our kids what they can *almost* do for themselves; and
3. when our parenting behavior is motivated by our own ego.[16]

Levine said that when we parent this way we deprive our kids of the opportunity to be creative, to problem solve, to develop coping skills, to build resilience, to figure out what makes them happy, to figure out who they are. In short, it deprives them of the chance to be, well, human. Although we overinvolve ourselves to protect our kids and it may in fact lead to short-term gains, our behavior actually delivers the rather soul-crushing news: *"Kid, you can't actually do any of this without me."* It increases our kids' chances of suffering from depression, anxiety, to become cutters, and to have suicidal thoughts.[17]

By the time Levine was through, the energy in the room had shifted from tense posturing to more of a "we're all in this together" feeling, and I sensed that maybe some folks would find the courage to make some change at what I call the local-local level of their own dining-room table, where parents can have some impact on the quality of our kids' lives, even if we can't change the larger societal rules operating outside the home.

Then Levine opened the floor for questions. After a few questions—one about how to motivate a "C" student, another about a kindergartener who doesn't sit still at circle time—a parent sought Levine's advice on how to motivate her fourth grader. The question went something like this: "My daughter really loves to write and her teacher says she is unusually talented. I keep trying to encourage her to enter writing contests, but she won't. She says she won't win and she just has fun writing on her own. But I think she can do well. How can I get her to enter competitions?"

My husband and I looked at each other with raised eyebrows. Programs rustled and some people looked around as if to signal, "She doesn't get it." But Levine was up to the task and, smiling broadly, responded, "Your

daughter enjoys writing. That's a great thing! Leave her alone. Let her write."
A small smattering of parents applauded, and my husband and I were two
of them. By the sound of it, though, those of us who agreed with Levine
and felt comfortable saying so were outnumbered by those who did not, by
those who thought, *Don't force her to compete, what do you mean? Don't
you know you're in Palo Alto?*

THE MENTAL HEALTH COSTS OF "FAILURE"

Some parents champion an authoritarian parenting style where the parent
dictates a narrow path of academic and extracurricular goals and punishes
a kid for not achieving constant excellence. Such parents tend to disregard
or disbelieve the mental health concerns we've been discussing. I've seen
this kind of attitude in parents of all ethnicities and across the socioeconomic spectrum.

In her best-selling memoir, *Battle Hymn of the Tiger Mother*, about a
highly structured style of parenting she calls "Chinese-American," Amy
Chua asks us to believe that a child does best when a parent's direction,
goals, and values completely stand in for the child's own.[18] Famously on
Chua's list are that her two daughters must never: "attend a sleepover, have
a play date, be in a school play, complain about not being in a school play,
watch TV or play computer games, choose their own extracurricular activities, get any grade less than an A, not be the No. 1 student in every subject
except gym and drama, play any instrument other than the piano or violin,
not play the piano or violin."

This all sounds a little funny until you realize that Chua actually did
these things. She writes with pride about using verbal degradation and other
techniques to discipline her children about their violin and piano practice,
and about their tears, defiance, and resignation. She tells the reader that
these methods are all worth it in the long run because her daughters "made
it" to Carnegie Hall and to selective schools.

Frank Wu is an educator and activist. I'm not mentioning the race of
most people I talk to, but since Amy Chua made a point of naming this
overbearing parenting style as "Chinese-American," I wanted to consult
someone in the Chinese American community; Frank Wu, like Amy Chua,
is Chinese American.

Wu is dean and chancellor at UC Hastings, the University of California law school located in San Francisco, and has been affiliated with a wide

range of institutions, including University of Michigan Law School, the historically black Howard University, Gallaudet University for the deaf, and Deep Springs College, a two-year college enrolling only twenty-six students, all male. Now in his late forties, Frank has seen his fair share of so-called wounded tigers—children of overbearing "Tiger Parents," both in the United States and abroad. He's also lived the story himself.[19] He writes and speaks about his experiences extensively.

"After I wrote a piece for the *Huffington Post* called 'Everything My Asian Immigrant Parents Taught Me Turns Out to Be Wrong,'" Frank told me, "I thought my audiences would pelt me with tomatoes. Instead, all these other Asian Americans were nodding, and I realized 'Wow I'm on to something here.'" Having ascended to the heights of his profession as a law professor and dean, he says, "My mother is still hoping I'll go to med school." He's not kidding. He explains that like many Asian American parents, his parents believed law and humanities were for people who weren't smart enough to do STEM fields (science, technology, engineering, math). "Tiger Parent strategies may have been appropriate for a different time, place, or generation," Frank suggests, giving a nod to the struggles of families desperate to leave oppressive regimes and hungry to get an immigrant's first foothold in America, "but they're doing a disservice now."

Frank speaks to the stereotypically rigid definition of success held by Tiger Parents. "If you become a neurosurgeon concert pianist, good for you. Your parent pushed you. You don't get that without someone *making* you do your homework and *making* you practice. But for every one success story like that, there are probably ninety-nine kids whose lives have been *wrecked* by that." Frank knows. He hears from the ninety-nine, whose stories tend to fit this theme more or less: "Child of Asian immigrants who invested absolutely everything they had into the child, often at great cost to themselves. The child became an adult who went to a good school, entered a profession, married, has a nice house. By all outward appearances this person is perfectly successful. But the parents are ashamed because the person is successful, but not *perfect*."

When the valedictorian results are announced, Frank tells me, it's not the mediocre performers who are upset, it's the kids who are numbers two through ten who are absolutely crushed. "The people damaged by the pressure are not *un*successful people; they are *highly* successful, but because they are not *the* number one, they feel worthless."

By this point in our phone conversation, I've already spent more time with Frank than his assistant had allotted; still, he lingers on the phone with me as further stories pop into his head, which he relays in language that is part philosophy and part humor. He's about to be late for his next meeting so he concludes, "It's just untenable because 99 percent of us are not going to be in the top percent. If the choice is you must be *number one* or it's not worth trying at all, then none of us should ever get out of bed. That's an insane standard to set; it wrecks people's lives when they feel that no matter what they've accomplished it will never be enough." Desiree Baolian Qin, Associate Professor of Human Development and Family Studies at Michigan State University—herself a Chinese American—has produced research and scholarship attesting to the harm of which Wu speaks, including higher rates of stress and psychological problems in children raised with so-called "Tiger Parents."[20]

The data emerging about the mental health of our kids only confirms the harm done by asking so little of our kids when it comes to life skills, yet so much of them when it comes to adhering to the academic plans we've made for them and achieving more, ever more academically. They are stressed out of their minds *and* have no resilience with which to cope with that stress, and we continue along our pressurizing path, as if this trauma is not happening, or as if somehow our kids' struggles—this suffering—is, or will be, "worth it."

The guidance center bulletin from any typical U.S. school district will offer a reminder of adolescent counseling services or of the upcoming visit of a renowned expert who will speak about teen stress. I recently saw one such bulletin from Fairfax County Public Schools, which is in northern Virginia, near Washington, D.C., and boasts some of the top public schools in the nation. Fairfax County Public Schools was promoting a session on teen stress, wellness, and resiliency, which would include breakout sessions on topics such as "Pressures and the Life/School Balance," "Balancing Academic Expectations," and "Surviving the Admissions Process," and testimonials about dealing with depression. Then it concluded, "Students can receive community service hours for attending."

I applaud school districts for offering these programs. Thanks to our schools and other community entities, hundreds of thousands of us have seen *Race to Nowhere*, the 2010 documentary film by Vicki Abeles that takes a close look at the pressure of the "achievement culture."[21] Audiences leave that film speaking breathlessly about how bad things have gotten, often with tears in their eyes. But what are we *doing* about it?

We need to get in front of the problem. Think about it: That students get community service credit for attending sessions about the stress of the college admission process for the purpose of impressing a college admissions counselor is proof of the dystopian Stepfordian situation we're facing. Our kids' efforts to alleviate the stress of high school are evidence of their worthiness for college admission?

Academically overbearing parents are doing great harm. So says Bill Deresiewicz in his groundbreaking 2014 manifesto *Excellent Sheep: The Miseducation of the American Elite and the Way to a Meaningful Life.*[22] "[For students] haunted their whole lives by a fear of failure—often, in the first instance, by their parents' fear of failure," writes Deresiewicz, "the cost of falling short, even temporarily, becomes not merely practical, but existential."

Those whom Deresiewicz calls "excellent sheep" I call the "existentially impotent." And I think this is precisely what English professor Terry Castle was noticing when she wrote, "The cultivation of a willingness to defy, debunk, or just plain old disappoint one's parents, that is the absolute precondition, now more than ever, for intellectual and emotional freedom." As dean, I saw this lack of intellectual and emotional freedom—this existential impotence—behind closed doors. The "excellent sheep" were in my office.

THE RISING TIDE OF STUDENT DEPRESSION

As the overparented Millennial generation first began to roll up onto collegiate shores in the late 1990s, student mental health concerns were what those of us involved in academic advising and student life dealt with first. Increasingly, students' poor mental health affected their ability to operate in the classroom, dorm room, or campus community. By the early 2000s the changing dynamic in student mental health was the hottest agenda topic at our professional conferences. Administrators from four-year institutions across the United States—large and small, public and private, highly selective and open to everybody, religious and secular—gathered and looked to each other and to experts for answers. Every school was impacted. No one said, "This isn't happening on our campus." (I make a point of noting that this was happening at four-year institutions because the same cannot be said for community colleges. My hypothesis is that since community colleges serve a demographic that includes working-class students, students with children, and people returning to school later in life—all of whom can have a set of skills and wherewithal to cope born of a more challenging life experience—community colleges see fewer mental health difficulties on their campuses than do schools that have a more "traditional" undergraduate population.)

From 2006 to 2008, I served on Stanford's mental health task force, which examined the problem and proposed ways to teach faculty, staff, and students to better understand, notice, and respond to mental health issues. We also proposed money for more therapists who could put in more hours to handle these much more serious matters.

Occasionally I personally got involved by walking a student from my office to Counseling and Psychological Services (CAPS), where I'd sit with the student until an on-call therapist could see him or her. For the many more students whose needs were not acute, I made a referral to CAPS and followed up with a nudge to try to persuade them to go. Often these students were doing well academically, busy with classes and extracurricular activities, and pursuing prestigious summer work. But in my conversations with them, they often seemed existentially thin, automated—holding all of it in.

In my years as dean, I heard plenty of stories from college students who believed they *had* "to study science (or medicine, or engineering)," just as they'd *had* to play piano, *and* do community service for Africa, *and, and, and*. I talked with kids completely uninterested in the items on their own résumé. Some shrugged off any right to be bothered by their own lack of interest in what they were working on, saying, "My parents know what's best for me."

One kid's father threatened to divorce her mother if the daughter didn't major in economics. It took this student seven years to finish instead of the usual four, and along the way the father micromanaged his daughter's every move, including requiring her to study off campus at her uncle's every weekend. At her father's insistence, the daughter went to see one of her econ professors during office hours one weekday. She forgot to call her father to report on how that went, and when she returned to her dorm later that evening her uncle was in the dorm lobby looking visibly uncomfortable about having to "force" her to call her dad to update him. Later this student told me, "I pretty much had a panic attack from the lack of control in my life." But an economics major she was indeed. And the parents got divorced anyway.

Some students bided their time until they could finally get out from under their parents (usually by attending the parent-approved grad school).

Some expressed anger at their parents. I read the resignation in their eyes. I sensed their bewilderment at the dawning realization that they were living within a landscape full of possibility unavailable to them because they were on a leash and led down a path of their parents' making—that they'd spent years learning how to reach for and achieve their parents' ambitious dreams but were not allowed to dream dreams of their own. Often brilliant, always accomplished, these students would sit on my couch holding their fragile, brittle parts together, resigned to the fact that this outwardly successful situation was their miserable life.

A good example is Faith, a sophomore who grew up in the Northeast as the oldest of three children in an upper-middle-class family. When she came to my office her jaw tightened and her eyes grew fierce as she explained that her parents were making her go to medical school and that they reviewed her course schedule each term, planned her extracurricular activities, and preapproved her summer work options. I held my own judgment at bay by just raising my eyebrows in response and continuing to ask questions. I wasn't yet sure why Faith wanted to see me. She fought back tears as she explained what it would be like to tell her parents that she wasn't interested in doing the medical internship they had in mind for her this summer. I leaned forward, nodded, smiled softly, and focused my questions on how she was feeling. Her eyes lit slightly when she said that as long as she did well academically, her parents might ease up on her younger siblings. When I asked about her academic performance to date, she said with no discernible pride that she had earned over a 4.0 so far in her time at Stanford.

This conversation broke my heart. Faith was sitting in my office, poised, beautiful, and accomplished, but as I watched and listened, she seemed like someone trying to keep her head above water with a smile plastered on her face. Sure there's the chance that all of this striving for perfection, even in a field the student doesn't think she likes, will by some measure turn out to be "worth it" in the long run, or that a kid who never mastered anything in particular will later regret being allowed to quit piano. I will speak about setting up proper expectations later in this book (Chapter 17). For now, I'm focusing on what happens when harsh, not-necessarily-fitting expectations have been imposed on children and they have lived up to those expectations. A great many students experiencing such things sought mental health counseling. Some dropped out of school for a while. Some fell completely apart.

When it comes to tangible measures of success, I think a town's teen suicide rate is the better indicator than the number of kids with top grades or SAT scores. I think about this whenever I cross the train tracks in Palo Alto, where a number of teens took their lives in recent years, most of whom attended my kids' high school, Henry M. Gunn.

Security guards are now posted at our train crossings, and often when the Caltrain comes through the engineer and guard salute one another while the engineer blows the train whistle. When I'm sitting there in my car waiting to cross and see the salute and hear the sound of the lonely train whistle, I get tears in my eyes. We've got to stop pushing our kids to this brink.

8

THEY'RE BECOMING
"STUDY DRUG" ADDICTS

Approximately 11 percent of children in the United States have a diagnosis of attention-deficit/hyperactivity disorder (ADHD), and just over half of those (6.1 percent of all children) are prescribed stimulants such as Adderall, Ritalin, Vyvanse, or modafinil to improve their focus and concentration.[1] With an ADHD diagnosis, students are entitled to academic accommodations such as extra time on homework and tests.

My son, Sawyer, was diagnosed with ADHD in the fourth grade. He was struggling to get homework done, particularly writing. Night after night he'd just sit there at the dining table, staring out into the distance or picking underneath his fingernails with his pencil. He's very bright and I thought he should be able to breeze through schoolwork; I found it excruciating to watch him do nothing. Adding to this distress was the impact of his struggle on his dad, his sister, and me, as we tried to maintain a distraction-free place for him to study.

I was impatient. I wanted to solve it. I wanted a silver bullet, not so much for academic competitiveness—he was still managing to do well—but to bring my kid some relief from those long, nightly homework dramas, to bring some free time back into his young life, and to allow the rest of us to exhale as well.

I felt that perhaps Adderall had become necessary for him, just as I've found caffeine necessary for me. I know that caffeine isn't the most healthy lifestyle choice, but it's something I can take to help me get work done. *That's what I wanted for Sawyer.* I feared we were putting him at a disadvantage by not at least trying the medication. But my husband was worried about the medication's possible long-term health impact and urged that we focus instead on strategies, therapies, and other ways to possibly improve Sawyer's ability to focus.

Our dilemma—to medicate or not to medicate—is a common one among families in which a child has ADHD. But parents of kids with ADHD aren't the only ones considering ADHD medication for their child. In a 2006 interview with NBC News, Dr. James Perrin, professor of pediatrics at Harvard Medical School, told NBC that it was an increasingly common scenario for parents to request ADHD medication for their adolescent children, even though the child lacked any actual symptoms of ADHD.[2] Some kids take ADHD medication without having the disorder.

A Manhattan mom named Jessica is exasperated by this possibility.[3] She says she knows parents in her very affluent community whose kids "are perfectly normal" yet who plunk down $10,000 for a battery of tests that will "give" kids this diagnosis. Jessica fears that those kids are then "getting a 2350 on the SAT, and the extra time they get to take the test is not noted on their transcript so the colleges don't know." Jessica tells me, "It's just wrong."

Doctors and psychologists have had a hard time pinning down what exactly ADHD is. The diagnosis relies heavily upon the qualitative and highly subjective measure of what teachers and parents *observe* in a kid's behavior. The rates of diagnosed cases are higher in affluent communities, but is that because such parents can afford to seek medical solutions when their kids are struggling, or because an affluent childhood somehow exacerbates the potential for ADHD, or because parents want—and can "buy," as Jessica suggests—the "advantages" the diagnosis confers? Of course, the drugs and extra time are "advantages" only for *non*-ADHD kids; for those who truly have the disorder, the medications and extra time on tests merely approximate a level playing field. (For the child who actually has ADHD, parents and educators seek the accommodations, just as they also make sure to get eyeglasses for a kid who has poor eyesight.)

Is an ADHD diagnosis gameable? Are people making a living doling out ADHD diagnoses to parents in affluent communities? Perhaps. Or perhaps it's just an urban myth in parts of Manhattan and in other communities where parenting feels so high-stakes. If it's happening, it's deeply problematic ethically and medically. Where's the line between helping your kid in an appropriate way and manufacturing your kid to be someone else just so they can get into a "better" college? What matters just as much if not even more, I think, is that Jessica and plenty of other parents around the country *perceive* that this scamming is happening. And this perception and the fear that follows—that *our* kids won't get ahead if *those* kids are taking stimulants and getting extra time—fuel a drugs-for-high-scores arms race.

THE PRACTICE OF ACADEMIC DOPING

While there are no hard statistics on how many parents are seeking these drugs as a study- or test-taking aid for their children, studies indicate that teenagers certainly seek out the "good-grade pills," "study drugs," and "smart drugs" for themselves. The Partnership for Drug-Free Kids at drug-free.org ran an attitude-tracking study in 2012 that showed that one in eight teens (13 percent) reported misusing or abusing Ritalin or Adderall at least once in their lifetime and one in four teens (26 percent) believed that prescription drugs could be used as a study aid.[4]

The practice of academic doping continues in college. A 2013 survey of one hundred thousand college students by the American College Health Association indicates that 8.5 percent of students used Adderall and other stimulants without a prescription;[5] a nationwide study of five thousand college students the year prior reported 14 percent of students were doing so.[6] In a 2013 news report, NPR reviewed a number of surveys for data on the number of college students who said they have used stimulants to improve academic performances and found that the reports varied from between 8 and 35 percent.[7] Senior student affairs officers on hundreds of campuses nationwide call this "the biggest drug problem" at their schools.[8]

A 2013 post by James L. Kent on the blog *High Times* (which purports to be the number one resource for cannabis information and culture, so make of it what you will) calls Adderall "America's favorite amphetamine" and shares his reporting on the culture of Adderall use at college through the story of Sheri and Dan:[9]

> Sheri is a junior in college. In the mornings she attends class, and in the afternoons she works at a coffee shop. Sheri has attention-deficit disorder (ADD), and without her medication she has a hard time getting out of the bed in the morning and accomplishing even the most mundane of her daily tasks. Her medication is Adderall, preferably the 30-milligram Adderall XR (extended-release) capsules, but Sheri doesn't have health insurance and can't afford to shell out a couple hundred bucks for the doctor's visit and the $200 to $300 a month for the prescription itself. But Sheri is lucky, because she knows Dan, who sells Adderall XR to college students for $5 to $15 a pop, depending on how many pills they're buying. And Dan does good business, because Adderall is America's favorite amphetamine, especially among college students trying to maintain long hours of focus preparing their finals.
>
> Street-level Adderall dealers (or traders) can distribute to college students at cheaper-than-retail prices. For uninsured students like Sheri, the retail price of a monthly Adderall prescription works out to $6 to $8 a pill. Dan buys prescriptions for Adderall from students still on their parents' health-insurance plan or from members of the military, who get Adderall prescriptions like monthly paychecks. With a military or insurance discount you can buy Adderall XR for under $1 a pill and then sell it for triple to five times the original price. Dan knows he can get $15 to $20 a pill for 30 mg XRs from the right people, so a bottle of cheap XRs is like his savings account, his investment portfolio, and his spending money all rolled into one. And if he doesn't have the time or money to eat, he can just take an XR and he won't be hungry again for another six hours.

THE PRESSURE TO POP PILLS

Taking stimulants may be what an alarming number of college students feel they have to do to succeed, but not all of them are sanguine about it.

Adam (not his real name) recently graduated from a prestigious public university on the East Coast. After hearing about this book from mutual friends, he approached me, wanting to talk about the widespread use of

Adderall by students recreationally (meaning without a prescription), why young adults do it, and where this habit might lead. Because of the sensitivity of the topic, Adam wanted to be anonymous.[10]

My first question for Adam was how students acquire Adderall for recreational purposes. He said, "Everyone I know has a friend who is prescribed this stuff. Every friend group has at least one person with a prescription." Adam knows of a kid whose parent prescribes it for her, even though she has no diagnosis, just for the academic advantage. He added that many kids who have it legitimately are overprescribed it, so they have extra to share. He clarifies that this is an expensive drug, and he's only seen it used by wealthy kids.

"There's a ton of pressure to get great grades and a ton of different things to be doing. So there's a bond and union between all of us. If everyone is working on a big paper due tomorrow, or you're assigned an impossibly long assignment, or it's finals, friends help friends. Someone will say, 'Hey, I have Adderall if we need it tonight' or 'Let's work together. Pool our resources.'"

Adam's tone is ponderous and wary. He says he's uncomfortable telling me this, but he wants to talk about it because he is deeply concerned for his peers—his generation. He describes how his friends' personalities change when they are under the influence of Adderall: how people can go from being a normal student to being singly focused on the academic task at hand, putting their phones away and studying all day, pushing all personal and interpersonal issues out of their minds.

As Adam sees it, Adderall provides seemingly limitless short-term performance gains. I asked Adam whether he sees any downsides. "Definitely," he tells me. "There's a frustration that it's a work-hard/play-hard medication. It's gives you superhuman abilities. Suprahuman, actually. Go out and get the paper done, have a really active social life and academic life, and do everything." Who's frustrated? The kids who accepted their human limitations, didn't take the drug, and received lower grades. "The smartest kids I knew were questioning the ethical nature of it all."

I've contended with the allure of the short-term gain myself. When middle school came around for Sawyer, the homework increased to a level I thought might crush him. In what universe is it reasonable for a sixth grader to have three hours of homework a night? I started to feel remiss as a parent for not exploring the medication option.

One day when Sawyer was particularly distracted, I asked him what it felt like inside his body. "Like the fuzz you see on a television when it's not getting a signal," he responded. My moment to bring up medication had presented, and I seized it. I asked, "If there was a magic pill that took your distractedness away, would you want it?" "Yes!" he shouted. Then he paused. "Wait a minute," he said, looking up at me. "It would change my brain chemistry. It would make me a different person. So . . . no." I had tears in my eyes—for a kid who loved science so much that he knew the truth of which he spoke and for speaking up for that self. The tears were also for me, because despite how very badly I wanted Sawyer to try the meds—so we could all get some relief—the answer was going to be no.

Adam and some of his friends worry about their brain chemistry, too. Whether they are prescription or recreational users, Adam tells me, his friends question the as-of-yet-unknown long-term effects of Adderall. "The fact that there is very little research on that really scares me," he says. They also talk about what will happen when they go off into the workplace, whether they'll still seek out this drug that has helped them manage workloads, expectations, and performance standards all these years. "It's a question of how we will choose to live our lives."

I brighten at this comment. I am interested in young people becoming self-actualized, in making decisions for themselves, and living with the consequences. There is a richness for all of us in making our own way, going about the work of life, earning our keep, paying our bills, and coping with life as it comes. No matter how humble our pursuits, it is edifying when they are *ours*. These kids sitting around the hallowed halls of their prestigious university questioning the role Adderall plays in their lives actually gives me hope.

"We talk about how unfair the system is," Adam tells me. "It's not that Adderall is a great thing, it's just that there is *so* much to do. Taking Adderall is our way of pushing back against the pressure from parents, professors, and friends. Just a way to counter the thing we've been given."

At some point in his college career, Adam gave in to the pressure, envy, and allure. "You're in the library at two a.m. feeling like you're going to pass out and there are tables and tables of kids who are up and just charging away." So he began using Adderall. It helped. But he was still somewhat ambivalent about it. For one, he felt it disrespected his relationship with professors. So Adam only felt comfortable using it in large classes where he felt no personal connection to the professor. This is how he made his peace with it. "Personally I'm not proud of the fact that I took it," he says.

"But you'd be hard-pressed to find a young affluent college student on the East Coast who hasn't tried it."

If our kids are becoming chemically manufactured versions of their otherwise imperfect but quintessentially human selves, if they feel the need to do that in order to succeed in the world, when and where will this drug use end?

9

WE'RE HURTING THEIR
JOB PROSPECTS

In the mid-2000s when I and my university colleagues resigned ourselves to the fact that helicopter parenting was not a fad but was here to stay, I wondered what would happen to overparented young adults in the workplace. Surely if parents felt college was such high stakes that they had to be involved in the minutiae, and students needed and welcomed parental involvement, the workplace would seem to present even greater challenges. Would helicopter parents follow young adults there as well? As we'll see, the answer turned out to be yes.[1]

Millennials in the workplace have been called "orchids"[2] (can't survive outside the greenhouse) and "teacups"[3] (chip easily and then are ruined), but to me the most prescient metaphor for young adults sent out into the world after being overparented is "veal"—a term coined by Massachusetts educator Joe Maruszczak—meaning they're raised in controlled environments and led, metaphorically, to slaughter. None of us took a course called "how to hold your kid back," but overparenting appears to be seriously poor preparation for life in the work world.

In 2014, interested in this question of how helicoptered kids will fare in the workplace, faculty in the Department of Management at California State University Fresno surveyed over 450 undergraduates who were asked to rate their level of self-efficacy, the frequency of parental involvement, how involved parents were in their daily lives, and their response to certain workplace scenarios. "The study revealed that the clearest difference between those students with helicopter parents was their lack of belief in their own ability to complete tasks and reach goals, with researchers suggesting this should ring alarm bells for future employers. It found that students who experienced helicopter parenting through college were more likely to be dependent on others, engage in poor coping strategies and lack the soft-skills, like responsibility and conscientiousness, that employers value. A particularly intriguing finding is that over-parenting relates to maladaptive job search and work behaviours."[4]

What's a parent to do?

The twenty-first-century workplace is global, fast-paced, and constantly shifting. To succeed requires taking initiative, solving problems, and bouncing back from adversity, now more than ever. Employees need all the help they can get, whatever their age may be. In this environment, the pertinent question for parents of young adult job seekers and employees is: How do we help versus hinder?

Helping by providing suggestions, advice, and feedback is useful, but we can only go so far. When parents do what a young employee must do for themselves, it can backfire. For example, in 2014, a mother went on Craigslist offering a finder's fee in the thousands of dollars to anyone who could get her son a job. Is her son a hapless sort? Disabled? Recovering from serious hardship? No. He's a graduate not only of college but a prestigious law school, a former employee at two clerkships, and a member of the California bar. Hopefully none of his clients will find out about his mother's ad. I don't know about you, but I want the lawyer who fights for me to have gotten his own job.

CAUTIONARY TALES FROM HR

In 2005 a young man named Richard graduated from an Ivy League college and two years out of college was on the fast track at a prestigious New York investment bank. He made $250,000 annually—it was right before the 2008 crash—and worked extremely long hours. Richard's mother, Jan, thought to herself that, pay aside, Richard was being worked *too* hard. So Jan did some sleuthing and found the fairly well-concealed land line number for Richard's boss, and called him up one weekend to complain. The boss was polite but was seething inside. When Richard came to work on

Monday, instead of being permitted to enter the bank of elevators that soar to the skyscraper's top, the security guard handed him a cardboard box containing the personal items from his desk. On top of the box was the note: *Ask your mother.*

Is Richard's boss an asshole? Sounds like it. Could he have handled it differently? Yes. Did Richard want his mother to intervene? Who knows? None of that matters because the boss had all the power, as bosses do. This example is from the absolute worst end of the spectrum of possible outcomes when parents get involved in the work lives of their young adult children, yet it is fair warning of what can happen when we try to wield the kind of authority and control we wielded in our kid's childhood. Where colleges have to varying degrees accommodated a parent's interest in being very involved, I've found a lot of employers want no part of it. All they care about is what the *employee* can do, not the parent. Might employment be where even seemingly successful overparenting finally must come to an end?

Suzanne Lucas, the Philadelphia mom now raising her kids in Switzerland who went berserk over the zip-lines, hammers, and nails commonplace in Swiss playgrounds, is a leader in the field of corporate human resources (formerly known as "personnel departments"). I came to know of her because she writes full-time about HR matters based on her expertise as a former corporate human resources manager (an "HRM") in the pharmaceutical industry.[5] Lucas's online articles get hundreds of thousands of hits a month, and she hears from a broad spectrum of HRMs who are hiring and managing employees—including those encountering issues with young employees. She says what's typical today is to receive a call from a parent asking why a kid didn't get a job or internship. When she's on the receiving end of such a call, Suzanne's blunt response is, "Because it's you contacting me, instead of your kid; I need someone with drive."[6]

After having spent five years in Switzerland, Lucas finally shed her "American-bred fears" and became a convert to the Swiss mind-set toward child rearing, which includes encouraging kids as young as kindergarten to walk or take public transportation alone to and from school, and providing "forest play-group" for four-year-olds, a weekly four-hour excursion into the forest, rain or shine, where the children saw and file wood, and roast hot dogs over an open fire for lunch.

Lucas's piece, "Why My Child Will Be Your Child's Boss," told of how experiencing childhood in Switzerland was teaching her American son to make his own decisions, manage risk, and overcome setbacks, skills she well knows will make him a clear choice over his softer American counterparts in the workplace.[7] Her colleagues around the country have cause to agree.

Lora Mitchell was a human resources director in central Ohio who hired emergency medical technicians for an ambulance service that provided emergency response to nursing homes, state prisons, and the mental health system.[8] In recent years, some young men and women have brought their parents along for their EMT interview. "It's clear the parents don't realize we can overhear them in the waiting area," she says. They say things like, "You can do this! You'll be fine!" This can be a flag for human resources.

An even greater concern is a parent "clearly dominating the path" by filling out the application and wanting to sit in on the interview. "If someone in emergency services needs a parent along in order to get through the interview, that person may very well have difficulty making independent decisions in an emergency. You can't call mom for advice when you're trying to treat a felon or a mentally unstable patient." In times when the number of candidates exceeded the number of open spots, Lora would steer away from candidates who brought a parent along; in times when she was short-staffed, she may have had no choice but to hire such a person.

Lora has also faced young employees who expected their supervisor to "parent" them, as Lora put it, meaning they want every last detail explained to them before moving in a particular direction. "They tended not to last very long."

Carol Konicki is the HRM for an Albuquerque, New Mexico, health care organization.[9] A few years ago, a young woman sat through Carol's new-hire orientation, which included an in-depth discussion of health care and other benefits. At the end of the day, instead of turning in her forms, the young woman asked Carol if she could take the paperwork home.

The next morning Carol's phone rang and the caller identified herself as the young woman's mother. "My immediate thought was something horrible had happened," Carol said. Then the mother said she needed to go over the benefits with Carol, explaining, "My daughter doesn't understand it and is afraid of you. There's no way she can come back and ask you these questions, so I need to ask them and then I can help her." Carol reflected back on the orientation session. To her mind, it had been a perfectly cordial interaction. This young woman was *afraid*?

Carol was "a little irritated; I didn't feel it was appropriate," but she went ahead and explained things to the mother. The next day Carol called the daughter and said, "I talked to your mom. Do you have any further questions?" Carol was trying to signal to the young woman that in the workplace the appropriate relationship is between employee and HRM, and that the employee had dented her own reputation right out of the gate by getting her mother involved. "But the employee wasn't ashamed or embarrassed by what happened." As an afterthought Carol offers, "I could not imagine a world where I made that kind of call for my son."

When a parent contacts the employer on her own volition, it's unclear whether it's a case of an overinvolved parent who can't stay out of her kid's business, or an immature young adult who has turned to Mom and perhaps even asked Mom to get involved. This is an important distinction: the former being merely annoying to the employer, the latter leading to concern about the employee's capabilities.

Hope Hardison, director of human resources at the multinational banking and financial services company Wells Fargo, which employs over 260,000 people, found herself wondering which type of parent and employee (called "team members" at Wells Fargo) she was facing when she opened her mail one afternoon.[10] It was the winter of 2013 and Hope received a letter from a mother questioning her daughter's performance review. "This team member was significantly over eighteen. It took me aback. I wondered did she even know her parent had written? It's not good either way."

Hope didn't know the team member personally but felt bad for her nevertheless; in a situation like this one, the parent's behavior reflects poorly on the employee regardless of whether the employee knew about the letter or wanted it to be sent—as with poor Richard, whose mother got him fired from the investment bank. When Hope left work for the day, she saw in the letter a silver lining. "I was off to my twelve-year-old's parent-teacher conference and it was a reminder not to be 'that parent,'" she says with a laugh.

Sometimes, however, it is clear that the employee *is* still very dependent upon their parents, which will cause an employer to be concerned. Teach For America's general counsel Tracy-Elizabeth Clay says corps members sometimes try to set their parent up as an intermediary between themselves and TFA from the get-go.[11] They'll say to TFA, "I've been talking through this new-hire information with my parents, and could we just get them on the phone? It would be easier than me just repeating this all to them. I'd like to get their advice."

Of course our kids want our advice. Of course we want to give it. But an employer wants to see maturity and self-confidence in their young employees. Employers want employees who have the wherewithal to handle things—which means handle things on their *own*.

When a young adult employee needs to bring parents in on a discussion of the routine matters associated with hiring, it can raise an orange flag that will stay with the employee for some time. For example, at TFA, an interaction like the one above where the new corps member wants to get her parents on the phone "will give rise to concerns about whether the person will successfully navigate the challenging environments they're going to be working in. In our ongoing communication with regions, we'll give a heads-up to a staff member in the region in which the corps member is teaching that he or she appears very dependent on their parents." In case you have any doubt as a parent, that heads-up is not a good thing.

OUR DOING UNDOES THEM

I know from my own mother whose career is science education—teaching secondary school teachers how to teach science—that teaching is a notably challenging profession and that, nationwide, many teachers quit after only two years. Teach For America exists to provide an additional source of teachers for the largely urban, underfunded school districts where poverty and its impact are keenly felt. TFA takes nearly six thousand of the nation's best and brightest college graduates and places them in a work situation that may end up being the most challenging work experience they'll ever face in life, as some older TFA alumni have termed it. To find out whether Millennials have what it takes to do highly sought-after, highly prestigious, highly challenging work, there's no better place to drill deeply than TFA.

The leadership at TFA knows full well that the experience of being a corps member can be extremely challenging emotionally. As with other important service jobs such as the military, police work, firefighting, or emergency room care, the unexpected and unforeseen will regularly arise and must be handled. Because of the very nature of the work, TFA only hires young adults who have "grit" and "resilience"—two buzzwords getting a lot of attention these days that signal whether someone can withstand tough challenges and persevere. TFA both expects and respects that the young adults they hire will get a great deal of emotional support from their parents. TFA, too, benefits from parental support as advocates for TFA and in helping secure resources for the program and for specific schools.

Still, TFA leaders have been taken aback by the rising extent of parental involvement in the work life of corps members. They feel it's completely natural for a corps member to complain or vent about workplace challenges to their parents, but it's a sign of continued dependency between young adult and parent when the parent hears these complaints, becomes concerned, and feels it's their place to intervene. "I'm always caught off guard when parents are intervening on behalf of their children, who are adults," says Eric Scroggins, executive director of TFA in the Bay Area.[12]

A typical parent call to Eric might relay facts such as this: The parent has heard from their daughter that she's confronting some unsavory characters on the way to and from school each day, or that she was reprimanded by the principal for violating school policy by leaving in the middle of the day to do an errand, or that she had an intense, difficult interaction with a student or fellow teacher. The parent will say to Eric, "This is an inappropriate place for my daughter; she's unsafe," or "You need to switch her employment," or "She's not receiving the right support; you need to provide it," or "Someone should be in her classroom every day with her."

Sometimes the parent feels better after having had the chance to talk it through with Eric, or with Tracy-Elizabeth, who, too, fields these calls. But sometimes the concerned parent persists. The parent might begin to rant, for example, about their kid working for a "completely incompetent" principal in a school district with policies that "would never be tolerated in my company," concluding that "this is shocking behavior" that "needs to be addressed immediately."

These TFA leaders appreciate that it's hard for parents when a kid is struggling, and that many parental concerns are rooted in stereotype-based fears about low-income communities. They do their best to help a parent understand that first, they're only hearing one side of the story; second, schools have their own rules and culture that may differ greatly from the parent's own professional experience; and third, because TFA corps members are employees of the school district in which they're teaching, TFA couldn't provide these solutions even if it wanted to.

What it boils down to, Eric tells me, is that if all of our school districts functioned perfectly, there would be no need for TFA. In some ways this often dysfunctional, underfunded, extremely challenging environment—and high-stakes important work—is precisely what their kid signed up for. "But in the day-to-day parents can be quite shocked and upset that their kid is being 'subjected' to it."

As is likely the case with Richard at the investment bank, the TFA corps member who is the son or daughter of these ranting parents may have no idea the parent called the office. "Then when they hear about it from us," says Eric, "they realize whatever they've said to their parent that caused their parent to call us makes them come across to us as a bit immature. Typically that ends the situation. It's a learning exercise for the corps member. We try to help them understand the impact their words can have on their parents."

What Eric shares about parents and TFA reminds me of the sessions Dr. Denise Pope and I would conduct for parents of incoming freshmen at Stanford. We would walk parents through scenarios students would be likely to call home about and talk through how to listen and discern whether the student was asking the parent to "do something" or whether the student just wanted to "vent" and needed someone to listen. As is often the case, our kids want us just to listen, and knowing we care and love them is enough to give them the reassurance that they can get back out there to do whatever it is they need to do. We *can* raise them to a healthy, self-actualized independence and still play this listening role in their lives.

THE CHECKLISTED CHILDHOOD COMES HOME TO ROOST

Sometimes the problem in the workplace is, in fact, the young adult employees themselves and has nothing to do with parents showing up, or making calls, or ranting, such as an employee who suffers from a cognitive problem that likely stems from always having been told what to do and from never having been allowed to take risks.

"If you tell them to do A, B, C, and D, they are excellent at doing it, and they're hardworking and dedicated as they do so," TFA's general counsel, Tracy-Elizabeth, tells me.[13] "But if you tell them, 'Look, we're trying to get to D. We're going to show you A and give you half of C. Go innovate, solve it for yourself,' they really struggle. Their mind-set is, 'Tell me what the path is and I'll follow it, even if it's really hard. But strike out on my own and figure it out? That I can't do.'" This is the checklisted childhood at work.

"What I think we're seeing is a lack of autonomy and independence," says Tracy-Elizabeth. "Some corps members arrive with less experience at being truly autonomous, which makes them less equipped to engage in relationships at their schools. The median age in the teacher lounge is double theirs. There are also gender and race issues. We want them to forge relationships as colleagues; to be seen as peers, not as 'kids.'" Tracy-Elizabeth speaks of a tool kit of personal competencies TFA expects an employee of twenty-two or twenty-three years of age to have acquired through life experience and education: maturity, responsibility, initiative-taking, accountability, and the like. "If they don't come with a full tool kit we can build on, with the basics intact, it makes our job much harder."

Tracy-Elizabeth attributes this lack of a needed skill set to a "client-services, customer-service relationship" at colleges and universities. "We often feel the universities are setting us and other employers up badly, because the level of service students receive in college doesn't have a counterpart in the real world. A new corps member may have the mind-set, 'Isn't everybody motivated by doing what's best for me?' When they discover that competing interests are in play and their needs may not be foremost, they're really shocked, deeply demoralized, and feel that the interaction is very unfair. And that's when we hear from parents. They don't think their kid has been treated fairly when often what has happened is their kid hasn't received the customized treatment they may have gotten in college."

When Tracy-Elizabeth says this, I'll admit this stings slightly. More than slightly. I was one of those college people offering the programs and supports she seems to be criticizing. But with distance from the university I can appreciate both that colleges are under tremendous pressure to provide more services in exchange for hefty tuition, room, and board rates, and that in some areas our effort may have strayed toward hand-holding. But I disagree about the origin of the mind-set, and tell her so. Students who have this mind-set arrived to campus with it; it's hard to undo in four years the effects of eighteen years of overparenting.

WORKPLACE CULTURES MAY NOT CHANGE

Some businesses embrace the close relationships between Millennials and their parents. Google and LinkedIn launched a "Bring Your Parents to Work Day."[14] PepsiCo's CEO was featured in a *Harvard Business Review* article for her practice of calling parents during the recruitment process and writing to "thank them for the gift of their children."[15]

Many are getting ahead of the curve by adapting their workplace to the ways Millennials behave differently. Nancy Altobello, Ernst & Young global vice chair—talent, is one of them. Millennials make up over half of her workforce of 190,000 professionals and Nancy unabashedly loves them. But as with any great relationship, she had to get to know them to get there.[16]

"For ten years we wrung our hands over how to best work with our Millennials, examining the number of hours they wanted to work, where they'd work, their role in the team, and whether or not they were being heard." Retooling after the recession, and recognizing that Millennials will comprise a huge percentage of the workforce in no time, Nancy and her colleagues figured out how to adapt to Millennials and make the best use of their considerable talents.

"They come in wanting to be told what to do. If they don't see the context, they won't be engaged. They're concerned with fairness, so transparency matters. They want to know who's accountable for what. We also find they have a huge desire to work differently, and to have flexibility. This doesn't necessarily mean working less—they are most interested in having control over how they work. So we're really mindful of setting the context, explaining what we expect at the end, and then empowering them to think about how to get there. Our experience is if you give them interesting and challenging work, and if they understand how it's going to have a business purpose, they will work just as hard as—if not harder than— members of any generation and will deliver in an extraordinary way."

Nancy understands why parents play more of a role in employees' lives today. Still, she feels that sometimes it's too much. "I had a dad call me last year. He said, 'I just want you to be aware of the hours my daughter has been keeping. If she knew I was calling she'd be so upset.' I looked into it and the father was dead right. But I would have loved if that young lady had said to her dad, 'I'm really struggling. I need help but still want to be perceived well. What should I do?' If he'd sat with her and helped her prepare to have a discussion with us, the situation would have been better. That's a great role for parents."

As parents we can hope our kids end up with bosses like Nancy Altobello instead of that asshole in investment banking. But we can't control that. Our job is to raise them so that even in the rough places, they have a chance to thrive.

10

OVERPARENTING
STRESSES US OUT, TOO

Why is it that we are at sixes and sevens about the one thing human beings have been doing successfully for millennia, long before parenting message boards and peer reviewed studies came along? Why is it that so many mothers and fathers experience parenthood as a kind of crisis? "Crisis" might seem like too strong a word, but there's data suggesting it probably isn't.[1]

—TED Talk by Jennifer Senior, author of *All Joy and No Fun: The Paradox of Modern Parenthood*

Not only does overparenting hurt our children; it harms us, too. Parents today are scared, not to mention exhausted, anxious, and depressed.

Psychologists speak of the "parenting paradox"—the unparalleled joy on the one hand and, on the other hand, the anxiety and depression—resulting from raising offspring.[2] Parental joys are, of course, immeasurable, but our depressions can be quantified: American parents are depressed at twice the rate of the general population—that's approximately 7.5 million depressed parents. According to a 2006 study published in the *Journal of Pediatric Health Care*, over one third of women of childbearing and child-rearing years have depressive symptoms.[3]

Meanwhile, *Parenting* magazine caused a stir in 2013 when it published the piece "Xanax Makes Me a Better Mom" (Xanax is an antianxiety medication). In the article, women detailed the day-to-day stressors and fears that send them running for their pills, and a critic argued that the psychiatric and pharmacological industries have turned normal human sadness into a depressive disorder and that we shouldn't need meds to handle the "everyday roller coaster of parenthood."[4] Plenty of parents I know would take umbrage at the notion that there is anything ordinary about this parenting roller coaster.

Our kids see the strain we're under. Researcher Ellen Galinsky asked one thousand kids what they would most like to change about their parents' schedules. "Few of them wanted more face time; the top wish was for mom and dad to be less tired and stressed."[5] (Our kids are *affected* by our stress, too. Studies show that children of mothers and fathers with poor mental health are at higher risk for negative mental health outcomes themselves.[6])

THE PERILS OF PARENTING ALONE

"Children are not the problem," says author Jennifer Senior in her 2014 TED Talk and in her book *All Joy and No Fun: The Paradox of Modern Parenting.*[7] "Something about parenting, right now, at this moment, is the problem. If we aren't trying everything, it's as if we're doing nothing."

In her 2011 book *Adult Supervision Required: Private Freedom and Public Constraints for Parents and Children,* Wellesley associate professor of sociology Markella B. Rutherford traced a century of parenting behaviors by examining advice columns in parenting magazines over time. She argues that we've lost a sense that it takes a village to raise a child, and instead of being able to rely upon informal community networks to help us raise "our kids" in the public sphere, we're each left to raise "my kid" alone in the private sphere where we are anxious and alone in figuring out how to best prepare our kids for the world outside.[8]

A 2012 study published in the *Journal of Child and Family Studies* looked at 181 moms of kids under age five, and homed in on the kinds of parenting behaviors and attitudes that led to negative mental health outcomes. The researchers found that mothers who adopt an "intensive parenting attitude" are more likely to have negative mental health outcomes. Specifically, mothers "who believe women are the essential parent" had lower life satisfaction,[9] and those who believed that parenting is challenging and requires expert knowledge and skills were more stressed and more depressed than moms "who didn't think an arsenal of expertise was mandatory."[10] Sociologist Annette Lareau, who has taken a close look at the day-to-day of parenting, describes middle- and upper-middle-class parents as being wedded to "concerted cultivation," approaching child rearing as a "project."[11] In her 2005 book *Perfect Madness: Motherhood in the Age of Anxi-*

ety, author Judith Warner coined the term "Mommy Mystique" (playing off Betty Friedan's "Feminine Mystique") for this drive to incessantly nurture or control our children to the point of losing ourselves in the endeavor.[12] Psychotherapist Beth Gagnon sees this "concerted cultivation" and "mommy mystique" in her practice outside of Boston. "Highly educated women pour their skills into parenting. They become experts at parenting in their mind. I find women who are highly invested in their children, and even in the face of their tremendous stress, anxiety, or depression, if I even *suggest* they pull back a bit, it's very insulting to them. I have to walk a fine line between helping and offending them."[13]

MARRIAGES HANG IN THE BALANCE

Stacy Budin has seen firsthand the extreme stress and pressure parents are under.[14] She's a psychiatrist in Palo Alto, where anxious parents come into her office every day. Often her clients' marriages are hanging in the balance.

A couple's relationship may get put on the back burner when the kids are first born, and if over time it continues to be shunted aside as the kid's lives take a higher priority, the relationship may wither. When this happens both the couple and the kids are impacted. "You can't have a healthy family life if you're so focused on the kids that you lose connection with each other. Budin knows many people who are "hanging in there" with marriage until the last kid goes off to college.

Don's marriage is one that didn't survive. When he looks back at what went wrong, he puts a lot of blame on his wife's overparenting.[15]

Don is a senior executive in technology in Silicon Valley. By his late thirties he had reached the vice presidential level in tech, with a résumé boasting work at Hewlett-Packard, eBay, and Salesforce.com, among other large tech companies, and a lifestyle that included buying his daughter a Mercedes for high school graduation.

But Don didn't start life in the 1 percent. "I grew up in a blue-collar family which depended on church and government handouts to feed us whenever my father was laid off. I remember many days growing up where the dryer was broken or the washing machine was, and we had to walk down to the Laundromat with garbage bags full of our clothes, or the car was broken—something was always broken—or the lights had been turned off." From age eleven on, Don worked—picking berries, doing yard work, and performing other odd jobs—to pay for a ticket for the rides at the county fair, and for school clothes his friends "wouldn't laugh at." An average student and a better athlete, Don was recruited to play college football, but the scholarship wasn't enough to cover meals more substantial than Top Ramen and peanut butter and jelly sandwiches, so Don took a job to make ends meet. Next he landed an internship in the tech industry, where he excelled and was asked back. He lost his passion for football but found a passion for tech, and began to climb a ladder that would ultimately lead to enormous success.

Along the way Don met and married a woman who came from a very similar background. But when it came to raising their two children, they couldn't have been less like-minded about how to help their kids "make it." Don's wife wanted to help their kids as much as possible, which to her meant letting the kids enjoy their free time instead of doing chores, and hovering over them to ensure their homework was done. Don saw both of these seemingly helpful things as quite the opposite. "I've looked back at my life and I believe one hundred percent that the responsibilities I had taught me how to be self-sufficient, and that sometimes you have to do things you don't want to do but you suck it up and do it anyway, and that's what teaches you humility, work ethic, responsibility, and follow-through.

"My ex felt like she always had to observe our son and daughter, tell them what to do, and remind them of this or that. And when they didn't do the things she was constantly reminding them to do, she'd get frustrated and keep telling the kids, 'You need to start your homework'—nothing would happen—'You *really* need to start your homework'—nothing would happen. These repetitive reminders and requests went in one ear and out the other. And there were no consequences."

Don was disappointed but perhaps not surprised to see his daughter flunk out after her freshman year at an elite public university, and attributes her failure in large part to a childhood of no responsibility and no accountability. "I was doing things around the house at six and eight years old that today I don't even see teenagers doing. I built a tree house, and helped my dad build and fix things; these days no one knows how to swing a hammer."

Don and his wife have been apart for over five years now and share joint custody of their son, a high schooler. When the son is at Don's house, Don's ex-wife calls to tell him to go on to the parent portal and check what's due in their son's classes, to make sure he turned in all his work, and to call the teacher if there's a discrepancy between what their son says he's done and what the online system indicates. Don sighs heavily as he relays this.

"I will say to my ex's credit that she was more on it than I was. But I wanted to give my kids space both for me personally as well as for my child. I didn't want to have to look at the online parent portal every single day. That's ridiculous. My child should be accountable for their work. If they're not producing, there's a result and it's their problem to resolve it. Nowadays you can watch every single minute step. I think it's the wrong approach. At work we call it micromanaging versus empowerment. If I monitor every single tiny step of a person's work in the office, they call that micromanaging; if I give someone a lot of rope and let them take risks and make decisions, they call that empowerment. If I'm empowering my employees, why would I not also empower my kids?"

BAD MOTHERING IN AMERICA

Comparing the way we parent in the United States to parenting elsewhere in the world yields a sense of just how far we've strayed from what we might think of as the human norm.

A Hungarian woman who teaches violin to many kids in the Southern California town of Santa Clarita asked the mother of one of her students, "Why is everyone here so stressed out?" The mother explained, "Pretty much that's just how it is here."[16] An Israeli mom told me that after years of pursuing her education and doing highly skilled, professional work in Israel, she moved to Palo Alto, "and instead of working I've found I joined the crowd of the really accomplished women who do nothing but drive their kids everywhere and work on their kids' résumés."[17] The minivan is the ultimate symbol of our era: We protect our kids from the danger of the streets and strangers by shuttling them to each and every activity they'll need to have undertaken in order to make it into that elite college we crave for them.

In her 2012 book *Bringing Up Bébé*, author Pamela Druckerman urged us to take a page from the French, who prioritize the cultivation of their children's autonomy and find value in children muddling through to figure things out for themselves, which enables parents to maintain their own sense of self and sanity.[18]

In her 2009 essay collection *Bad Mother*, American author Ayelet Waldman lamented women's constant judgment of ourselves and of our fellow parents, and described her effort *not* to lose herself to parenting by taking a laissez-faire approach to child raising and by valuing her relationship with her husband over her relationship with her children.[19] But she drew heavy public criticism for daring even to speak of a mother's right to preserve her sense of self and sanity, a right that French mothers freely enjoy.

In 2014, I called Waldman to catch up on how her thinking might have evolved in the five years since her controversial book had been published, and it was immediately clear from the tone of her voice that she is unflappable and was unstung by what other people seemed to think of her. "We are beating ourselves up and stressing ourselves out to have the picture-perfect tableau," she said of parenting in the United States. "But it's not working. We're striving for an unattainable, inauthentic shell, and ignoring the real nut, the gooey inside." The gooey inside, she told me, is love, laughter, and fulfillment from simple things[20]—which sounds like it should be so simple.

When I ask parents why they participate in the overprotection, overdirection, hand-holding frenzy, they respond, "So my kid can be happy and successful." When I ask how it feels, they respond: "Way too stressful." I ask why the stress is worth it; they respond, "So my kid can be happy and successful." We're wrapped up in a tautology—the dog chasing its tail—and are too overwhelmed to unwind the illogic that a process so stressful could contribute to our kids' happiness, let alone our own.

Author Jennifer Senior cautions against having a goal of our kids' happiness and self-confidence, which makes us "the custodians of their self-esteem." This is an elusive goal, she says, because we can't teach our kids to be happy or confident the way we can teach them to plow a field or ride a bike. "Happiness and self-confidence can be the by-products of other things, but they cannot really be goals unto themselves. A child's happiness is a very unfair burden to place on a parent."[21] And, I would add, vice versa.

MISPLACING OUR EGOS

Many of us parents, particularly us moms, are "doing parenting" the way we did college, perhaps grad school, and, if we chose it, the world of work, that is, throwing ourselves at it full bore, running the PTA or soccer snack schedule the way we ran our student groups or corporate meetings, leaning in to our kids' lives as if they are the metrics and deliverables of our little private corporation. How our kids look, what they eat, how they dress, what activities they pursue, what they achieve have become reflections of us. Of how we see *ourselves*. Like *their* life is *our* accomplishment. Like their failures are our fault.

Many of us derive a sense of self and purpose in life from the way our children dance the dance, swing the bat, or take the test. Here are some examples I heard from moms around the country:

- Wilhemina is a Dallas mom whose three-year-old competed in a speech contest at school and won. "Now it's the second year, and *we* have a reputation to uphold. When it was her turn to go, my heart was beating hard. I thought to myself, 'What are you doing, she's only four!' There's this sense that it's partly my responsibility to make sure she does well."[22]

- A Menlo Park, California, mom named Melissa calls her friends' use of social media an "expansive, unyielding platform to brag about their kid's success, and their own."[23]

- A Seattle parent named Tina says, "It's a culture of fabulousness. People do PR for their own kids. And maybe for themselves."[24]

- A Southern California mom named Maurina was in her forties when she had her first child and is ten to twenty years older than the moms around her. "I am not of the generation that got a trophy every time you turned around. You either won or lost, you got the part or you didn't, and you learned to suck it up. But now, the moms *and dads* have been told how fabulous they are their whole lives. They seem to have a need to be told they're such a good mommy or daddy. It's so about them. The kids are *supposed* to be the beneficiaries of all this attention but they're not, because the parents are doing it to benefit themselves."[25]

- Dallas mom Nikki has five kids. "I need to put out champion-caliber children who are at the top of their field," she says, "making an impact and changing the world in some way. I am responsible for creating the individual who is capable of that. They are my legacy to the world."[26]

Not only are we measuring our worth by our children's accomplishments, but we've set the bar for achievement so high that it requires our constant and intense involvement.

And even if waking them up, taking them to and from school, reminding them of deadlines, bringing them forgotten assignments and lunches, standing on the sidelines of their games rain or shine, having the hard conversations with coach and teacher, doing projects and essays with and for them does manage to make some of us feel valued (for now), these responsibilities take time, energy, and effort that deplete us.

Says Mia, an entrepreneur in Dallas and mother of a grown daughter, "I realize that when my daughter was growing up, every decision was about whether I was going to manifest as a good mother—like the *character* of a good mother versus an actual person."[27]

Says Nikki, a former corporate engineer and mother of five in Dallas: "I take my parenting to the extreme. It is personal for me and if they don't get that sense of confidence and limitlessness I will feel I failed them as a parent. I tend to get lost in my identity as a mom. I think I forget about myself as a person. I don't do those things I need to do for myself."[28]

Says Wilhelmina, a corporate lawyer and mother of two in Dallas: "Once or twice a month I stay up all night just to stay in the game, not even get ahead. I'm up at five a.m. every day, even Saturday and Sunday. I don't know how long this can continue."[29]

These comments resonate with the totalizing nature of American motherhood Judith Warner describes.[30] Mothers shed their identity as individuals in order to attain the epitome of modern motherhood.

A Silicon Valley mom named Quinn described to me how this totalizing nature of motherhood pushed her to the brink.[31] She wanted to be that "do everything" mom, and with three kids spread over six years, doing everything meant doing a lot. She tried to be "super mom," which meant being an officer in the PTA at the local public school, running the school auction, running the book fair, going on every school trip, driving her kids everywhere, and knowing where they were at all times.

"Everything I was doing involved my children. I had no idea what I liked, complained about not having as much money as everyone else, hated my husband, felt I was competing with all the other moms, and was incredibly insecure. I'd leave the house, go buy myself a new outfit, put a smile on my face, and then go pick up my kids." Clothes shopping was a little something Quinn could do for herself and was a way to have a bit of choice in a life that seemed out of control.

For Quinn, at some point keeping up with the people who set the standards in her school began to take its toll. "When you're a woman in this area that isn't a CEO of a company, you feel you have to do all this stuff to prove you are capable—of something. The politics of the PTA are brutal. Who's doing what and why. Who's *not* doing what and why. Designing around this person because of her propensity for this and that. All the while smiling and nodding and going for coffee with each other. It was completely running me into the ground. I was literally losing my mind. When you find yourself in the self-help portion of the bookstore, that's a sign." One day a close friend told Quinn, "You're miserable. You're angry with everyone. You're overreacting to everything. You're unpleasant to be around." This tough love from Quinn's friend was a wake-up call. Quinn says, "She was right."

"Wanting our kids to be successful is natural," says Palo Alto psychiatrist Stacy Budin. "But the less healthy part comes from the hyper drive in our communities for kids to set themselves apart and shine in one way or another, or in *all* ways. There's so much pressure for kids to achieve that it can become the focus of the mother's life to ensure that high achievement happens. Some mothers seem to have nothing but their kids' SATs and accomplishments to talk about. Then, when college admission offers come, the competitiveness, bragging, and comparisons are hard for all but the few who have the most to brag about. It's not great for kids and it's not great for mothers."[32]

And what's more, this great achievement race is all calibrated to a college admission system that is very, very broken.

11

THE COLLEGE ADMISSION
PROCESS IS BROKEN

What's the best restaurant in New York City? There is no one right answer—what's "best" all depends, of course, on who you are and what you want. The same is true for colleges, but thanks to *U.S. News and World Report*'s annual Best Colleges issue, you wouldn't know it.

For the past thirty years that magazine has made its fortune convincing increasingly anxious parents and students that an undergraduate experience can be reduced to the sum of a few of its measurable parts, a sum that has little to do with the quality of the education a student will experience there.[1] Billionaire Mortimer Zuckerman is the sole owner of the parent company U.S. News & World Report, LP, and his company profits mightily from our hunger for this (mis)information. When *The Chronicle of Higher Education* tried to interview Zuckerman about the controversy surrounding the legitimacy of the *U.S. News* college ranking system in 2007, "he became rather curt and defensive" and ended the interview after a minute and a half.[2]

There are approximately twenty-eight hundred accredited four-year colleges and universities in this country. Pick ten people you admire or think are successful and look them up on LinkedIn and you're likely to see seven to ten different colleges attended. Ask an academic for advice on where a kid can get the best college education and they'll tell you that places offering undergraduates regular, close interaction with faculty—in the classroom, in research, in mentoring relationships—are the places to go. Great undergraduate educations are to be found across America, at small liberal arts colleges, at community colleges, at both public and private schools, and even at some of the schools with the biggest brand names. Brand may be brawn but it isn't always best. Anyone inside academia knows the *Best Colleges* ranking is meaningless when it comes to assessing excellence in education, yet the rankings are powerfully persuasive in steering applicants to just a tiny fraction of America's great possibilities.

Yes, the elephant in the room during all discussions of overparenting and its harms is college admission. It's time we talked about it.

When I applied to Stanford in 1984 it was fairly competitive. Approximately 19,000 students applied for approximately 2,400 slots, and 1,600 accepted the university's offer. That's an admission rate of 12.6 percent and a yield rate (percentage of students who accept) of 67 percent. In 2014, 44,000 applicants applied for approximately 2,200 slots for an admission rate of 5.02 percent—the lowest rate in Stanford's history and the nation. The number of admission slots went down because more Stanford admits accept their offer of admission these days. Having increased the class size to approximately 1,700 recently, Stanford was expecting an admissions yield of 77 percent in 2014. Dean of Admission and Financial Aid Richard Shaw relayed to me that Stanford's *actual* yield rate was 79 percent, which probably sent my former colleagues scrambling to find more beds for those extra students![3] As an alumna and former dean, I am excited that Stanford has risen from regional to national to world prominence over the past fifty years. But it's hard as hell to get in. Like most Stanford alumni today, I can look at those stats and lament, "I wouldn't get in now."

Sid Dalby, the admissions dean at Smith College we met in the part of the book about the kinds of applications that strike an admissions officer as interesting versus the kinds of activities and opportunities parents want their kids to have, gives talks at high schools and community centers in her local area to students and parents about how to approach the college admission process. After talking about finding a school that's a good match for a student, she tells her audience, "If there's a 5-to-10 percent chance of rain, do you wear your raincoat? No? But if people hear 5-to-10 percent chance of admission, they don't assume they'll be part of the 90–95 percent."[4]

This may surprise you, but until Sid said that same line to me on the phone in spring 2014, I had been expecting that my kids would attend one of these most selective schools. My rationale was this: *My husband and I both went to Stanford. Why would I expect anything different (less?) for my kids?* I've felt that way since before they were born, and probably before. But in the weeks since Sid and I spoke I've been mulling that 5-to-10 percent number in my head. With so many kids with top grades and standardized test scores plus everything else colleges want to see in a young adult, I began to think more rationally about what it would take for my kids to make the cut.

Why was I so sure previously that my kids would beat these odds? And why was I so sure I *wanted* them to beat those odds? As former Yale professor and social critic Bill Deresiewicz sees it, by pushing our children toward something unlikely—and not often fitting for them—what we're doing to kids is hubristic, stressful, misguided, and wrong. "Will we continue to maintain an artificial scarcity of educational resources, then drive our children into terror and despair by making them compete with one another for the spaces that are left?" asks Deresiewicz in his 2014 book *Excellent Sheep: The Miseducation of the American Elite and the Way to a Meaningful Life.*[5]

THE U.S. NEWS AND WORLD DISTORT
(A.K.A. THE ANNUAL COLLEGE RANKINGS)

A college degree is necessary today. In 1975, 21.9 percent of Americans aged twenty-five to twenty-nine had a bachelor's degree; today the number is 33.5 percent.[6] The shift from one fifth of the job seekers to one third of the job seekers having that credential means whereas once a high school diploma could lead to good-paying white-collar jobs, today you need a bachelor's degree to even be in the running.

Yes, college matters. But what seems to be causing much of the ramped-up, twenty-first-century stress about college admission is a sweeping misperception of *which* colleges matter. Each September, *U.S. News and World Report* publishes "Best Colleges," a special report that purports to accurately rank over fourteen hundred universities and liberal arts colleges. Over 75 percent of a school's ranking is based on what appears to be objective data[7] (but sometimes is manipulated by the schools or *U.S. News* itself) such as retention rate, student-faculty ratio, class size, SAT/ACT scores, acceptance rate, per-student spending, graduation rate, and alumni giving.

The final 22.5 percent of the ranking is from the "reputation" survey, where senior administrators rate the academic program at *other* schools on a scale from one (marginal) to five (distinguished), a process known among college presidents as the "beauty pageant."

When it is published each fall, the "Best Colleges" issue flies around the Internet commanding 10 million page views in comparison to the five hundred thousand average views the magazine receives in every other month. While college presidents and trustees study it, knowing that a change in ranking—up or down—can directly impact their financial bottom line, the majority of readers are parents of high school and college students, who mistakenly regard the rankings as the true indicators of the relative value of each college's education.

The college application process has become like an international arms race. The grades, the SAT scores, the essays, the extracurriculars, the recommendations, the ability to pay (!), and so on are like stockpiled weapons. And some weapons (a 4.0 GPA) are considered more powerful than others (a 3.5 GPA). Whoever has the most weapons and the most powerful weapons will win. What will they win? They win admission to one of the top-ranked colleges. And, like nations stockpiling weaponry: power. A powerful spot in the world. Or so the misguided thinking goes.

The twenty-five schools atop the *U.S. News* list get so many applications because they are deemed the top schools; then they become even more selective year after year and are able to boast entering classes of students with increasingly extremely high average SAT/ACT scores, and average GPAs near or above what used to be regarded as perfect (4.0). Borrowing from Freud, Bill Deresiewicz calls this "'the narcissism of small differences'— the meaningless distinctions people make to feel superior to those who are exactly like them."[8] However meaningless they are as the measure of a human, these are the only elements that a student can influence in the admission equation, so they appear to be all that's important in an applicant. Students and parents steer a course toward the high end of these "small, meaningless distinctions" because they know that such distinctions can affect the student's chance at a highly selective college—and they have been falsely led to believe those colleges offer the best education and the best chance at a successful life. This arms race leads students to take more advanced placement courses and clamor for every possible point on each homework assignment and test. Often schools have multiple students with the highest grade point average, computed out to the ten-thousandth decimal point. A kid is criticized by peers and parents for having gotten a higher grade in Advanced Chinese—and therefore becoming valedictorian (a powerful weapon)—because he is a native speaker. It's petty.

UNRELENTING PRESSURE TO BE PERFECT

With the college admission system as it is, students (and their parents) feel pressure to achieve perfection, with every homework assignment, lab, paper, quiz, and exam. Even middle school kids are affected. In math, many districts begin "tracking" or "laning" students based upon sixth-grade performance. Kids who didn't earn superior marks in sixth-grade math—due to their skills, lack of interest, poor teaching, life circumstance, or daydreaming—will not be able to take algebra in the eighth grade (the standard in some districts is now even higher—geometry) and can find themselves shut out of the top math lane in high school, which many colleges will all but require in asking that students take the most advanced courses available (and get As in them). When students get less-than-hoped-for college admission results, they and their parents may find themselves blaming an academic experience six years earlier.

I've been there. As a ninth grader, my son, Sawyer, was in the middle math lane—geometry, but not the super-duper geometry that will allow him to take the calculus BC AP test as a senior. I worried about it for about five minutes, and then realized that my kid doesn't like math, is doing well in regular geometry, and if a college doesn't want him because he didn't take the hardest-possible classes in every subject, then to hell with them. (Or at least I was able to be that strident on some days. On other days, I'm as anxious as anyone else.)

In 2013, Blaike Young, a graduating senior at the Latin School of Chicago, wrote an article for her school newspaper equating the stress she and her classmates face from this academic arms race to that experienced by patients in insane asylums in the 1950s.

I spoke with Blaike on an April day in her senior year when she and her classmates were considering their college acceptances and when the Latin School's tradition of seniors wearing their future college's sweatshirt to school on May 1 was very much in mind.[9] All that matters to Blaike and her classmates is the brand name of the college they'll attend. "We know studies show a better education is to be had elsewhere but we ignore them. It goes back to wanting to impress people. Everyone knows every-thing about everybody. You can't be secretive about things with social media."

When we began talking Blaike's voice was cheerful and polite. She spoke with gratitude about being lucky enough to attend the best private schools, and with satisfaction that the long, arduous process of college admission was over. "Finally, I'm learning for the sake of learning," she told me, "not for admission to something or to prove anything to anyone else."

Looking back, Blaike recalled "freaking out about college" as early as the fourth grade. "I would always do my homework to a level that wasn't very normal. Several hours a night." By the time she was a junior she was doing upward of seven hours of homework some nights. She's had to "push, push, push, push, push" these last eight years, which she attributes to her peer group and the academic environment in Chicago. Thinking about her admission results, Blaike pauses and says that she regrets not having had stronger math skills, which she blames on her first-grade math class. "I never understood math then. If I was taught better in first grade, I'd be in a higher math class right now. It still bothers me."

Blaike will be attending one of the nation's most highly ranked public universities, but I can hear in her voice what the process has done to her. We are now thirty minutes into the interview and her initially sunny lan-guage is now blunt, her attitude weary, her tone resigned.

Blaike wrote her article "Go Insane, Go Insane? The Extent of Stress at Latin" during spring break junior year, out of frustration that AP history homework had been assigned over break. Her comparison of the mental health status of high school students to that of patients in an asylum wasn't based on data. "It was really just a wish that if we *did* have evidence that we are at the extreme, that this is as *far* as a person can go, then we'd *know* we were working hard enough. That's something we need to *know*. The amount of anxiety people feel is so ridiculous, so out of the roof. People at school talk about 'having a panic attack' and 'not being able to breathe.' In a sick sort of way, people are proud of it."

Blaike's article concluded with an explicit wish: "I hope that there will eventually be the restoration of childhood. Maybe one day we won't be stuck with paralyzing stress, just the stress that pushes us forward in positive ways." I ask her what she means by a restoration of childhood. "Freedom. You can't have a summer anymore. You have to be working, interning. You can't just enjoy it. You can't enjoy having no homework—that's impossible.

There's no place where you can just be a kid. You're tied down by everything. You can't just have fun, be carefree for even a moment because you're tied down to your phone, to school, to standards. There's no room for spontaneity. You can't go to the pool in the summer. It's like, 'No I have to go do work.' You can't be happy because you'll feel guilty that you're not doing something that's defined as more important." She feels like she's been institutionalized. In some sense, she has.

As I'm thanking Blaike for her time I hear the dead bolt in my front door slide open, signaling that my own high schooler, Sawyer, is home, facing three to four hours of homework. As I walk down the stairs to greet him, I think to myself that as a mom and as an educator, I am contributing to the problem. I want to apologize to Blaike for being part of this system everyone says will be worth it. Later, I shared the transcript of Blaike's interview with Sawyer, and, in response to that last sentiment on the restoration of childhood, Sawyer said, "Yep. She nailed it."

THE SAT—WHAT'S IT GOOD FOR?

The parental–college admissions coresponsibility for this pressure might be nowhere more ubiquitous and obvious than in the persistent use and abuse of SAT scores as measures of student worth. (You literally get more financial aid to colleges if your SAT scores are high.) To assist students in acquiring their munitions for this arms race—the higher SAT scores, and the improved grades, the AP scores, the notable college application essays—a gigantic college-prep industry has arisen, in the form of tutoring centers in strip malls, $14,000 essay-coaching weekends, and personal coaches who will come to your house. This has become a multi-billion-dollar enterprise annually.[10]

Barbara Cronan is head of marketing for the College Board in New York—the organization behind the SAT, PSAT, and AP tests. (The ACT, a test similar to the SAT, is run by a competitor organization, ACT, Inc.) The mission of the College Board is to help kids—including first-generation kids and those from other underserved backgrounds—learn the importance of a college education, how to apply, and how to pay for it. Barbara is the first in her family to have attended college, and she feels great personal satisfaction in being part of the organization.[11]

The College Board sees the PSAT and SAT as equalizers, offering students from all backgrounds the chance to attend competitive colleges. The

PSAT is taken in the sophomore or junior year and more kids take the PSAT than any other standardized test. The College Board sells the PSAT score data to colleges, so that kids with a certain level of aptitude can get onto a college's radar screen—in particular students from underserved communities and under-resourced schools who would otherwise not have meaningful access to such colleges. This starts the flow of college brochures arriving in homes and email in-boxes that won't let up until the college admission season is over one to two years later. This is why the College Board believes in its testing products and the role they play in college admissions.

But what use do colleges make of the tests? There's widespread criticism that colleges buy the PSAT results data so they can send brochures to students they're never going to admit just to boost their number of applications, which in turn will boost their apparent "selectivity," which in turn will boost their *U.S. News* rankings. As for the value of the SAT in the college admission process, it purports to predict a student's likelihood of success in the freshman year of college. Yet virtually every admissions dean I've spoken with takes issue with the SAT to at least some extent because it measures not aptitude but one's ability to study for the test, which boils down to wealth. Here's how: SAT scores improve as a student studies for and retakes the tests. The more test prep and testing a student can afford, the higher their scores. This means that SAT scores correlate highly with socioeconomic status rather than cognitive ability. Acclaimed writer Ayelet Waldman, who raised eyebrows by unveiling her laissez-faire parenting style in her book *Bad Mother*, also has things to say on this topic. "When I think of how much money I've spent on test prep for my carefully nurtured children who can take these standardized tests, it's reprehensible. It's grotesque that universities would continue to use as a measure something that only measures parent neurosis and capacity to pay."[12]

Colleges know that the SAT measures wealth. The bond agencies that rate colleges also know this—they see high SAT scores as evidence that the college has well-heeled parents capable of paying its bills.

The College Board knows this, too. And, given their mission, they bristle over it. In 2014 they radically redesigned the SAT in part to try to get the test out from under the thumb of the test-prep industry that caters to the affluent. They hope the new test will better assess a student's ability to apply knowledge (not just memorize things), as they will need to do in college and in life. They expect the changes will make the test less a function of how often you've prepped for and taken it and more a function of what you intrinsically know—but they've also recognized the value of test prep by partnering with Khan Academy to provide free SAT prep services to anyone and everyone who wants it. The College Board is attempting to realign their test with their ideals. Whether the SAT will indeed end up being more of an equalizer instead of a tool used by the privileged to gain access to elite schools remains to be seen. The new test comes online in 2016.

CRITICISM OF TESTING AND RANKINGS

While many college officials take issue with the purpose and value of the SAT, an even greater number disagree with the purported value of the *U.S. News* rankings survey they receive each year—particularly the "beauty pageant" portion of the survey in which they're asked to rate their fellow institutions. Many believe that some of the nation's best teaching takes place at schools "no one has heard of." So why don't they stop going along with *U.S. News*? The same reason they won't give the SAT far less weight in the admissions process. It'll hurt their ranking if they take these steps, so none wants to do it without their peer institutions doing the same. And they can't seem to band together to make a change, which is not to say they haven't tried.

Lloyd Thacker founded The Education Conservancy in 2004 to tackle the stress of the college admission process and realign it with higher education's values.[13] He pulled together a group of like-minded college presidents and deans of admission to see if something could be done. Lloyd's passion and impatience are palpable, but you wouldn't be off for thinking it quixotic zeal. His opponents are a nation's mind-set, college leaders' fears, and a billionaire's pocketbook.

A few schools had already opted out of the entire *U.S. News* survey—Reed College in Oregon being the most notable—refusing to send in their own data or opinions on other schools, and taking the ratings hit that came. Sarah Lawrence College in Bronxville, New York, stopped accepting the SAT in 2005 because it "did little to predict how a student would do at our college" but did "much to bias admission in favor of those who could afford expensive coaching sessions." *U.S. News* then informed Sarah Lawrence that if they didn't submit SAT scores, it would assume the students had *lower* scores than at peer schools and would assign to Sarah Lawrence an average SAT number approximately 200 points lower than peers.[14] That is,

U.S. News would make up something deliberately designed to punish Sarah Lawrence for not cooperating.[15]

Thacker sought to aggregate these one-off efforts to stand up to the rankings stranglehold. If most institutions were too fearful to take the steps Reed and Sarah Lawrence had taken, perhaps there would be strength in numbers. Lloyd soon published *College Unranked: Ending the College Admissions Frenzy*,[16] a collection of essays by institutional leaders. These leaders also gathered to create a holistic college search tool—BigFuture, a robust, interactive website with much more information than could ever be found in *U.S. News*, hosted by the College Board (www.bigfuture. collegeboard.org). Despite these efforts, the *U.S. News* rankings currently remain the most looked-to source of information on colleges.

In 2007, *PBS NewsHour*'s Gwen Ifill picked up on the brewing criticism of the rankings and interviewed *U.S. News* editor in chief Brian Kelly. She asked whether his college rankings issue "is a marketing tool . . . like a *Sports Illustrated* for academia swimsuit issue sort of thing?" Kelly replied, "You know, from our end of it, certainly we're in business. We are a journalistic organization. We're a publication, but we also make money. We sell the journalism that we produce, so we're not shy about saying that. . . . But, you know, it's a little bit out of our hands once the actual rankings are published."[17] Ifill was wise to equate *U.S. News*'s college rankings issue with *Sports Illustrated*'s annual swimsuit issue; for each of those publications the fiscal health of the entire magazine franchise rests on that single issue.[18]

Like Lloyd Thacker, Bob Sternberg has been on a quest to fix the system. Sternberg is a professor of human development at Cornell, who developed a theory of successful intelligence that is much broader than the theory of general intelligence that serves as a basis for the analytical assessment of the SAT.[19] From his years researching standardized tests and their use in the college admission process, as well as his time as a faculty member at Yale, dean of arts and sciences at Tufts, and provost at Oklahoma State University, Sternberg tells me, "Usually two thirds of college applicants to selective universities are academically qualified. Deciding on them on the basis of whether the SAT is 710 or 730 or the GPA is 3.7 versus 3.9 is really trivial. To the extent you want to make a better society, you're not achieving that by looking to SAT scores or grades."

Sternberg and his colleagues developed, over the years, a series of assessments, called "Rainbow," "Kaleidoscope," and "Panorama" (depending upon the campus at which they were used) to measure his theory of broader intelligences—which included the analytical skills measured by the SAT but also measured creative, practical/common sense, and wisdom/ethical skills. In the early 2000's, he and his colleagues ran a study using Rainbow, supported by the College Board, with roughly one thousand student participants, which showed that his test doubled the prediction over the SAT alone of students' success in the freshman year of college. The differences in performance across ethnic groups were reduced as well. Those results were very promising, and the study was selected to be the lead article in the best journal in his field.[20] But the College Board discontinued its support of the project out of concern that it would be impossible to "scale up" Sternberg's test for meaningful use at a nationwide level.

Larry Momo is director of college counseling at the elite New York college prep school Trinity, and the former admissions dean at Columbia University, and he's fed up with the system.[21] He once stood up at a College Board forum and challenged the new president to *do something* to lessen the importance of standardized testing in college admission. He also wants change in how colleges admit. "After the first read, once the applicant is judged academically capable, why not take the scores off the docket so no one is staring them in the face in committee? Make decisions solely on all the other stuff. If that drives down your average score in a given year, so what?"

The only institutions that could pull off that kind of change with little negative consequence are the colleges that have the biggest brand names and will still have a strong brand even if their average SAT scores go down. A whole book could be written on that subject; this is not that book.

THEIR MORTGAGED CHILDHOODS

For the purposes of this book, the broken SAT system is but one piece of a whole broken college admissions process in which a rich high school learning experience is sacrificed for test scores, and a healthy childhood and young adult development is sacrificed to a corrupt and false ideal. In *Excellent Sheep* Bill Deresiewicz writes, "It comes to this: the elite have purchased self-perpetuation at the price of their children's happiness. The more hoops kids have to jump through, the more it costs to get them through them and the fewer families can do it. But the more they have to jump through, the more miserable they are. . . . You think you're screwing other people's kids, but you also end up fucking up your own."[22]

The system is broken. Our kids are mortgaging their childhoods. But it doesn't have to be like this. There are other options and better ways, as we'll discuss in Parts 3 and 4 of this book. We are going to have to work very hard, together, toward change—for our kids' sakes and for our own.

PART 3

ANOTHER WAY

12

THE CASE FOR ANOTHER WAY

Before the mountains call to you, before you leave this home
I want to teach your heart to trust, as I will teach my own
But sometimes I will ask the moon where it shined upon you last
And shake my head and laugh and say, "it all went by so fast."

—Singer/songwriter Dar Williams,
"The One Who Knows," from the album *The Beauty of the Rain*

Dar Williams is one of my favorite recording artists. Her lyrics are minia-
ture stories, her voice is etched with breathless realism, and she picks the
guitar well. I've sung along to her song "The One Who Knows" hundreds
of times but have yet to get through the final stanza (above) without chok-
ing up. Parental love is piercing, fierce, and beautiful. It is hard to comprehend that we'll be able to cope with our kids leaving home, let alone that at
times we won't even know where they *are*. Yet we gave them life. And life
is to be lived.

And we are mammals, after all. We may be mammals with clothing and
cell phones; nevertheless, we are mammals. In the wild, our mammal counterparts raise offspring until they can fend for themselves. Regardless of
the duration of the raising period—weeks, months, or years—at some point
the young mammal becomes independent. In fact, it is the job of a mammal parent to put itself *out* of a job by raising offspring who will be able to
thrive in the absence of the parent, and who in turn will be capable of raising the next generation. This is our biological imperative. But our fellow
creatures are much better than we are at letting go.

Of course, we're not living in the wild, and we're fortunate that neither our own mortality nor that of our offspring needs to be the predominant motivator of our twenty-first-century middle- and upper-middle-class American behaviors. Yes, it is scary out there. Terrorism lurks and looms, the economy is at times perilous, the middle class is shrinking, a college degree is necessary for a good job, student loan debt is an enormous burden for many, and it's hard to predict what kinds of jobs will lead to success in a constantly shifting information- and technology-based economy. Moreover, from the poor economy, to unemployment rates for young adults, to the high cost of living, there can be good reasons for providing our grown kids some financial support until they can stand on their own, for using our networks and knowledge to help them negotiate the world of work, and for allowing our adult children to move back home when times are tough.

But what will become of our children if we lose touch with our basic mammalian imperative to position them to begin their own adult life, maybe even with a partner and kids of their own one day? Parents protect, direct, and handle so much for children today that we prevent them from the very growth that is essential to their development into adult human beings. And precisely because we're so helpful and supportive, we take away their need for what was once a common adolescent and young adult cry for independence. Today's kids are, for the most part, grateful for our presence, which feels damn wonderful. But have we bred the desire for independence right out of the next generation? Clark University psychology professor Jeffrey Jensen Arnett, purveyor of the new concept of "emerging adulthood," has a new book out called *Getting to 30: A Parent's Guide to the 20-Something Years*.[1] Really? A *parent's* guide? Darwin must be rolling over in his grave.

THE CORE OF THE SELF

Between their late teens and early twenties, we want to launch a kid who still loves us and wants to see us, but who also has the wherewithal to make his or her way in life, with a lot of skills and a mind-set of "I think I can, I think I can!" Another word for that mind-set is "self-efficacy," a central concept within the field of human psychology developed in the 1970s by eminent psychologist Albert Bandura. Self-efficacy means having the belief in your abilities to complete a task, reach goals, and manage a situation.[2] It means believing in *your* abilities—not in your parents' abilities to help you do those things or to do them for you.

Self-efficacy is more than just believing in yourself like that small blue train in *The Little Engine That Could*. Self-efficacy is about having a realistic sense of one's accomplishments (neither overblown nor undersold). It's about learning that when at first you don't succeed you can indeed try, try again and you're likely to make progress perhaps even to a point of recognizable achievement and maybe even to a point of mastery. Self-efficacy is different than self-esteem, which is the belief in one's worth or value. Self-esteem influences self-efficacy, but self-efficacy is built by doing the work and seeing that success came from effort.[3] Self-efficacy is built in large part by the repeated trial-and-error opportunities afforded by childhood. It's in fact what the years we call "childhood" are for in the life of a developing human, what these years have always been for, what these years have always offered until relatively recently when we parents began doing so much of the work of life for our kids.

Believe it or not your kid will be eighteen one day, and although you adore them and love doing for them, you don't want to keep them dependent upon you until they turn eighteen and then dump them out into the real world cold-turkey and wave good-bye; we're supposed to raise them—to parent them—in a manner that inculcates in them a sense of how to be adult in the world, in age-appropriate ways, beginning in early childhood.

So again I'll ask, what does it mean to be an adult? We began to look at this question at the start of Part 2, in the chapter "Our Kids Lack Basic Life Skills." For guidance I turned to someone I know and greatly admire: Professor William (Bill) Damon, professor of education at Stanford and director of the Stanford Center on Adolescence. Bill is one of the world's leading scholars of human development and has raised a handful of humans of his own who are now in their thirties and forties. Based on his research, Bill coined the definitive description of "adolescence" as "that period of time between the onset of puberty and a firm commitment to an adult social role."[4] I visited Bill in his office on the Stanford campus on a busy day in the fall quarter of 2014 to ask him to unpack the latter portion of that phrase: What does it mean to make a firm commitment to an adult social role, and how can parents help a kid mature to that point?[5]

Bill explains that an adult social role is one that is intrinsically not about *you*. A wide range of things qualify, including being a parent, having a commitment to a vocation (job), or joining the military. Inherent in these adult social roles is that you have responsibilities and obligations beyond your personal care and pleasure. So, how can we approach our job as parents so that we raise kids who are able to make firm commitments to adult social roles instead of living in a prolonged adolescence (and dependence upon us)?

WAYS TO PARENT

In the 1960s, University of California–Berkeley developmental psychologist Diana Baumrind researched different parenting techniques and their impact on children. Her 1967 paper articulated three distinct types of parenting—permissive, authoritarian, and authoritative—which were considered standard in the field for the ensuing fifteen years. In 1983 psychologists Eleanor Maccoby and John Martin modified Baumrind's classification, replacing "permissive" with "indulgent," and adding "neglectful." Developmental psychologists around the world now, mostly, regard these four types as definitive.

The four types of parenting describe the extent to which a parent is more or less demanding of a child, on the one hand, and more or less responsive to a child, on the other. They can be plotted on a simple Cartesian chart where the x-axis goes from less demanding on the left to more demanding on the right, and the y-axis goes from less responsive at the bottom to more responsive at the top.

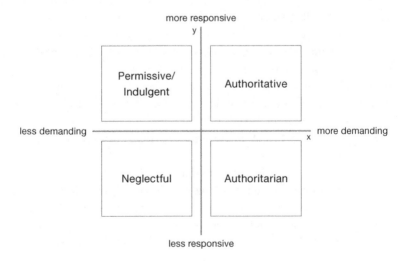

The four types are described as follows:[6]

- AUTHORITARIAN: *demanding and unresponsive.* These parents are strict, expect obedience and respect, and punish their children for failing to comply. They don't explain the reasoning for their actions—they are the "because I *said* so" type. They value achievement, order, discipline, and self-control. Their children have a lot of responsibility in the home and few freedoms outside of it. These parenting characteristics were particularly important during the agricultural and industrial eras. Today this style of parenting is more prevalent in poor and working-class families, immigrant families, and in African American and Chicano/Latino households. However, the affluent, Chinese American, self-described "Tiger Mom" Amy Chua may fall into this category as well, if her fear-based approach and complete dismissiveness of her daughters' own interests is more truth than satire (she's indicated her book *Battle Hymn of the Tiger Mother* is part parody, so we don't know quite how authoritarian she really is).

- PERMISSIVE/INDULGENT: *undemanding and responsive.* These parents tend to attend to their child's every need and comply with their child's every request. They are reluctant to establish rules or expectations, and thus have little basis for or need to discipline. They remind to the point of nagging, but the behavioral consequence they threaten rarely comes. They "give in" regularly and are reluctant to say no or to enforce consequences when they do say it, and feel their kid can do no wrong. Some are very present physically in their child's life. They want their child to like them, and act more like friends than parents. Some are very present at a surface level without being engaged in what their child is actually doing. Permissive parents tend to be wealthier and more educated than other parents.

- NEGLECTFUL: *undemanding and unresponsive.* These parents are, at best, "hands off," and at worst criminally negligent. They are uninvolved in their child's school and home life, are emotionally distant, and often physically absent. They can be unreliable when it comes to providing the necessities of food, shelter, and clothing. They are more likely to live in poverty, and their neglect may be caused by that, or by mental health problems such as depression and anxiety.

- AUTHORITATIVE: *demanding and responsive.* These parents set high standards, expectations, and limits, which they uphold with consequences. They are also emotionally warm, and responsive to their child's emotional needs. They reason with their kids, engaging in a give-and-take for the sake of learning. They give their child freedom to explore, to fail, and to make their own choices.

Helicopter parenting tendencies fall into one or both of two types: authoritarian and permissive/indulgent. They are authoritarian if they bring a heavy hand of direction to their kids' academic, extracurricular, and home lives, instilling a fear of failure with little regard for what each kid wants to pursue. They are permissive/indulgent if they are focused on pleasing their kid, praising their kid, protecting them from failure or harm, and sticking up for them in the world, with little regard for building skills, a strong work ethic, or character. The third type of parent—"neglectful"—is the antithesis of a helicopter parent as they exhibit disinterest in the developmental needs of the child.

The fourth type of parent—"authoritative"—sounds like a combination of "authoritarian" and "permissive," and rightly so. Like authoritarian parents, authoritative parents enforce rules. But unlike authoritarian parents, authoritative parents explain the reason behind the rules, treat their child like an independent, rational being, and are emotionally warm with their children. Authoritative parents also share some traits with permissive/indulgent parents—they are involved in their kids' lives and are responsive to their needs, but unlike permissive parents, authoritative parents don't let their kids get away with things. Authoritative parents balance warmth with strictness, direction with freedom. For this reason, investigative journalist Amanda Ripley describes "authoritative" parents as sitting at "the sweet spot"[7] between "authoritarian" and "permissive" parents.

In her *New York Times* best seller about the world's education superpowers, *The Smartest Kids in the World*, Ripley examines the role of parenting in explaining why American students have a lower degree of academic achievement compared to their peers in dozens of countries around the world. She describes the authoritarian style of parents who "go too far with the drills and practice in academics," and the indulgent/permissive style who raise kids with a "coddled, moon bounce of a childhood." She concludes that the authoritative style of parenting is best—with its balance of strictness and warmth that gains kids' trust and respect. She supports her conclusions with the work of another researcher, Northwestern University's Jelani Mandara, who in a study of close to five thousand U.S. teenagers and their parents found that children raised by authoritative parents have higher academic achievement, fewer symptoms of depression, and fewer problems with aggression, disobedience, and other antisocial behaviors.[8]

We can look at these parenting types and the evidence presented and come to some quick conclusions about the type of parent we think we are, and want to be. But it's not that simple. Many of us derive real pleasure from feeling like our kid's best friend. Many of us are fearful that if we don't force our kid to study or pursue what we're sure is best, they will become failures in life. Amy Chua herself says, "All decent parents want to do what's best for their children. The Chinese just have a totally different idea of how to do that."[9] Indeed, we're all trying to do the right thing.

So, Part 3 of this book is about specific ways to cultivate an authoritative parenting style. It's not easy. It will take practice. We will stumble and have moments of tremendous satisfaction and accomplishment, only to stumble again. But by cutting ourselves some slack, widening our definition of success, and focusing on how to unconditionally love our kids and ourselves, we can, in fact, get it right.

It'll involve letting go of an illusory sense that we can control or manufacture everything in our children's lives, and letting them go about the important work of figuring things out for themselves. It'll involve making them do for themselves, so they develop competencies and confidence. It'll involve teaching them to think for themselves rather than rely on others to tell them what's what or what matters. It's also about being adult enough to set standards and expectations about our children's character and effort, and being able to enforce those standards and expectations. And about accepting our own imperfection—and theirs; neither we, nor they, will get things right all of the time and life is so much more joyously lived when we accept this.

We've been given the awesome, humbling task of helping a young human unfold. What they need most of all is our love and support as they go about the hard and joyful work of learning the skills and mind-sets needed to be a thriving, successful, adult. The "sweet spot" of authoritative parenting—halfway between permissive and authoritarian, and not in any way neglectful—will help us raise our children to truly succeed in life, where we can be proud not only of them, but of ourselves.

13

GIVE THEM UNSTRUCTURED TIME

We were so independent, we were given so much freedom. But now it's impossible to imagine giving that to a child today. It's one of the great losses as a society. But I'm hopeful that we can regain the joy and experience of free play and neighborhood games that were taken for granted growing up in my generation. That would be one of the best gifts we could give our children.[1]

—Hillary Rodham Clinton, 2001

An overscheduled, checklisted childhood doesn't afford time or opportunity for real free play; instead play is planned and organized by parents for a future date when both parents and children are available, and parents accompany the play, often generating ideas for play and watching out for those *just in case* moments when the children aren't getting along or someone is misbehaving. Parents scheduling play seems necessary in our densely packed lives (if it ain't on the calendar, it ain't happening), but even if we must create and protect the time parameters for play, we really need to get out of kids' way as they play. Play is the first real developmental "work" children are supposed to do.

PLAY MATTERS

American historian Howard Chudacoff is one of the gurus of play. His 2007 book *Children at Play: An American History*[2] examines play in American childhood over the last four centuries and details the degree to which, today, free play is really anything but. He traces the shift from ad hoc free play to formal, structured, supervised activity, and concludes, "For preadolescents at least, we need to think more carefully about how *play*—in Tom Sawyer's meaning of *something one is not obliged to do*—should be the private domain of childhood. . . . Perhaps we should consider how and when to give kids more independence to explore their environment, create playthings, interact with other kids, and simply enjoy being young."[3]

Boston College professor Peter Gray takes Chudacoff's musings a step farther, articulating how free play is essential to a child's mental health.[4] For healthy psychological development, Gray says, kids must be involved in activity that is freely chosen, directed by the kids themselves, and undertaken for its own sake, "not consciously pursued to achieve ends that are distinct from the activity itself." If you're not sure what counts as play, quips Gray, "When there's an adult there directing things, that is not play."[5]

Richard Louv is the chairman of the Children & Nature Network, a not-for-profit organization dedicated to reconnecting children and their families with nature. In his 2005 best seller *Last Child in the Woods: Saving Our Children from Nature-Deficit Disorder*, he details the great benefits of outdoor play and the harms accruing to children as they increasingly live life in structured environments and indoors. In our efforts to value and structure time, he writes, we may unintentionally be "killing dreamtime."

Even the United Nations has weighed in on the importance of play, stating in its *Convention on the Rights of the Child* that "children have the right to relax and play."[6] We often think the United Nations exists to assist people in distant lands who suffer from extreme scarcity or violations of their human rights. And it does. But let's not be blind to the abrogation of time for kids to relax and play happening right here, not only under our noses, but by our own hands, through our own mind-set, and courtesy of our own efforts.

In short, play matters.

HOW TO LET YOUR KID PLAY

When and where your child can have the liberty to play freely is clearly a function of your kid's age, his or her capabilities/special needs, your home and neighborhood environment, and how much time is available. Taking those limits into account, consider the following suggestions for how to enhance the degree of free play experts say is critical for a child's psychological health, personal development, and preparedness for the world of adulthood:

1. **Value free play.** Whether your kid is five or fifteen, you—the parent—must value it; like sleep, if it's not valued it will be encroached upon and give way to more pressing, seemingly more important, things. Embrace play as a developmental necessity for your child, and figure out how to fit free play into your family calendar. Ask yourself where you can allow your kid more freedom.

2. **Know your kid.** You know your kid best. What degree of freedom is he or she ready for? Set the limits—amount of time, location, type of activity—with which you're comfortable, knowing you want to balance your concerns about safety, on the one hand, with your job as a parent to build the independence and competency that come from free play, on the other.

3. **Create agreements with other parents.**
   - Your kid wants to play with other *kids*. With so many kids' and adults' lives being overscheduled, at first you might need to help ensure that your kid can find someone to play *with*. So you've got to band together with your kid's friends' parents to carve out times on weekends or after school when nothing is going on, so that free play can happen. Having to structure time for free play may sound like an oxymoron, but until our lives and our kids' lives are a little less compressed, we may have to go out of our way to make time for it so as to ensure that free play can happen.
   - Instead of presuming play *always* has to be scheduled in advance, try for spontaneity. Have your kid call up another kid's house to see if that kid can play. Weekends are more likely to work here. Try to be flexible when the call comes your way.

4. **Offer materials and equipment that foster imaginative play.** Most modern toys have taken the imagination right out of play. For example, a basket full of a thousand Lego bricks just waiting for a kid to shape them into something—anything—supports the development of the imagination, whereas the Lego set that gives step-by-step instructions for building a

structure does not (unless the kid goes rogue and ignores the instructions). Provide materials—wooden blocks, plastic cups, fabric, pots and pans, dolls, boxes, sporting equipment, Lego bricks, Lincoln Logs, Tinkertoys, arts and crafts materials—but let your kid decide what to do with those things. There's a reason behind the joke that kids prefer the manufacturer's box over the toy inside; the box can be a ship, a sled, a house, a bed, a fort, a hole, a stage, a mountain. The toy is whatever the manufacturer says it is.

5. **Let your kid decide how and what to play.** As I've said, have all kinds of stuff readily available so they'll have things to play with. But—and this is key: Leave your kid to it. Wave your hand in the direction of stuff they can play with if you must, but don't structure how the play will unfold or come up with activity ideas. Let your kid figure it out. Let them do what they want, even if it seems silly, unproductive, or unimportant to you. Even let your kid be bored—finding one's way out of boredom builds the problem-solving skills they're going to need down the road.

6. **Work on creating space between you and your kid.** If you feel the need to observe your kid playing in the house, yard, or elsewhere outside, practice being at a greater distance than usual, and continually increase that distance as your child ages and as you grow more comfortable. Remember that the statistics on stranger abduction have been hyped by the media and in reality are incredibly low. If you accompany your kid to the park, sit on a bench and distract yourself with a book. Resist the temptation to intervene in disputes over sharing or taking turns—your kid needs to figure these things out for themselves. Resist the temptation to narrate everything they do as it's happening; let them come to you and tell you all about it. When they do, you can ask them good questions that demonstrate your interest as well as develop in them a deeper understanding about what they've experienced and learned. (More on how to ask these questions will come in the chapter on teaching kids to think.)

7. **Develop a capacity to wince but not to pounce.** Your kid might get hurt and that's okay. Be ready to provide a hug or a Band-Aid and the reassurance that they'll be okay, instead of preventing the upset, scrapes, and sprains that will inevitably happen when kids play freely.

8. **Create a culture of free outdoor play.**

    - Meet more neighbors. It's not just we parents who have changed; our neighborhoods have changed, too, to a point where we're more coexisters than neighbors. Do you know your neighbor on either side well enough to go next door for a stick of butter or a cup of sugar, which used to be the paradigmatic definition of a good neighbor? (Maybe the culprit is our good eating habits—no one eats butter or sugar anymore!) If you don't already know a number of your neighbors, introduce yourself and your kids to the neighbors on your street. Hold a block party. Once you know and trust your neighbors, let them know that your kid is going to be playing outside more often. Let them know how to reach you if they have concerns.

    - Designate safe outdoor spaces. Join with neighbors, friends, and local officials to make your neighborhoods more inviting and safe for play, where kids can run, explore, and create. It could be a particular segment of a street or an entire street, a set of adjoining back or front yards, a park, a vacant lot, a school yard, or an area a few blocks square, all depending on your community, your comfort zone, and your kid's age and readiness for increased independence. In some municipalities local authorities have agreed to officially close a street to car traffic at designated hours so kids can play.

    - Designate block parents. If you've designated places or times where kids are going to be roaming outdoors, figure out which parents will be watching out for the kids during those times—not to hover, direct play, or intervene over turn-taking or hurt feelings, but to provide some supervision as well as snacks and access to bathrooms, and to give kids, particularly little kids, the sense that an adult is around if needed.

    - Give your kid a cell phone. If your kid has a cell phone, you'll feel much safer when they're out in the world beyond your eyesight and earshot. Make sure they've memorized their address and phone number instead of just relying on those things to pop up when they push a button on a smartphone.

    - Enforce limits on electronics. Yes, the cell phone is a handy tool for keeping in touch and for reeling them back in when it's time for dinner or the next thing on the calendar, but it's sad to see a pile of kids outdoors on the grass on a beautiful day all staring down at their phones. You're the parent. Make a rule. Band together with your kid's friends' parents to enforce it.

9. **Get inspired.**

- Visit places deliberately constructed to offer kids the chance to explore, create, and tinker, such as Adventure Playground in Berkeley, California, or Children's Garden in Ithaca, New York. Read Hanna Rosin's 2014 article "The Overprotected Kid"[7] about one such place in the United Kingdom called "The Land" and think about how to create that kind of place, or provide more informal ways for your kids to play this way in your own community.

- Send your kid to a summer camp focused on free play. One such place is Gever Tulley's Tinkering School—a sleepover summer camp in Half Moon Bay, California (half an hour south of San Francisco, on the Pacific coast).

- Consider schools that value student-driven learning and play, such as Montessori schools, which exist nationwide.

10. **Encourage change in your community.** Be an active proponent of free play in your community. Speak about it with your book club, or at the PTA, or at your community center. Talk to your local elected officials and local law enforcement agency. What can your community do to provide a safe, welcoming environment for kids so they can play and be more independent? What can your community do to unpack the schedule kids live by? What can you do to help?

11. **Model play.** Adults play, too (or should). When your kid sees you and a friend sitting in a lawn chair in your front yard or backyard, or on your porch or sidewalk, chatting, laughing, and enjoying yourselves over the beverage of your choice, you're modeling for your kid that a joyful life includes relaxation and hanging out with friends. Adult play also includes the various hobbies and things we do "for ourselves" or "just for fun." Let your kids see you tinker in the garage, practice your guitar, roll a skein of yarn, work a thousand-piece jigsaw puzzle, or whatever it is you do that constitutes *fun* in your own life. (And if you're thinking, "What fun?" take notice of that and do something about it.)

YOU CAN DO IT: THE *PLAYBORHOOD* EXAMPLE

Mike Lanza is bringing play back to his neighborhood in Menlo Park, California. A successful Silicon Valley entrepreneur, Mike, along with his wife, were determined that their three young boys would have the chance to play freely in their home, in their yard, on their street, and in their neighborhood. Their friend Gregory Gavin runs Riveropolis—an organization that creates furniture and sculpture that "brings the magic of running water" to schools, museums, and public places—so they bought one of Gavin's rivers for their front yard. Nearby, toward the street, a set of cozy benches sit around a large wooden table. Near the driveway is plenty of chalk. The backyard has a playhouse with a pitched roof, and right below it is an in-ground trampoline that is best accessed from the playhouse roof. Mike wrote a book called *Playborhood*, which documents these efforts, and more, as well as his overarching philosophy.[8]

I sat with Mike in his front yard one day to learn more about his approach, and the day-to-day routine with his boys.[9] While we talked, his four-year-old rode a trike from the driveway and into the street, and the squeak of a garbage truck down the street jostled my attention. Mike noticed. "Don't worry," he said. "My kid knows to pay attention and get out of the way." What? I also learned that Mike's second grader bikes alone not only the one-and-a-half-mile route home from school but into town to meet his dad for a haircut. If Mike is late to the barber's, the kid settles into the chair and into conversation with the barber on his own. When the haircut is done the kid bikes over to the bike shop and gets his brakes adjusted. The kid is eight. You won't be surprised to learn that I like Mike, or that some of Mike's neighbors think he's crazy.

Mike believes the neighborhood is the unique place in which children can develop their own agency. "They need to be helped to develop who they are in the world and how they can do things on their own. They also need to be nurtured. The neighborhood is a special zone outside the four walls of the home but not so far that you have no idea where they are and don't know the people they're interacting with. It's a place where they can test out different things, do different things, *be* different things."

Mike and his wife often invite other kids in the neighborhood to play freely with their own. He's got a photograph of kids roaming in a pack down the street where, with smudged faces and dirty clothes, they look like a band of pirates. He recalls, "The real formative experiences of my childhood were about me and my friends in my neighborhood exploring, learning, playing, having a flow experience all day. Doing one thing, then another thing, having that total freedom." Mike designed Playborhood to give his own three kids, and his neighbors' kids, some semblance of that childhood. "Kids learn by doing, not by sitting in a cocoon waiting for their brains to develop," he says.

I leave Mike, thinking to myself that his kids are certainly in a unique situation, and also lucky. Like the children Hanna Rosin observed in that throwback UK playground, Mike's Playborhood offers an alternative way to play that children *crave* because there just aren't enough places like that.

UNLEASH CHILDREN AT SCHOOL

To play is to unleash one's mind and enjoy exploring the moments unfolding. The tenets and benefits of play shouldn't be left behind when children enter school. Some schools embrace this approach to learning.

Take Montessori education, for example, which for over one hundred years has applied student-centered, active-learning approaches to K–12 classrooms. Students guide their own learning, particularly figuring out what step to do next on their own. Assessments depend on well-trained teachers, not standardized tests. Montessori "unfolds" students instead of "molding" them.

Montessori graduates are known for their creativity and freethinking. Graduates are wildly successful across every industry, and include Jeff Bezos (founder of Amazon.com), T. Berry Brazelton (pediatrician, child psychiatrist, Harvard professor), Julia Child (celebrity chef and author), George Clooney (Academy Award–winning actor and producer), Sean "Diddy" Combs (Grammy Award–winning musician), Anne Frank (author), Katharine Graham (Pulitzer Prize–winning author, former owner and editor of the *Washington Post*), Helen Keller (political activist, author, lecturer, one of Gallup Poll's most widely admired people of the twentieth century), Beyoncé Knowles (Grammy Award–winning musician), Gabriel García Márquez (Nobel Prize–winning author), Sergey Brin and Larry Page (Google cofounders), Jimmy Wales (founder of Wikipedia), and Will Wright (video game pioneer and producer of the Sims, SimCity, Spore, and Super Mario Brothers), to name just a few.

Speaking about his Montessori education to the *Wall Street Journal*, video game pioneer Will Wright said, "Montessori taught me the joy of discovery. It showed you can become interested in pretty complex theories, like Pythagorean theory, say, by playing with blocks. It's all about learning on your terms, rather than a teacher explaining stuff to you."[10]

Despite the evidence that Montessori's student-driven learning approach is a springboard to success in life, Montessori has yet to become a mainstream model for education in the United States. However, it is on the rise, not only in the upper-middle-class and white communities in which it has always had a foothold, but increasingly in both private and public schools, and with diverse student bodies including low-income students, such as Urban Montessori Charter School in Oakland, California, which is new and thriving.[11]

As CNN reported in March 2014, Montessori is also on the rise in China, whose Ministry of Education is concerned that its students are great at sitting in rows and memorizing things but not great at the heuristic skills that come from thinking outside the box.[12] The CNN report followed a 2013 story by the *Washington Post* that reported that the Chinese Ministry of Education was calling for less time in school, less homework, and less reliance on test scores as means of evaluating schools. According to University of Oregon professor Yong Zhao, an internationally known scholar, author, and speaker whose work focuses on the implications of globalization and technology on education, "The Chinese have seen enough damage done by an overemphasis on testing and academic work on creativity, innovation, and student psychological and physical well-being."[13]

If 1.3 billion Chinese are being encouraged to embrace a freer-thinking style of education, perhaps here in America we should, too.

HELP THEM EXPERIENCE "FLOW"

Earlier, Playborhood's Mike Lanza described his desire for his kids to experience "flow." Flow is the thing we feel, or the place we're *in*, when we're interested in or talented at something and the challenge or situation is just slightly beyond our current capability. It's a concept from the field of positive psychology discovered and coined by Mihaly Csikszentmihalyi (pronounced ME-high Chicks-SEND-me-high).[14] I learned about Csikszentmihalyi from professors at Stanford's Design School (a.k.a. the D School) who were training me to teach a class on design thinking, and Csikszentmihalyi's work was on the syllabus.

When we're "in flow," the challenge we're facing slightly exceeds our skill level, and, striving to keep at it, we lose track of time, don't notice our hunger or tiredness, and feel like what we're doing could go on and on and on. We're intrinsically motivated—whatever we're doing becomes it's own reward. The analog for flow in sports is being in the "zone." In music it's called being in the "groove."

Good old-fashioned natural free play provides an environment in which kids can experience flow. But kids who live highly structured lives, where academic, extracurricular, or athletic pursuits are part of a checklist that must be completed in order to achieve some other thing—such as the very concrete goal of college admission, or the very subjective and at times elusive goal of a parent's approval—may have little opportunity to experience flow.

In 2011 and 2012, when I had the chance to teach Stanford undergrads about flow, I was struck by how many said they hadn't felt it in years. Many dug way back to early childhood for an example. But some were feeling it at college and could describe how academic pursuits such as a biology lab, an English paper, or an engineering problem, or extracurricular efforts like a long bike ride put them in that place. Noticing when we're in flow means noticing what we love doing. When we can look back on an experience and realize we were in flow, we've gotten a great clue from our*selves* that we're doing something that matters to us, which can lead to meaningful work and hobbies.

I now set a goal to look back on my day and notice when I was in flow (by definition, you can't really notice it while you're in it, because the act of noticing takes you out of it). I strive for as much flow as possible in my life. More important, I want to see my kids experience flow, and unstructured playtime is the environment in which flow can best happen for them. On its website, the George Lucas Educational Foundation features an interview with Csikszentmihalyi about how kids can experience flow and how parents can increase the possibility for such experiences in their kids. Csikszentmihalyi said that kids who are in flow have parents with high expectations and who give them opportunities. "For instance, we find that kids who are in flow often at home have a place where they feel private, where they can be by themselves. And at first we thought, 'Oh, well the rich kids have that.' No. Rich kids have no more chance to have privacy than poor kids. It's not having a big place, it's just having a place where you feel, 'Okay, here I can do what I want to do.' It may be a basement, a corner of the basement, whatever. Having a TV in a kid's bedroom is one of the worst things because then they end up taking the easy way and when they're bored they turn on the TV, etcetera."[15]

BENEFITS FOR A LIFETIME

Play is good for kids in the moment and aids their development as students and thinkers. It also directly builds capabilities valued in the workplace. Nancy Cotton, a clinical developmental psychologist living in Vermont, wrote a piece in the journal *Child Psychiatry and Human Development* that beautifully captures the four ways in which the arena of play develops competencies needed for adult work:

1. Play provides the opportunity for children to learn, develop, and perfect new skills that build *competence*;
2. Play is the child's natural mode to master anxiety from overwhelming experiences of everyday life, which builds the *capacity to cope with the environment*;
3. Play helps build the ego's capacity to mediate between unconscious and conscious realities, which enhances *ego strength*; and
4. Play repeats or confirms a gratifying experience that fuels a child's *investment in life*.[16]

Recall how (in Chapter 9, "We're Hurting Their Job Prospects") Tracy-Elizabeth Clay at Teach For America spoke of some TFA corps members who can go from A to B to C to D quite successfully, but when you tell them to get to D on their own, they're lost? These are the very skills that *could have come* from free play.

Dr. Stuart Brown, founder of The National Institute for Play, which advocates for the importance of play in the lives of all humans, concurs. In his 2008 TED talk, Brown explains that employers such as Jet Propulsion Laboratory, NASA, and Boeing won't hire a research and development problem solver—even if the person is a top graduate from one of the top engineering schools—unless they know that the person did stuff with their hands early in life. Tinkering, making stuff, fixing stuff, being curious enough to do all that, and the key learnings that arise, are seen as essential prerequisites for problem solving in the aerospace industry, and presumably others.[17]

———

Hanna Rosin's 2014 article about the UK playground that offers kids a tantalizing degree of freedom and a whole bunch of stuff with which to make things and play struck a nerve in the United States nationally. *PBS NewsHour*'s Judy Woodruff interviewed Rosin about the playground, and about what Rosin had learned as a parent from seeing it. Rosin told Woodruff, "Emotionally we like to intervene before anything bad happens. That's what it means to be a good parent these days. In my mind I think of [what I learned from observing that playground] as slightly shifting the definition of what it means to be a good parent. Keep a kid safe *and* create opportunity for a child to think independently and take risks, build character— that's part of being a great parent. I'm not failing or neglecting them by doing that—I'm doing what's right for their future."[18]

14

TEACH LIFE SKILLS

> The mountain climber takes pride in planting his flag at the top because it took a lot to get there. If he took a helicopter it wouldn't feel the same. In facilitating success parents are paradoxically guaranteeing that a kid can't achieve it on his own.[1]
>
> —David McCullough Jr., teacher, Wellesley High School,
> author of *You Are Not Special: and Other Encouragements*

Compared to their less-advantaged peers, children in middle- and upper-middle-class families often have the tasks of daily life done for them by their parents (or other caregivers, or hired help). We absolve our kids of these tasks—things like waking themselves up, keeping track of their own belongings, and making meals—in part to show our love, in part to make life easy and nice, also perhaps in part to ensure that these things are done correctly, and even at times out of a need to feel a greater sense of purpose in our own lives. We also do it because the mountain of homework and slew of extracurriculars our kids face leave little time for regular old life stuff. It's not that the parents of less-advantaged children love their kids any less; it's that they're busy working multiple jobs with inflexible hours just to keep a roof over everyone's heads and to put food on the table. Being able to do so much *for* our kids is very much a function of extra money and leisure time.

When we do everything for our kids, we do so with the best of intentions. But when it comes to getting ahead in life, skills like getting to places on time, being in charge of your own backpack or briefcase, and knowing how to cook turn out to be as important as schoolwork, piano lessons, and competitive sports. However accomplished our kids may be in a résumé sense, a young adult lacking life skills is not prepared to succeed in life without a full-time concierge, personal assistant, valet, or parent by their side. Would you rather always be there for them, or have confidence that they can do for themselves when they leave home, and in that unwelcome future time when you're gone?

LIFE SKILLS MATTER

A person hand-held through life—where things are always taken care of for them—doesn't have the opportunity to develop the concept of *mastery* at the heart of psychology professor Albert Bandura's theory of "self-efficacy," which is the belief in your abilities to complete a task, reach a goal, and manage a situation.

Having things done for you and having no control over those outcomes can also lead to a kind of "learned helplessness," a concept developed by psychology professors Christopher Peterson and Martin Seligman that describes how humans shut down when they feel they have no control over situations. Learned helplessness was originally thought to occur only when *bad* events were uncontrollable. More recently, Seligman has written that learned helplessness can also occur when *good* events are uncontrollable, as when a parent rewards a child with praise regardless of what she does.[2] According to Seligman, it's crucial that humans experience "contingency"— which means "learning that your actions matter, that they control outcomes that are important." Young children who experience "noncontingency" between actions and outcomes will experience "passivity, depression, and poor physical health."

Beit T'Shuvah is an addiction treatment center that has been serving the Greater Los Angeles area for decades.[3] Historically their clientele were people in their thirties and forties. Recently the staff has seen a sharp increase in young adult clients, many of whom appear to suffer from this "learned helplessness" and lack of "self-efficacy." With this changing demographic in mind, the staff of Beit T'Shuvah conducts prevention outreach programs at schools and community centers in the Greater Los Angeles area and elsewhere across the nation. Their target audience is parents, and they focus their message on how the seemingly benevolent act of handling everything for one's kids can lead those kids down a path toward alcohol and drug addiction.

Rachel (not her real name) was one such kid. I spoke with her in the spring of 2014, when she was twenty-three years old and had been clean and sober for three years, thanks in large part to the support she found at Beit T'Shuvah. I asked her to detail the sequence of behaviors and experiences that led to her alcohol and drug addiction.[4]

Rachel is from an affluent and Conservative Jewish family in Los Angeles, and her parents always had very high expectations for what she and her three younger siblings would achieve academically. It was not hard for Rachel to meet their expectations; she was self-motivated, worked hard, and earned straight As throughout her years in middle school and at her private high school. But at an early age she began to experience a "meaninglessness" that became pervasive, and she turned to disordered eating, drugs, and alcohol to get through each day.

"A lot of things were done for me growing up. Even simple things like making my bed or doing laundry—I never did any of that. I never did anything for myself." Rachel experienced some relief by taking control over what she ate. She was ten years old when her eating disorder began. Her parents were not aware of this problem for years.

By the time Rachel was in high school, her parents were handling matters both in and outside of the house for her. For example, if she had a conflict with a friend, or an issue arose at school, her parents would take it into their own hands. "There was always a 'fix it.' It wasn't of my own doing. I was going through the motions. Doing life. Not really participating in it. It was scary." Rachel began using cocaine at fourteen along with alcohol and other drugs. "The thing I could do best was drink and use; it took me out of feeling life was completely pointless." At the start of Rachel's senior year in high school her mother managed all aspects of Rachel's life, and in particular her college admission process, "like a secretary."

When the college admissions letters came Rachel had a number of exciting options. She decided to attend a prestigious private university in the South. There, she pursued a rigorous premed program and earned all As, but she was starting to experience the cost of all of those years of overparenting, with devastating results.

"When I got to college, I had no living skills whatsoever. I had an unbelievable ability to do well in school, but that was it. Nothing else. Not only was I in an environment where I knew no one, but I had to fend for myself and I didn't know how." Rachel soothed this bewilderment over how to manage her day-to-day life by drinking daily. She also became addicted to Adderall. At nineteen years of age, in December of her sophomore year of college, Rachel attempted suicide. Rachel's parents pulled her out of school and took her to Beit T'Shuvah for treatment of her addiction.

Rachel's story is extreme. But it illustrates the reason for the mounting concern about what's happening to affluent kids today. In her 2013 paper in *Psychology Today*, "The Problem with Rich Kids," researcher Suniya S. Luthar shares her studies on kids like Rachel from well-educated, high-income, two-parent families who were found to abuse drugs and alcohol at much higher rates than their peers at the other end of the socioeconomic spectrum (which was a surprise to Luthar, who expected the opposite). Luther writes, "Across geographical areas and public and private schools, upper-middle-class youngsters show alarmingly high rates of serious disturbance."[5]

HOW TO TEACH LIFE SKILLS

There's a scarcity of information on how one *acquires* life skills, presumably because children who are otherwise healthy and developing normally used to develop these skills naturally in the normal course of childhood, and we're only just beginning to recognize that these skills are missing in many children and must be affirmatively taught.

However, researchers, therapists, and advocates who work with kids with special needs, and parents of kids with special needs, think about life skills as a matter of course; their aim is to help children acquire such skills in order to function in the world independently out in the mainstream one day. Perhaps ironically, children with special needs who get good interventions are, often, getting life skills training (as well as developing grit that comes from failing and trying again) that many of today's "typically developing" kids lack.

My friend Stacey Ashlund is part of this community of parents with special needs kids.[6] She has two children, one of whom, her son, is both hearing and vision impaired. Having sought the best possible resources to support their son in his growth and development, Stacey and her husband learned about the applied behavior analysis (ABA) method, a system for behavior change derived in the 1960s by a group of faculty at the University of Washington, based on the work of behavioral psychologist B. F. Skinner, and applied to the autism community in the 1980s. ABA changes behavior by offering rewards for the desired behavior. They also learned about the Relationship Development Intervention (RDI), an approach to supporting children with developmental disabilities developed by internationally known researcher Dr. Steven Gutstein. RDI focuses on the growth that comes when the relationship between caregiver and child is developed in a step-by-step way, and specifically teaches that failure equals learning and focuses on the process, not the end result. Influenced by the ABA, RDI, and other sources, Stacey pulled together the following strategy for building skills in her children.

- first we do it *for* you,
- then we do it *with* you,
- then we *watch you* do it,
- then *you do it* completely *independently.*

This philosophy and strategy neatly sums up not only the intrinsic purpose of parenting but the practical path toward independence for all kids. It also aligns with psychologist Madeline Levine's warning: Don't do for your kid what your kid *can already* do, or can *almost do.* When we overparent we delay moving from the first bullet point to the second, we really get stalled at moving from the second to the third, and we may never get to the fourth bullet point at all. But we must. The real world will demand that our kids be able to execute bullet point four.

Stacey's son is achieving in ways neither doctors or educators initially predicted. He is exceptionally bright, and that, plus access to great resources and tremendous engagement of his parents, including how they've implemented the applied behavioral analysis and Relationship Development Intervention approaches, have likely made the difference. As Stacey well knows, though, this method of teaching skills to a child can be applied to any child, regardless of needs or ability. Her second child is developing "typically" (that is, has no special needs), yet Stacey and her husband parent *both* of their children using this same wise approach.

SAMPLE SET OF LIFE SKILLS KIDS MUST ACQUIRE

Rachel, the student from Los Angeles who ended up in the Beit T'Shuvah treatment facility for addicts, said she felt a sense of helplessness because her parents were taking care of everything for her. But what exactly were her parents doing for her instead of requiring that she do for herself? As with *how* to teach living skills discussed in the prior section, there's of information on just what exactly these living skills *are*.

A 2012 article by Lindsay Hutton, associate editor at the Family tion Network, outlined such living skills by age category. Family Education Network, owned by education publisher conglomerate Pearson, was founded in 1996 and claims to be the oldest site for parenting advice on the Web. The following tips appeared in Hutton's article. Remember, to be an authoritative parent, you have to set out rules and expectations. This list of things your kids should be able to do for themselves is a great set of expectations with which to start.[7]

AGES 2 TO 3: SMALL CHORES AND BASIC GROOMING. This is the age when your child will start to learn basic life skills.

By the age of three, your child should be able to:

- help put his toys away
- dress himself (with some help from you)
- put his clothes in the hamper when he undresses
- clear his plate after meals
- assist in setting the table
- brush his teeth and wash his face with assistance

AGES 4 TO 5: IMPORTANT NAMES AND NUMBERS. When your child reaches this age, safety skills are high on the list.

She should:

- know her full name, address, and phone number
- know how to make an emergency call

She should also be able to:

- perform simple cleaning chores such as dusting in easy-to-reach places and clearing the table after meals
- feed pets
- identify monetary denominations, and understand the very basic concept of how money is used
- brush her teeth, comb her hair, and wash her face without assistance

- help with basic laundry chores, such as putting her clothes away and bringing her dirty clothes to the laundry area
- choose her own clothes to wear

AGES 6 TO 7: BASIC COOKING TECHNIQUES. Kids at this age can start to help with cooking meals, and can learn to:

- mix, stir, and cut with a dull knife
- make a basic meal, such as a sandwich
- help put the groceries away
- wash the dishes
- use basic household cleaners safely
- straighten up the bathroom after using it
- make his bed without assistance
- bathe unsupervised

AGES 8 TO 9: PRIDE IN PERSONAL BELONGINGS. By this time, your child should take pride in her personal belongings and take care of them properly. This includes being able to:

- fold her clothes
- learn simple sewing
- care for outdoor toys such as her bike or roller skates
- take care of personal hygiene without being told to do so
- use a broom and dustpan properly
- read a recipe and prepare a simple meal
- help create a grocery list
- count and make change
- take written phone messages
- help with simple lawn duties such as watering and weeding flower beds
- take out the trash

AGES 10 TO 13: GAINING INDEPENDENCE. Ten is about the age when your child can begin to perform many skills independently. He should know how to:

- stay home alone
- go to the store and make purchases by himself
- change his own bedsheets
- use the washing machine and dryer
- plan and prepare a meal with several ingredients
- use the oven to broil or bake foods
- read labels
- iron his clothes
- learn to use basic hand tools
- mow the lawn
- look after younger siblings or neighbors

AGES 14 TO 18: MORE ADVANCED SKILLS ARE LEARNED. By the age of fourteen, your child should have a very good mastering of all of the previous skills. On top of that, she should also be able to:

- perform more sophisticated cleaning and maintenance chores, such as changing the vacuum cleaner bag, cleaning the stove, and unclogging drains
- fill a car with gas, add air to and change a tire
- read and understand medicine labels and dosages
- interview for and get a job
- prepare and cook meals

YOUNG ADULTS: PREPARING TO LIVE ON HIS OWN. Your child will need to know how to support himself when he goes away to college or moves out. There are still a few skills he should know before venturing out on his own, including:

- make regular doctor and dentist appointments and other important health-related appointments
- have a basic understanding of finances, and be able to manage his bank account, balance a checkbook, pay a bill, and use a credit card
- understand basic contracts, like an apartment or car lease
- schedule oil changes and basic car maintenance

You might wince when you read this list—I certainly did. Looking over the list and looking back over the years spent raising Sawyer and Avery, I see that my husband and I did way too much for our kids instead of welcoming them to the joy of doing more and more things on their own. I'll admit it was often easier just to do these things ourselves, plus we *liked* doing things for them. My kids were tweens when we realized the error of our ways, and what they lacked in life skills they made up for in analytical reasoning. "Why now?" they asked. "If this matters, how come we haven't always been doing it?" (They were used to our indulgent/permissive tendencies.) Sorely tempted to resort to the "*because I said so*" mantra of the authoritarian parent, I managed to eke out a more reasoned, authoritative response: "Because you need to know how to do these things and we should have been teaching you all along." I took responsibility and now they were going to do the same. I was ready to teach these tasks following Stacey's bulleted approach, knowing that for some tasks I was stuck on bullet points one and two—doing it *for* them, and doing it *with* them—and needed to zoom ahead to bullet points three and four.

GETTING TO BULLET POINT THREE:
THEN WE WATCH YOU DO IT

If the first two bullet points in Stacey's approach to teaching life skills— first we do it *for* you, then we do it *with* you—are rather easy to execute, bullet point three—then we *watch* you do it—can require a huge leap of faith not only in our kid but in the environment in which the task will be done, particularly when that environment is outside of our locus of control.

In September 2010 Sawyer was starting sixth grade and middle school. He was to register the day before classes began, and registering might have been simple if *only* the two hundred kids in Sawyer's class had shown up. But parents were there, hundreds of parents, with an assortment of younger siblings along for the ride. Yes, two or three times the necessary number of people were standing in barely moving lines. The sixth graders themselves tended to be loitering with friends, waiting around for parents like me to do the registering. Yes, I was one of the parents waiting to do what my kid could have done for himself.

Here was a blatant example of being stuck at bullet point two (doing it *with* them), but I had good reason to think Sawyer was capable of more. Midway through my wait in the long line, I called him over to me, had him read through the forms, and briefed him on what he could expect when he turned them in to the person behind the table at the front of the line. By the time I got to the front of the line I was ready to go for bullet point three: Instead of hovering next to him to hear the staff person's questions and instructions, I told Sawyer that I'd hang back while he handed them in and responded to whatever questions the staff would ask. There were further steps after handing in the forms and another line for the ID card/yearbook picture, and I told him he needed to figure out those next steps for himself. It all went fine. Back at home, I kicked myself for having stood with him through the process, for having even been there at all, really. If I couldn't hang back and let him try out registering for sixth grade, was I going to show up in seventh grade? Eighth? Was I going to accompany him to high school? College? If sixth grade was such high stakes that I needed to be there, and the stakes only get higher in life, then wasn't I really consigning myself to play this role forever?

Adam Mindel is on the executive management team at Beit T'Shuvah, where he directs a parent program he lovingly calls "Mothers Without Borders"—the support groups for addicts' parents who are often entirely too involved in managing the lives of their adult children. "They can't tolerate letting their children struggle or have fear. They grasp for control in every way, and don't allow their children to figure it out. We have 'children' who are twenty-three, twenty-four, twenty-five years of age, with parents chronically looking to manage their activities. It's like they're still holding them in their arms; what I'm trying to teach parents to do is *put their children down*."[8]

The second child is often where we redeem ourselves, where we grow more comfortable putting our children down—getting to bullet points three and four more quickly—and I did so with Avery. On the eve of her sixth-grade registration, we talked through the process at home and she felt she could handle it, so off she went alone (bullet point four), and both she—and I—did just fine.

My next chance to get it right with Sawyer came during the summer before seventh grade, when he was headed to western Canada for a twelve-day summer program with People to People, an organization that sends American kids to other countries to build cultural awareness and understanding. When the brochure arrived, I saw it as a chance for Sawyer to build some life skills (and also learn a lot of cool stuff in Canada). Six months of anticipation and planning and fifteen hours of orientation later,

Sawyer and we were ready. His dad had taught him to pack a suitcase, keep track of his stuff, and handle money. Meanwhile I was trying to fatten him up a bit because I worried that my picky son would find little to eat there. (As it turned out, I was wrong.) Meet-up time at San Francisco International Airport was 4:30 a.m. sharp. There we stood like all the other parents, huddled a respectable distance from our twelve-year-olds, pretending we weren't worried about our baby leaving us to go to another country for close to two weeks.

When the ticket counter for the Vancouver flight opened for business, two types of parents became evident. Group A were those who handled the entire check-in procedure for their child while the child stood alongside, listening or not (who could tell?). Group B hung back and had their kids check themselves in. We were in Group B; our feeling was, if the airport check-in process is going to be hard, let it be hard here at the home airport while we're still loitering nearby so our kid has some confidence in his skills by the time he has to change planes in Vancouver. In other words, let's see if we can implement bullet point three before he has to execute bullet point four.

Many parents from Group A stayed clumped near their kids right up to the security line, when the stern face of TSA authority prevented further accompaniment. But my kid was going free range. I was both *so* afraid of what could happen to him out in the world, on the plane, in the security line, really from the moment he left our gaze, yet on the other hand, I could feel my chest swell with pride, even admiration, for him as I watched him walk away from us. Sawyer came back home twelve days later with a lot more swagger, and 98 percent of his stuff. It was Mission Accomplished for both mother and son.

GETTING TO BULLET POINT FOUR:
THEN THEY DO IT COMPLETELY INDEPENDENTLY

Lorie and Eric are neighbors of ours with four kids aged ten to sixteen, the eldest of whom, Zachary, is Sawyer's friend, and they turn out to be way ahead of my husband and me at teaching life skills to their kids. Some years ago when Zachary was over at our house and I was making lunch for the boys, he announced that he and his three younger siblings were responsible for making their own breakfast on school day mornings, and for packing their school lunch box.

I just about dropped my coffee cup. Surely his youngest sibling—then about five—wasn't left to fend for herself? I was wrong. As Zachary's mom, Lorie, would later tell me, from the time her kids were four they were expected to make their own breakfast, freeing up Lorie and her husband, Eric, to work out, shower, and get ready for the day. I couldn't even picture it. How did the littlest one reach anything? The next time Zachary came over I asked him to tell the story again so I could see how it actually worked, while my own kids tried to avoid eye contact with me while muttering, "Don't get any ideas." Zachary responded matter-of-factly, "The cereal is in the bottom cupboard, so are plates, and cups, and the milk is on a low shelf in the refrigerator. They showed me how to do it when I was little and my brother and sisters figured it out by watching me." Not rocket science. And Zachary sounded proud as he rattled off further things he was expected to do—and could do—on his own. Proud, and confident. In contrast, my own kids were rather content to have stuff made, solved, done *for* them.

In the 2013–2014 school year, a public elementary school located one town over from mine in Menlo Park, California, called Oak Knoll School, consulted with Lenore Skenazy—author of *Free-Range Kids*[9]—as part of the school's annual theme that year, which was "building confidence." School psychologist Jenny Ryan had read *Free-Range Kids* and brought the school's leaders together to think about incorporating Skenazy's wisdom into their school community in the form of "free-range projects."

When the projects were over, I spoke on the phone with Jenny, and Oak Knoll's coprincipals, Kristen Gracia and David Ackerman.[10] "We hear all the buzzwords about grit and self-reliance," Ackerman told me. "We want kids to have all these attributes. But then we have no plan for developing them other than talking about it. How do you give kids actual practice you can look at, monitor, and coach? We said, 'Okay, we're going to have a "free range" project.'"

These school leaders got parents on board by inviting them to think of tasks they'd done as a kid or freedoms they'd had that they wouldn't let their own kid experience today, and why. They then launched it to the kids, telling them to pick something they wanted to do on their own (with their parents' approval). Though the project was optional, close to 150 kids participated. Projects ranged from biking or walking alone, going into stores and buying things while parents waited in the parking lot, and making a meal at home for themselves or the family. The kids were picking things they'd already done *with* their parents, or with their parents *watching*, so this was their chance to implement bullet point four.

Five students were chosen to be on a panel to share the details of their project and field questions from an audience filled with kids, teachers, and parents. A fifth-grade boy reported enjoying walking alone to the library in his neighborhood. He said, "It gave me a little *me* time." One audience member asked, "Were you guys nervous?" The response was both adamant and enthusiastic. "No! I wasn't nervous, *I picked this!*" replied a second-grade girl.

"As parents, we tend to be the worriers," Principal Gracia told me. "When the kids are given the chance to pick something, they stretch a little and feel way more confident after, that's for sure." School psychologist Ryan added, "The kids really did seem to beam afterward. Like maybe they'd grown a couple of inches!"

Parents and students raved about the free-range projects. Gracia felt the best part was giving students and parents a new lens to look through. "Now the parent is better equipped to think through 'why am I fearful?' as opposed to giving a quick response of 'no, you're not doing that; you're too young.' We've given them tools to think about whether doing that thing on their own can be an avenue for a child to build confidence."

LETTING GO OF PERFECT

In addition to lingering concerns about safety, one of the hardest aspects of letting our kids do the stuff of life for themselves is giving up on an ideal of perfection that *we* can most likely achieve but our kids most likely can't. For example, sometimes I cringe at how my kids have loaded the dishwasher. But I know that if they open it the next day when it's clean and see that I secretly realigned everything, they'll be crestfallen; the better approach is to wait until the next time we're at the dishwasher together, tell them that lining the dishes up neatly leads to cleaner dishes, and demonstrate how. Allowing freedom within limits to try and fail and get better is the only way children (or anyone) will ever learn how to do things for themselves. Perfectionism is not only the enemy of the good; it is the enemy of adulthood.

With the support of the Beit T'Shuvah community, Rachel began to construct a new life. After being sober for one year, she went back to school and completed her undergraduate degree in psychology and neuroscience at a Los Angeles university, for a total of only three years in college. But she no longer got straight As.[11]

"As a daily drug user, I'd still always managed to get straight As—that was very important to me and my ego. When I went back to school, I got my first B, in ethics, of all things. I had this moment: Wait, I'm sober and I'm getting a B, which I'd always thought of as failing? Then it hit me that I'm okay and can live with this. I don't have to be perfect. Perfectionism is so wrapped up in self-loathing."

Rachel is now getting her master's in nursing at UCLA, and she may go on for the PhD. She's also fascinated with what she's learned about evolutionary psychology. "Tens of thousands of years ago young kids were learning to fend for themselves and provide for their families. Today everything is done for children. We're biologically programmed to want to fend for ourselves, to operate out of this survival mode, but the way we live now completely contradicts everything our genes have programmed for us. I'm a big advocate for the idea that a lot of the unhappiness we experience comes from us not following our evolutionary path. When you start to learn how to do things at a young age, it gives you purpose—this idea that I can fend for myself."

15

TEACH THEM HOW TO THINK

[A student] told me she'd love to have a chance to think about the things she's studying, only she doesn't have the time. I asked her if she had ever considered not trying to get an A in every class. She looked at me as if I had made an indecent suggestion.[1]

—William Deresiewicz, social critic and author of *Excellent Sheep: The Miseducation of the American Elite and the Way to a Meaningful Life*

Often we catch ourselves daydreaming about what our kids will be like when they grow up, what they'll do to earn a living, and how they'll construct a meaningful life. Our hearts swell in anticipated pride when we imagine them competent and successful at work, productive and engaged as citizens, valued in their community, and perhaps playing the roles of partners and spouses and fathers and mothers themselves one day.

In that dreamed-of future state, our kids will need to know how to think—that is, to be able to really think things through and figure things out for themselves. They'll need to be able to hold a thing in their hands and examine it, or to hold a concept in their brains and reason with it and, after examining or reasoning with it, to decide how to approach solving it if it's a problem, or if it's a concept, whether and to what extent and why they agree or disagree. We don't want our kids to be robots—mechanistically giving answers or going through motions dictated by someone else. We want them to be thinkers. But too many schools today promote rote memorization and regurgitation, and in our homes we're doing too much over-directing, overprotecting, and hand-holding. We end up doing way too much of our kids' thinking for them. They need to think for themselves. René Descartes said, *I think, therefore I am.* If we're not letting our kids think for themselves, are we not letting them *be*?

And, it turns out, thinking is not only an existential necessity (as if that weren't enough!) but, increasingly, an economic one.

THINKING MATTERS

In his 2009 best-selling book *Drive: The Surprising Truth About What Motivates Us,* Daniel Pink describes how being able to figure things out is especially essential for an employee in the twenty-first-century workplace. He shows that jobs requiring "algorithmic" tasks (ones in which you're given a set of instructions that you follow down a single pathway to one conclusion) have been outsourced or given over to computers, whereas 70 percent of job growth in the United States today is for jobs entailing "heuristic" tasks—where you must think through the task, experiment with possibilities, and come up with a novel solution precisely *because* no algorithm exists.[2] Workers in the twenty-first century will need to be able to think for themselves.

The Foundation for Critical Thinking, an educational nonprofit focused for over thirty years on inculcating critical thinking in students, agrees, warning, "In a world of accelerating change, intensifying complexity, and increasing interdependence, critical thinking is now a requirement for economic and social survival."[3]

In 2000, a German researcher named Andreas Schleicher developed the Program for International Student Assessment test (PISA) to help nations determine whether their teenagers had the thinking skills necessary to succeed in the twenty-first century at college, in the workplace, and in life.[4] PISA didn't ask kids to answer equations or give definitions (things kids can memorize and cram into short-term memory) and didn't use a multiple-choice format (which narrows an infinite set of possibilities down to four or five choices from which the correct answer can often be deduced or "figured out"). Instead, it asked them to take whatever knowledge they had in their brains and apply it to real-world situations and scenarios that require critical thinking and effective communication (such as whether a graph explains what it purports to explain, or whether a public health poster is effective at convincing the reader to get a flu shot). Put simply, PISA's purpose is to reveal which countries teach kids to think for themselves, says investigative journalist Amanda Ripley in her best-selling 2013 book *The Smartest Kids in the World: And How They Got That Way.*

The first PISA test was given in 2000 to teenagers in dozens of countries, including the United States. It has been given every three years since. As Ripley shows, high scores on the PISA had nothing to do with school funding, race, or class. High scores came in countries where educators and parents promote rigor in learning (having very high standards, and engaging in the effort toward learning those standards) and mastery (a deep level of understanding demonstrated by being able to apply concepts learned).

In the United States, year after year, teenagers' results on the PISA test were only average, which stings for a nation that prides itself as the world leader across many realms including education, economic productivity, leadership, and innovation. PISA scores for the United States reveal that American kids aren't being exposed to rigor and aren't being held accountable for mastery, and therefore they are not learning to think for themselves. These results predict that U.S. kids will not possess the skills of complex decision making or effective communication they'll need in order to thrive and lead in the real world.

In 2006 the American Institutes for Research, a behavioral and social science research organization, reported outcomes supporting those dire predictions. "More than 50 percent of students at four-year schools and more than 75 percent at two-year colleges lacked the skills to perform complex literacy tasks" such as "analyzing news stories and other prose, understanding documents, and having math skills needed for checkbooks or restaurant tips."[5]

Critical thinking isn't just about being able to understand the news and balance your checkbook (which is itself an outmoded concept). It's much broader and richer than that. In *Excellent Sheep*, Bill Deresiewicz describes the "sheep-like" state of many young people who, in his view, jump through the various hoops parents, educators, and society place ever higher in front of them, and end up with high grades and scores and accolades for things they've done. While the doors to elite colleges, and to a narrow set of elite professions, are open to these kids, Deresiewicz argues that their minds are closed. They haven't been taught to wrestle in the intellectual gray areas, to contend with the right and wrong of the matters they've memorized. They're doing what they think they're supposed to, without pausing to ask if it's what they actually want for themselves, and why. Both the "teach to the test" schooling and a home life with authoritarian or indulgent/permissive parents, situated in a larger societal and cultural milieu that values achievement and accomplishment over thinking and learning, are to blame.

UNDERMINING THINKING AT SCHOOL

In her 2001 book *"Doing School": How We Are Creating a Generation of Stressed Out, Materialistic, and Miseducated Students,*[6] Denise Pope—Stanford educator and cofounder of the nonprofit organization Challenge Success—wrote about the so-called teach-to-the-test mentality endemic in U.S. K–12 schools, and how kids educated this way behave like robots: info comes into their brains in the form of instruction, and they spit the info right back out onto homework, school exams, or standardized tests. The federal policy No Child Left Behind, promulgated in 2002, has only furthered the "teach to the test" mentality of which Pope initially wrote in 2001, instead of promoting the rigor and mastery necessary to develop thinkers. In her nationally acclaimed 2010 film *Race to Nowhere,* filmmaker Vicki Abeles put a human face on the kids Pope studied.

Pope's research shows that kids "do school" but don't end up *learning,* that they experience tremendous stress (not good stress, but psychologically damaging stress) from this approach, and that they adopt a "whatever it takes" mind-set in order to get the right score or grade or to simply get all of the homework done, which, Pope found, includes cheating at epidemic rates. Homework is valuable if it engages students more deeply with the material, but not when it's just busywork.[7] But "there is a lot of confusion between rigor and load on the part of teachers, administrators and parents,"[8] Pope has said more recently. Author and social critic Alfie Kohn took a critical look at a wide swath of research on homework and concluded there was no proven benefit to it at all.[9] Yet, as we all know, the homework just keeps coming.

The Foundation for Critical Thinking refers to the "teach to the test" type of teaching as the "mother robin" approach, because it's akin to mentally chewing up everything for kids and putting it into their intellectual beaks to swallow. The foundation reports that kids taught this way can repeat things back but they don't actually learn, and they will lack the ability to apply that information in different scenarios, and in that sense will not really *know* it. According to the foundation, kids then adopt a mind-set that they can't understand anything unless told exactly how and what to say, think, or do. They need things figured out *for* them. They don't want to be challenged to do anything more than repeat back from the parent, teacher, or textbook.[10]

UNDERMINING THINKING AT HOME

In our homes, many of us are caught up in the "mother robin" approach to homework, testing, activities, choices, and tasks—instead of letting our kids figure things out for themselves. Recapping Part 1 of the book, here's how we do this:

1. **We overprotect:** We are their bumpers and guardrails. We assess risk for them, tell them when it's safe to cross the street, whether Halloween candy can be eaten, and not to climb trees or use tools. We are risk averse, prefer for them to be within our sight at all times—at stores, outdoors, going to and from school—and tell them never to talk to strangers. We praise them at every turn—taking their side over the judge or teacher who found them subpar, and calling every effort "perfect."

2. **We overdirect:** We tell them what to play, what to study, what activities to pursue and at what level, which colleges are worth looking at, what to major in, which career/profession to pursue. We solve problems for them and shape the way they dream.

3. **We hand-hold:** We go to bat for them with teachers and coaches. We act as concierge for the logistics of their life. We second-guess the decisions of authority figures. We correct their math homework, fix their essays, and overly edit or outright write their applications.

Essentially, when we overparent, it's as if we get inside our kid's head and live there—like our personal rendition of *Being John Malkovich*. We supplant our thinking for theirs with our constant, vigilant, determined presence in their lives, and via cell phone. We do all of this because we think this is what love looks like, and to ensure they "make it," that is, succeed professionally, grasp the brass ring of life. But when we parent this way, childhood hasn't been a training ground for our kids to *learn to think for themselves*; they merely "do" the various things on the checklisted child-hood. We haven't prepared our kids for success in college, work, or life if we haven't taught them—*made* them, *allowed* them—to think.

WHAT WE CAN DO ABOUT IT

At the school level, when it comes to teaching kids to figure things out for themselves, things seem to be in a bit of a mess, to put it mildly. The Common Core State Standards Initiative arose in 2009 partly in response to PISA's warning that in the main, U.S. kids lack critical thinking skills, and thus are unprepared to succeed in college, work, and life. Yet the Foundation for Critical Thinking, based at Sonoma State University in California, has for over three decades worked at teaching educators to teach critical thinking to kids, and their research reveals that even most *educators* don't know what critical thinking is, let alone how to teach it. Improving how critical thinking is taught in schools is a complex problem—and is not the focus of this book.

But in our own homes we parents can and should take up the task of teaching our kids to think—to figure things out for themselves—instead of having them go through the motions of processing information and life experiences mechanistically, by improving our conversations with our kids about what they're learning, experiencing, and deciding.

Here's how. At its most basic, the term "critical thinking" means "thinking" itself, and can be understood simply as "figuring things out" and "applying knowledge to new situations." The concept of critical thinking dates back to Socrates, who developed a back-and-forth style of questioning with his students—most notably Plato—which opened students to the rationale for their ideas and led to deeper understanding of the soundness or fallacy of their reasoning, which then allowed them to apply their understanding in different circumstances.

As a law student at Harvard in the 1990s I was treated to "the Socratic method" style of teaching and learning. The vast majority of law professors use this approach, as do professors in many other disciplines. It's a tried-and-true method for bringing a person to a real level of understanding of a matter and stands in contrast to rote memorization, or being told how to solve something, what the "right" answer is, or what to believe.

Children who have figured out a problem, concept, or idea for themselves can talk about the why and how of the matter rather than the mere fact of its existence, and can apply what they've learned to new situations. Some contend that the Socratic method is inappropriate for children, because it teaches them to question authority. To others, such as the Foundation for Critical Thinking, the Waldorf Schools, and some Montessori educators, a simplified version of the Socratic method—helping someone understand information or make a decision by continuing to ask them questions about it—is a trusted method for helping children figure something out for themselves instead of the teacher (or parent) supplying the information or the answer. Educator Jennifer Fox, author of *Your Child's Strengths: A Guide for Parents and Teachers*, would agree. In her book she explains that you can help kids get to the heart of understanding a matter by asking them the question "Why?" five times.[11] I call it the continual questioning approach.

TIPS FOR TEACHING YOUR KIDS TO THINK FOR THEMSELVES

If we want our kids to be able to think for themselves, we have to be willing to open up a dialogue with them and resist the natural temptation to give the answer, say what we know about a situation, solve the problem, and in other ways shut the dialogue—and their thinking—down. When our kids are infants and toddlers it's highly appropriate for us to engage in a running monologue about their environment—that's how they learn the language—but once they are toddlers and can carry on a bit of conversation, we want them to be doing their share of the talking in response to our good, open-ended questions.

Since conversation is the best mechanism for practicing and seeing the results of critical thinking, below are sample dialogues between parent and child that demonstrate ways you can teach your kids to think for themselves. These dialogues employ the continual questioning approach, which boils down to you, the parent, being always interested in the "what," "how," or "why" underneath whatever your kid has just said. This method will work regardless of your kid's age, though the subject matter will change and grow more complex as the child matures and becomes more intellectually sophisticated. Note that when a child is very young, your questions might be more "leading" (in that you know the answers to the questions you're posing and are guiding them in that direction), but as a child ages, you may know less about the subject at hand; nevertheless a good set of continual questions on your part will bring them (and you) to a deeper understanding of the situation. Following are variants of how this continual questioning approach can teach kids of all ages to think for themselves. (Don't stress out about this—we're all busy and don't necessarily have the time or mental space to sit around philosophizing like Socrates—you don't have to have these kinds of dialogues all the time; just try to incorporate some continual questioning whenever you see the opportunity and are able to make the time.)

1. TALKING WITH PRESCHOOLERS

First is an example of a conversation that applauds a child for what he knows but doesn't teach him to think.

> CHILD: A butterfly!
> PARENT: Yes, that's a butterfly. Good job! What color is it?
> CHILD: Orange and black.
> PARENT: That's right! You're so smart.

Using the same scenario, here's how you might open up the conversation using the continual questioning approach:

> CHILD: A butterfly!
> PARENT: Ooh, what's the butterfly doing?
> CHILD: It's on that flower. And now it's on another flower!
> PARENT: Why do you suppose it likes the flowers?
> CHILD: Because they're pretty?
> PARENT: Maybe. Can you think of another reason?
> . . . etc.

A conversation with a little kid can go on for a surprisingly long period of time. Continual questioning helps the child unpack what they already know and helps them figure out the next set of concepts related to what they already know. They're learning. And your attention itself is an even greater prize.

2. TALKING WITH ELEMENTARY SCHOOLERS

In elementary school, conversations between parents and kids often surround a logistical problem—my bike tire is flat; I left my homework at school—that our kid might expect us to handle for them. Here are sample dialogues about a situation to be managed and how we can help our kids come to their own solution. First, a poor dialogue:

> PARENT: How was school?
> CHILD: Fine. But I forgot my backpack.
> PARENT: Oh no! I'll drive you back to school so you can get it.

This parent hasn't taught the kid how to think about the problem and instead zoomed ahead to solving the problem for the kid. Not only does the kid not know how to pick apart the situation and devise a solution, the kid is more likely to forget the backpack again in the future because she hasn't suffered the consequences of having forgotten it. (A similar scenario would be a kid who can't wake up on time and whose parent continues to wake him up and/or makes alternate arrangements to get him to school if he's missed his usual mode of transport.) The better dialogue:

> PARENT: How was school?
> CHILD: Fine. But I forgot my backpack!
> PARENT: Oh no.
> CHILD: What am I going to do?
> PARENT: I'm not sure. What do you think you can do about it?
> CHILD: I don't know! Will you drive me back to school to get it?
> PARENT: I'm sorry, but I can't—I've got other things to do this afternoon. What do you think you can do about it?
> CHILD: I could call my friend and ask what the homework is.
> PARENT: Okay.
> CHILD: But I might not have what I need if it's in the backpack.
> PARENT: Hmm. Yeah.
> CHILD: Or I could e-mail my teacher and tell her I forgot it and see what she says.
> PARENT: Those both sound like good ideas.
>   . . . etc. Let the child go through the work of trying out the solutions.

The kid learned that the parent doesn't feel responsible for the problem and that he is going to have to figure it out for himself. This "tough love" approach may be particularly hard for permissive/indulgent parents, but keep in mind that the most loving thing to do here is not to do it for them but to teach them how to do for themselves. Elementary school homework is rarely of consequence in contrast to middle or high school (the same goes for being on time for school). It's better for her to learn the lesson of how to remember that backpack (or to wake herself up) *now*, than for her to still be facing those issues when she's in a higher-stakes school environment and where you'll feel tempted to help her avoid those harsher consequences.

3. TALKING WITH MIDDLE SCHOOLERS

Middle schoolers are still our little kids, but they're rapidly changing into teenagers. We call them "tweens" in recognition of this in-between phase. They want us to be involved and interested in their lives but can be quick to close down if we seem overly focused on what to them feels like the wrong thing. First, a poor dialogue:

PARENT: How was school today?
CHILD: Fine.
PARENT: How'd you do on the Spanish test?
CHILD: I got an A!
PARENT: Great!

The parent focused on grades, not on what the child was learning or found interesting in the class. A better dialogue might go something like this:

PARENT: How was school today?
CHILD: Fine.
PARENT: What did you enjoy most?
CHILD: Spanish.
PARENT: Great! How come?
CHILD: It's my favorite class!
PARENT: How come?
CHILD: I always get a really good score on tests and homework is never hard and I'm never lost. I raise my hand all the time and when she does call on me, especially when other people aren't getting it, I feel "Yay! I've got this, let's go!"
PARENT: How can you tell you're good at it?

CHILD: Well, when my teacher is explaining something, I can guess what she's about to say because I already know exactly how it works. I know what's coming next. I can explain it to my friend.

. . . etc. Keep asking why and how.

It's one thing for a child to know she likes a subject, but as this dialogue demonstrates, what we really want is for a child to be able to home in on *how she knows what she knows*.

4. TALKING WITH HIGH SCHOOLERS

A high schooler's interior world is full of feelings and fueled by hormones; they can be a mystery to themselves, and also to us. Typically when we ask high schoolers about their day, we get a short answer like "fine." As their parents we are craving more information, and we also want to help them get to the why and how of what they learn and experience so they can develop a deeper understanding of themselves, other people, and the world, and can make better choices and decisions. We can get past a teen's typical one-word response by repeatedly (but thoughtfully and creatively) asking "why" or "how" in response to their statements—just as with the preschooler and the butterfly—until they reveal the nugget of their experience or learning. When we engage in these critical thinking dialogues, we behave as active listeners, an added benefit of which is that we demonstrate to them that we're actually interested in them beyond the transactional issues of life such as whether they got their homework done, what grade they got, or whether their team won or lost. These conversations become *quality time*. First, a poor dialogue:

PARENT: How was school today?

CHILD: Fine.

PARENT: What kind of homework do you have?

CHILD: I have a ton of math, some chemistry, and an English essay draft due (heavy sigh).

PARENT: But I thought you were enjoying reading *Cyrano de Bergerac*.

CHILD: Yeah. I like *reading* it, but that doesn't mean I want to write an essay about it.

PARENT: Come on, you can do it. Just think of what you like about Cyrano and . . .

CHILD: Mom. It's not that simple.

PARENT: I know. But you're so smart. I just want you to have confidence that you can do it.

CHILD: I just want to get it done.

The parent supplanted his thoughts (you like *Cyrano*) for the child's own (I'm dreading this essay). The parent then tried to build the child's confidence with his own words rather than have the child come to feel that his own effort could make a difference. Here's a better dialogue:

PARENT: How was school today?

CHILD: Fine.

PARENT: What did you enjoy most?

CHILD: Well, we're reading *Cyrano de Bergerac* in English.

PARENT: Mmm. And why was that fun?

CHILD: Well, we were reading out loud and I got to be Cyrano.

PARENT: How'd it go?

CHILD: It was really cool.

PARENT: Why?

CHILD: Because I like Cyrano.

PARENT: Why do you think you like Cyrano?

CHILD: I don't know. Maybe because all of the things Cyrano does to aid Christian and Roxanne's romance. Even though maybe he shouldn't.

PARENT: What do you mean? Why does he do that?

. . . etc.

The child moved from a cursory sense *that* he likes Cyrano to a more nuanced understanding of *why*, which will aid him in classroom discussion and in writing that essay he has to write.

DON'T LET THEM JUST "DO SCHOOL"

As Denise Pope outlined in *"Doing School,"* kids today have tremendous pressure to simply get the work done—to "do school"—rather than to learn. They learn to do tasks, to produce every element the teacher wants to see in a five-paragraph essay, or to memorize every term in bio and every formula in math. They think their next task is to get into certain schools in order to be a success in life, and this mind-set often then extends to career and professional pursuits.

I called up Jeff Brenzel, dean of admission at Yale, to ask him what he was seeing by way of "doing school" versus freethinking in his undergraduates.[12] "I see a continuing tendency in some to play it safe, to view what they're doing here as a kind of career-building step. It leads them to a perfectionism and a reluctance to experiment, fail, or rebel, and actually serves them poorly in the long haul. I suspect that twenty years down the road they'll be having midlife crises, feeling they were in a straitjacket. Failure to recognize that an education has to be seized rather than delivered to you is the harm that's really done."

I saw and heard about this mentality at Stanford, too, where students had difficulty contending with the open-ended and the uncertain and just wanted to continue in the manner to which they had grown accustomed, which was to be very good at delivering on what they were told to do. A faculty member in Stanford's equivalent of freshman English told me of what is now a common scenario in her field—handing a paper back to student scrawled with feedback—*say more; how do you know?; what's the motivation here?; and then what*—to which undergraduates plaintively plead, "I don't know what you want. Just tell me what you want me to SAY."

On the other side of campus—engineering—John Barton, director of the architectural design program within the Department of Civil and Environmental Engineering at Stanford, sees a similar dynamic playing out.[13] Barton teaches an introductory drawing course (an architect needs engineering skills but also needs to know how to draw) and many students approach him wide-eyed, worried that they don't have the skills even to begin. "They say they had never had a drawing course in their life. I see this regularly now."

Students tell Barton things like, "Well, I knew that I wanted to get into a really good university and I took as many AP courses as I could. And yes, my school had an art requirement, but not at an AP level and I fulfilled it by being in the jazz band, a student play, or some such approach that shows better on college application. Further, my mom and dad did not want me wasting my time in soft subjects. They took away from one more AP course."

Barton paints a scene for his students of what learning looks like in high school. He says, "When you took AP chemistry, I would guess the teacher told you that you needed 95 points for an A and valued every assignment and test. Further, he/she gave a possible 120 points if you came in early and helped set up the lab or stayed late to wash beakers. Thus you could do C work and still get an A in the class. Further, all tests were scantron forms with no essays or explanatory elements and your lab reports were on a form outlined by the instructor." His students look at him like he had been in their class alongside them, and they all nod their heads yes.

Then Barton tells his students how his class will be different: "I tell them accuracy and exactness are not important but process and reflection are. That I expect them to break the rules and to climb up to the highest branch and saw it off behind them. I tell them that risk and open-ended problems are what we do in design. Design is a problem-solving methodology not a 'task' and this will be hard because they have only had tasks so far in their education. Because they are Stanford students they do not freak out, but the stress level rises. But this is what they thirst for and they then embrace it. It takes a little time for them to stop asking if they *can* do X. My response is either 'ask for forgiveness not permission' or 'can you?' By week five some group of students will answer for me with one of those responses. That is when I know I have brought them to the human side of education."

Barton isn't letting his students "do school." He's teaching them to think. But with some he has quite an uphill battle.

TEACH THEM TO PERSIST AT THINKING

Of all the things that comprise our kids' lives, their academic pursuits and progress seem to be the most intense crucible, and the present methods and approaches to teaching children emphasize memorizing and regurgitating information and getting good grades on homework, exams, and standardized tests. Often we meet their positive results with comments like "You're so smart!" But research shows that such feedback from parents actually undermines academic success rather than enhances it.

Stanford psychology professor Dr. Carol Dweck is the internationally recognized pioneer of the concept of "growth mindset" as a way to continually grow, learn, and persevere in our efforts.[14] Dweck found that kids who are told they're "smart" actually underperform in subsequent tasks, by choosing easier tasks to avoid evidence that they are not smart, which Dweck calls having a "fixed mindset." In contrast, Dweck found, kids who are praised not for their smarts but for their effort—with praise specific to the effort made, and not overblown—develop what Dweck calls a "growth mindset." They learn that their effort is what led to their success, and if they continue to try, over time they'll improve and achieve more things. These kids end up taking on tougher things, and feel better about themselves. "Emphasizing effort gives a child a variable that they can control," Dweck has explained.[15] "They come to see themselves as in control of their success. Emphasizing natural intelligence takes it out of the child's control, and it provides no good recipe for responding to a failure."[16]

Dweck's website, mindsetonline.com, teaches a step-by-step approach to developing "growth mindset."[15] She says, "How you interpret challenges, setbacks, and criticism is your choice. You can interpret them in a fixed mindset as signs that your fixed talents or abilities are lacking. Or you can interpret them in a growth mindset as signs that you need to ramp up your strategies and effort, stretch yourself, and expand your abilities. It's up to you." A growth mindset is all about being motivated to persist at figuring things out and it leads to better critical thinking.

TEACH THEM TO THINK ABOUT MORE THAN THEMSELVES

A kid's academic and extracurricular lives and personal matters seem to be all there's time to think about these days. But you can also develop critical thinking in kids by talking about what's going on in the world around them and encouraging them to form an opinion about things.

Educators and psychologists have a mantra these days: No matter how hectic the schedules of your family members may be, make time to have dinner together. Research shows that family dinners help kids feel they matter to the parent, and as a result they have a positive impact on kids' mental health and lead to greater self-esteem and greater academic achievement. In addition to talking to our kids about their day or their lives, talking to them about current events scales the level of critical thinking up a level— to a level of theoretical challenge, to a degree of interest in the world around them, and to a degree of humility about what they don't yet know. It makes them hungry to know more.

Once your kid is in elementary school, they can express opinions and be challenged as to what they believe. *You* get to decide which issues are appropriate topics for your family, given your interests, beliefs, values, and the ages of your children. Here is how you can engage in a conversation about current events so as to develop stronger thinking skills in your kid.

1. **Come up with a topic about which there are different perspectives.** It could be from a book you've read, a movie you've seen, a television show you watch as a family, a school policy, an issue in your local newspaper, or a topic with which the local PTA or school board is concerned. As long as there are at least a few differing, reasonable perspectives, the conversation will work. Present the issue at an age-appropriate level, erring on the side of what your elementary schooler can stretch to understand.

2. **Ask your kid what they think.** Ask what they think about the topic, and *why* they think what they think. On what values or prior assumptions do they base their opinions? What do they think would happen if their perspective did not win out? What would be the consequences? Why would things be better if their perspective did win out?

3. **Play devil's advocate.** Whichever "side" your kid took, now it's your turn to play devil's advocate. This means you express the counter opinion, in about the same amount of words your kid used to express their opinion. Tell why this is the better point of view, on what values or assumptions you base this opinion, and the consequences of your view being adhered to or not. Be encouraging and playful, not demanding or overly critical.

4. **Encourage your kid to respond to your point of view.** Encourage them to come up with a reason they didn't state when they presented the issue first time around. Gauge your kid's readiness and willingness to engage in this intellectual banter and don't push it beyond their comfort zone. (I know some grown women whose father—a lawyer—pushed them to the point of tears in dinner table conversations where they had to defend their point of view. Don't go that far!)

5. **FOR THE ADVANCED: Switch sides.** Now start over, reversing roles, and see if your kid can articulate the argument and values underlying the perspective that is *against* their original point of view. Or start with a new topic and when your kid says what they initially think, stop them and challenge them to start arguing from the other point of view.

Having family dinner conversation about events in the world isn't just a great way to achieve stimulating dinner conversations in your house each night. In *The Smartest Kids in the World: And How They Got That Way,*

Amanda Ripley explains that around the world the kids whose parents engaged them in conversation about books, movies, and current events scored better on the reading portion of the international PISA test.

LET THEM SPEAK UP FOR THEMSELVES

In an earlier chapter (Chapter 3, "Being There for Them"), I included a vignette about a Stanford freshman who came with his parents to talk to me about doing research while at Stanford. In our meeting, the parents did all of the talking, even though I posed questions directly to the kid and redirected my eye contact to him as often as possible. At the end of our twenty-minute conversation, I couldn't tell what, if anything, the kid was thinking about the matter, or whether he was interested in doing research at all. It was just clear that his parents were *very* interested in the topic.

My daughter, Avery, told me a story from the sixth grade, when she'd been selected to be in the group of students who would show visiting fifth graders around the middle school. Instead of letting the sixth graders speak to the fifth graders, however, the teacher involved in the effort ended up doing all of the talking. Then he turned to the sixth graders standing beside him to see if they had anything to add. They didn't—except that he'd gotten the location of the library wrong, as it would be moved before the fifth graders arrived and they'd been instructed to discuss its new location. Avery and her friends just stood there, smiling, trying to look responsible and important, but feeling instead like idiots. What was the teacher so afraid would happen if he'd let the sixth graders actually speak for themselves?

We have to get out of our kid's way and let them speak up for themselves in the world. Here are my thoughts as to how.

1. **Value it.** Your child needs to be able to think for themselves and to be able to initiate and respond to conversation with the people they'll meet. Whether it's exciting news to share, an explanation of their interests or desires, or a problem that needs to be raised, your kids will need to be able to handle these things completely by themselves one day, and childhood is meant to offer practice.

2. **Make a goal for yourself.** Decide that you will let your child speak for him- or herself whenever possible, and increasingly so as they—and you—

gain confidence in their abilities. Every time you succeed, you're telling your child you believe in their capacity to think for themselves.

3. **Practice it.** When you know your kid is going to be talking to an adult about something—say, the coach of their team, or the leader of a camp at which they'd like to work—let them know in advance that you want them to do the talking, that you know they can handle it, and that you'll be there to fill in any information they don't have. Teachers, store clerks, dance teachers, and coaches alike love when a child can come to them with a question, idea, or concern. Let your child see the joy on the face of the adult with whom they're talking. Caveat: You know your kid best—if your kid is introverted or shy, they may welcome your doing the heavy lifting for them, and if they have special needs, they may need you to do so. But even if you're speaking for your kid, be mindful that you are not them and are not literally able to speak for them. You can say, "Jasmine told me she's feeling . . ." or "Jordan told me he's interested in . . ."

4. **Resist, resist, resist!** Instead of nudging them to speak or whispering in their ear, resist the urge to step in. Give them the chance to do it for themselves. At a store, or with an instructor or coach, you might even physically hang back and avoid eye contact so that it's clear to the adult that your child will be doing the talking.

5. **Add your thoughts when necessary.** Until they are grown, chances are you will always know more than they do about a subject, and you will always have your own opinion and thoughts on the matter. Your thoughts matter, but as additions to whatever your child wants to say, not instead of. Like a good manager in the workplace, let the junior person in the room (your kid) speak first, then support what they've said, adding only what you feel is essential. This empowers them.

THEIR THINKING, THEIR LIFE

Every Friday afternoon at Stanford I held office hours where, in thirty-minute increments over the course of three hours, I'd hear from students who wanted advice about academic and personal matters, such as the choice of major or grad school, a set of competing summer opportunities, or which classes or activities to drop in order to have a bit more breathing room or to pursue other things. Whatever their question, I'd respond with questions of my own, such as, "Why do you think you want this versus that?" "How will your long-term plans be impacted, and why?" "What would you lose if you didn't do that, and why?" "What would you do if you could do whatever you wanted, and why?" By inquiring further in various ways, multiple times, I peeled back the layers surrounding my students' question. I was conducting the kind of continual questioning critical dialogue we discussed earlier in this chapter.

Sure, I had my opinions on the various matters my students presented to me, but it wasn't my job to come up with answers. My job was to ask a student good questions that opened her further to her self. I'd try to tease out the values underlying her ideas, her sense of her own strengths and areas for development, and her fears and her dreams. Then I'd help her interrogate the choices available in light of what she knew of her self. I was teaching her to develop a rationale for the choice she would ultimately make, rather than letting her fall back on the advice from an authority figure (me) or the rationale that she "should" do such and such because "everyone else is" or because "it's expected that I will," which often tumbles out of the mouths of young adults. It was both humbling and exciting to be in the presence of a human unfolding, thinking for herself, figuring things out.

In *The Smartest Kids in the World: And How They Got That Way*, Amanda Ripley writes about the dismal level of critical thinking ability in American teenagers, but she also reported on the various pockets around our country where better teaching and learning occurs, and students score extremely high on the PISA. Ripley concludes with optimism: "Without a doubt, American teenagers can perform at the top of the world on a sophisticated test of critical thinking."[17] Through better teaching *and* better parenting, we can give them the chance.

16

PREPARE THEM FOR HARD WORK

I realized I needed to have a plan bigger than waiting for someone to recognize my stunning brilliance.[1]

—Stephen Parkhurst, Millennial, filmmaker

They're so entitled. They think they're amazing and just want to be given a pat on the back for showing up. They want to be told what to do all the time. They have no work ethic.

So goes the conventional wisdom on Millennials in the workplace.

In 2013, a twenty-nine-year-old aspiring film director named Stephen Parkhurst parodied the older generation's take on Millennials in a video—*Millennials: We Suck and We're Sorry*—that went viral, with over 3 million views and counting.[2] In his script, Parkhurst cleverly combined an acknowledgment of Millennial behavior with a critique of the parents who raised them, so I called him in February 2014 to ask about his motivations for creating the video.

Parkhurst lives in New York City and works as a digital tech/projectionist at Deluxe, a company with offices worldwide that provides a wide range of postproduction services to the film and television industries. He graduated from New Hampshire's Keene State College as a film production major in 2007, smack into the worst economy since the Great Depression. By 2014, he was working full-time at Deluxe while plugging away on his own films on the side. His video, narrated by four Millennials, begins: *"We suck and we know it. We're self-centered, we're entitled, we're narcissistic, lazy, and immature. And we're super sorry about that. We're the worst! If only we could be more like our parents."* The voices are male and female, white, urban, twentysomething, and hipster-looking, speaking from their sunny couches, their front steps, and the sidewalk outside their New York brownstone apartment, in faux-apology for the relative entitlement, failures, and apathy of their generation.

"We don't know what happened!" they go on. *"You raised us to believe we were special. So special we didn't have to do anything to earn it. I got this trophy for existing in soccer [shows trophy]. That's pretty special. No idea what went wrong. You tried your best."*

Quickly, the voices move from satire over at having been raised with too much praise to more macro issues, such as the economic and societal impact of baby boom policies and actions that led to: two wars, the housing bubble, the Great Recession, the dearth of full-time work, the destroyed manufacturing industry, gutted unions, the meteoric rise in college tuition prices, the student loan burden, and an environmentally devastated planet.

The crescendo of irony comes when one woman ponders, *"Man, it'd be crazy if there was a generation that recklessly awful, huh?"* And the video concludes, *"So on behalf of all the Millennials we'd like to apologize for being so terrible. From now on we're going to be just like the baby boomers. Cuz you guys? You NAILED it!"*

Parkhurst created his video in response to the spate of articles published in recent years about Millennials' lack of work ethic, such as Joel Stein's 2013 article in *Time* magazine called "Millennials: The Me Me Me Generation," and a 2013 piece in the *Boston Globe* by Jennifer Graham, "A Generation of Idle Trophy Kids." Criticism tends to be directed at the Millennials themselves, as if they caused their situation. But blaming them is patently unfair. Having known thousands of Millennials, and hundreds of them quite well, I know that they're full of hope and heart, and, like every generation before them, they want to be successful. The negative characterizations of their behavior in the workplace reflect not some flaw innate in their beings but in the way they've been raised. I was glad to see Stephen Parkhurst fighting back.

THE MISSING WORK ETHIC

But, blame aside, the claim that Millennials aren't showing up in the workplace with the kind of stick-to-itiveness and pitch in mind-set of their predecessors is more than just a sardonic sound bite. In 2013, Bentley University commissioned a study on workforce preparedness. Of the more than thirty-one hundred respondents, including leaders of higher education and business, corporate recruiters, high school and college students and their parents, and recent college graduates, 74 percent of non-Millennial respondents believed Millennials lacked the work ethic of older generations in the workforce and 70 percent believed that Millennials were not willing to "pay their dues." (In contrast, nearly nine in ten Millennial respondents [89 percent] stated that they did have a strong work ethic.[3] At the least, the mismatch in perceptions is striking and suggests a critical generational divide over the definition of work ethic.)

We parents can help turn around this work ethic/workplace mismatch. By following the strategies already discussed in Chapters 12 (the case for another way), 13 (give kids unstructured time), 14 (teach kids life skills), and 15 (teach them to think for themselves), you'll have gone a long way toward preparing your kid to be the kind of person who will be treasured in the workplace.

In this chapter we'll look at strategies that build on those prior chapters, and teach kids to work hard—to pitch in and see a job through to its completion—so they'll be prepared for active citizenry and the world of work. We want them to become—and they can become—people able to say, *I should do this*, and *I'm determined to do a good job.*

BUILDING A WORK ETHIC: THE ROLE OF CHORES

The life skills we discussed in Chapter 13—basic grooming, taking care of belongings, making meals, and keeping the home clean—are things each of us must do to look after the *self*, which is, for any of us, our first obligation. In this chapter we'll use that list as the baseline of a larger set of tasks we'll ask kids to do in order to teach them to pitch in, put some skin in the game, and see a job through to its completion for the betterment of the family, household, team, or other group. The authoritarian parents are already requiring these kinds of things of kids, but in a dogmatic way; the permissive/indulgent parents are not requiring it much at all. Taken together, teaching life skills plus a "stick-to-itiveness and pitch in" mindset builds a work ethic in kids and is evidence of great authoritative parenting.

A kid who does chores has a greater chance of success in life, according to Dr. Marilynn "Marty" Rossman, professor emeritus of family education at the University of Minnesota. Rossman defined "success" as not using drugs, having quality relationships, finishing education, and getting started in a career. She relied on data from a longitudinal study conducted by the definitive authority on parenting styles, Dr. Diana Baumrind (the parenting researcher discussed in Chapter 12), and concluded that those who were most "successful" began doing chores at three to four years of age, whereas those who waited until their teen years to start doing chores were comparatively less successful. Rossman never published this particular research in a formal study, but many scholars and authors have subsequently cited Rossman's conclusions on the value of starting chores early in life.[4]

George Vaillant's famous longitudinal study of Harvard students from their time as undergraduates through their entire adulthood also concluded that chores in childhood is an essential contributor to success in life. In an interview for a 1981 *New York Times* article, Vaillant explained that "work plays a central role in an individual's life"—so much that it trumped having a strong family background as a predictor of mental health in adulthood.[5] Edward Hallowell, a psychiatrist, author, and former faculty member at Harvard, says chores build the kind of "can-do, want-to-do feeling" that leads a person to feel industrious rather than incapable.[6]

So, chores matter a great deal. Yet children today spend significantly less time doing chores than did previous generations. A 2008 study from the University of Maryland found that children between the ages of six and twelve spend only twenty-four minutes a day doing housework, which is a 25 percent decline from 1981.[7] In reporting on this study the *Wall Street Journal* opined, "In the glacial realm of sociological change, that amounts to a free fall."[8]

Wellesley College sociology professor Markella Rutherford examined changing societal expectations about children and chores by reviewing articles in *Parents* magazine—the longest-running and currently most popular magazine about parenting—written between 1926 and 2006.[9] She found that through the 1930s, '40s, and '50s, chores were a common subject in articles written by experts and laypeople alike; children were doing much of the work to maintain a household, including fire-tending, meal preparation, carpentry, maintaining household accounts, and looking after sick family members. Chores all but dropped out of *Parents* magazine discourse in the 1960s, '70s, and '80s. When, in the 1990s, chores returned as a topic of expert and lay opinion, the chores referenced were "trivial tasks" compared to chores done by children in earlier decades, such as picking up after themselves, taking care of a pet, clearing the table after dinner, and sorting dirty laundry. Since the 1990s, articles in *Parents* about chores have tended to focus on how to motivate kids to do chores with external rewards such as "points" to be "cashed in" for spending on toys or other items a child might like, whereas in the past, the articles spoke of chores as ongoing work necessary to the functioning of family life and on children feeling "pride in a job well done."

If we're middle- or upper-middle-class, our daily lives are not taken up with the hard work that consumed our forebears. Much of the work of keeping a home has been outsourced to machines, technology, or to other humans we hire to assist us. Instead, our daily lives are taken up with our child's schoolwork and enrichment activities. University of Pennsylvania sociologist Annette Lareau terms these activities—sports, the arts, tutoring—and a parent's dedication to driving kids to and from them, "concerted cultivation."[10] And she notes how it exhausts us. With all that is on the typical family calendar, it's a wonder, really, that any work gets done around the house at all.

And then there's the pressure of homework—which often automatically excuses a kid from having to do any work around the home. In a talk given in September 2014 during the Challenge Success organization's annual conference for educators, parents, and kids, psychologist Wendy Mogel, bestselling author of *The Blessing of a Skinned Knee* and *The Blessing of a B Minus*, said all a kid has to do is say "I have a test" and we parents wait on them hand and foot as if they are "fascist dictators" or "handicapped royalty."[11] The old cliché "my dog ate my homework" has gone by the wayside; now kids do mountains of homework and don't have time to look after— or play with—the dog.

Extracurricular activities, tests, and homework are important, but equally important is that we teach our children the skills and values that come from doing chores. Through chores, they will learn:

- responsibility for contributing to the work of the household or the team;
- autonomy in handling tasks;
- accountability to meet a deadline and a particular level of quality;
- determination to get a job done well;

- perseverance when challenges are met; and
- the value of taking the initiative instead of waiting to be asked.

Even if our child's sweat equity is not *needed* to ensure the smooth running of our home, they must contribute, know how to contribute, and feel the rewards of contributing in order to have the right approach to hard work when they head out into the workplace and become citizens in the community. In short, chores build the kind of work ethic that is highly sought after in our communities and in the workplace.

BEYOND LIFE SKILLS: BUILDING A "PITCH IN" AND "JOB WELL DONE" MIND-SET

Chances are your kid can understand the importance of learning the life skills listed in Chapter 13. If they're young they'll enjoy doing for themselves and helping you out, and they'll want to be given more to do. If you're not getting started until they're tweens or teens you might face some resistance and resentment about the things you're *preventing* them from doing because you're *making* them do such and such. But the advantage you have with your tweens and teens is that they can see high school graduation looming; a simple reminder that they'll be out of the house before they know it and will need to be able to wake themselves up, deal with laundry, and feed themselves is probably enough of a rationale to get them to do the various life skills that are about looking after the *self*.

A work ethic, though, is about taking care of more than number one. It's about pitching in to help in a situation even if there's no direct benefit to you. It's about the old adage my mother always used to say: "If a job's worth doing, it's worth doing well." If building life skills means you know that your kid can pour himself some orange juice and clean it up if he spills, work ethic means knowing that your kid will pitch in and help when *someone else* spills something, instead of thinking "that doesn't concern me" and walking away.

But how do we get our kids to feel the impulse to help with things that aren't intrinsically about them? Unless they're that rare child born with a sense of empathy and obligation to help others, they need to be taught. For how to do this, Rossman's research is instructive, as is the work of parenting experts Jim Fay and Foster Cline, coiners of the term "helicopter parent" back in 1990 and founders of the company Love and Logic Institute,

Inc., as are the oodles of articles on the Web such as Patricia Smith's 2009 article in education.com, "Pitch In! Getting Your Kids to Help with Chores," Esther Davidowitz's 2012 article "Get Kids to Pitch In" in parenting.com, and freelance health writer Annie Stuart's piece "Divide and Conquer Household Chores" for WebMD.com. Based on my review of various sources and my own life experience, here are my tips for how to get kids to step outside of the comfort of doing as little as possible and into the zone of doing one's part.[12]

1. TODDLERS AND PRESCHOOLERS

The theme for your littlest ones is "cash in on their enthusiasm," says Esther Davidowitz, former editor in chief of *Westchester* magazine. Little ones love to feel like grown-ups so they'll delight when you ask them to stack a set of magazines, when you give them a cloth to dust with, or if you point to a pile of laundry and ask them to take it to the laundry room and sort it into whites and colors. Don't expect perfection. By having them participate and contribute, they develop a sense of competence about doing a task and confidence that they're following instructions and are valued for it.

2. ELEMENTARY SCHOOLERS

These guys can give you lots of help around the house. Take the kitchen, for example. They can bring groceries in from the car, unpack groceries and put them away, set and clear the table, and load and unload the dishwasher.

Break each task down into simple steps. When unpacking the groceries, for example, tell them to separate out the freezer, refrigerator, pantry, and other items. Then send them off to deliver some of the items to the proper places—veggies and fruits are usually stored lower down in a refrigerator, so have your little ones be responsible for putting the produce away. Have an older kid put away the things stored higher up, such as milk and juice. Have a younger one stuff your cloth grocery bags into one larger bag for easy retrieval next time. Again, don't expect perfection. It's no fun for them if you ask them to do something and then micromanage every step. They won't do it as well or as efficiently as you—accept that—but they'll get better and better over time.

Kitchen spills are a great opportunity to build that "pitch in" mind-set. When it happens, call out to whichever kid is in the vicinity, "I need your

help." They won't know how to be most helpful until they've had some practice cleaning spills, so tell them, specifically, how they can help—tell them
to wet the sponge and start mopping up the juice, or tell them to grab a
broom and dustpan from the hall closet and to sweep while you hold the
dustpan. Don't rest until the task is done completely. Then express satisfaction that it was a "job well done." Be sure to thank them, not with an
over-the-top amount of praise that treats them like they've climbed Mount
Everest, but with eye contact and a smile, perhaps a hand on the shoulder,
and a kind, simple "thank you." Giving that type of feedback to a kid will
make them want to experience that type of praise for effort again.

3. MIDDLE SCHOOLERS

These guys can venture out of doors to do tasks that won't lead a prying
neighbor to worry that your child has been "left alone." Have them wash
your car when the weather is right. Have them shovel the snow from the
front walk. Have them do yard work such as weeding, transporting a mound
of dirt from the driveway to the flower beds, raking leaves, tossing the post-
Halloween rotting pumpkins into the compost, or setting up holiday deco-
rations. Have them bike to your local convenience store to pick up an item
you need. If by this age they haven't been asked to do much by way of helping out, you're likely to get a raised eyebrow or an outright "what?" or "why?"
or an excuse as to why they can't. Unless the excuse is legitimate, press forward. Your rationale need be nothing more than "I need your help." Many
parents find that a cause-and-effect approach helps move kids along, such as
saying, "I need your help. Please rake those leaves. When you're done we'll
go to the store and get the materials you need for your school project."

Life is full of so-called grunt work, and doing the icky, yucky unglam-
orous tasks are a great way to build work ethic. Someone has to clean that
spill, wash out the trash or recycling bin, deal with the ant infestation, move
all the boxes that got mildew because of a roof leak, or shovel the dog
poop. Why not your middle schooler? Remember to show your gratitude,
again, not as over-the-top, jaw-dropping praise, but as a simple, sincere
"Thank you. I know that was gross. I appreciate it."

By this age you can develop your kid's work ethic further by asking them
to anticipate the next steps involved in a task, or the longer-term sequence
of related tasks, rather than waiting to be told what to do next. You can ask,
"I want to be sure that garbage doesn't overflow next time. What can we

do about that?" Or, "We keep running out of toilet paper in the bathroom. What can we do about that?" Being able to be proactive about next steps is critical for our kids' success as citizens and workers. If they don't seem to know what to do next, ask them what they think the next steps are. Resist the temptation to create that checklist for them.

4. HIGH SCHOOLERS

These guys are big enough to do most of the things *you're* doing, and can be responsible with machinery, heights, and other such risks. Inside the house they can clean out the refrigerator (chuck old stuff, wipe down the shelves and interior); wipe down the oven, microwave, and stove; and change the bag in the vacuum. Outside they can wash windows, mow the lawn, and go onto the roof with you to clean the gutters.

You want to see them sweat. Have them haul the Christmas tree to the curb. Have them work alongside you with hammer and nails to mend the fence. Have them help you organize the attic or garage. When they put in that kind of physical effort, it improves their concentration (as any parent of a kid with ADD/ADHD knows), builds their strength and stamina, and gives them that workman's pride in accomplishing a physically demanding task.

Work ethic is about rolling up your sleeves and doing what needs to be done, anticipating the steps involved, and being proactive about it instead of waiting to be asked. Is there an elderly neighbor who struggles to bring in her newspaper every morning or to bring her trash cans to the curb? Tell your teen a story about a time you helped a neighbor out. You just might find that your teen starts to anticipate ways to be helpful like that in your life or in the life of a neighbor.

THIS IS A PARENT'S RIGHT AND RESPONSIBILITY: DON'T SHRINK FROM IT

1. **Model it.** Don't tell your kid to go do work while you lounge on the couch. The best way to teach work ethic is by example. Pitching in is what every family member is expected to do, regardless of age, gender, or title. Let them see you working. Ask them to pitch in. When you're setting out to do something in the kitchen, yard, or garage, call to a kid, "I need your help with this."

2. **Expect their help.** You're not a concierge. You're their first teacher: their parent. The greatest impediment to instilling a work ethic in our children just might be ourselves, particularly if we've been on the permissive/indulgent side of the parenting spectrum and have tended to be very focused on our kids' happiness and enjoyment while being quite aware of how busy they are with homework and extracurriculars. But we're trying to grow our kids to adulthood, where they'll need the skills that come from chores. Chores at home become the "grunt work" of employment—the stuff they do to "pay their dues" and advance up the employment ladder. They may not like being asked or told to do things, and they'd certainly rather be on their phones or some other device, or with friends, or really doing almost anything else, but they will come to feel a sense of accomplishment for having done whatever you've asked.

3. **Don't apologize or overexplain.** A hallmark of parenting in middle- and upper-middle-class families today is that parents talk-talk-talk. Talking through a kid's day at school to unpack what they experienced and learned is a great way to build critical thinking skills, as we saw in the prior chapter. Talking a problem over with a child is a great way to help them come to a decision and to show you care, which is a hallmark of authoritative parenting. But chores are an arena where the authoritative parent articulates the rules and values of the household. Talking their ear off about the why and how behind your request that they do chores, or how you know they won't like it but they really need to, or how you feel badly asking them to do it, isn't useful. Overexplaining makes you look like you feel the need to justify your request. And if you apologize in the asking, along the way, or after the fact, you'll undercut your own authority as a parent who has the right and responsibility to ask your kid to help out. Your kid might grumble in the short term, but in the long term they'll thank you.

4. **Give clear, straightforward instructions.** Figure out what you want done and say so. When a task is new to a child, explain the steps. Then back off. Don't hover as they do it. Don't micromanage. You're not trying to get them to do it exactly the way you would. You're just getting them to do it. They won't learn how to do it for themselves if you're there nudging them to do it this way or to try it that way. They won't feel a sense of accomplishment and a desire to do it again or to do more if they haven't actually done it

themselves. They won't learn to be proactive next time if you're there to tell them precisely what needs to be done. Let them try and fail and try again. Tell them, "Let me know when you're done and I'll come over and see how you did." Then, unless it's something dangerous where your supervision is required, walk away.

5. **Give appropriate thanks and feedback.** Don't overpraise. When our kid does the simplest thing—takes out the trash, brings their dishes in from the table, feeds the dog—we tend to overpraise it with a "Great job, buddy!" or a "Perfect!" However, a simple, kind, confident "Thank you" or "Nice job" is sufficient. Save your over-the-top praise responses for when they've really gone above and beyond in their effort, or accomplished something truly exceptional.

Chances are they've done a decent job, maybe even a pretty darn good job, but they'll also need some constructive feedback on how to improve— as will be the case in the world of work one day. A friend of mine is a senior manager at Google overseeing a team of Millennials. Often when she gives constructive feedback to her young employees she hears, "What? It can't be me. I've never gotten feedback like that before. It must be you or Google that's the problem." Don't let your kid's first performance evaluation in the workplace be the first time they receive constructive feedback.

The bulk of the time you'll be able to point out one or two things they might do differently next time: "If you hold the trash bag like this, less stuff will fall out." Or, "You see that stripe on your gray shirt? It's because you washed it with your new jeans. It's better to wash new jeans by themselves the first time, or else they'll bleed onto the other stuff."

And if your kid didn't actually complete the task, or completed it but not at a high quality level, you need to let them know. Say, "This was a good start at cleaning up after dinner. I see you did the dishes. But those pots still need to be hand-washed, and the counter needs to be wiped down." Then smile—you're not angry with them, you're teaching them—and go back to what you were doing.

If, as your child gets more accustomed to helping out around the house, she starts doing things without being asked, that's the more appropriate time to reach out with words, eye contact, and body language that communicates, "I noticed what you did, and I really appreciate it." Even then, that's enough. Don't belabor the point. Just walk away or go back to whatever you were doing. Know that your kid will be beaming inside.

6. **Make it routine:** If you set expectations that some chores are daily, others are weekly, and others are seasonal, your kids will get used to the fact that something always needs to be done in life, and that pitching in and helping out is a way to feel useful and good and will be recognized. Over time if you've been saying to your kid, "Hey, I'd like you to pitch in and help me with this," and if, when you see them struggling, you pitch in to help them, your kid will start to look for ways in which they can "pitch in" when they see another family member, friend, neighbor, or coworker in need.

THEY MUST WORK FOR THEIR DREAMS: BELIEVING IN THEMSELVES IS NOT ENOUGH

Stephen Parkhurst's video is his response to media critiques of Millennials with which he disagreed. Still, looking around at his peers, Stephen saw some truth in what was being said about his generation. "Yes, we have a sense of entitlement. I've felt it myself," Stephen told me.[13] His parents always said that he just had to believe in himself and he could do anything. For a while, he behaved as if that was literally true; he was all self-esteem and no work ethic, and it didn't get him very far.

"When I first got out of college I bounced from job to job trying to get somewhere with my films, but nothing was happening. I sort of had this idea that the problem was where I was living, like, it wasn't me, it was that I wasn't in the right place yet. I remember thinking, 'I'm twenty-five! Why am I not a famous director by now?' We went to college and did what we were supposed to do, and weren't immediately rewarded as we thought we should be."

In April 2009, just after the financial markets crashed, Stephen gave up and moved back home to Portland, Maine. He set his filmmaking dreams to the side and took a job working as a valet at a hotel just to make ends meet. Two years later, he had what to him was a horrifying thought—that he'd still be a valet at age forty.

Something clicked for Stephen in those moments of despair parking other people's fancy cars. He came to realize success in film wasn't going to be handed to him. "No matter how much I may think 'I'm great,' nobody else cares about that. In the valet years I came to realize that instead of just moving about, I needed to have a plan bigger than *waiting* for someone to recognize my stunning brilliance."

Stephen moved to New York to build his network and skill set by working in the film industry as a digital tech/projectionist at Deluxe. Even though he'd rather be making his own films for a living than working behind the scenes on someone else's, he now knows it will take a lot of hard work to achieve his dreams of being a filmmaker, and a plan, which is now unfolding. He has a lot of student debt but feels good about the life he and his girlfriend are carving out for themselves in New York, and about his work at Deluxe and on his own films. "I feel that I'm on the right path, whereas for quite a few years I wasn't on any path at all, I was just stumbling through the wilderness. Now it's like, 'There's my career, it's up ahead,' instead of 'Hey, *where's* my career?'"

HOW WORK ETHIC COMES ACROSS IN THE JOB HUNT

Stephen is willing to do the grunt work in order to pay his dues and move up the ladder. Alexa Gulliford wishes she saw more young employees like him. Alexa is managing director at Groupe Insearch, a corporate search firm that places recent college graduates in support positions at Bay Area technology companies, financial services companies, and corporate retailers. (Think Twitter and Salesforce.com, venture capital firms and hedge funds, Sephora and Restoration Hardware.) These companies want great young adults for entry-level positions, so Alexa is out there "sorting and sifting" candidates. Too often she sees candidates who roll their eyes in interviews when the "grunt work" (a.k.a. administrative tasks of a job) is discussed. What Alexa and her corporate clients are looking for are people who are eager to roll up their sleeves and pitch in.[14]

Alexa turned her observations and client feedback into tips for young applicants about how to demonstrate work ethic:

1. **Be interested in the work itself.** Don't say, "It's okay, I'm *fine* with doing the administrative part." Say, "I'm going to *kill it* with the administrative part." Say "I'm so excited to do this job and the work that goes into it."

2. **Be interested in paying your dues.** Don't suggest that this job is a pill you're willing to swallow to get your foot in the door. "Foot in the door" is a no-no phrase because it demonstrates in quick summary fashion that you're only interested in promotion and

something down the road, not the actual job you're interviewing for. No one wants to hire the foot-in-the-door candidate.

3. **Once on the job, be proactive and take the initiative.** Be able to anticipate the next steps. Think to yourself, "He asked for X for this meeting. I'm going to have to do Y and then Z after that." Alexa says if employees can't think to themselves, "I know what happens next, I know how to stay ahead of the game," and then act upon those instincts, it will prevent them from advancing.

Listening to Alexa share her corporate recruiting experience, I can see how the checklisted childhood might have been helpful for a third grader, or even seventh, but if we've led them to believe someone will always do the grunt work and will always provide the next steps for them, we've basically led them astray. Reading my mind, Alexa adds, "We teach our kids to wait for cues. To wait for instruction. That's what keeps them from having the type of mind-set employers want to see."

HARD WORK AT HOME LEADS TO PROMOTIONS IN THE WORKPLACE

Hannah is a twenty-five-year-old Millennial who has exactly the mind-set employers want to see. She works as a senior project manager at a Texas financial services firm where she's been promoted a number of times in the few short years since she earned her political science degree from Duke.

"I didn't realize how *differently* I was raised until I got to college," she tells me.[15] She is the eldest of three kids in an affluent Bay Area family where much could have been done for her but wasn't. "My parents raised me and my siblings to be very independent. They gave us many chores and reinforced the value of doing things by yourself and not getting help all the time." In college Hannah saw students whose parents "babied them" by flying in to decorate their kid's college apartments, buy them groceries, and do their laundry.

During her senior year at Duke, when she started going through the job application process, she narrowed her focus to companies that are big sports sponsors and "decided I would be willing to do *anything* there." Except for showing her parents her résumé, "I went through the process on my own, and got the job on my own merits." A number of Hannah's friends took for granted that they'd get a job through their parents' connections. "In today's economy there's nothing wrong with that, but I really valued getting a job on my own, being successful on my own, paying all my bills from the beginning." Her voice brims with confidence as she says this. "In contrast, a lot of my friends' parents pay their rent and their car insurance, and so they stay in this comfort zone of halfway to adult but not having to deal with what's stressful or hard about being an adult."

Hannah knows being "halfway to adult" doesn't bode well in the workplace. "If you start to behave in ways that are consistent with the stereotypes about Millennials, it will impede your progress at work. Being hand-held as a kid and having entitlement in the workplace tend to go hand in hand. If a kid wasn't forced to do chores or their parents helped them with anything that was hard, the workplace may be the first time they've had to deal with that."

I ask Hannah about the chores she had to do as a kid and she rattles off a list: "Making our beds every day; putting away our toys, books, and clean laundry; helping do the dishes and make dinner; helping with laundry; weeding and watering plants and helping with gardening; running errands for my mom (once I could drive); washing the windows; general spring cleaning; sweeping out the storage area; dusting our baseboards; and cleaning the cars."

Hannah continues, "The opportunity to rise to the occasion and prove yourself to managers and coworkers is there, but I've seen people go the other route." Some of her friends have "gone the other route" and are on their third jobs after only eighteen months out of college. "They quit because they didn't love it. They can't grasp the concept that their first job is entry level and the purpose is to *learn*. It can force you to step up, or you can have parents who continue to support you by helping with bills as you job hop."

"I have a coworker, my age, who has a super-inflated sense of self, doesn't work very hard, delegates a lot, and thinks her current role is a little beneath her. When the promotion cycle came up, she was shocked not to get promoted. For a week or two after not getting the promotion, she left work at 2:00 or 3:00 p.m., sulking. She's tarnished herself in her manager's eyes because she sulks like a little child instead of working hard. Her parents humor this behavior. They tell her, 'Oh, if you don't get what you want, you can just quit.' She never learned to throw herself into her work. Her parents have always told her how great, amazing, and awesome she is. It totally colors her ability to honestly assess herself vis-à-vis her peers."

While Hannah's coworker is sulking around the office, Hannah continues to get more responsibility. Often she's asked to sit in on interviews. The company is trying to screen for someone who knows what she wants and is willing to work hard to get it; what they want is another Hannah.

17

LET THEM CHART THEIR OWN PATH

I could pressure my son, but the skill of reacting to pressure I put on him is not the skill I want him to have.[1]

—Sebastian Thrun, cofounder and CEO of Udacity, developer of Google self-driving car and Google Glass

What do you want to be when you grow up? What are you going to major in? Adults constantly ask children and college-bound students these questions, and, depending on the answer, the grown-up will offer a beaming face, a quizzically raised eyebrow, or a frown in response. Even when the kid is a stranger to us, we're pretty sure we know which pursuits are worthwhile and which aren't.

I've already confessed to you that when my daughter's nursery school teacher took me aside and highly praised her paintings, I thought to myself, "Yeah, yeah, yeah, *but that's not gonna get her into college.*" Avery was only four years old, but what she "ought to" do was already on my mind. I didn't yet understand how dismissing my child's artistic talents might be harmful to her. Soon enough, though, in my work as Stanford's dean of freshmen, I understood the error in my thinking. I sat with far too many students describing what "everyone" expected them to study or pursue. And too many responded through tears when I asked, "Yeah, but what do *you* want to do?" I developed mantras that I'd fold into formal and informal conversations with my students, one of which was "Find your voice and honor what you hear." This was my way of saying: *What you're going to be and do in the world is up to you. Look to yourself for clues about what really matters to you. Give yourself permission to be and do those things.*

And at home, I did a 180. I stopped expecting that Avery or her brother would become any particular *thing* (a doctor, a lawyer, a teacher, an entrepreneur, and so on). I stopped thinking of them as little bonsai trees that I could prune carefully, and I began treating them instead like wildflowers of unknown genus and species that would reveal their unique and glorious beauty as long as I gave them the proper nourishment and environment. I began hoping foremost that my children as well as my students would find what Stanford professor of education and director of the Stanford Center on Adolescence William ("Bill") Damon calls "purpose."

PURPOSE MATTERS

Damon's research indicates that a sense of purpose is *essential for achieving happiness and satisfaction in life.* He defines purpose as a person's "ultimate concern," that which, when known, becomes a person's ultimate answer to the questions "Why am I doing this?" and "Why does this matter to me?" Damon distinguishes purpose from short-term desires— such as an A on a test, a date to a dance, a new piece of technology, a spot on the team, or admission to a particular college. A short-term desire may or may not have longer-term significance, Damon says. "Purpose, by contrast, is an end in itself."

In 2003, Damon and his colleagues began the Youth Purpose Project, a nationwide four-year study of purpose in people aged twelve to twenty-six. Only 20 percent of those studied had found something meaningful to which they wanted to dedicate their lives. Another 25 percent were "drifting" with no sense of what they really wanted to do and no intent to develop that knowledge. The rest were somewhere in the middle. Twenty percent who've found their purpose is too low a percentage for Damon, who wrote his most recent book, *The Path to Purpose: How Young People Find Their Calling in Life*, not only as a culmination of his work in human development but out of a sense that in society today too many young adults are experiencing a sense of emptiness.[2]

This emptiness does not arise from a lack of interest in having a purpose. A 2012 study by Net Impact, a nonprofit organization devoted to helping people make a difference in their world through their careers, found that 72 percent of college students feel that having a job that makes a positive social or environmental impact is very important or essential to their happiness. And Millennial Adam Smiley Poswolsky, whose best-selling 2014 career guide *The Quarter-Life Breakthrough* has shown thousands of young adults how to pivot their lives toward purpose, writes of the desire he and so many of his generation have to find "meaningful work."[3] For Poswolsky, meaningful work "provides personal meaning reflecting who you are and what your interests are, allows you to share your gifts to help others, and is financially viable given your desired lifestyle." And meaningful work stands in contrast to "mediocre work," which pays the bills, passes the time, doesn't align with one's values, and may make you financially successful but "doesn't allow you to make your unique contribution to the world."

"So many young people I talk to end up pursuing paths out of parental pressure rather than personal alignment," Poswolsky told me. "This leads to confusion and resentment, and sometimes unhappiness. Parents (especially in a job market completely different than the one they experienced as boomers) may not know what is best for their kids."

As dean, I became very interested in helping my students home in on their purpose as a way of starting them on the road toward meaningful work. I'd tell them to forget what you think "everyone" expects you to study or do for a career. I'd say, *Study what you love, and the rest will follow.*

"When you study what you love," I'd say, "you're motivated to go to every class. You do all the reading. Maybe even the supplemental reading. You speak up in class. You go to office hours. You synthesize what you've read with what was said in class and with what you discussed with the professor and fellow students afterward, and you formulate your own thoughts about the material. When you study what you love, you probably end up with a great grade because you were intrinsically motivated to master the subject matter. But even if you don't get a great grade, if you've studied what you love, you've put your heart into whatever grade you got. You've made a real effort. And regardless of the grade, through all of this effort you've got a professor who can write you a very meaningful letter of recommendation about your curiosity and determination. And even more than that, you'll be able to speak about the subject in a compelling manner in a job interview. If you have the guts to study what you love regardless of what other people say, it leads precisely to the kind of success you're looking for."

Rick Wartzman, executive director of the Drucker Institute, a social enterprise that is part of Claremont Graduate University dedicated to a mission of "strengthening organizations to strengthen society," agrees with my "study what you love" mantra.[4] When I spoke with Wartzman in 2014 to get his insight into this concept of life path and purpose, his daughter had just graduated from college, and Wartzman, a highly acclaimed writer, had just written an open letter to her about deploying management guru Peter F. Drucker's principles in her life; he published the letter in *Time* magazine.[5] "Chances are," he wrote to his daughter, "what you love plays to your strengths and it's where you're going to have the most success." In our conversation Wartzman added that if you start doing work you love when you're young, "you've got the best shot of reaching excellence and mastery, because you have that much more *time*."

Meanwhile, Sebastian Thrun, the German-born Silicon Valley genius behind the self-driving car, Google Glass, and the free online university Udacity, believes that a sense of purpose will lead not only to happiness and to meaningful work, but also to success.[6] When I called him in 2014 to ask his thoughts on parenting, the first thing he said to me was, "I'm not an expert in child education. I know the world is full of opinions and I don't know any more than anyone else." With that caveat out of the way, he proceeded to tell me that whenever young people ask him for career advice, he gives them the simple message: find your passion. When he told me this I cringed slightly; although "find your passion" was once a lovely philosophical ideal, it has become utilitarian, as in, find your passion—as if it's hiding over there on the bookshelf or under a rock—and find it quickly!—so you can tell a college admission dean about it. I push back on Sebastian to get at the values that for him underlie this standard platitude.

"I say, 'Listen to yourself, listen to your intuition,'" he says. "Many kids have a complete disconnect with their inner feelings; instead they're attuned to 'tell me what to do and I'll do it.' If you're passionate about what you do, then you're going to find a job. Relatively few people are actually passionate about what they do, and when you're passionate you're twice as good as anybody else. When you hit the working world and you want to be really successful, there's no one around to tell you what to do. You've got to know yourself well enough to know what you want to do.

"How to make a kid truly successful in life is more important than getting into Stanford. I find a shocking number of people who have a perfect pedigree but don't have the passion. And look at Steve Jobs, Zuckerberg, Gates. Their pathways weren't neatly laid out. This model of dragging the kids to exactly the same stuff at the same time is a broken model. Parents mean extremely well, and are willing to endure a lot of hardship themselves. But for their kids, their independence of thought and mind, and the ability to derive pleasure from their own actions, all of that is left by the wayside."

Rick Wartzman and I spoke about the potential downside of doing what you love—that is, that it might not make you well off financially. This is a hard subject, particularly for upper-middle-class parents, to swallow. Wait, our kids might have a lower standard of living than us? They won't live in the manner to which they've grown accustomed? They won't be able to buy a home in the kind of neighborhood we live in? Perhaps. The state of the economy and the cost of living may make it so. But here's where it's worth interrogating what success actually means. A kid may come home to more modest digs, and have to make do with less, but if she's doing what she loves, she swells with immeasurable happiness, contentment, joy, and, yes, *purpose*. Who are we to say that's not a meaningful life?

"Children," says Damon, "must have a sense that they are finding their way toward purposes of their own choosing, and parents cannot make these choices for them." Parents cannot *give* a child purpose, define what it should be, or force a sense of purpose onto a child, Damon warns, "any more than the parent can choose the child's personality or write a script for the child's life."

So, what can a parent do to help kids chart their own path?

FIRST, EMBRACE THE KID YOU'VE GOT

"Embrace the child you've got" is an obvious point, yet it deserves an underscore. When we decide it's our job to determine what our kid should explore, study, or do for a living, we run the risk of focusing on who they *aren't* (but we wish they would be), and explicitly not seeing, valuing, and loving the person they actually *are*.

A friend named Jennifer Ayer is head of the Palo Alto independent school, The Girls' Middle School, and mother of three teenage girls.[7] As a child, she was a "teacher and parent pleaser" and had no idea what she really wanted to do. "I knew how to do school, jump through hoops, get all the grades. I remember being told that I was a natural leader and wondering what on earth I was supposed to lead. It took me until age thirty to learn to hear to my inner voice over the cacophony coming from society." She plows these lessons learned into her parenting and into her role as educator. "I have faith that kids can learn to listen to their inner voice much sooner than I did. Setbacks, struggles, and failures are essential to the process."

Jennifer's eyes were opened to the importance of helping a kid find their own passion more than a decade ago, when she invited Challenge Success cofounder Denise Pope to speak at her home, as part of a fundraiser for Bing Nursery School. Until Denise's visit, Jennifer, a mother of three then-preschool-aged girls, had not given much thought to the perils of having her daughters follow the same paths she and her husband had taken and attend elite schools from childhood through graduate school. "But as Denise spoke I was riveted by what she was saying," Jennifer told me. "After everyone had left, I turned to my husband and said, 'I want our girls to be healthy, ethical, and to still love learning when they leave our home. Nothing else matters.' He said, 'But secretly you still want them to go to Dartmouth.' I responded, 'We have to let go of that. If it is meant to be, it will take care of itself.' As parents of preschoolers we changed our mind-set and our parenting. 'Help them discover and develop their interests and talents' has been our mantra ever since."

From my conversations with educators and parents nationwide, as well as my own observations, I know this shift in focus toward who a kid *is* and what a kid *can* do as opposed to who they *aren't* and what they *can't* do is sorely needed in our communities and in our homes. Time and again I hear something such as this, from Michele, who lives on the Upper East Side in New York: "We've got to celebrate kids for who they are. That's what's missing here. There's too much working on what's 'wrong'—deficient in this and deficient in that. There's little celebration of what's good about kids."[8]

Holley, a parent from northern Virginia, took this shift in focus to heart after hearing a talk by psychologist Madeline Levine.[9] Holley told me, "What I found out between Madeline Levine's talk and my own experience is that just because my daughter is said to be 'gifted' doesn't mean she's gifted in *every* subject, at all times, forever. She *hates* history and English. She loves math and science. But I made her do honors English anyway, and she got a D. I changed my mind after hearing Madeline Levine. Why did I keep saying she had to take *all* the gifted classes? Why do we make them do things they absolutely *hate*? I realized we shouldn't expect our kids to be perfect at everything. My daughter is taking honors chem, and is pulling a B. And she loves every moment of it."

I had a similar moment with Sawyer during his sophomore year of high school, when he was handling many challenging subjects including honors chemistry and algebra two/trigonometry but positively drowning in his third year of Spanish, which I'd required him to take. Night after night he'd go through the motions of his Spanish homework along with his five other academic subjects, getting farther and farther behind in his comprehension as he went through the rote motions to complete the homework. He was spending upward of four hours a night on homework, rubbing his already red eyes in exhaustion as the hours ticked by, and waking up the next day with no optimism about school or life. He spent two weekends devoted to getting ahead in his Spanish homework so as to lighten the load in each coming week, yet the load never seemed lighter.

After observing this for two weeks and feeling some measure of "this isn't right" as we relaxed into family weekend activities while our son plodded away at his Spanish, my husband and I decided to offer him a lifeline. Spanish had been our idea, based on my regret over not ever having developed fluency in the language. We talked with him about how to achieve more balance and offered up the idea of dropping the class as one way of doing so. He immediately brightened considerably, but then faced the weighty question: *Should I, or Shouldn't I?* He e-mailed his guidance counselor that night and the next day went to see the counselor to talk it through—on his own. His counselor, very predictably but understandably, said, "Colleges want to see three years of a language." Sawyer countered, "But I'm completely stressed out and it's impacting my ability to do well in my other classes. If I drop, I'll have a prep period where I can get started on my homework in the classes I care most about. And I'm not doing well enough in Spanish to have the kind of comprehension a college will want to see." Sawyer also talked with his Spanish teacher. Ultimately, he dropped the class. Homework is now still a very demanding but more manageable three hours per night. He had a choice in the matter and has had a spring in his step ever since.

As for my husband and me, this was not an easy decision—we very much value our kid learning a second language. It's an important practical skill and will open him to valuable cultural experiences and other types of awareness. But the stress Sawyer was experiencing every afternoon and evening was becoming unmanageable; it was compromising his sleep and his overall life outlook. We decided we'd rather he squeezed the most out of the subjects he loves—science, history, English, and photography—than see him compromise all of that while being squeezed to death by Spanish. As for colleges, some admission deans may question this decision and decide he's unfit for their freshman class because of it; but I have confidence—tremendous confidence—that the right college for Sawyer will understand why he made this choice.

SECOND, WHEN THEY'RE YOUNG, LISTEN FOR CLUES

Damon's research and that of others shows that until around the middle school years, most children aren't developmentally capable of reflecting about their identity or thinking about the future, both of which are prerequisites to being able to think about their purpose. So no matter how much you as the parent might want to push your kid to know themselves and get going on developing that all-important sense of purpose, a kid *simply can't* until that developmental milestone of being able to "self-reflect"—which will be different for every child—is reached. With younger kids, your job is to observe who they are, expose them to different things, and take an interest in what interests them.

"What a parent *should* do," Bill Damon asserts, "is lead a child toward promising options. A parent can help a child sort through choices and reflect upon how the child's talents and interests match up with the world's opportunities and needs. A parent can support a child's own efforts to explore purposeful directions, and open up more potential sources of discovery about possible purposes. These are supporting roles rather than leading ones, because center stage in this drama belongs to the child. But while the most effective assistance parents can provide is indirect, it is also invaluable."[10]

Google Glass inventor Sebastian Thrun's young son makes many of his own choices and has fewer extracurriculars than most other kids as a result. "I could probably *make* my son play chess really well or ski really well, but I don't want to deprive him of the ability to discover things on his own. I could *pressure* him, but that skill of reacting to pressure is not the skill I want him to have. When I'm not around anymore, he has to be able to do things on his own. The metric is not whether I can *make* him do things, it's whether *he* can do things. Rather than pushing him to think about this or that, I want to encourage him to find the world on his own."[11]

Or, as Poswolsky puts it, "The best thing parents can do is allow their kids to be creative, experiment, and follow their bliss."[12]

THIRD, ESPECIALLY WITH TWEENS AND TEENS, REMEMBER: WILDFLOWERS, NOT BONSAI TREES

How can we parents help our kids develop Damon's sense of purpose and Thrun's sense of passion without going overboard and charting their path for them? Based on the research of Damon and the advice of Poswolsky, as well as my own personal experiences and observations, here are my tips for how to support your kid in charting their own path, especially during those years when the external pressures of college and the internal pressures of your seemingly combustible teen heat up:

1. **Accept that it's not about you, it's about *your kid*.** Set aside your definition of a successful career, what you'd be proud to be able to say to others about your kid, or what you'd always assumed or hoped your kid would be or do. This is no small feat. It requires a fundamental commitment to the belief that their life isn't about you. Many parents struggle with this piece, but it's essential that you get there. Being able to differentiate your life from theirs is an essential contributor to their mental health—and yours.

2. **Notice who your kid actually *is*** —what they're good at, and what they love. This is your kid's precious, unique life unfolding, and the possibilities are infinite. Whether you're at home or out in the world, the clues to what your kid is skilled at and interested in are everywhere. For example, which subjects do they pursue with vigor, discuss excitedly, and persist at when there's a challenge? What kinds of books and magazines do they read? What topics do they post about on Facebook, tweet about on Twitter, or pin on Pinterest? When are they curious, asking questions, and lighting up with interest? What are they so *into* that it becomes hard for you to tear them away? What are they bothered about in the world? What kind of injustice concerns them?

   Also pay attention to how your kid likes to participate in the world. Do they enjoy interacting with people? Are they good at organizing things? At solving problems? Do they articulate the big picture? Are they interested in every small detail? Are they idealistic or practical? Do they like knowing a lot of information? Are they a numbers person? A people person? Highly competitive? Persuasive? Do they like to use their hands and make stuff? Do they like to help others?

   Your kid has a great chance of living a meaningful and purposeful life at the intersection of what they're good at, what they love, and what they value. There, they'll experience Mihaly Csikszentmihalyi's concept of "flow"—where the challenges presented are just slightly ahead of the talent or skill they bring, and their interest and motivation are strong. They'll feel good about themselves and their contributions. Even if you don't really understand what it is they do, their joy will be palpable. And that's what matters.

3. **Explore with diagnostic tools.** The concept of "strengths"—the ways of being in the world that energize you and, if utilized and honed, can lead to professional success—is the work of Donald O. Clifton of the Gallup, Inc., opinion poll organization. Through the Clifton StrengthsFinder test (which can be accessed for free if you've already purchased a copy of a *StrengthsFinder* book, or can be purchased by going to www.gallupstrengthscenter.com), a person can learn their top five strengths out of the thirty-four talents or skills most common in humans based on Gallup's research. Writer Marcus Buckingham, author of international best sellers *First, Break All the Rules* and *Now, Discover Your Strengths*, among other titles, is a leader in bringing the "Strengths Movement" to the workplace. Jennifer Fox, author of *Your Child's Strengths: A Guide for Parents and Teachers*, fashioned the "Strengths" concept into an entire high school curriculum and pedagogy when she was head of school at Purnell School, a private, all-girls school in New Jersey.

   Parents may find the Clifton StrengthsFinder test to be a fun and useful tool for gaining insight into how a kid is going to find meaningful and purposeful work in the world. It's appropriate for persons aged fifteen and older. Similar types of tools are the Strong Interest Inventory, which seeks to match a person's interests with possible careers, and the Myers-Briggs Type Indicator (MBTI) personality inventory, which can help a person better understand how they enjoy functioning in the world and the kinds of careers that they might find rewarding. All three of these tools are used by high school guidance counselors and in college career services centers throughout the nation. For younger kids, the strengths movement offers Strengths-Explorer, a tool for ten- to fourteen-year-olds.

4. **Be interested and helpful.** When a parent senses a spark of interest in their kid, we can be enormously helpful at "fanning the flames," as Bill Damon puts it, to help our kid and us better understand their

interest and where they might want to take it. Family dinner conversations are a great time to sense a spark and then fan the flames. Start by talking about their day and what was most enjoyable at school, or after school, and why. Keep up the continual questioning to get at the nugget of what made the experience enjoyable—and resist the impulse to fill in your own answer or make assumptions. Once we begin to develop a sense of our kid's interests, we can support them by a willingness to seek out school activities, summer camps, and other forms of enrichment that can help them develop their interests.

5. **Know when to push forward, know when to pull back.** None of us wants our kid to squander their talents, or to have given up on something when it started to get difficult, such as playing a musical instrument. But we need to look to our kid for clues that they are genuinely interested in a particular pursuit before we decide that this is something worth cultivating at great effort, time, and perhaps expense. If your kid has the budding talent for something *and* a good deal of interest in it, by all means support it to whatever degree you can. But if your kid lacks the interest, that's a red flag that no matter how talented they might be, it's not likely to be something they want to do with their life. If you push them anyway, they may end up bitterly resenting you no matter how much they've "succeeded" at it or how proud you are to be able to say they've done it.

6. **Help them find mentors.** According to Damon's research, "virtually all the highly purposeful youth whom we studied had mentors outside the homes, and these mentors contributed importantly to the youngsters' quests for purpose." So we can also fan the flames by introducing our kid to people farther ahead on the same path who can become mentors and help them deepen and strengthen their interests. Many grown-ups in our kids' lives can be great role models for how to live a life of meaning and purpose. Does your kid love science? Encourage them to ask their aunt, the scientist, about when she first got interested in her particular field and the steps she took to develop that interest further. Does your kid love airplanes? Introduce them to your college friend who builds or flies them and ask that same question. Does your kid have a favorite author? Take her to a book signing and encourage her to meet the person. Encourage

her to follow up with a letter asking the author how he or she got their start. Every kid has a teacher, or two, or three, who loves what they do for a living. Encourage them to approach a favorite teacher to ask how they got their start. Even if your kid isn't interested in teaching, talking to a person who has a sense of purpose helps a kid understand what purpose looks like and they will hunger to feel it for themselves.

Kids of any age can feel nervous at the thought of engaging an adult in conversation, but as with the professors I advised my undergraduates to go meet in office hours, almost any adult is happy to respond to the simple, thoughtful question "You seem to love what you do. When and how did you figure out that's what you wanted to do?" This question is an icebreaker any kid can ask any adult, and the dialogue can then proceed toward what this person would recommend a young budding scientist/pilot/engineer/writer do to deepen their exposure to the subject.

7. **Prepare them for the hard work to come.** As was the case with Millennial filmmaker Stephen Parkhurst, parents often tell kids that they can be anything they want to be or that their dreams will come true; both platitudes are half right—believing in yourself and having dreams is really important—but the other half of the equation, which there is simply *no* way around, is hard work. When we overpraise our kids—telling them everything they did was "great!" or "perfect!" we give them a false sense of what it'll take to achieve their goals in the real world one day. Being able to give a kid a reality check and constructive feedback are crucial.

    We do this by telling our kid what it actually takes to succeed in the real world—hard work, relationship-based connections, perseverance, resilience, and some amount of good luck. Says Damon, "Impress upon them the importance of sticking with something in order to really master it, but also be prepared to give honest, frank feedback." We've got to share with them what we know of the challenges and limitations that exist—not to derail them or make them feel foolish, but to prepare them for just how hard they'll have to work to make those dreams come true.

    For example, a parent of an aspiring professional football player can say, "Son, only three to four percent of high school football players will get the chance even to play in college and a small fraction of them will make it to the NFL . . ." and follow that up with encouragement about what it will take to get to the next level: "If this is what you want, you're going to need to double up your practices and work on your strength. I think you can do it *if* you're willing to put in the work. I'm here to support you."

8. **Don't do too much for them.** When you're highly excited about your kid's interests, you may find yourself wanting to do too much to further things along. Your kid must be in the driver's seat. They must be the one to make it—whatever "it" is—happen.

Little mini-businesses or social-entrepreneurship activities are all the rage for kids these days, in part because we think "colleges want to see" it on the application. Those motives aside, they can be great opportunities for a kid to develop more skills and nurture their budding sense of purpose. But remember, if you construct the enterprise, order the items being sold, or devise the storage method for the items being collected, deliver it to the school or sidewalk, troubleshoot along the way, and pack it all up when the day is done, and all your kid does is make a sign or poster, stand there with a smile, and take people's money or donated items, you haven't helped your child develop any of these traits at all. And you'll have done nothing to further your understanding of your kid's purpose. A Seattle parent I spoke with refers to this as "parents acting like the sous-chef and the kid acts like they're Julia Child." The right thing for you to do is stand well to the side and observe—take note of what sparks in your kid: Is it handling money and making change? Is it bringing in new customers? Is it engaging in conversation? Is it speaking about the purpose behind the thing being collected or sold? These observations can yield clues as to what your child's purpose will one day be.

9. **Have your own purpose.** Here's where we parents get to put our own selves front and center. Too often, our kids hear us complaining about things; let them hear what pulls you toward work instead of what pushes you away from it. Do you derive meaning and purpose from the work you do? If so, why? Are you experiencing personal growth through it? Are you helping others? Are you making a contribution to your community, or to society more broadly? Are you

proud to be earning a living that keeps the family safe, warm, and fed? Is your work about personal expression? Share with your kids whatever it is about your work that gives you a sense of purpose and meaning. If you're a stay-at-home parent, let your kids hear you say why you enjoy raising children and running a household. If you work outside the home, talk about something meaningful that happened at work that day. Too often today kids are dabbling in everything and end up as dilettantes who know a little bit about a bunch of things but lack the depth they would have acquired if they were truly interested in it and had the time and inclination to pursue it further. If you help them understand how *you* became a person with purpose, you'll inspire them to want to do the same.

If, on the other hand, as you read this question, you're one of those many midcareer people who realizes you're not deriving much satisfaction from what you currently do for a living, you can be honest with your kids about that, too. Don't be overly pessimistic—you don't want them to fear that your job or their home life could be disrupted—but do let your kids know what you "really want to do" someday. Let your kids be inspired by that passion you have for that thing, whatever it is, and let them hear you talk about your plans, and see you making strides, toward making that dream come true.

WANT TO KEEP THEM CLOSE?—GOTTA LET THEM GO

We think we're playing it safe when we chart our kids' course toward what we see as prestigious, and as offering honor, title, and money. Many parents badly want those things for their kids' sakes, but also as evidence of great parenting. So we become architects drawing up plans for someone else's life. Sometimes it "works"—meaning our hunches or ideals align with what our kid was intrinsically motivated to pursue. Sometimes it just *looks* to us and to the world like it works—because they became a doctor, lawyer, engineer, concert pianist, pro tennis player, or whatever else we may have had in mind for them—but, in this case, the kid at some point sheds the blinders, sees the landscape of other options around them, and claims their life for themselves, having experienced some degree of angst, if not suffering.

As we've seen, Bill Damon is a strong proponent of the role parents can play in helping their kids discover their purpose. Still, he cautions, "A parent cannot simply give a purpose to a child, and indeed any too forceful or controlling effort to do so is likely to have adverse repercussions."[13] In the summer of 2014 I heard about one such case of serious adverse repercussions. A grown man I did not know reached out to me on Facebook to tell me he was glad I was writing this book, and wished his mother had read a book like this when he was growing up. Minutes later we were talking on the phone, and he relayed the following story:

Tyler (not his real name) represents the epitome of professional success for many.[14] Close to thirty years of age, he's an associate at a prestigious corporate law firm in Los Angeles, and a graduate of Harvard University and Stanford Law School. But when it comes to how overparenting can hamper a kid's ability to find their purpose, Tyler's story is an instructive one. He began telling the story of his upbringing in a voice that was strong, eloquent, and warm:

"As a kid I was an *extremely* hard worker. My parents really valued that, and there's nothing wrong with that in and of itself. They weren't doing my homework for me but in every class they knew exactly what was going on and they were involved in every single assignment. When I was twelve or thirteen they sat me down and told me grad school wasn't optional, it was required, and that it would be law school; both of them are lawyers. If that's what they said I was going to do, I was going to do it. I *always* did what they said. Their message was 'This is the path; keep on it' and anything outside of that path was frowned upon."

At Harvard Tyler majored in government. "My mom called me multiple times a day and my parents visited me all the time." This impacted not only on his academic choices but his ability to form relationships with others. He graduated from college and after a few years working at a casting agency in New York, his parents said, "It's time for law school."

Tyler chose Stanford in part to get away from his parents, but they came along anyway. "They picked out an apartment for me. They negotiated with the landlord. They paid the rent. I didn't have to do anything. They even *decorated* it for me. My friends would moan about having to pay their own way, but I'd tell them, 'There's something to that. You're making it in the world. I'm still trying to please my parents.'"

In law school Tyler noticed his peers "seemed like they were there on their own volition. But I was there because this was the next step in the path laid out for me by my mom. I knew deep down that all of this help was problematic. But how could I say no? My parents had both lost a parent when they were young and I knew it was bringing them so much joy to be so involved and do these kinds of things for me."

During his first term in law school, his mom was still calling him every day and often multiple times a day. "I'd been a quiet and shy kid but one day it got to the point where I just didn't want to talk to her anymore. I had no control over the emotion that was coming out of me. It just bubbled over. I yelled, 'Your voice is the only voice in my head! I have to hear my own voice.' It was the beginning of the process of putting myself back together."

That phone call led to a drastic change in Tyler's relationship with his mother. "I stopped talking to her for about six months. It was really, really, really hard for her. I told her, 'I'm not going away forever, but it's the right and necessary thing to do.' Then I started intensive therapy."

Tyler was in therapy for the better part of two years. I asked him when he first sensed something was wrong. "As a kid, whenever I did something purely on my own—like writing songs and recording music—I was reproached. The piano lessons were great as far as my mom was concerned because they went on the résumé. But when I was fifteen and brought home a little CD of songs I had written and recorded, my mom said, 'Did they say you were the next Elvis? No? Okay, that's what I thought.' Sometimes my grandma would say something like 'Oh, Tyler, you have such a nice voice' and my mom would say, 'Oh, let's not go too far.' I don't see how she could've possibly worried there was a risk of me dropping out of school or not going to college. The fact that she couldn't even acknowledge the pure joy I got from that hobby—that she tempered my joy, tried to dial it down so much that my grandmother felt the need to stick up for me—was problematic."

Tyler's voice becomes gravelly as he reflects back on what he says was a huge depression. "I'm so thankful every day I wasn't an abused child, but in some sense, those people at least know they're supposed to be angry. I didn't know I had any right to have any resentment or anger. It's a kind of reverse neglect. In therapy I dealt with feelings that were always there but I didn't feel justified in acknowledging. It took over two and a half years."

It's hard for anyone, including Tyler, to criticize an abundance of opportunity and counsel provided by educated, loving parents. "You feel you have security that you should be grateful for. Someone is literally laying out the path for you. You think it's a good thing. You think you're lucky. But then you see people who are truly independent, truly passionate about what they do, and you realize you don't know yourself at all. You're trying to be the best person for your mom that you can be, with no other goal for yourself. You feel your parent doesn't ever see you as an individual. Ever. You're an outgrowth of them, following the path they want you to take. It's not your safety and security. It's about fulfilling their ego. It just makes you resentful of someone who thought they were trying to do a good job."

In his final two years of law school, having completely changed the dynamic between himself and his mother, Tyler soared socially. "I loved it. It wasn't the study of the law per se. It was that I began to feel for myself at age twenty-six the freedom that kids are supposed to start to feel as college freshmen. I was finally able to carve out something for myself."

Tyler had family allies in those two years. "My father had never smothered me; he just passively went along with whatever my mom said to do. In the past if he and I talked it was always superficial. But when I cut off communication with my mom, my dad was the interlocutor. He would go to my mother and say, 'Tyler has a point.' Meanwhile my mom would tell her friends, 'Tyler's mad at me.' Her friends would say, 'Well, leave him alone, he's a twenty-five-year-old man.' Her friends could see that, but she couldn't; she just saw the son she could control. She didn't see me as a grown man until that cycle of control was severed completely."

"Now she and I talk one or two times a week. Everything is different, and much better. She'll say 'I'm sorry. I know I did a better job with your sister.' It's hard for her to go much farther than that. I think she would say she needed to pay more attention to herself and less to her kids. I think if she had taken twenty percent of the attention off of me and spent it on herself, I think we all would have been better off. When you have a kid it's 'Oh I can focus on this. I can make this thing perfect. Finally here's something I can control.'"

Tyler credits author Eckhart Tolle's words for sparking the sense that he could change his life. "In an interview Tolle spoke about children who really aren't themselves because they're living as extensions of their parents. That language spoke to me immediately."

Bill Deresiewicz concurs. In *Excellent Sheep* he says, "There is something that's a great deal more important than parental approval: learning to do without it. That's what it means to become an adult."[15]

18

NORMALIZE STRUGGLE

Together we will cry and face fear and grief. I will want to take away your pain. But instead I will sit with you and teach you how to feel it.[1]

—Brené Brown, researcher, author, motivational speaker

Some years ago my Stanford colleague Adina Glickman noticed that increasing numbers of our students lacked the wherewithal to cope with adversity (including Bs). Adina is an academic skills coach who oversees academic support programs and coaches students in time management, overcoming test anxiety and procrastination, note taking, and other study skills. Concerned by the increase in the number of students who were having trouble coping with anything less than the perfect level of performance that characterized their childhood, Adina consulted with Harvard's Abigail Lipson, who had started the Success-Failure Project there and produced a booklet called *Reflections on Rejections*. Together, Adina and Abigail determined that more and more students today are "failure deprived."

If students are in their late teens or early twenties when they first face their own very normal human trait of imperfection, they'll lack the "brush it off, get back on the horse, try again, persevere through it" mentality they could—*should*—have cultivated in childhood. Adina went on to found the Stanford Resilience Project, which includes an online library of videos and PDFs from members of the Stanford community—including students, a Supreme Court justice, a favorite computer science professor, and me—who share their struggles, failures, and rejections, how they coped with them, and what they learned.[2] The aim of the project is to "normalize" struggle— to give students a sense that struggle happens to everybody, and that they need not be ashamed when they experience it—and to demonstrate that struggle teaches us lessons and opens up new possibilities. Early studies suggest the Stanford Resilience Project is having a positive impact on undergraduates.

But a fear of failure and lack of ability to cope with struggle isn't only a problem among young adults at Stanford or Harvard. It's a growing facet of life in middle- and upper-middle-class America today as well as elsewhere in the world.

The internationally known educator Sir Ken Robinson, whose 2006 TED Talk on how we're killing creativity in children is the number one TED talk of all time, clocking in at over 28 million views, said in that talk: "We're now running national education systems where mistakes are the worst thing you can make. [But] if you're not prepared to be wrong, you'll never come up with anything original. By the time they get to be adults, most kids have lost that capacity. They have become frightened of being wrong."[3] Even kids intending to be officers in the military are not immune. "We talk at West Point and in the army about young men and women today being less resilient than they ever were," Colonel Leon Robert, professor and head of the Department of Chemistry and Life Science at West Point, told me.[4] "With some of our new cadets right out of high school, if you raise your voice they get teary-eyed. Like no one has corrected them on a behavior before. You've got to be able to have a setback, pick yourself up, dust yourself off, and drive on." A lack of resilience is common among addicts. Harriet Rossetto of the Beit T'Shuvah rehab facility in L.A. says, "The best predictor of success is a sense of resiliency, grit, capacity to fail and get up. If you're prevented from feeling discomfort or failure, you have no sense of how to handle those things at all."[5] A lack of resilience will also impact young adults in the workplace. Phil Gardner, the Michigan State University collegiate employment expert, told me, "Employers like kids with work ethic and resilience, which can often be the middle- and low-income, or blue-collar kids."[6] Eric Scroggins, executive director of Teach For America– Bay Area, concurs: "We select for grit and resilience. We're not just pulling randomly from the population of twenty-two-year-olds; we are taking the top 15 percent of the high achieving who show a record of perseverance."[7]

Back at Stanford, my sense of what was happening went something like this: If you take a culture of high academic achievement at all costs and add a parent's vigilance at smoothing the rough spots of life—in play, in academic outcomes, in interpersonal relations, *and* you heap on exaggerated praise like "great job" and "perfect" regardless of whether the task or accomplishment had any objective merit—you can actually set a kid up for a breakdown in college where consequences such as Bs, Cs, Ds, or even Fs *will* happen, along with misunderstandings with roommates, and rejection from teams, clubs, fraternities, and sororities and from opportunities, and *where parents can no longer fix those outcomes.*

Remember Stephen Parkhurst, the aspiring filmmaker who created the Millennials video? One day when he felt he was wasting away working as a valet while wondering when his stunning brilliance as a filmmaker would be recognized by others, he recalled his mother's frequent refrain: "All you need is a positive attitude and great things will happen." While as a kid it had made him feel good, when he was struggling out in the real world he resented it.[8] "What she had been saying was bullshit; it was that coddling parent thing," he recalls thinking. He knows his mother was only saying what parents in that era had been encouraged to say, and that she was doing her best. Still, his advice for parents *today* is that *yes, of course*, tell kids they can achieve greatness. "But remember also to tell them just how hard you have to work to accomplish these things."

Colonel Robert at West Point agrees with Stephen Parkhurst on this point.[9] "People need to take personal responsibility and accept the objective quality of their own work," Robert says. "We are not all superstars and we've got to stop telling everyone they are." Bill Deresiewicz also laments this superstar mentality. "You want to make it to the top?" he asks. "There is no top. However high you climb, there is always somebody above you. . . . I can tell you right now where you're going to end up: somewhere in the middle, with the rest of us."[10]

Depriving our kids of the chance to struggle and to learn to persevere, while we focus instead on prepping them to be the number one at all things and tell them how awesome they are, is a prime example of our best intentions gone awry. Perhaps we didn't realize that "protecting" our kids from falls and failures could hurt them. But it can. We need to redefine success as being a good and kind person, and as making a strong effort whether they ultimately win or lose. We need to help our children gain resilience to cope when things don't go their way. But how do we do this, since none of us can easily stomach seeing our kids suffer?

Sometimes I joke that when parents in communities like mine get wind that colleges value skills like perseverance and resilience, they'll start up a hardship summer camp instead of closely examining what it is about childhood that deprives kids of developing these traits naturally. Could this happen? Elite college admission seems like a holy grail and at times we do truly wacky things in order to obtain it—such as writing our kid's application for them. But we can't buy resilience for them in the way we buy tutoring, coaching, test prep, and college counseling. Resilience is built from real hardship and cannot be bought or manufactured.

So how *do* we prepare middle- and upper-middle-class kids to thrive, then, to lean in to life, to persevere, when the rough edges of life have been sanded off by the very privilege we worked so hard to be able to provide for them? How do we raise them not to be veal running for home in the face of the world's slaughter but to be warriors? How can they aspire to achieve excellence and hunger for success if they've been given so much and have never hungered for much at all? James Willcox, CEO of the Aspire Public Schools, who educates underserved kids at work while raising his own three daughters amid affluence at home, says, with a deep sigh, "We've got to let our kids fail. We've got to let them struggle. It seems really basic, but it's very hard to do."[11]

At an intellectual level we may understand the value of letting go and letting them make mistakes or fail, yet it's a deeply unsatisfying directive because as parents we want so much to affirmatively *do something*. There is good news: There is something we can do to normalize struggle for our kids and help them build the toughness they'll need in order to thrive as adults in the world. We can help them become resilient.

BUILDING RESILIENCE IN KIDS

Resilience is the ability to bounce back from adversity. It's what gives us the will to go on. Wisdom and advice on how to build resilience in children come from an abundance of sources representing various fields—from medicine, to psychology, to social work, to youth mentoring, to religion and spirituality, to literature. Here are a few examples:

Carol Dweck, the Stanford psychology professor who pioneered the concept and practice of "Growth Mindset" we discussed in Chapter 15 ("Teach Them How to Think"), is a great place to start.[12] Focused on undoing the "fixed mindset" that comes from praising kids for being smart and results in kids avoiding harder challenges because they don't want to receive results contradicting this "smart" label, Dweck teaches that we must instead teach kids that it's their *effort* (something they have control over), not some innate level of intelligence (something they have no control over), that leads to ever higher levels of achievement. The mantra with growth mindset is to keep going, keep trying, and learn through effort that you can get where you want to go; in a sense, Dweck is teaching resilience when it comes to learning.

New York Times best-selling author, researcher, and beloved storyteller Brené Brown teaches what I think of as the resilience of spirit. In recent years, through inspirational works such as *The Gifts of Imperfection: Let Go of Who You Think You're Supposed to Be and Embrace Who You Are* and *Daring Greatly: How the Courage to Be Vulnerable Transforms the Way We Live, Love, Parent, and Lead*, Brown has become the nation's thought leader on subjects most of us have a very hard time discussing: vulnerability, imperfection, and shame.[13] These are the very emotions in which we stew when something has gone wrong or when we anticipate a bad outcome happening, and the very emotions that can erode resilience if we give in to them. Brown's 2010 TEDxHouston talk (currently the fourth-most-watched TED Talk ever at more than 16 million views) touched this nation's nerve.[14] Through her research and empathetic manner of storytelling, Brown helps her audiences and readers appreciate how accepting our fears, imperfections, and vulnerabilities can lead us to a more joyful, happy life. She coined the term "Wholehearted Living" and describes a "Wholehearted" person as someone who can go to bed each night thinking, "Yes, I am imperfect and vulnerable and sometimes afraid, but that doesn't change the truth that I am also brave and worthy of love and belonging."

University of Pennsylvania researcher Angela Duckworth developed the concept of "grit," which is the ability to sustain interest in and effort toward a very long-term goal.[15] Her research shows that a high level of grit leads to outcomes as diverse as surviving the arduous first summer of training at West Point, reaching the final rounds of the National Spelling Bee, retention in the U.S. Special Forces, retention and performance among novice teachers, and graduation from Chicago public high schools, over and beyond talent measures such as IQ, SAT, or other standardized achievement test scores and physical fitness. Grit also correlates with lifetime educational attainment and, inversely, lifetime career changes and divorce. I think of grit as resilience for the long haul.

Best-selling author of more than twenty-five books, Dr. Tim Elmore is the founder and president of Growing Leaders, an Atlanta-based nonprofit organization. He writes and speaks about leadership training for young people and corporations. In his book *Generation iY: Our Last Chance to Save Their Future*, Elmore writes about "seven lies" we've told to the Millennial generation: "You can be anything you want to be; It's your choice; You are special; Every kid ought to go to college; You can have it now; You're a winner just because you participated; and You can get whatever you want." He asserts that these "lies" have led Millennials to reach adulthood "emotionally unstable and socially naïve."[16] For Elmore, being honest and straightforward with kids build resilience.

Pediatrician and adolescent development specialist Dr. Kenneth Ginsburg has written a comprehensive and perhaps definitive text on building resilience in children—*Building Resilience in Children and Teens: Giving Kids Roots and Wings*, published by the American Academy of Pediatrics.[17] In it he teaches that resilience is comprised of competence, confidence, connection, character, contribution, coping, and control, which he terms the "7 C's," and which emanate from the positive youth movement, itself an outgrowth of the positive psychology movement.

Taking a look at my Stanford students and their struggles, as well as what I've experienced over the years in my own life and in raising kids, and drawing upon the work of Carol Dweck, Brené Brown, Angela Duckworth, Tim Elmore, Kenneth Ginsburg, and others, my definition of resilience is simply this: It's the ability to say to ourselves, "I'm okay. I can choose to figure this out, or figure out another way, or decide it's not what I want after all. I'm still me. I'm still loved. Life goes on." The following are my thoughts about how to build that kind of thinking in our kids.

TIPS FOR BUILDING RESILIENCE IN KIDS

1. **Be present in your kid's life.** Overinvolved parents are known for hovering and swooping down when needed, yet, paradoxically, research indicates some are not making meaningful emotional connections with their kids or spending meaningful time with them. Here's how you can build resilience in your kid by being present in their life:

- **Show your love.** When your kid gets home from school or activities, or you get home from work, set aside what you're doing, step away from your computer, put down your smartphone, and let them see the joy their presence brings you. We need to know we matter to each other. We *all* need to know this. Something as seemingly simple as eye contact is enormously important; it's the first step toward showing love, and feeling loved helps us be more resilient.

- **Take an interest in them.** Seek to get to know your kid a little bit more every day by taking an interest in *their* interests, ideas, experiences, and concerns. Choose your moment—after school, while cooking, over dinner, in the car, while walking the dog, at night before bedtime. Expand the stereotypical parent/child conversation from *"How was your day?" "Fine,"* into *"How was your day?" "Fine." "Really? Why was it fine? What happened that was great or not so great? And how did that make you feel?"*

- **Show them you care.** Setbacks are a great time to demonstrate you love your kid unconditionally (no matter what). When they've had a setback, sit with them. Say that you can see it hurts. Perhaps do something to take their mind off of it. Help them think through ways they can achieve a different outcome next time. Tell them the story of something similar that happened to you. But don't fall into the trap of blaming poor outcomes on someone else—the bad teacher, the biased judge, the unfair coach, the mean friend. And don't try to take matters into your own hands. Instead tell them that sometimes these things happen in life, and yet, they also have a lot of control through their own efforts. Reassure them that you love them.

2. **Also, back off.** If we're right there with them as they do everything (or checking up before, during, and after by cell phone), we're undermining their confidence by indirectly sending the message "I don't think you can do this without me." Here's how to build resilience in your kid by letting them have their own experience.

- **Let them make choices and decide how to do things,** such as: what to wear (if they're small), whether it's cool enough to take a coat (if they're in middle school), in which order to do their evening activities, homework, and chores (if they're in high school). Don't micromanage them by checking in with them on every detail or nitpicking every piece of the outcome. It's only through actual experience that kids develop skills and learn to trust their judgments, make responsible choices, and face difficult situations.

- **Let them take risks and make mistakes.** Making mistakes is the only way to learn. Unless your kid's health or safety is truly at stake, risks taken and mistakes made when they've done something that was initially scary or hard will provide a tremendous sense of authentic accomplishment.

3. **Help them grow from experience.** You're not meant to do *nothing* for them—you're just not meant to do *everything*. Here's how to help them grow from their own experiences.

- **After the experience, decision, or choice has been made, engage in a questioning dialogue to unpack what your kid learned from the experience.** If there's a problem, help them think for themselves how to solve it. Say, for instance, *Hmm, that sounds really tough. How do you think you want to handle that?* We can offer advice. We can model a solution in our own lives. But we mustn't do it for them.

- **Continue to set the bar higher.** Humans want to grow and learn, to be capable of more and more and more. As your kid demonstrates her trustworthiness and good judgment, you can give her more responsibility, opportunity, challenge, and freedom. This builds competence, which builds confidence, both of which build resilience.

- **Combat perfectionism.** The phrase "just do your best" is quixotic. *Just* do your *best*? The best is the very best you can give; there is nothing better. How is a child—or any one of us, for that matter—going to manage to always perform at that high standard without losing their minds? What we mean when we say "just do your best" is something more like "do the best you can in that moment" or the even more forgiving "try to give it your best effort." These phrases acknowledge that in any moment a number of factors could weigh against our ability to do our actual best *and* that it's the trying, the effort, that matters.

4. **Build their character.** Too often today our focus is on our kid's academic and extracurricular outcomes and admissions results, instead of on who they are as human beings. Too many of us struggle well into middle age with whether *our* mothers or fathers are proud of what we've done with our lives. Everyone wants to be valued for who we are. A human's worth

comes not from our GPA but from our character, which is our degree of kindness, generosity, fairness, and willingness to work hard, among other things. Character boils down to what we do *even when no one is looking or keeping score*. People of good character are met with kindness, praise, and gratitude from the world, which helps bolster them against the inevitable setbacks they'll experience. Let's build resilience in our kids by showing them it's not their grades and scores and trophies that make us proud; it's their good *character*.

- **Notice them being good.** We can build character by noticing them being good and reflecting back on it with them afterward. For example, if they helped someone reach an item on a grocery store shelf, during the car ride home you can say, simply, "It was very kind of you to help that woman." Or if they gave a sibling or a friend a chance to go first, or the extra turn, you can say, simply, "I saw when you [did that thing], and it was nice of you." These are *not* the moments for "Perfect, wow, you're amazing!" All you need to convey is: *I saw you. I noticed. You're a good person. When you do things like that it makes me proud.* It will feel tremendously good to your kid to hear this, and they will seek to produce more of those moments.

- **Help them develop perspective.** Being aware that there are others who are worse off than they are allows your kid to recognize what they're grateful for. Service doesn't need to be done in a faraway country; in your local community there are people who are struggling to afford food and shelter. Doing service work as a family not only helps the person you're serving, and feels good, but helps your kids develop perspective that will serve them in the moments of their own doldrums and over the long haul.

5. **Give specific, authentic feedback.** Late boomer, Gen X, and early Millennial parents are known for overpraising and for an inability to critique or discipline. Words like "perfect," "brilliant," "amazing," "wonderful," and "great" sound like compliments when they trip off our tongues, but over time they are daggers in the soul of a developing kid and end up undercutting resilience. Using terms like these at every turn gives our kids an inaccurate sense of their skills and talents, and leaves them fearful that any evidence to the contrary means that they are no longer good enough. As a result, as Dweck's research shows, kids are motivated to play it safe in the

classroom and in extracurricular activities rather than take on a higher-level challenge (which may lead to evidence that they are not so brilliant after all). Or they'll push, push, push themselves to the extreme, becoming perfectionists who will do whatever you, their boss, or whomever else's opinion they value wants. We want our kids to build real and lasting self-esteem that comes from making efforts and seeing good outcomes, not from what some third party (including a parent) seems to think of them. Here's how authentic praise and constructive criticism can build resilience in our kids:

- **How to praise.** In the realm of school and activity-based accomplishments and achievements, it's more loving and resilience-building to offer praise that is specific to the task accomplished. For example: (1) For a little kid—*I like how you used all kinds of colors in that picture*; (2) For an elementary schooler—*I noticed how you pointed your toes throughout your whole ballet performance, just like your teacher asked*; (3) For a middle schooler—*You did a good job maneuvering the glue gun to make your school project. That can be so tricky*; (4) For a high schooler—*Your essay on Cyrano de Bergerac made such detailed references to Cyrano's emotional turmoil. You really managed to get inside his head.* Specific praise like this builds confidence because it shows we've paused for a moment to pay attention to what the kid has actually done.

- **How to criticize.** We want our kids to learn and grow, to better themselves, and to develop. The only way they can do that is by having a realistic assessment of their current performance. As with praise, we need to make sure to target the actions or efforts, not the person. Saying *"You left your lunchbox in the hallway overnight and now there are ants swarming all over it. Please go wash it out. No, not later; it'll only get worse."* is much more effective at correcting behavior than saying, *"Why don't you listen to me? I told you not to do that. Now we have ants."* And of course if we swoop in and handle the ants ourselves, we've taught them nothing. We want to criticize the action (which can be corrected) as opposed to saying or implying that our kid is a bad *person* (which can't be changed).

6. **Model it.** As psychologist Madeline Levine said in her talk at our local high school, our kids see us as successful and aren't aware of the twists and

turns and setbacks we experienced—and continue to experience—in life along the way. One of the best ways to normalize struggle and build resilience is to let our kids know when we have, or have had, a setback—such as a failure or disappointment at work, or a falling out with a close friend—and that it got us down for a bit. Let them hear you say that maybe you did some things wrong, or could have done things differently, and you've learned for next time. Let them hear you reflect, and see you smile and move on.

LETTING THE BAD THINGS HAPPEN

Humans make mistakes. We always have, and we always will. Children are no exception; in fact, childhood is the training ground where mistakes are made, lessons are learned, and competencies including coping skills and resilience are developed. Deciding to allow our kids to have those essential experiences—to flail, fail, and fall—isn't just a good way to help them learn and grow, it's the best way. Mistakes can be life's greatest teacher.

Jessica Lahey, teacher, writer for *The Atlantic* and *New York Times*, and author of *The Gift of Failure: How the Best Parents Learn to Let Go So Their Children Can Succeed*,[18] has observed the phenomenon of overparenting in her classroom and written extensively about it. She says that when children make mistakes, parents must remember that "the educational benefits of consequences are a gift, not a dereliction of duty." She writes, "Year after year, my 'best' students—the ones who are happiest and successful in their lives—are the students who were allowed to fail, held responsible for missteps, and challenged to be the best people they could be in the face of their mistakes."

And what about life's so-called curveballs? We *make* mistakes. But sometimes negative consequences result even when we've done everything right. When life throws our kids a curveball, we do them no favors by jumping up and catching it for them unless it's truly a matter of health and safety. They've got to be able to learn to catch those curveballs—or get out of the way—on their own.

In the 2000s, psychologist Michael Anderson and pediatrician Tim Johanson—both practicing in the Minneapolis area—began seeing kids and young adults who seemed to lack the perspective and perseverance that come from making mistakes and experiencing curveball moments. In their 2013 book *GIST: The Essence of Raising Life-Ready Kids*, they write that the main task for parents is to keep their children safe while raising them to adulthood, yet "in many homes, there is more concern about safety, followed by an emphasis on performance, but not nearly enough focus on preparation."

"Preparation," as Anderson and Johanson write about it in *GIST*, means being able to deal with whatever comes. They've fashioned the following list of the kinds of tough situations that offer kids the right preparation for adulthood. Caution: Things on this list might make you wince—which turns out to kind of be the point:

MISTAKES AND CURVEBALLS YOU MUST LET YOUR KID EXPERIENCE[19]

- Not being invited to a birthday party
- Experiencing the death of a pet
- Breaking a valuable vase
- Working hard on a paper and still getting a poor grade
- Having a car break down away from home
- Seeing the tree he planted die
- Being told that a class or camp is full
- Getting detention
- Missing a show because she was helping Grandma
- Having a fender bender
- Being blamed for something he didn't do
- Having an event canceled because someone else misbehaved
- Being fired from a job
- Not making the varsity team
- Coming in last at something
- Being hit by another kid
- Rejecting something he had been taught
- Deeply regretting saying something she can't take back
- Not being invited when friends are going out
- Being picked last for neighborhood kickball

Not only must you let your kids experience these things, you must appreciate their importance. Anderson and Johanson argue that parenting well means "learning to see events you might otherwise try to avoid or dread in your child's life as *growth-producing* events" that build wisdom and perspective. When they occur, we parents should say silently to ourselves, "Perfect, that's perfect—it's just what he needed to happen at least once in his childhood."

Best-selling author and psychologist Wendy Mogel would agree with Anderson and Johanson on this point. In *The Blessing of a B Minus*, Mogel says that letting these kinds of events happen to our kids is the equivalent of "giving them good suffering," which prepares them to deal with the much more serious disappointments and difficulties that will arise in their adult life. By the time our kids leave home, Mogel says, our kids should be familiar with the "wave pattern of feelings" that will go like this: *"I was feeling bad, but now, because I talked to my friend/went running/spoke to my professor/got some sleep/confronted my roommate about her boyfriend sleeping over/wrote up a plan to improve my soccer skills/went to the health center/actually finished some of my work, I notice that I feel better, and my parents had nothing to do with it."*[20]

"I feel better, and my parents had nothing to do with it," the young adult in Mogel's imagined scenario concludes. Indeed. Even though our impulse is to protect and prevent upset, we must step back, muzzle ourselves, and sit on our hands—whatever it takes so that they can figure out that they are capable of handling their discomfort, devising solutions, and moving on.

Eric Scroggins, executive director of Teach For America–Bay Area, has witnessed the right kind of parental engagement giving rise to resilience. "TFA is a tremendous opportunity for growth and leadership for the teacher. The most productive parents see that and try to serve as a sounding board for their children but not for excuse-making. They'll say, kindly, 'You signed up for this. Anything that is worth doing is challenging. What did you expect? How are you seeking out the resources you need and accessing the support available?' The counterproductive parent—the enabler—will say, 'You are in an unfair situation. I am going to do this and do that for you.'"[21]

HOW PRIVILEGE LEAVES US LACKING

In a rather ironic twist, poor and working-class kids, whose parents lack the financial resources, social capital, and sheer amount of time needed to engineer perfect outcomes at every turn, are sometimes fortified by their tougher life experiences and may end up much stronger than their affluent counterparts in the long run, a phenomenon Paul Tough considered in *How Children Succeed: Grit, Curiosity, and the Hidden Power of Character.*[22]

At Aspire Public Schools, a national nonprofit headquartered in Oakland, California, the motto is "College for Certain." The organization offers a comprehensive K–12 education to low-income kids, and Aspire's motto is drilled into the kids beginning in kindergarten. By the time Aspire kids graduate from high school and go on to college, they've been hearing this phrase practically their whole lives. After fifteen years in the business, Aspire now runs thirty-eight schools in California and Tennessee, and has become one of the nation's highest-performing high-poverty school systems. For the past four years, 100 percent of Aspire graduates have been accepted to college. Its teacher training program was profiled on the front page of the *New York Times* in October of 2014.[23]

At Aspire's annual fund-raising gala in 2014, one of Aspire's graduates, Rena Stone, now also a college graduate, spoke about how Aspire shaped her life.[24] "Aspire became my home. It's where I felt safe. Sometimes I would walk to Aspire Monarch Academy and sit in the parking lot. Or, I would sit in Ms. Reed's classroom until eight p.m. bothering her while she tried to work. She never complained. Instead, she would offer to drive me home." Rena then shared a very difficult time she faced in college at Fisk University, a historically black, private liberal arts institution in Nashville. "My sophomore year at Fisk University seemed a barricade, slowing my progression. It was my breaking point and the true test of both my strength and my resilience. The challenge was simple: I could not afford food and housing along with tuition. I had to make a choice between my future and the bare essentials needed to survive. At Aspire, they told me I could change the outcome of my life. Education was the key to changing that outcome." Rena chose to be temporarily homeless and continue with classes. She graduated from Fisk and is now a teacher.

Aspire CEO James Willcox, a graduate of the United States Military Academy (West Point) who served in the army for close to eight years before heading to California to pursue a dual degree (MEd and MBA) from Stanford, has three daughters in their late teens and early twenties. He spoke with me about kids like Rena Stone and his "other (Aspire) kids."[25] He talked of the enormous, largely untapped potential that low-income students have and how they possess a degree of drive and perseverance that's built through hardship and struggle. He openly shares that his own affluent, privileged children simply haven't had the same struggle and hardship, and have never had the chance to build the same skills.

Willcox thinks of resilience as a toolbox with multiple trays of tools. One tray is filled with what your parents gave you. Another is filled with skills from your time in school, and the third tray is filled from life experiences. Every student goes off to college with a toolbox.

"Life experience is where I think students like Rena get an enormous number of tools that kids like mine will not have. The tools Rena has are forged through incredible hardship, and persevering over hard times, actually *seeing* hard times, experiencing them, experiencing very tough choices and tough trade-offs. Most middle-class and upper-income students just don't face the same kinds of tough choices or truly hard times. Rena was homeless for a period during high school as well, and I am certain that experience is a piece of who she is. My children have never had an experience like that, and so they will lack that whole tray of tools when they go to college and start experiencing 'hard times' on their own, for the first time. Rena and every low-income student has huge untapped potential and incredible tools to navigate college and life. The rest of us need to figure out how we're going to give our own children the same kinds of tools, in some other kind of less traumatic way.

"On the flip side Rena went off to college *without* a set of tools that the middle-income and upper-income kids do go with, which is the *expectation* that they will succeed, the belief system that they belong in college. If we can prepare students like Rena with those expectations—with the 'college for certain' mind-set—they are unstoppable. With the grit and perseverance they have inside them, their mind-set becomes not 'Do I belong in college?' but 'Get out of my way.' They can be so much more equipped than kids who really haven't deeply struggled in life. With a college degree and a great education, they're going to change the world.

"The life experience that Rena and other Aspire students have is as cruel as it is invaluable. If we can support them through it, they will have tools that will give them the perseverance and grit to get through anything. And, that's the tool that's the hardest to replicate."

But it can be done.

19

HAVE A WIDER MIND-SET
ABOUT COLLEGES

We live in a Lake Wobegon bubble. We're socioeconomically advantaged.
All the parents have degrees from great schools. You could fill the Ivy
League just with our local high schools. The academics are ridiculous.
The kids who get rejected are in the 98th percentile on the SAT, they're
curing cancer in their free time, and they're building houses. It's crazy for
the parents and it's got to be crazy for the kids.[1]

—William Rivera, father, McLean, Virginia

Over drinks one night with friends, a Palo Alto mother announced that
her son just came home with a B and she had said to him, "What are you
thinking? You think you're going to get into Stanford with a grade like that?
You're going to get into Arizona State and if you think I'm going to pay for
Arizona State, I'm not!" This mother obviously doesn't think highly of Arizona State. Apparently she didn't know that it's in the top ten U.S. produc-
ers of Fulbright Scholars, that one alumna is Susan Cartsonis, producer of
the second-highest-grossing romantic comedy movie of all time, *What
Women Want*, or that the designer of her very own handbag—Kate Spade—
went there.

The truth is that most of us have no idea how to judge a college's suit-
ability for our kids. We salivate over the *U.S. News* college rankings, even
though the list mostly reflects how hard a school is to get into and what a
group of other educators think of it, which is a function of how hard it is to
get into. In his 2007 book *Creating a Class: College Admissions and the
Education of Elites*, Stanford professor of education Mitchell L. Stevens
critiques the widespread use of admission selectivity as a proxy for prestige

or educational quality.[2] He writes that absent a system for accurately evaluating educational quality, the admissions statistics have become not just a proxy for status but "status itself." He considers this a tautology: "The more people want to be admitted to a place, the more elite its diploma." The admissions selectivity stats relayed by *U.S. News* convey absolutely nothing about the quality of the undergraduate education offered at a school or whether it'll be a great match for our kids; nevertheless, we drool.

And our kids notice us drooling. Most kids pick up their Ivy League myopia not only from the *U.S. News and World Report* "Best Colleges" list, but from us, their parents, according to Barry Schwartz, author of the best seller *The Paradox of Choice: Why More Is Less*[3] and professor of behavioral psychology at the liberal arts college Swarthmore. Schwartz has found that "parents communicate to their kids that only the best will do. They communicate this standard inadvertently, but kids adopt the same mindset. And the pressure cooker to get into schools is worse than pointless. My research shows if your attitude to decisions is that only the best will do, this is a recipe for paralysis and dissatisfaction."

When Barry Schwartz gives talks on this subject around the country, he likes to show his audiences a *New Yorker* cartoon by the late Leo Cullum depicting a young woman wearing a sweatshirt that says, BROWN BUT MY FIRST CHOICE WAS YALE. "Today we have a large number of students at great places who feel they really ought to be someplace else. If you walk around with that mind-set, it's going to wreck your college experience. All of these places are *gifts*, but they aren't treated as gifts, because students spend all their time thinking they should have gotten in to a different school. They end up dissatisfied with their college experience for no good reason."

In my view, the parental thinking that leads to kids being dissatisfied with their college experience for no good reason is itself a product of the perspectives of our friend group, our ethnic and social communities, our professional milieu, and our families. This mountain of opinion about status, prestige, and worth (all couched as quality) makes us feel—fear—we can only *really* be proud of our kid—*and perhaps ourselves*—if our kid gets into one of the *most highly selective* schools. This feeling, this fear, becomes a set of blinders we give our kids to wear so they can stay focused on the checklisted childhood we set out for them. It's our kid's life, our kid's journey, our kid's race to run, but those of us who give our kids these blinders then ride our kids like racehorses toward the desired finish line. They run harder and harder, bit between their teeth, careening down this track doing whatever it takes to beat the almost impossible odds, as we nudge and cajole, steer, spur, and whip. Occasionally, our kid is fully prepared to run that race. But many kids would choose a different kind of race, and perhaps a chance to enjoy the ride of childhood instead of racing right through it. Some, we know, are just barely hanging in there.

Remember Larry Momo, the college counselor at New York's prestigious Trinity School, and former Columbia admissions dean? He sees plenty of kids with blinders on.[4] Larry says he knows that his students can be perfectly happy at any number of varied colleges and universities and that part of his challenge is to get his families to think more broadly about an array of options. But he is concerned by a growing trend among his highly able seniors to make the college process into a game to be won rather than a match to be made. "Among the questions we ask students is one that has them tell us the specific schools that interest them among those they believe are competitively realistic. All too often these days, they tell us, 'I'll apply early to Yale and if that doesn't work, I'll apply regular to Harvard, Princeton, and Stanford.' This attitude ignores the different academic and campus cultures of these schools and is about winning the ultra-selective college lottery. We call it the HYPS phenomenon." Larry believes that the hyperselectivity among our most competitive colleges and the eagerness of many others to follow suit is creating a class of college-goers who have "internalized the gamesmanship of the college process making them anxious, risk-averse, overly strategic in their thinking, and old before their time."

The parental mind-set, and the blinders kids wear, lead to more students submitting more applications at the most selective schools. According to the National Association for College Admission Counseling, the number of students who apply to seven or more schools was 9 percent in 1990, 12 percent in 2000, and 29 percent by 2011—and this rise in applications makes already selective schools *appear* to be even more selective than they actually are; it's not that there are *that* many more qualified students applying to top schools, it's that more of those students are applying to *many* more schools.[5] (And at the end of the day each kid can only occupy a spot at one school.) Still, there's no getting around the fact that the odds of getting into the most highly selective colleges are between 5 and 10 percent. That is, the chances are dismal.

Remember Sid Dalby, the admissions officer at Smith College who said,

"If there's a five to ten percent chance of rain, do you wear your raincoat? No. But if people hear five to ten percent chance of admission to a college they think somehow they or their kid'll make it into that five to ten percent." Sid's the one who helped *me* see I'd been kidding myself about my kids' chances of getting into the schools that have those kinds of odds.

Let's look at the odds using a different set of numbers. The twelve schools whose 2013 admission rates were under 10 percent (Stanford, Harvard, Columbia, Yale, Princeton, U.S. Naval Academy, Cooper Union, MIT, University of Chicago, U.S. Military Academy—West Point, Brown, and Alice Lloyd College) have roughly a combined fifteen thousand spots in their freshman classes. There are roughly thirty-seven thousand public and private high schools in the United States. If every high school valedictorian— the student with the highest GPA at each high school—wanted a seat at one of these twelve most selective schools, there'd be room for only 40 percent of them, and not a single spot for anyone else. Add to that the fact that most of these schools admit a good number of international students, and the odds for the U.S. valedictorians, let alone all other kids, decrease further.

We have to pull back those blinders and widen our kid's perspective and our own, or—can't you see—most of us are going to end up at the end of the process, exhausted, dejected, feeling like failures—making our kid feel like failures when instead they should be incredibly excited about this next phase of their lives.

STEP ONE: BE REALISTIC ABOUT THE ODDS

If those of us who place a premium on college *selectivity* could have the courage to pull the blinders back just a tad so as to bring a bit more of the landscape of college into view, we'll find the next most selective schools—a group of thirty schools, which in 2013 admitted between 10 and 20 percent of their applicants. And pulling the blinders back ever so slightly more, we'll find another fifty plus schools that are considered moderately selective, with admission rates between 20 and 33 percent. That makes one hundred schools in total that have admission rates below 33 percent and are considered the "most selective" of the nation's twenty-eight hundred accredited four-year colleges and universities where the overall average admission rate is 63.9 percent. *If* a college's degree of selectivity is our concern (and there's good reason to think it *shouldn't* be; as we'll see later in the chapter, some of the schools offering the best undergraduate education are, as of yet, undiscovered jewels and don't receive a slew of applications and therefore aren't very selective at all), then let's pull back the blinders at least far enough to see the full hundred "most selective" schools. These schools attract very strong faculty and students who are very talented, motivated, and interesting. They are well resourced. Their alumni make a good living, have rewarding jobs, find friendship, and are happy. Isn't that what matters?

I've told you twice that Sid Dalby's straight talk on the admissions odds to highly selective colleges got through to me. Well, I'm not the only person whose mind she changed. One day a New England state court judge approached Sid and said, "I remember when you spoke at our local high school. That talk was the best advice anybody ever gave me. Thanks to you, I was prepared for the outcomes." I asked Sid to put me in touch with the judge. Here's what the judge (who is required by the rules of her job to speak anonymously) had to say:[6]

"I was as competitive as anybody. I went to Yale myself, my husband went to Johns Hopkins, and my daughter, Stefania, can run circles around me intellectually. So we figured she'd go to those schools. I wanted that edge for my daughter."

Prior to Sid's talk, the judge was trying to bring a heavy hand to Stefania's college application process, even though Stefania, a public school kid, eschewed parental involvement, as well as the private college counseling and extra test prep her friends were getting. Stefania's best friend had a "handler" through the process, and the judge thought her daughter should have one, too. Stefania refused. She also refused her mom's offer—request— to review her essays. "What parent *doesn't* review them?" the judge asked me. The judge was left to hover on the sidelines, saying, "You should let me do this! I can help you!" Stefania was undeterred. She wanted to do it herself.

That's about when the judge heard Sid's talk. "I will admit that while I held back, as Stefania wanted, internally I didn't handle it well. I knew how competitive it was to get into these schools. I knew you needed all of those advantages, any little edge you can possibly have. I was willing to spend the money. I fell prey to the fact that everybody else was giving their child that advantage. I was trying to level the playing field. I knew the playing field was stacked and that Stefania was already in the stacked part of the playing field. I wanted the extra goal, so to speak. I tried to find ways to convince Stefania that I was right."

Once she heard Sid's advice, the judge "pivoted," as she calls it. "Once you do that pivot, you feel better," she says with relief, "and you can be a better parent. You can be there for your kid, be supportive of your child."

Stefania applied to a bunch of Ivies and didn't get in, but began to embrace her other options. She chose Barnard, an august, small liberal arts college in New York City, which is affiliated with Columbia University, and which in 2013 had an acceptance rate of 20.5 percent. "Thanks to Sid we had pivoted toward some schools being 'a reach' and we emphasized the positive things at the other schools," the judge says. "Sid saved me. These days a kid can have everything—top grades, volunteerism, athletics—and not get into one of the very top schools; if they don't get in they need you to be 100 percent supportive and say, 'You've pleased us. We're happy. It's all about your having a great experience in college.' That's what matters."

The judge's daughter, Stefania, thrived at Barnard and exemplifies this point made by writer Dan Edmonds in his 2013 article in *Time* magazine: "Students who meet the academic and extracurricular thresholds to qualify for competitive schools will still get into a selective college; it's just less likely that they'll get into a *specific* competitive college."[7] Put differently, if you widen your blinders, college admission isn't a game of musical chairs; everyone is likely to find a place.

STEP TWO: BRAG ABOUT OTHER BRANDS

The judge admits she'd "ruffle" when other parents said, "Barnard? I haven't heard of it." "I would think, 'Well, you *should* have heard of it. What do you mean you haven't heard of it?' I remember being mildly miffed about people not recognizing it. Now I realize I shouldn't have felt that way. I've kind of learned from it. People are in the moment when those college acceptances come. Many parents feel that the choices your children make reflect on you, and therefore you have a vested interest. I think that's probably not a good attitude. It's the child's future, not yours. Your vested interest should be in the well-being of your child."

If you know of Barnard, it's hard to imagine anyone boo-hooing over it, let alone not even knowing about it. This story is a great illustration of the brand-name brouhaha plaguing so many of us. So, some people haven't heard of New York's highly regarded Barnard. For others it's Wisconsin's Beloit, or Maine's Bates, Ohio's Antioch, or Oregon's Reed. These are just five examples of the fantastic colleges at least some swath of people "haven't heard of." We're obsessed with the brand name of colleges as if we're teenagers obsessed with designer jeans all over again, dying to have what it seems everyone else has, too immature or lacking in confidence to break out and go with what fits us—our kid—best.

To combat the brand-name brouhaha, when I'm out and about in Palo Alto I try to sprinkle the names of the top hundred schools "no one has heard of" into conversation. And I encourage my friends to do the same. Oh, and the dance I did when Minnesota's St. Olaf's College began sponsoring my local NPR station! I could picture moms and dads listening to the radio while commuting to work or kids' activities saying to themselves, *"St. Olaf? What's that? Must be good if it's promoting itself on NPR."* Indeed. When more of us can start bragging about the great education our kids are getting at schools "no one has heard of," our peers will start to pay attention and it'll help them pull back their blinders and give their kids—all kids—permission to survey the fuller landscape of possibility and make the choice that's right for *them*.

STEP THREE: UNDERSTAND THE ADVANTAGES OF GOING TO A LESS SELECTIVE COLLEGE

In 1999, researchers Stacy Berg Dale and Alan Krueger studied what happened to students who were accepted at an Ivy or a similarly highly selective institution but chose instead to attend a "moderately selective" school (that is, within the top hundred).[8] It turned out that such students had on average the same income twenty years later as graduates of the elite colleges. Krueger and Dale found that for students bright enough to win admission to a top school, later income "varied little, no matter which type of college they attended." In other words, the student, not the school, was responsible for the success.[9] Today admission deans at the most highly selective schools acknowledge that thousands, even *tens* of thousands, of their applicants are qualified for admission. With the number of spots in the freshman class at these schools ranging from a minimum of 150 to a maximum of 1,700, the vast majority of those qualified thousands will have to go elsewhere. The good news is, Krueger and Dale's research indicates they'll do just as well financially. Might they perhaps do even better, by other measures?

That is, can going elsewhere *help* you? A few thought leaders think so. In *Excellent Sheep*, Bill Deresiewicz notes that at *U.S. News's* top twenty universities, usually over 90 percent of students graduated in the top 10 percent of their high school class. "I'd be wary of schools like that," he says. "Not every ten-percenter is an excellent sheep, but a sufficient number are for you to think very carefully before deciding to surround yourself with them. Kids at less prestigious schools are apt to be more interesting, more curious, more open, more appreciative of what they're getting, and far less entitled and competitive. They tend to act like peers instead of rivals."[10]

Lou Adler, a guru in corporate recruitment and author of Amazon best seller *Hire with Your Head* and *The Essential Guide for Hiring and Getting Hired*, agrees. He cites students at Ivy League university Cornell as an example.[11] "When you meet Cornell kids, they're all smart but they're different kinds of kids. They just seem to be more grounded. They think they're in the 'bottom' tier of the Ivy League and all these people are 'above' them according to some people's measure. It may have deflated their ego, but they emerge with stronger interpersonal skills, are more down to earth, and aren't full of themselves."

Malcolm Gladwell goes so far as to say that attending the most highly selective schools can even *harm* you. In his best-selling book *David and Goliath: Underdogs, Misfits, and the Art of Battling Giants*, Gladwell explains that most kids *shouldn't* attend the most prestigious schools they get into, because at *every* college it's the top kids who get the most attention, resources, and opportunities that lead to greater success in grad school.[12] Going to a place where you will be in the bottom half of the class not only means you won't get goodies such as attention from faculty and access to select experiences in your chosen major, but it also damages your self-esteem, says Gladwell. If you want college to be the strongest possible springboard for what will come next in your life, Gladwell advises going to a college where you know you can be in the top 5 or 10 percent *there*. The only exceptions to this rule are students from underrepresented backgrounds for whom attending a name-brand school seems to provide a bump in after-college options regardless of where they rank in their college class.

The list of undergraduate schools attended by first year students at Harvard Law School illustrates Gladwell's point. The approximately 540 members of their class of 2016 came from 171 different undergraduate schools.[13] The complete list of colleges attended—featuring some schools you've heard of and many more you surely haven't—is in Appendix A.

Hiring information from the nation's second-largest recruiter of college graduates—Teach For America—makes the same point. TFA hired fifty-nine hundred incoming teachers in 2013 who came from a whopping eight hundred different colleges. You can find the sixty schools that contributed the largest number of corps members in Appendix B.

And then there's Google. In an interview with *New York Times* columnist Thomas Friedman, Google's senior vice president of people operations Laszlo Bock stated it's not the GPA or the school you attend, it's your skills that determine whether you'll be hired—things like the ability to learn on the fly, to know when to step up and step back as a leader, ownership, and humility.[14] Of Google's hiring philosophy, Friedman writes, "Beware. Your degree is not a proxy for your ability to do any job. The world only cares about—and pays off on—what you can do with what you know (and it doesn't care how you learned it)." Bock warned Friedman of the pitfalls that can come from having too successful a pedigree: "Successful bright people rarely experience failure, and so they don't learn how to learn from that failure."

There's that failure thing. Rearing its head. Again.

STEP FOUR: USE BEST COLLEGE LISTS OTHER THAN THE *U.S. NEWS* LIST

U.S. News's rankings have us by a stranglehold, but their algorithm has nothing to do with the quality of an undergraduate education, about the undergraduate experience more broadly, or about career and life outcomes of graduates. Whether a young adult will find a true sense of fit and belonging at a school—and therefore make the very most of it, soar, and thrive—is a function of so many more variables than *U.S. News* surveys. We parents will get much relief, and lessen the stress both we and our kids experience as our kid approaches the college admission process, if we take a broader view of what makes a college great, and worth our considerable expense.

U.S. News's competitors are many, and each in its own way attempts to provide a feel for what it would be like to be a student at a particular school, and get an education there. They include the *Fiske Guide to Colleges*, currently the best-selling college guide, authored by Edward B. Fiske, a former education editor at the *New York Times*. The *Fiske Guide* prides itself on making a subjective analysis of each school based on its extensive contacts at hundreds of schools nationwide, and recently has begun ranking colleges based on the quality of the experience and their price tag, which they term "Best Buys." *Forbes* magazine produces its "America's Best Colleges" list, ranking schools based on the quality of the education they provide, the experience of the students, and how much they achieve in life after graduating. *Niche* produces the "College Prowler" rankings, a result of surveys of over 300,000 college students, as well as objective data pulled from elsewhere. Schools at the top of its lists focus on student happiness, academic strength, diverse community, healthy environment, and low student loan default rate. The *Princeton Review*'s college rankings are solely comprised of student opinion, based on surveys of 130,000 college students nationwide, and looks at everything from best classroom experiences and professors, to financial aid, to politics, to the social scene, to the beauty of the campus, to happiest students.

A different kind of list entirely is *Colleges That Change Lives*, a short list bearing the names of only forty very small schools utterly focused on building the kind of living and learning communities in which undergraduates engage in rigorous work done in close contact with faculty and with one another, and emerge well prepared for the world of work, and to be an engaged citizen of the world.[15] The list was originally compiled by Loren Pope, a former education editor at the *New York Times* who became one of the nation's first experts on college admission with the publication in 1990 of his best-selling book *Looking Beyond the Ivy League: Finding the College That's Right for You*, which profiled two hundred schools.[16] To create his list of the very best schools for undergraduates, Pope visited campuses to get a feel for the gestalt, the ethos, and the vibe. The forty schools that made Pope's cut were those for which the resounding sentiment of students, alumni, faculty, and administrators alike was "this school changed my life."

Pope died in 2008, but not before the nonprofit organization Colleges That Change Lives (CTCL) was founded to carry on his legacy. It's a small operation—the website is updated by volunteers, the executive director is a part-time consultant, and there are no paid staff—but there are enough committed resources and workers to ensure that Loren's philosophy lives on. Most of the colleges on the CTCL list are moderately to not particularly selective, admitting in the range of 50 to 80 percent of applicants. A few have lower admission percentages owing to their bigger brand name (such as Reed College in Portland, Oregon). The website is www.ctcl.org.

Another eye-opening resource is *The Alumni Factor*, a list that's been around only since 2013 and offers another twist on the typical college rankings paradigm (www.alumnifactor.com). Founded by a corporate titan and father who found the *U.S. News* college rankings data woefully lacking in information that would allow his kids to make meaningful choices, he turned his focus to how alumni from various schools fare out in the world, and how they feel about themselves and their lives. He surveyed hundreds of thousands of alumni from over 225 colleges and universities about these life outcomes:

intellectual development

social and communication skills development

friendship development

preparation for career success

immediate job opportunities

willingness to recommend the college to a prospective student

value for the money

would you choose the college again for yourself?

average income of graduate households

percentage of high-income graduate households (>$150K annually)

average net worth of graduate households

percentage of high-net-worth graduate households (>$1million)

overall happiness of graduates

In addition to these factors, *The Alumni Factor* ranks schools based on alumni views on social and political issues such as immigration, gun control, gay marriage, affirmative action, abortion, racial profiling in law enforcement, school prayer, and media bias. A prospective student and their parents can see the schools at which alumni are most likely to be in favor of or against such issues, which provides a sense of whether a student would feel a sense of inclusion or exclusion in the sociopolitical environment at the school, in its classrooms, and in its dorms.

Perhaps most fascinating is *The Alumni Factor*'s "Ultimate Outcomes" section, which ranks schools according to a combination of two attributes, such as schools whose alumni have attained great financial success *and* intellectual capability, financial success *and* happiness, or friendships *and* intellectual capability, among others. The seventeen schools ranking in the top fifty on all six of the "Ultimate Outcomes" are, in alphabetical order:

Bucknell University

College of the Holy Cross

Dartmouth College

Gettysburg College

Middlebury College

Pomona College

Princeton University

Rice University

Scripps College

Swarthmore College

United States Air Force Academy

United States Coast Guard Academy

United States Military Academy

United States Naval Academy

University of Notre Dame

Washington and Lee University

Yale University

Sam Moss, chairman of the board at the Association of College Counselors in Independent Schools (ACCIS), the professional organization for college counselors at private high schools, was an early adopter of *The Alumni Factor*. Moss is dean of college guidance at Darlington School in Rome, Georgia, a hundred-year-old college prep school, with kids from twenty-two states and forty countries. Moss has been in college counseling for forty years. This is a guy with every conceivable college guide on his shelf. He tells me *The Alumni Factor* "completely changed the dialogue I'm able to have with students and parents."

Sam counsels his students as follows: "Look, if you apply to one of the super-selective 'reach' schools, you have to understand you're as good as anyone but 95 of 100 will be denied. Those denied look just like those admitted; you can't consider it failure. It's like the Georgia lottery. If I win I'm thrilled but I'm not going to spend the next nine months worrying, when the odds are better elsewhere *and* you can be equally as successful and happy at those other schools." That last bit is what *The Alumni Factor* shows really clearly, he tells me. "Whether it's financial success they care about, intellectual rigor, or happiness in life, there are an awful lot of schools whose alumni achieve it. It has kids and parents focus on colleges in a different light. Outcome versus input. What I like best is it doesn't ask respondents to rate other institutions, it only asks them to comment on their own institution and their own satisfaction with the education received."

Sam heard about *The Alumni Factor* when he went back for his college reunion at Sewanee—The University of the South, located in Sewanee, Tennessee. In his remarks that weekend, University Vice-Chancellor (equivalent of President) John McCardell Jr. told the gathered alumni, "There's a new way of looking at evaluating colleges and our alumni seem to think pretty highly of us." Given that Sam advises students about college selection for a living, his ears perked up. McCardell—formerly president at Middlebury College in Vermont—had good cause to be pleased by Sewanee's results in *The Alumni Factor*: sixteenth overall among liberal arts colleges, first in intellectual development, first in social development, second in whether alumni would recommend it to a current student, fourth in friendship development, and ninth in preparation for career success. I'll confess I had never even heard of Sewanee, but knowing all of this made me excited to dig in and find out more. I learned Sewanee boasts twenty-six Rhodes Scholars, and one notable alumnus is Samuel F. Pickering, the inspiration for the character Mr. Keating in the film *Dead Poets Society* played by the late Robin Williams. It's also one of the test optional schools (which we'll discuss in the next section) and has a very welcoming 61 percent acceptance rate.

LinkedIn's University Rankings—launched in the fall of 2014—is also likely to make a huge splash with college counselors, prospective students, and parents. Currently the world's largest professional network, with 100 million users in the United States and over 300 million members worldwide, LinkedIn has more data than any other source on which schools' graduates have the greatest chance of being hired in any industry. LinkedIn can also see what happens to people who major in any field, including so-called useless fields—such as English or philosophy—not only answering the question "Will I get employed?" with a loud "yes," but showing "the long tail" of career options for people with those majors. Their new University Rankings pages rank schools based on how successful recent graduates have been at landing desirable jobs in every conceivable field.

Whereas every type of list we've discussed so far is based on a qualitative or quantitative survey of some kind, LinkedIn's rankings come from data it continually receives from its ever-growing, ever-updated information on hundreds of millions of professionals. In that sense it is "evergreen," says

Christina Allen, the former director of product management at LinkedIn who oversaw the new rankings product.[17] These alumni career outcomes are the proof in the pudding that successful professionals come from all kinds of schools and majored in all kinds of things. "The beauty of these data and the system," says Allen, "is that you can look at a broader list of schools, or at fields of study your parents hope you won't choose, and you can make an argument that yes, those graduates do go on to have good careers." These data are full of surprises. Allen tells of a computer scientist at LinkedIn who came out of Maharishi University of Management in Iowa— not a school that comes to mind for most people when they think of great places to get a computer science degree. Yet this guy was an incredibly well-trained computer scientist, so Allen was intrigued. "When I looked at my data on Maharishi graduates, I saw they're placed in very high level individual contributor and management roles at companies like Microsoft, Google, and Amazon." The LinkedIn data (www.linkedin.com) may well disrupt the *U.S. News*–led stereotypes about which colleges are worth applying to.

STEP FIVE: CONSIDER COLLEGES THAT DE-EMPHASIZE TEST SCORES

In addition to expanding our list of which colleges are worth a serious look, it's worth examining colleges that take a more holistic view of candidates instead of letting test scores drive the review process. Applying to such schools can not only lessen the stress of the process but can facilitate a better student–college match.

According to FairTest: The National Center for Fair and Open Testing,[18] over eight hundred schools are SAT/ACT optional or "flexible." These eight hundred schools will look at your SAT/ACT scores if you submit them, but they're far more interested in other measures of academic capability and potential, as evidenced in high school grades, the essay, letters of recommendation, and, in the case of test "flexible" schools, in other types of testing. The list of test optional universities and liberal arts colleges can be found at www.fairtest.org, and includes the following schools that will be familiar to those who peruse rankings:

American University

Arizona State University

Bates College

Bowdoin College

Brandeis University

Bryn Mawr College

Clark University

College of the Holy Cross

Dickinson College

Franklin and Marshall College

Mount Holyoke College

Pitzer College

Sewanee—The University of the South

Smith College

Wake Forest University

Wesleyan University

Worcester Polytechnic

One school made headlines in 2014 for being not-*even*-test-optional; that is, they don't want to see your scores. Period. That school is Hampshire College, located in Amherst, Massachusetts.[19] In Hampshire's press release announcing the decision, dean of admission and financial aid Meredith Twombly stated, "The SAT is essentially one test on one day in a given year. Students' high school academic records, their history of civic engagement, their letters of recommendation from mentors, and their ability to represent themselves through their essays trump anything the SAT could tell us." Hampshire is on the "Colleges That Change Lives" list, has a notable alumni community that includes Netflix chief communications operator Jonathan Friedland, documentary filmmaker Ken Burns, cognitive scientist Gary Marcus, and Academy Award–winning actress Lupita Nyong'o, among others. In 2014, Hampshire had a 70 percent acceptance rate.

Bard College, located a few hours north of New York City in Annandale-on-Hudson, New York,[20] made headlines in 2014 for its "revolutionary college-admissions experiment,"[21] which gives applicants an option: go the usual Common App route or respond to four of twenty-one essay questions instead. If an applicant chooses the latter, their essays will be reviewed by

Bard faculty and if each essay gets a B+ or higher, "You're *in*, period. No standardized test, no GPA, no CV inflated with disingenuous volunteer work."[22]

In a 2014 article in *Slate*, Rebecca Schuman calls the new Bard entrance exam "the country's only true alternative application to an elite school."[23] She continues, "The Bard Entrance Exam aims for exactly the kind of student who, for any number of reasons, doesn't fit inside that infernal perfection cage—who is instead, as Bard's vice president of student affairs and director of admissions Mary Backlund told me, 'someone who really likes learning,' but perhaps 'couldn't be bothered with what they saw as the "busy work" of high school, and instead invested themselves in things not perceived as "academic" in some places, like music or the arts—or just reading on their own.'" Bard's 2014 acceptance rate was 38 percent.

One of my favorite examples of an elite school that does things differently is Tufts University in Medford, Massachusetts. Now, Tufts is in a different category of selectivity from the two other schools above—admitting only 17 percent of applicants in 2014. But I've got them here because they're a great example of an elite school that sees testing as *one* element of their holistic admissions process rather than *the* element that guides their evaluation process. "We are willing to see testing in a more elastic context," says Lee Coffin, dean of undergraduate admissions.[24] I have some sense that Coffin's methodology gets it right because in 2014 they admitted a smart, fabulous, hardworking Palo Alto kid I know who was passed over by the higher-ranked schools. I also like Tufts because they've embraced the "gap year" concept, to offer students the chance to build maturity, confidence, and leadership skills before starting college.[25]

Coffin is known in his field as a "throwback dean." While many deans talk the talk of a more holistic approach to college admission, Lee is known for walking the walk. Most school leaders eye their annual position in the *U.S. News* rankings and attempt to move themselves up on the list by pushing for more and more applicants (even while turning away 80 to 95 percent of them). Lee credits the Tufts board of trustees and university president for being "very sane" by comparison. When he was hired some years ago, the president told him, "I'm not going to be obsessed about application volume, acceptance rate, or yield. I'm more interested in having you deliver a class to Tufts each year that has a higher degree of intellectual engagement than the class who came before it."

Lee's been at the task ardently ever since. "Our first task is to certify an applicant's eligibility for success in our curriculum—to know they can be successful with the rigorous curriculum we'll make available to them." But as at so many schools, 75 percent of Tufts' nineteen thousand applicants make that cut. So, Lee tells me, next they look for the kinds of qualities that reflect Tufts' founding ideals: community mindedness, using the intellect to make a difference in the world, ability to be a creative thinker, and kindness. "Kindness?" I say to Lee. "Yeah," Lee says. "I don't want an undergraduate community of cutthroat robots." Stanford's dean of admissions and financial aid Richard Shaw often expressed the same philosophy to me. To get at the kindness factor, Lee looks well beyond grades and scores in his review of each applicant.

Why doesn't he just skim the top of the academically qualified list and call it a day? It would certainly take less time. One reason is to "shape a class," as Lee and his admission colleagues around the country call it. Also, he wants the academically excellent but not necessarily "the *best* in that pile; the *best* often don't have a whole lot else going on. I'm not going to admit a statistical supernova just because they're a statistical supernova. You've got a big GPA and supercharged scores via aggressive test prep, but are you intellectually *engaged*?" A political science professor at Tufts told Lee he was noticing an interesting pattern with seniors at Tufts who are applying for the very prestigious Truman and Rhodes Scholarships. "The ones with the biggest numbers don't always interview as well as the person who is maybe a half step behind them in the statistics—the A- student versus the A student, or the A instead of the A+. The person a half step behind is intellectually engaged and has something to say. They seem to be more fully formed humans. The ones who've been coached to take tests and get As don't always do as well when you get them off script."

Lee asks applicants "what makes you happy?" as one of the options for the supplemental essays. Critics call this question silly, but to Lee, "Happiness is such a primary human need. Asking a high school senior 'what makes you happy' is such an important question." One young woman wrote about old books—the way they smell, feel, and sound when you flip the pages. One young man wrote about babysitting his three younger brothers. Of all the options for the supplemental essay, this question was the most popular *and* was the one with the highest acceptance rate.

FOCUS ON FIT AND BELONGING

Over the course of my career in academia, prospective students and their parents sought my advice on how one should go about choosing colleges. My standard answer was: "It's all about fit and belonging." I'd say, visit schools and after all the official hoopla—info sessions, videos, tours—go find some real students not employed by the school and say, "Hi, I'm thinking of applying here. How do you like it?" After that icebreaker question, then ask, "So what would you change about it, if you could?" The answer to the second question speaks volumes about an institution. (It might also speak volumes about the idiosyncrasies of that particular student, so be sure to ask three or four different students.) In the end you'll have a wealth of information not only about the school but about yourself. What resonated? What turned you off? You want a sense of the faculty—are they involved in undergraduate teaching or will you be taught by grad students? What about your fellow undergraduates—do you want to be with those kids in the classroom, in the dorm room, on the quad, in the lab, in clubs, and just hanging out? Finally, I tell students, ask yourself, "Can I be *myself* there? Will I be valued for who I *am*?" A gut feeling of "yes" in response to those final two questions is what I mean by having a sense of fit and belonging.

Now that I've left Stanford, I've gotten involved in some college admissions counseling myself, where I try to serve students (though it's their parents who hire me) as an antidote to a virulent process. A multibillion-dollar industry is devoted to telling kids how to manufacture their childhood so as to "be" what colleges seem to want. Self-described "packagers" marauding as professionals, and other third parties (including parents) heavily edit or outright write the most personal, private part of the process, the college essay, for kids.

As dean I didn't enjoy interacting with manufactured kids, and as a parent I find the whole concept distasteful. I can't change that system, but when I have the chance to sit down with a high school senior I'm interested in the actual kid in front of me and try to put them front and center in the application. Who are they? *Not who do they think they're supposed to be, but who are they, actually?* What makes them tick? What bothers them in the world? What enchants them? How do they know what they know? We toss the phrase "find your passion" around as if most seventeen-year-olds have one or should hurry up and find one, but the truth is that most don't yet. They're young human beings with only a budding sense of self and of what they might want to be and do in the world. That they're engaged in learning is what counts. That they're curious. That they want to grow, and serve, and one day do something of purpose and meaning in the world. That they're en route to figuring out what that is. To me, that is enough. If through continual questioning I can help a high school student identify those truths about themselves, they can write a meaningful essay that will be appreciated by a college admission officer.

Parents thank Lee Coffin at Tufts "for running an admission process that felt humane." What we can take from Lee's approach, and from the admissions approaches at Hampshire and Bard, and the colleges that are SAT/ACT optional or flexible, is that there are processes for college admission that can feel like much less of a grind. What we can take from *The Alumni Factor,* "Colleges That Change Lives," and LinkedIn's University Rankings is that adults who are successful in life—across personal and financial measures—have attended all kinds of colleges and universities, some of which we've heard of and most of which we haven't. What we can take from all of this is that if we focus on encouraging our kids to look for schools where they can feel a sense of fit and belonging, there are a number of tools to help them figure that out. And if we pull back those blinders that have us and our kids focusing on only the most highly selective schools and be proud of where our kids apply and get admitted—as did the judge profiled earlier—things will turn out just fine.

A college experience is four long, potentially wonderful, potentially life-changing, years in the life of a developing human. Frank Sachs, director of college counseling at The Blake School in Minnesota, says, "College is a match to be made, not a prize to be won." Indeed. The prize is when our kids go to a place that's truly right for them and thrive.

20

LISTEN TO THEM

As parents have become increasingly hell-bent on manufacturing kids who might gain admission to the *U.S. News* top twenty, Anne Ferguson has been one of the many high school guidance counselors standing ground on the front line guarding the kids. She is the senior associate director of college counseling at Phillips Academy in Massachusetts (known as "Andover"). I spoke with her on the phone in February of 2014, right after she'd kicked off the college admissions process with her current batch of juniors and their parents.

"When we first meet our eleventh-grade students we ask them several things: 'Write down on an index card the first word that comes to mind when you think about college.' The most common responses were 'SAT, stress, freedom, independence, applications.' Then we ask, 'If you could say one thing to your parents, what would it be?' The kids scrawl messages on index cards, things like, 'I know you love me and you're trying to do the best, but can you just back off?' Next Anne meets with the parents of these eleventh graders and has them take an index card and write a note to their child. If she hasn't shared the student cards with the parents first, the parents write things like, "Strive for the best," "I know you think you can't get into Harvard but try." However, if she has shared the student cards, the parents write things like, "You are completely in charge," "I'll totally supportive of you."

When Anne shares the students' messages with parents, they squirm.

They then write their more encouraging message to their kid, and "it gets very warm and fuzzy and parents say 'that's not what *we're* doing,' and everyone commits to doing the right thing." But when the application process starts to heat up, "the magic of that parent session wears off. A lot of parents go back to being their neurotic selves."

Anne sees the parents' anxiety impact students. An eleventh grader came to Anne's office to initiate the conversation about college applications, and as Anne assembled her thoughts and materials, trying to decide how she wanted to proceed with this particular child, she looked over at him and saw him sitting with his head in his hands. She stopped talking, put her materials aside, and paused. Then she asked him if he was okay. The child said he was not. He told Anne his father wanted him to attend Andover so he would get into Harvard. Then he confessed, "I'm not doing well in math. Harvard's not going to happen." The boy said he wasn't sleeping well and had nightmares.

"We college counselors are the ones who try to be the gatekeepers, to look out for the children," Anne tells me. Anne will try to say to the boy's family, "This is a lot of pressure on your kid. Why not let him enjoy this experience and see what happens?" In the meantime, she took a compassionate tone with the kid holding his head in his hands in her office. "I know you're not going to believe this, but there is nothing more important than your health. The specific college is not important. If your health isn't good, you won't survive at college." He believed her. I imagine he was relieved to be with someone who cares.

Many of us parents are used to exerting a good deal of control over our kids' lives to achieve specific outcomes. But with more kids applying to more places, colleges make tough choices and the secret sauce for admission to any particular school these days is anyone's guess. As a result, the state of the college admissions game, and a parent's lack of control over it, leaves parents "terrified." Anne knows if she can just get parents to think more broadly, by opening them up to a wider range of wonderful possibilities, the whole process can be much less stressful. But it's extremely challenging to navigate what can feel like a minefield—for parents, for kids, and for Anne.

In striving, ambitious, and competitive communities, such as the one in which I live, not taking time to listen to our kids starts early. I asked a former Palo Alto mom named Maeve, who moved to Bend, Oregon, for a less high-strung quality of life, for her impressions of the different parenting environments.[1] "Where it works well in Palo Alto is where parents have a consciously communicative relationship with their children and can invest a lot of time in them," she said. "Where it doesn't work in Palo Alto is the constant running around and not hearing what your child is saying. We found we couldn't really communicate within our family in the middle of all the busyness and external obligations. We wanted the chance for unstructured communication and just hanging out with each other."

Maurina, a mom from Santa Clarita, California, said something similar to me: "We're yelling at them to get out of the house. Yelling at them to get ready for baseball. Yelling at them to get their homework done. Home is not an oasis. Home is a disaster."[2] What if we—all of us, stay-at-home parents and parents who work outside the home—disengaged from some of the craziness of all the external activities so as to make more time to just consciously *be* with our loved ones?

HOW TO REALLY LISTEN TO YOUR CHILDREN

The American Psychological Association advises that listening and talking are key to a healthy relationship between parents and children— particularly teenagers. The following is based on the APA's "Communication Tips for Parents."[3]

1. **Be available.** If you have more than one child, focus a bit of time on each one-on-one. Pick the time when you know that child is most willing to talk. Is it bedtime? The car ride to practice? A weekend morning when little is going on? When you've found the right time, initiate the conversation. Don't start with a question that's on *your* mind—show an interest in what they've been doing or what matters to them. Teenagers often feel their parents only want to talk about grades, accomplishments, or college applications. Show them you care about *them*—their interests, joys, and concerns. If you do that, then you'll be in a better position to raise the topics you're concerned about, such as when they're going to start drafting their college essay.

2. **Let them know you're listening.** Stop what you're doing and listen. Make eye contact. Listen without interruption, even if what they're saying is hard for you to hear. After they've spoken, repeat it back to them. You might say, "So it sounds like you're really enjoying this. . . ." or "I'm hearing you say that this is really stressful. . . ." Ask them if they want your advice or specific help in problem solving, or if they just want you to listen while they vent.

3. **Respond in a way they will hear.** Kids often test us by telling us part of the story and gauging how we react before saying more. If you listen carefully and encourage them to talk, you may hear the whole story. Kids will tune us out when we start to get emotional or angry, so be mindful about how you're coming across. Focus on their feelings, but try to keep your own very balanced. Say what you feel and think without dismissing their perspective. Don't argue about who is wrong or right. You might say, "I know you disagree with me. This is how I feel about it."

In the process of researching this book, I had the opportunity to listen to many young adults. As a way of practicing your ability to "listen" and as a way of learning why it's so important to listen, I offer up three young adult stories for you here. It was hard to choose whose stories to share. I went with a college freshman, a college senior, and a grad student, who embody the values and capabilities I think we'd all like to see in our adult children.

BRANDON'S STORY: FREE TO BE ME

Brandon hails from the suburbs of Dallas, Texas, where high school football is like *Friday Night Lights*. He played multiple positions on his high school team, including safety, receiver, cornerback, tight end, and linebacker. When I spoke with him in the summer of 2014 he was nineteen years old and had just completed his freshman year at the very selective Rice University in Houston.[4]

Brandon's mother had him when she was in college, and "she would pass me around from person to person," he chuckles. "I was free to discover what I wanted, learn what I wanted, and do what I wanted from an early age." He spent three years at Carroll Senior High School, a public school in Southlake, Texas. When his mom and stepdad got divorced his junior year, he moved to the Bay Area to be with his father and stepmother. He spent senior year in San Mateo and attended Aragon High School, also a public school.

"I've always behaved independently. In sixth grade I played trumpet out of pure interest, not because my parents forced me to do it to get ahead. I played for two years, and was good at it, but I didn't like it as much as football so I quit. My parents were fine with that. A lot of my peers here at Rice used to play the violin or piano. But when I ask them why they don't play here—there's a piano in our common room right down the hall—they'll say, 'I'm not interested. My parents made me play it. I didn't choose it. It's just something I've always done.'"

"In high school I chose a lot of advanced classes. Going into my junior year of high school I *hated* English. I planned to take AP chem and math, but I told my mom I wasn't going to take AP English. She pushed back. 'What's your reasoning?' When I said I didn't want to work that hard, she said, 'You should *always* work hard. You shouldn't be saying that.' She asked questions and built upon what I would say in response, like a questioning counselor. She pushed me but what I did was my choice.

"My stepdad, being a guy, was a little more authoritarian. He was like a head coach. He'd train me off the field, do all he could to prepare me for the battle on the field, which was life. But on the field there was nothing he could do for me. The direction I would move was up to me.

"When it came time to write the college essay, I wrote that thing completely on my own. I had my parents read it once, and then came my mother's dreaded red pen. I talked with her about it and then, as always, I went upstairs and decided which changes I wanted to make and which not. Often I ignored the red pen because I thought my way was better. Whether on my schoolwork or my college applications, the red pen was never the ultimate authority.

"Many of my peers' parents were as involved in the college admissions process as their kids were. They were writing the essay together, or they were paying someone else to write it. The essay is supposed to be coming directly from the student's heart, not from their parents or somebody they paid. It should be a representation of the person's character in its purest form. They're supposed to be revealing themselves for who they actually are.

"When it came time to apply, I chose schools where I could be more successful and have the resources I wanted available to me. I applied to Stanford because it's a great school, but I didn't get in. I applied to some Ivies, Rice, and some state schools in California. When it came down to it, it wasn't my parents' decision where I'd go to educate myself for my life. It's not their life or their education. It's mine. That's what I thought. That's how I always viewed it."

Brandon wasn't recruited to play football for Rice, but early on they approached him about playing. He wanted to put his academics over athletics, and said no. "The irony set in four months later when I wanted to play but it was too late." So he joined the rugby team instead. "I hung out with a lot of cool guys and met a lot of new people around campus. It was a really good choice for me. I'm going to stick with it all three years if I can." There's an expansiveness to Brandon's voice, like anything is possible.

Brandon is premed, as is 70 percent of his class by his estimate. To fulfill the premed requirements he is majoring in biochemistry and cell biology. "I'm also really interested in Latin so I am doing a double major in classical studies. Maybe I'll go to Rome senior year and dig in the archives. I'm also interested in the neuro part of health. So maybe I'll do some neuro research." Brandon sounds just plain excited.

"I see a lot of very rigid students doing premed because their parents were like 'You're going to be successful. Premed is the best thing to do. You don't have a choice in the matter.' With my parents both being in finance, I suppose they'd want me to do that. But I can explore and study what I want. If I observe something interesting, I decide hey I want to learn more about that. I have intellectual freedom. My interests come from within."

Brandon knows students who say they were "helicoptered" growing up. "They're not driven by anything internally. Knowing what you want to do and how to go about doing it is a life skill. Take applying for classes. Kids who had overinvolved parents have trouble doing that in college. I see kids who may say they 'want to be a doctor.' An adviser has told them what they need to take but they don't know how to go about preparing themselves for the medical field because they don't understand the *how*. They've never had to contemplate the *how*. They've always had someone telling them *how*. A friend of mine talks to his mom and dad once a day to review his schedule and what he did that day. He's not able to set his own goals. Even now, he has to ask his parents if it's the right thing to do. I want to say something but I have to let him be who he is.

"I don't want to downplay the role my parents have played," he concludes. "They've been great. They've been really supportive and provided all the means. The best choice they've made in regards to raising me is letting me choose my own path."

EMMA'S STORY: MY SO-CALLED USELESS DEGREE

None of us want our kids to have a "useless" degree and end up flipping burgers for the rest of their lives while living on our couch. So when I came across a 2014 article in *Time* called "Why I Let My Daughter Get a 'Useless' College Degree," I wanted to hear more.[5] A week later, I was on speakerphone with the writer, Randye Hoder, and her "useless-degree"-holding daughter, Emma.[6]

We spoke in the spring of 2014, mere days after Emma graduated from Scripps College, an elite, small liberal arts college for women located southeast of downtown Los Angeles, along with its four sister colleges—Pomona, Claremont McKenna, Pitzer, and Harvey Mudd. Emma's so-called useless degree is in American studies. It happens to have been my major as well.

Emma's college experience began two thousand miles to the east, at Oberlin, another highly regarded small liberal arts college, located in Ohio. While Oberlin turned out not to be the right fit for Emma, a first semester course there called Introduction to American Studies turned Emma on to the field that would become her intellectual home.

"When I started college I didn't have this sense of 'I want to be a lawyer, I want to be a doctor, or whatever,'" Emma told me. Looking through the Oberlin course catalog she was drawn to the topics that the AmStud class would cover, including colonialism, Native American history, the prison industrial complex, and urban food issues. The sheer breadth of topics on the syllabus, plus an "incredibly captivating" professor, hooked Emma. "American studies allowed me to explore and end up studying what it turns out I wanted." When she decided to transfer from Oberlin, she was pleased to discover that Scripps, too, offered a strong program in American studies. When she arrived at Scripps she was proactive about meeting with the department chair and declaring the major. Her focus became food, politics, and culture.

As Randye's *Time* article had made clear, she and her husband were supportive of Emma's choice to major in American studies. They embrace the philosophy that a person is best served in life by having gotten a great education and by finding their passion, both of which were happening for Emma. But Randye told me she could appreciate the concerns of parents whose kids want to pursue a field with no obvious career ladder. "There's a tremendous amount of information out there now on the whole idea of 'return on investment' with college. As a parent you're anxious about whether your kid is going to get a job in this economy and in this world if they're an English major, American studies major, or, God forbid, a major in the politics and culture of food!"

"It's the fastest-growing field!" Emma yelled from the background, overhearing her mother. "I got awesome internships!"

"But we didn't *know* that at the time," said Randye, laughing. Even for someone like Randye, who embraces the value of the humanities and has written that "STEM subjects should not be society's only answer to helping the next generation thrive in a competitive world," recent articles equating a major with financial success were a bit nerve-racking.

At times, Randye also found it challenging to explain Emma's choice of major to friends. Over time, however, she realized she was feeling a need to *justify* Emma's major and decided she no longer had to do so. "I was over-explaining in an attempt to rationalize how Emma's chosen path will turn into a steady paycheck. It's as if her employment status were a referendum on the choices that my husband and I have made about her education. In retrospect, I'd hit a common pitfall: equating Emma's personal success with my own success as a parent."

If Emma was hip to any of these concerns, it didn't affect her. Her senior thesis was "First We Cook: An Exploration of Why Americans Should Return to the Kitchen—And What It Will Take to Get Them There." In it she examined the trend of fewer people cooking food at home, the cause of this mid-twentieth-century lifestyle change, and efforts to reverse this trend such as community gardening, food education, and combating food deserts. She'd had a fantastic summer internship the summer prior with a website called Food52, founded by *New York Times* food editor Amanda Hesser, where she tested recipes, contributed to the editorial side of the house, and had great female bosses, all while living in the very happening city of New York. And when she returned to campus and began plugging away at her thesis, her classmates were working on completely different, fascinating topics. "One girl was writing about how country music has changed post-9/11, another was researching a historical figure who wrote women's guidebooks, someone else wrote about grief from a psychological angle. It was so stimulating."

I was on the phone with Emma so I couldn't see her face as she spoke. But her language was rapid, her tone was weighted with authority, and her voice was confident and clear. Emma reminded me of a former student of mine, Jeff Orlowski, who was also pretty sure he knew what he wanted to study, even if it made some others ask, "What are you going to do with *that*?" When Jeff got to Stanford he considered philosophy and other subjects that allowed him to explore human existence. He decided to major in anthropology, which he hoped to combine with his considerable skill in photography. His dream, he told me during his freshman year, was to work for *National Geographic*. A few years after graduating Jeff became the director, producer, and cinematographer of *Chasing Ice*, the Sundance and Emmy Award–winning film that drew a nation's attention to melting glaciers and the impact of climate change, which he *sold* to *National Geographic*. I know nothing about the politics and culture of food, yet was captivated by Emma's explanation of her studies and interests. It was like listening to Jeff Orlowski all over again. Sure, some people might raise a questioning eyebrow. But none of that mattered to Jeff, or now to Emma. They know themselves. They've got purpose. This is what passion looks like.

STEFANIA'S STORY: I HONESTLY THOUGHT
I COULD DO IT MYSELF

Stefania—the daughter of the New England judge we heard from earlier, who refused her mother's oft-offered help in the college admissions process—is now twenty-six. After graduating from Northampton High School, her public school in Northampton, Massachusetts, Stefania did indeed go off to Barnard, and she thrived. As Malcolm Gladwell suggested might occur in such a situation, as a top student at Barnard she was admitted to many prestigious law schools. In a complete turnaround, her mother, the judge, wanted her to go to a lower-tier law school that was offering a full ride. But, true to form, Stefania refused. She was wait-listed at Harvard Law and then admitted. She is delighted to be a student there, loans and all. When I caught up with her she was a rising "3L" (third-year student) spending a summer splitting her time between a law firm and a nonprofit organization in Washington, D.C.[7]

"Everything really worked out for me. Ultimately how I went about the college application process was very important. I learned I could get into Barnard on my own and that's pretty awesome, and I gained confidence from that; and I did really well there all on my own, which was also a big confidence builder in the long run.

"Applying to college, well, *I honestly thought I could do it myself*," she tells me. I find her emphatic tone of voice incredibly poignant; it tells me how atypical it is for students to undertake the college application process entirely on their own. "I did my own work in high school and did well, so I thought I could do well in the world without help. Also my friends similarly situated to me in the hierarchy of high school had parents who were going the route of SAT tutoring and having people help them with college apps. I said to myself, 'Well, I'll do it alone, and I'll show you that I can do just as well as you without getting any help.' So that definitely motivated me. In hindsight this mind-set was immature, kind of like cutting off your nose to spite your face. I certainly would have felt that way if I'd been rejected all around." But she wasn't.

Her friend had a "college handler" and went to an Ivy League school, and is now in a Harvard graduate program. "We ended up in the same place. She wasn't a very spoiled hand-held person; I think she would have gotten where she was without help."

I ask how "spoiled hand-held" people fare in college. "People like that complain a lot. *A lot.* Students will put up with complainers to varying degrees but professors will not. They are real professionals. They really care about their subject area. To them this is not just a career, it's a passion. They have no respect or tolerance for the student who thinks, 'You're here to serve me.' When students act like they're entitled to their education or complain about the quality, professors can spot it a mile away. It's detrimental to their relationships with people who will end up mattering in terms of mentorship and grades.

"Knowing that I had the integrity to do the college application process by myself kind of set a benchmark for me in my head. Every time I made that choice to do my own work, it reinforced that value for me. In high school I saw a lot of parents effectively writing their kids' college essays. I saw plagiarism in college. We see a lot of that in the workplace as well. I feel that when you know you have to do your own work that knowledge builds on itself.

"I'll honestly admit that's the long view of my experience. For teenagers, and parents looking at teens, I think there will be that disappointment and struggle; it's emotional not getting into schools you want to get into. But that's not necessarily a bad thing. There are a lot of hidden lessons in that. Starting off in a place where I didn't have everything I wanted made me work *so much* harder to get what I didn't have. I ended up loving Barnard. And I feel really, really blessed to have a spot at Harvard Law, and I really do not take it for granted.

"When people ask for advice on which college to apply to, the thing I say most is you really can turn any college experience into something to brag about. The name on the diploma doesn't matter. No matter where you go to college, you can find something—grades, work, extracurriculars—that will allow you to craft a really impressive narrative for grad school or jobs.

So, don't go for the brand name. Go to a place where you can be happy and do well. I guarantee when it comes to applying for jobs or grad school, you'll write that narrative and they will choose you over the person who went to a 'better' school but has nothing impressive to show for it because they were unhappy the whole time. The dud from Harvard is not going to succeed over the really vibrant person from George Washington University. I was happy at Barnard, and was able to succeed there and turn that success into something more successful. Go to a college that will allow you to craft the best narrative."

I ask Stefania how parents are helpful in college. "What I saw that worked well was parents being there on an emotional level, especially as a freshman. It's a pretty turbulent time in someone's life. What I saw parents doing was being that person on the phone. 'Mom, I'm so stressed, I got a bad grade, I don't think people like me.' You just need to vent or cry and you don't know anyone yet, and even later on when you do, you're more comfortable being that vulnerable with your parents about that stuff.

"But I have a friend who graduated Barnard with me who really still doesn't make a move without them. Not to say you shouldn't discuss big-life decisions with your parents, but it's more than that. Their opinion means so much to her that I don't think she would ever go against it. So they still have an enormous amount of control over her. She has a job in a city she hates that's not really going anywhere and she knows it, but she won't leave because they tell her, 'You made a commitment; you don't even believe what you're saying.' She really relies on them for life advice and emotional support. When you're twenty-six you know your life better because you're not living at home, and you know your experience, feelings, and desires. It's detrimental because she's not following her heart or taking risks. Her parents are risk averse. But a parent is always going to play it safer than you would because you're probably the most valuable thing in their lives. There is no downside to *them* of you playing it safe."

PART 4

DARING TO PARENT
DIFFERENTLY

21

RECLAIM YOUR SELF

> Nothing has a stronger influence psychologically on their environment and especially on their children than the unlived life of the parent.
>
> —Carl Jung

Catharine Jacobsen, a Seattle parent and senior college counselor at Lakeside School, got an important reality check when as a young mother she called her own mother to complain about being cold, wet, and muddy on the sideline at her kid's soccer game.[1] Catharine's mother was not especially sympathetic. "I have no idea why you're standing out there," she said. "You aren't showing your kids anything. If you want to show them that athletics are important, you should be going on a run yourself. Or if you want to show them what is valuable to you, go home and read a book, or get together with some of your own friends, or go to a play and then come home and talk about it. Why don't you go do some stuff of your own? That's you getting a life. Your kids will observe that and think, 'Okay, that's how you get a life.' And they'll want to go get one. But the way it is, they're going to get to be twenty-five and think, 'I never saw grown-ups living a life. I only saw them doing stuff for me, driving around, standing somewhere on a Saturday morning.'"

In middle- and upper-middle-class families, we practice what sociologist Annette Lareau terms "concerted cultivation"[2]—where, thanks to a packed family calendar, plus the belief that to be a good parent means to always be there with and for our kids, and the looming threat that the Joneses are doing more to get their kids ahead than we are, every day feels like a leg in a race of unknown duration, and every task feels to be of consequence. Whether we work outside the home, are stay-at-home parents, or have fashioned a hybrid of these options, the background noise crowding our thoughts as parents is, *Did our kid do well in life today, and if not, what does that mean for me*—her, *what do I need to do about it, and how can I fit that solution*—*whatever it may be*—*into my already incredibly hectic life?*

With all that is on our calendar and on our minds related to our kid's care, and academic and extracurricular support and enrichment, there is little room for us to focus on looking after our own adult selves. According to *Parenting* magazine, parents experience depression at twice the rate of the general adult population.[3] According to a 2010 survey conducted by the American Psychological Association, the average parent reports experiencing a level of stress that is twice the level parents themselves consider healthy.[4] In her book *The Sweet Spot: How to Find Your Groove at Home and Work*, University of California–Berkeley sociology researcher Christine Carter reports that 66 percent of working parents say they aren't getting everything done that they want to, 57 percent feel like they don't spend enough time with their families, and 46 percent feel they have no time for leisure.[5] Award-winning journalist Brigid Schulte calls these persistent feelings "The Overwhelm" in her 2014 book *Overwhelmed: Work, Love, and Play When No One Has the Time*.[6] Even if we are not among the depressed or highly stressed in the parent population, if we are overparenting there's a good chance we are still doing some degree of living life through our kids instead of living our own life, which is healthy neither for us nor for our kids.

Each of us humans is on a life path that ought to be constructed by our choices, paved with our experiences, and aimed in the direction of our dreams. For parents, our path included having children who in turn have their own paths to follow. But our path continues on. If we walk our kid's path with and for them, we're not only depriving them of the chance to build self-efficacy—that basic human need to do for *oneself*—we're also depriving ourselves of the chance to continue to construct our own path. If you've ever mistaken your child's achievements for your achievements, your child's happiness for your happiness, your child's life for your life— even if this confusion happens only every now and then—this chapter is especially for *you*. You see, you still matter even though you've become a parent. You've got to make sure you're walking your own life path—not only for your own sake, but for your kid's sake, too.

The research shows that kids think of parents as their *heroes*. They look up to us more than they look up to any other adult figure in their lives. We are their biggest role models. But when they look up to us, can we be proud of what they see? Do we show them a harried, stressed-out person who is constantly staring at a smartphone, tablet, or computer and who seems to care only about whether homework has been completed, and grades and scores have been obtained, and the soccer carpool runs on time? Or do we show up in their lives as a person who walks through the world feeling good about ourselves, doing work that plays to our strengths and resonates with our values, and who makes time for meaningful human connection with them and with others? Our kids notice *everything* we do and don't do. As Catharine Jacobsen's mother pointed out while Catharine stood on the soccer sidelines that cold, wet day, instead of showing kids that a parent's primary purpose and function is to hover over a kid and facilitate all of their interactions and activities, we need to show them—through the choices we make, the activities we undertake, and the principles we value— what it actually means to lead a fulfilling adult life.

It's not selfish to make ample room for the things we value in life: It's critically important. In order to be good role models, we need to put ourselves first. This may sound completely incongruous to you (women in particular may struggle with this, as often we are raised to put others' needs before our own), but an airline's worst-case-scenario directive about putting on your own oxygen mask before helping others is extremely practical advice for living life generally. The same advice comes from financial planners who tell us to save for our own retirement before saving for our kids' college expenses, and from eminent twentieth-century psychologist Carl Jung, who admonishes parents to lead our own lives so our kids don't end up dealing with the neuroses that come when we don't. Whether from air travel safety videos, financial planning, or the field of psychology, the wisdom boils down to this: We humans are at our most capable and are of most use to others when we've first looked after ourselves.

All of the previous material in this book has addressed how to successfully raise your kid to adulthood. The question *this* chapter asks is *Are you an adult?* Do you take care of your basic needs, think for yourself, work hard, and make time for relaxation? Are you resilient? Do you chart your own path? Can you look past what others think is popular or best and make choices that feel right for you, all things considered? Of all of these attributes that characterize a self-actualized adult, I'd wager that most of us who overparent have in common a wobbly ability to think for ourselves, that is, sometimes we let the powerful tide of other people's fears and opinions sweep us through life. Sure, we're hard at work and at parenting, often to the point of exhaustion, but toward what end? Working hard to lead a life dictated by the neuroses of others leaves us little wherewithal for relaxation and enjoyment, to look after our basic needs, and to weather the struggles that inevitably come. And of course, the notion of charting our own path goes by the wayside when we're caught up in keeping up with others or living our child's life as if it is our own.

So what can you do to reclaim yourself and be the kind of human and parent you really want to be? Drawing upon the work of positive psychology researchers Christine Carter, Barbara Frederickson, and Martin Seligman, as well as my own lived experience, here are my thoughts about how to do so.

HOW TO LOOK AFTER YOURSELF
(YOU'LL BE A BETTER PARENT AS A RESULT)

1. **Discover your passion and purpose, and chart your path accordingly.** If you're overfocused on your kid, you're quite likely underfocusing on your own passion. Despite what you may think, *your kid is not your passion.* If you treat them as if they are, you're placing them in the very untenable and unhealthy role of trying to bring fulfillment to *your* life. Support your kid's interests, yes. Be proud—very proud—of them. But find your own passion and purpose. For your kid's sake and your own, you must.

After years of living well astray from it, I eventually found my passion. I had gone to law school to pursue my interest in social justice work, and while there I developed a keen interest in family law where I could work on behalf of neglected kids. But I found myself swayed by the value others placed on the prestigious and lucrative career of corporate law and chose to go that route instead. Nine months into my career as an associate at a great law firm, I had high blood pressure and a knot in my stomach every Sunday at around noon at the thought of having to go back to the office the next day (sometimes, of course, I was in the office on Sundays). I was working long hours but that wasn't the problem. The problem was that I didn't care much about the issues central to the work. I was making plenty of money but feeling purposeless. And purposelessness was turning into hopelessness. I was twenty-seven years old.

One weekend I sat bawling in my backyard, thinking, "This is *not* what

I thought I'd be doing with my life." Visualizing my life as a map, I realized that I had strayed to the periphery. The added trouble was, I didn't know what a more rewarding and fulfilling path through life might be. I tried to figure this out on my own by taking a piece of paper and brainstorming a list of what I thought I was good at (skills) and what I loved doing (interests and values), and then I searched for an intersection of the two lists because my sense was that meaningful work lay there. That exercise showed me that I was a people person (skills) and I want to help marginalized people thrive (interests/values). It was also validation that family law just might have been the right path for me; unfortunately, by this time I had had it with law. Instead, I decided to seek a job where I could support students. On my fourth attempt after three years of job seeking, I landed a temporary job at Stanford. I knew if I could just have a chance to demonstrate what I could do, I might find permanent work. And that's what happened.

That little exercise was how I found my passion—helping humans on their path—then I had the courage to embrace it, and then I found meaningful and fulfilling work accordingly. Your passion might be something you pursue through employment, or volunteer work, or a hobby. But whatever part of your day is reserved for your passion, have you found that pursuit yet? Take some time to think this through. Make a list of what you're good at and your interests and values, as I did way back when, and, I'd add, ask yourself how you want to *be* in the world (meaning how you want to show up and behave in the lives of others) and what you want to *do* in the world (meaning the type and manner of work that appeals to you). For further guidance you can turn to any number of sources, from the teachings of life coaches such as Barbara Sher, author of seven best-selling books including *I Could Do Anything if I Only Knew What It Was: How to Discover What You Really Want and How to Get It*, to the insight that comes from knowing your Myers-Briggs type (www.myersbriggs. org/) or "Strengths" (www.gallupstrengthscenter.com/), to the wisdom and research of spiritual leaders such as *New York Times* best-selling author Eckhart Tolle, whose works include the *A New Earth: Awakening to Your Life's Purpose* (an Oprah selection).[7] Your passion and purpose can be absolutely anything you want, as long as it's not "my kid."

2. **Learn to say no.** If you're going to live in furtherance of your passion, you're going to have to do fewer of the things that don't align with your passion, and get good at saying no. The overparenting herd always has more

ground to cover: one more field trip, bake sale, school auction, PTA meeting, volunteer opportunity, community meeting, social obligation, soccer practice, and carpool. Don't get me wrong—these things matter to the well functioning of the school and community. But you may be doing well more than is needed, and for the wrong reasons (to keep up with the Joneses). University of California–Berkeley sociologist Christine Carter urges that to live a happy life, 95 percent of our time should be spent on the five things that matter most to us.

So, step back. Compare your sense of passion and purpose to how you're presently living your life. Is there alignment? What needs to change? What needs to go? Take a look and ask yourself if you really need to do all of it and to the degree the herd seems to require. Resist the urge to make the PTA meetings run like a corporate board or to treat your turn making soccer snacks as a referendum on your worth as a human. Can you do these activities in a manner that is good enough rather than "perfect" so you can have time for the other things that matter more to you? Can you say no to the things that feel like petty obligations? Keep in mind that no one will say no for you. You have to start speaking up for yourself even if others may resent you for wanting to step back (or for having the guts to say so). And when we need to explain why we can't do whatever is being asked of us, often less is more. Try saying with a firm smile, "I'm sorry, I can't"; it will go a lot farther than a rambling, apologetic explanation that leads others to second-guess your decision.

3. **Prioritize your health and wellness.** We're of less use to our kids, loved ones, colleagues, and friends if we're not physically and emotionally well. When was the last time you had a physical? Are you eating in ways that are good for your body, exercising in a form you enjoy, and removing unhealthy addictions from your life? Consider reducing your stress and increasing your self-awareness through meditation or yoga. If you ever think, *I can't start exercising, learn to meditate, or cut down on my bad habits right now because I need to get my kid through this baseball season or their school applications*, I'm suggesting that you stop that kind of thinking and, instead, seriously consider that you have your priorities—or, at least, the way you address your priorities—backward. In the spirit of putting on your own oxygen mask first, these are not things to deal with once everything else falls into place—these are things you should deal with *so that everything else can fall into place.*

4. **Make time for your most important relationship(s).** Harvard psychiatrist George Vaillant, the main researcher behind the longest study of human experience ever conducted (known as the Harvard Grant Study), found when looking at the study's subjects at the end of their lives, "The only thing that really matters in life are your relationships to other people," and "Happiness equals love—full stop."[8] If you're in a relationship, are you giving it enough attention? Do you look each other in the eyes, let each other know you matter, take time to talk and listen at the end of each day (about more than your kids)? Is there enough intimacy?

This love of which Vaillant writes need not be romantic—we can love and be loved by friends, neighbors, our children, and other relatives. Vaillant says it's the "capacity for empathic relationships" that matters. Being in empathic relationships with other humans helps us feel good about ourselves and stay focused on the things that matter most to us.

5. **Interrogate your relationship with money.** First, if you are one of the few among us who are wealthy, ask yourself if money is what you value most. If so, all right, that's your choice, but allow that your kid may want to live by a different value system. Also, if you take a moment to think about it, valuing money above all else may be a *cause* of your overparenting, because you're seeking to ensure that your kid also reaches high-income-earning heights. Remember how overparenting hurts kids, particularly when a parent is determined for a kid to pursue a certain lucrative path. Your kid's life is more important than an assets comparison lifestyle.

Second, if you are among the vast majority of us who aren't wealthy, take a serious look at your financial situation. Are you running on fear? Do you worry, *How will my kid support themselves in this economy? How will we pay for college if they don't get a top SAT score and the financial aid that will come from that?* Are you racking up coaching, tutoring, private school, and summer camp bills in a desperate race, fearful that you are not keeping up with the Joneses? Your fear is not going to help your child succeed in the world. Put on your financial oxygen mask first by (1) finding work that is meaningful to you, (2) living within your means, and (3) tending to your retirement fund. Looking at your own financial situation may be scary, but eventually being more on top of things will reduce your stress level and fear. And by educating yourself to behave better with money, you will begin to model for your child a better way to live. If you don't qualify for much financial aid (don't assume this will be the case; check out the College Board's website—www.bigfuture.collegeboard.org—to familiarize yourself with the financial aid rubric), your kid can get a terrific education at a more affordable institution, such as a state school or city college that doesn't have the brand heft but nevertheless features smart kids and great professors. Your kid has a long life ahead of them and is going to do fine. And they'll be even finer if *you're* fine.

6. **Practice kindness and gratitude.** Learning to say no is so important because we can't do all the tasks people ask of us if we're going to live the life we want to live. But what we *can* always offer—which is free of cost, takes little time, and benefits others as well as ourselves—is kindness and gratitude. Do kind things for people you know, or for strangers. Let someone into the long line of traffic in which you're sitting. Open a door for someone (and thank the person who holds the door for you). Smile at the cashier or barista and ask them how *their* day is going. Don't rush past other people's needs—the dropped keys, the ripped bag, the holding-too-many-things-so-I-can't-open-my door—help them out. Do something even bigger like volunteering on a regular basis to help those in need in your community.

Where kindness is about *doing*, its partner, gratitude, is about recognizing what's been *done for* you. It's acknowledging the cook, whether he or she is a stranger or your own partner. Or the janitor. Or the store clerk, the nurse, your colleague, or your kid. When someone does something that makes your day brighter, more beautiful, easier, or less painful, look them in the eye and say so. Tell them you appreciate what they've done and be specific. Your words will make them feel valued and will make you feel happier, too.

Kindness and gratitude suffer from seeming simple—so simple that some of us are tempted to discard them as fluffy, unimportant nonsense. But not only should they not be discarded, they're essential to our well-being. In *Raising Happiness: 10 Simple Steps for More Joyful Kids and Happier Parents*, Christine Carter summarizes numerous studies on the positive health effects of helping others and concludes people who are kind and helpful to others live longer, healthier lives, have fewer aches and pains, and experience less anxiety and depression.[9] And in her book *The Sweet Spot*, she writes of a study at the Greater Good Science Center at Berkeley that showed that people who jotted down something for which they were grateful, every day for just two weeks, showed higher stress resilience and greater satisfaction with life and reported fewer headaches, less congestion, and a reduction in stomach pain, coughs, and sore throats.[10] Over time if you offer more kindness to the world, and notice and speak up about what you're grateful for, you'll be inviting a great deal more happiness—and good health—into your life. And you'll be a better parent.

YOUR KID NEEDS A HUMAN PARENT—NOT SUPER MOM OR SUPER DAD

Remember Quinn from Chapter 12—the Silicon Valley mom who was trying to be super mom? After being told by a close friend that she seemed miserable and was making others miserable as well, Quinn saw a psychiatrist who said she sounded anxious and depressed. Quinn saw her kids, her husband, and her friends who were seemingly ever more successful as the causes of her less than robust mental health, and the doctor didn't disagree but offered medication nevertheless. Quinn agreed to take Lexapro—and joined the community of 1 in 4 women who receive notable relief from prescription medications for anxiety and/or major depressive disorder.

But to Quinn's mind what mattered just as much as the medication were the major changes she made to her life once the most urgent symptoms of her anxiety and depression were stabilized. "I began to look at things more clearly and decided to drop out of the mom competition game. I quit the PTA. I took a step back and started to say no to things. I stopped trying to prove I was super mom. I let my kids do their own thing, make their own mistakes, fight their own battles. I was happier. My kids didn't care that I wasn't running the book fair anymore. They laugh a little bit about that. I'm so much closer to my kids now that I let them go and do things on their own. The only child who noticed the change, I think, was my oldest (now a college sophomore). I think when I was stressed out and trying to do too much, I took everything out on him. I also hired a babysitter so my husband and I could spend more time together. That was like the best thing. I've felt so at peace."

And remember Rachel, the straight-A student from Los Angeles who, while maintaining a 4.0 in college, was a daily user of alcohol and Adderall who ultimately tried to take her own life? Well, Rachel is not the only member of her family to have undergone a profound, positive transformation after that devastating experience; her mother reconceived *her* way of being in the world as well.

"My mother was a stereotypical neurotic Jewish mother," Rachel says.[11] "What was fascinating for me was that as I began to change, as my life began to take a different turn, my mom began to change also. She had been very controlling—not out of malice; she just loved by trying to take care of things. She has changed more than I have. I've watched her parent my younger siblings. She no longer needs to control every single detail. She now coaches other parents on how to let go."

After speaking with Rachel, I spoke with Rachel's mom, Leah, about how her mind-set changed in response to Rachel's addiction, and about what she tells other parents experiencing similar struggles.[12] Leah tells parents that she learned a key lesson the first time she was in Beit T'Shuvah director Harriet Rossetto's office with her husband seated beside her: Rossetto, a formidable presence behind her vast desk, asked Leah and her husband what was most important to them, and Leah replied, "I just want Rachel to be happy." Turning her deep, probing eyes on Leah, Rossetto laid into her with advice Leah now passes on to other parents: "Saying you just want your kid to be happy puts enormous pressure on the child. They feel if they're not happy, they're failing. Periods of unhappiness are okay and our kids need to know that; it's the struggle that makes you who you are."

Rossetto advises that the goal of a kid's happiness is actually a dual burden, negatively affecting both child and parent. "The whole family system has to change," says Rossetto. "The child is addicted to pleasure seeking. The parent is addicted to controlling a child's choices and behaviors and creating a perfect human being, so their emotions are a mess. If the child is having a good day, Mommy and Daddy are happy, and if he's not having a good day Mommy and Daddy are in despair. Severing that umbilicus is what our family program does. A parent's well-being can't be dependent on whether or not the kid is having a good day."

In addition to counseling other parents, Leah puts Rossetto's wisdom into daily practice with her two youngest children, who still live at home. She says, "At times we make life too easy for kids by not letting them experience things we think of as traumas but that are, in reality, not all that bad, and we solve problems for them instead of letting them stew over some things. When my kids are storming about the house, it's tempting to feel 'My kid is angry at me' and to want to do something about it. Now, I can accept that they can be unhappy or angry, and I don't need to soothe their feelings; it's okay."

Rossetto has impressed upon Leah the importance of separating her own identity from that of her children. So Leah's overarching advice for other parents is "Spend time working on your*self.*" Leah says, "My happiness—Rachel and I joke now—is really independent of hers." And that's a very good thing.

22

BE THE PARENT YOU WANT TO BE

We need not wait to see what others do.

—Mahatma Gandhi

Mahatma Gandhi is credited with the pithy phrase "Be the change you wish to see in the world," but it appears that he actually said something both more philosophical and more practical: "If we could change ourselves, the tendencies in the world would also change. As a man changes his own nature, so does the attitude of the world change toward him. . . . We need not wait to see what others do."[1]

What if changing the way we parent didn't involve waiting for all of society to change but was as simple as acknowledging the ideas presented in this book, and pivoting our approach to raising our kids accordingly? What if we pivoted toward these principles:

1. *The world is much safer than we've been led to believe, and our child needs to learn how to thrive in it rather than be protected from it;*

2. *A checklisted childhood designed to lead to a narrow definition of success robs children of the proper developmental opportunities of childhood and can lead to psychological harm;*

3. *A child learns, grows, and ultimately succeeds by diving into what interests them, doing and thinking for themselves, trying and failing and trying again, and developing mastery through effort; and*

4. *A family life is richer and more rewarding for all when parents aren't hovering over and facilitating every moment of a kid's life.*

Many of us can visualize a life lived according to these beliefs and can almost feel the relief that would come if only we could make the changes in our family routine that would lead to this new life. But making such changes is not psychologically simple. In communities in every region of this country, the overparenting model is like the popular kid we want to follow, or the bully we have trouble standing up to because we fear being harmed, ridiculed, or left out. Even when we know we want to parent differently, says author and sociologist Dr. Christine Carter, it can be frightening to "stray from the herd." In her book *The Sweet Spot: How to Find Your Groove at Work and Home,* Carter says we need to "muster extra courage" to do things that will likely be perceived by others as threatening to the status quo, dangerous, or just plain stupid in the context of their worldview.[2] It really can seem to require Gandhi-like faith and fortitude to be willing to be the first in our extended family, our neighborhood, our kid's school community, or our professional milieu to stray from the herd and stop overparenting. Who among us dares to go first?

STANDING UP TO OTHER ADULTS—SIMPLE SCRIPTS FOR COMPLICATED MOMENTS

Healthy lives are lived in communities with others. So how can we parent differently from our community and still get along? If you want to be an authoritative (*not* authoritarian) parent and aim to raise your kid to be an independent adult, be decisive and inclusive in what you say. Make sure to give other parents a psychological "out." What you do or say in any situation will vary based on the age of your kids, the situation at hand, and your readiness to speak up about what you believe, but these samples of things to say may remind you of your new path and help you speak up.

1. **When parents referee.** When there are disputes over toys and turns, don't get involved. If another parent approaches you, politely and confidently say, *Maybe I'm old-fashioned but I really prefer to let the kids try to work it out. I know it can be hard to step back, but I think it's how kids learn.*

2. **When parents chauffeur.** If another parent wants to drive your kid somewhere, but you want your kid to walk, bike, or take public transportation, say (again politely and confidently), *No thanks, I really prefer that she go on her own. I'm confident she has the street smarts she needs, and I want to help her become more independent.*

3. **When parents fetch and carry.** If you overhear parents lamenting about having to drive their kid's forgotten lunch box, backpack, or homework to school, be as straightforward as you dare and be gentle; you're just sharing a different perspective. You might try with a smile or a laugh, *I make my kid suffer; otherwise, he'll keep assuming I'll do it.*

4. **When parents are personal assistants.** Let your friends know that you're putting an end to playing concierge and will no longer do for or clean up after your child beyond an age when it's appropriate to do so. Try, *Of course I can do it faster or better, but she's got to learn this stuff for herself. I'm not going to be that parent who shows up to do everything for them in college!*

Say you're with some friends, out for a walk, having coffee or cocktails, or at book club, the golf course, or the PTA, and your kid texts or calls you with a minor catastrophe. Let your friends hear you say, *Sorry to hear that, honey. How are you going to solve that?*

5. **When parents do their child's homework.** Whether your kid is in kindergarten, twelfth grade, or somewhere in between, raise your hand at Back to School Night and ask, *What is your policy about parental involvement in homework? Can you help us understand where and how to draw the line when it comes to math/essays/school projects?* If you do this in every class, you risk becoming *that* parent. But someone has to get this point across and it might as well be you.

If your kid wants you to be overly involved in homework by solving it, figuring it out, or writing it for them, try saying, *I've been a fourth/sixth/eighth grader before. Now it's your turn.* And let your friends know how you handle "the homework problem"; try, *I could do it for them but then I'll always be doing it for them. I don't want them to feel like they can't do it without me.*

6. **When parents do all the chores.** Be an advocate for the importance of chores. Let people know that homework and extracurricular activities don't give kids a pass from household chores. Without chores, kids miss learn-

ing how to pitch in and how to work hard at tasks that may be unpleasant. Share what your kids do for chores, and maybe you'll hear other great chore ideas from friends.

When you're at PTA, Scouts, or some other meeting involving projects, parents, and children, be the voice in the room that says, *How can we give our kids more responsibility for this job/activity/event/project? I don't want them to just stand around while we do all the work.*

7. **When parents chart their kid's life path.** Picture yourself at a social function where people are checking in with each other about their kids. When you're asked what your son or daughter is interested in, or is headed toward academically or career-wise, say, joyfully, *I really have no idea; it's entirely up to him,* or *I want her to just figure out what she's good at and what she loves, and to make the most of that, whatever it is,* or *He's really into hiking/painting/books/puzzles/numbers; I'm not sure what he'll do with that but I'm supporting him in developing that talent and interest.*

When you hear people say that their kid "has to" do a certain activity at a certain level "for college," laugh or sigh with a smile as you say, *Well, we've stopped trying to predict what some small set of colleges may want, and we've started just living our life, which turns out to feel much better.* Be prepared for stunned silence. Smile big and say, *Seriously!*

8. **When parents have a narrow (sometimes very narrow) mind-set about colleges.** I've told you I've joked that if we all memorized the names of five good colleges that "no one has heard of" and strategically name-dropped those colleges into conversation with our friends and colleagues, we would start to shift the perception about these places both in our community and in our own minds. But now I'm not joking. I think we should give it a try. Go to the College Board's Big Future website (www.bigfuture.collegeboard .org) and play with their highly interactive college search tool. Read up about the Colleges That Change Lives (www.ctcl.org). Check out *The Alumni Factor*'s list of colleges whose alumni achieve the "ultimate outcomes" of financial success *and* happiness, or intellectual growth *and* friendship (www.alumnifactor.com). Find five to ten colleges you can get really excited about and start to envision your kid attending them instead of going wherever "everyone" (including perhaps you) thinks your kid "should" go. Tell your friends, *I'd just love it if my daughter would consider Carleton or Whitman or our strong City College,* and offer one reason why.

Note: this task isn't about getting your kid to go anywhere in particular—that's their decision, remember? This is about widening your own mindset while letting your kid hear that you're excited about colleges that don't have cutthroat admission standards and dismal acceptance rates. Also, stop referring to the college application process in the first person plural (we)! *We're* not doing the applications (remember?) and *we're* not the ones going to college.

Finally, talk openly about how the odds of getting into certain schools are horrid, and the stress simply isn't worth it. In talking with friends, shrug your shoulders and smile and say something like, *The most highly selective schools have to reject thousands of qualified applicants. That's life. A great college education is to be had at many, many places. We're not going to stress about it.* Also, your kid really needs to hear this come out of your mouth, so say this in front of them as often as you can.

9. **When parents don't listen to kids.** Our kids wish we were less stressed out about their every outcome. They want to be loved for who they are. They want to be encouraged to do more of what they're good at. They want to do for themselves. Think about whether you can be that person in your friend group who says, *My kid wants me to back off from their activities/their high school work/their college applications/their college choices, and I am. It's better for both of us. We've tried to set expectations and instill good values. The rest is up to them.*

At least one of your friends is likely to say, "Isn't that risky?" but know that at least one other parent is thinking, "You're so brave," even if they don't feel comfortable saying so.

BUILD A COMMUNITY OF LIKE-MINDED ADULTS

There are parents everywhere who, like you and me, feel it's time to say enough is enough. Right now we may be in the minority. But we need to stop going along with a manner of raising kids that we know is wrong; we need to summon the courage to do things differently. Banding together will help us find the courage to do what our gut tells us is right, and be the parents we want to be.

1. **Get your partner on board.** If you're rearing kids with someone else, talk with them about how to raise healthy, independent adults. When it comes

time to stop following the herd by refusing to sit on a soccer field sideline all weekend, forcing your kid to study what everyone else's kid is studying, or hiring a college application "handler," your partner is the person who will join you in walking away from the herd, even while others may be whispering and pointing at you; you need to know you've got each other's backs.

2. **Find like-minded parents.** You don't have to change other people's minds, but do strive to be in community with people who are bringing a similar approach to parenting. Look to the people whose way of raising kids feels right to you.

And consider broadening your community beyond those you already know. I guarantee if you post on Facebook, your neighborhood's Listserv e-mail, or some other forum, that you're starting a conversation in your community about how to end overparenting and raise kids to independent adulthood, you'll find like-minded people eager to jump on your bandwagon. Or, if you're not the bandwagon-creating type, then be clear that you want to get the conversation going—have confidence that a leader *will* emerge. Change needs to happen; let it begin with *you*. But don't worry, you don't have to go it alone.

3. **Connect with thought leaders.** Use the Web, Twitter, and Facebook (FB) to connect with leaders on various topics addressed in this book:

- On giving kids more freedom and independence, follow Lenore Skenazy (www.freerangekids.com; @freerangekids; FB: Free Range Kids).
- On embracing the importance of play and adventure in kids' lives, follow Mike Lanza (www.playborhood.com; @playborhood; FB: Playborhood) and Gever Tulley (www.tinkeringschool.com; @Gever; FB: Gever Tulley).
- On letting kids do their own academic work, follow Jessica Lahey (www.jessicalahey.com, @jesslahey, FB: Jessica Lahey).
- On reducing academic stress in schools and at home, follow Challenge Success (www.challengesuccess.org; @chalsuccess; FB: Challenge Success).
- On raising psychologically healthy kids, follow Madeline Levine (www.madelinelevine.com) and Wendy Mogel (www.wendymogel .com; @drwendymogel).

- On how to motivate kids, follow Dan Pink (www.danpink.com; @ DanielPink; FB: Daniel Pink).

- On helping kids bring more happiness into their life, follow leaders in the field of positive psychology including Christine Carter (www .christinecarter.com; @RaisingHappines; FB: Christine Carter) and Barbara Frederickson (www.positivityratio.com).

- On helping kids accept their vulnerability and imperfections and build resilience, follow Brené Brown (@BreneBrown; Facebook: Brené Brown).

4. **Join me.** Visit my blog (www.deanjulie.com) and share your story and your ideas. Follow me on Facebook (www.facebook.com/How To Raise An Adult) or Twitter (@raiseanadult). Spread the word by sharing this book with friends or assigning it to your book club.

DO A REALITY CHECK

Pivoting away from overparenting and toward raising an adult may be all well and good philosophically, right up until your kid is the one who has no one to play with because everyone else is at an activity, or your kid is the only one without a parent on the soccer sideline, or until you're the one whose kid is at a college that "changes lives" but your sister's kid is at Harvard. What are you going to do in those moments of real aloneness or social discomfort? Try to sit with the reality that reflects your values and embrace it.

Vulnerability expert Dr. Brené Brown writes that being able to experience our vulnerability, our fears, and "the torture chamber that we call uncertainty" exposes us emotionally, which is actually a really good thing. "There's no equation where taking risks, braving uncertainty, and opening ourselves up to emotional exposure equals weakness," she writes. Many of us can't fathom allowing ourselves to experience or express such emotions because we feel a need to be perfect or appear to be perfect at everything we do; we worry a great deal about what others may think but it's those feelings of vulnerability and fear that, if unexamined, can keep us going along with the herd, even when we know there's a better path.

If your kid is at home with unstructured time but no friends to play with, remember that you put that unstructured time in their life for a reason. Seize that moment for some family time. Read together, or do a puzzle, or go for a walk, or completely veg out staring at the clouds and sharing something you're each grateful for or looking forward to. If you have more than one kid, encourage siblings to do something together. As a Palo Alto dad named Brian tells his kids, "You're going to know each other longer than you know anyone else; you need to spend time together and you can't do that if you're always off at some activity." Or, let your kid be alone to figure out how to fill their time. There's a lot of value in that, too.

If yours is the only kid without a parent on the soccer sideline (trust me, it won't be this way for long once some other parents see your example as permission to not *be there all the time*), emphasize that soccer should be an enriching experience for *your kid*. And tell your kid that just as soccer is important to them, you have things going on in your life that matter to you, be it work, a hobby, time alone, or time with friends. Ask them to pick a few games to which they'd really like you to show up and commit to being there. At dinner on the day you *didn't* go to the soccer practice or game, when everyone shares something about their day, make sure you share about what you did while your kid was playing soccer.

I've taken this approach with my daughter, Avery, now an eighth grader, who takes dance classes throughout the week and on weekends, and competes throughout the winter and spring. "Dance Mom" types are as ubiquitous as "Soccer Moms," but I assure you I'm not one of them. I've told Avery to pick the performance she'd like me to come to, and I'll be there with bells on. This frees me up to do all the other things I couldn't do if I was at every performance, and makes that particular performance she chooses for me to attend a very special one for my girl and her mom.

If your kid is at a college that changes lives, or starting off at a good community college, and your sister's kid is at a very well-known college, you've got to learn to say "so what?" in your head (really believing it helps). What matters is not where kids are but that they are blossoming where they are. When you talk to your college kid on the phone, ask them what they're enjoying most, and why. For the academic studies they are most enjoying—the class in U.S. history, the biology lab, the anthropology seminar, whatever it may be—encourage them to think about ways to get even more out of their pursuits, such as by getting to know faculty. I gave this kind of advice to my students all the time. I remember a former student who came in to see me at the start of his junior year, brimming with obvious pride over his academic achievement, which he reported to me as a 4.0 GPA. I congratulated him and praised his hard work. Then I said, "So how many faculty know you by name?" To which he replied, "Um . . . none?" To which I said, "Well, you may have a 4.0 GPA, but if you just do the work required and don't get to know faculty, you're making a 'B' effort. Getting to know faculty (and all that follows, such as a deeper understanding of the subject and the confidence that follows, getting research opportunities, and the possibility of a great letter of recommendation) is how to squeeze the most out of this place." Those rewards can come for students at *every* college, and *may be even more likely to happen at small liberal arts colleges* instead of universities because faculty at universities face that fabled pressure to "publish or perish" and, as a result, the important task of mentoring undergraduates may get put on their back burner or not be a priority at all.

BE ALERT TO AND INSPIRED BY THOSE WHO WALK THE WALK

It's one thing to "talk the talk" of ending overparenting and raising adults, but another to be among the parents who have figured out how to "walk the walk," who are choosing to not overparent. These early adopters include:

PARENTS APPROPRIATELY INVOLVED IN THEIR KIDS' SCHOOLING

Maurina is a stay-at-home mom in Santa Clarita, California, a town north of Los Angeles.[5] While educators in underresourced districts across the nation wish for *more* parent involvement, parental involvement is by no means lacking in Santa Clarita's schools. Unlike many of her fellow parents, Maurina hangs back. She believes that her kids should feel like school is *their* territory, not yet another place where their mother is present. "At open house my kids get excited to show me *their* place instead of school being another place where their mommy is all the time." Being less involved in her kids' schools means Maurina is "that mother" in the eyes of some of those parents who hover at the school door. But Maurina is older than many of the other parents and I can hear in her voice that she really could not care less about anyone's judgment. She recoups time that would otherwise be spent at school or on school activities and uses it to create a home life that is relaxed and to do things for herself, such as exercise. "We say we're 'stay-at-home moms,' but we're never home! Disengaging from all the craziness means I have tons of time to create a positive, happy, home."

Lisa is a mother of two in an upper-middle-class Minneapolis suburb where "activities and honors are very important and competitive to get into."[6] When her daughter applied to the National Honor Society as a sophomore, Lisa and her husband expected her to do it all on her own, though other students had parental assistance. "She had all the criteria nailed—service, academics, et cetera, but she failed to fill out one form and was rejected." A year later her daughter applied again, in a process that was much harder. And she got in. It was hard for Lisa and her husband to see their daughter go through the more challenging process. "It was not a slam dunk, like the previous year. Nobody was more thorough in their application than she was, I'm sure, because she had the failure and the learning from the previous year. It was better to have had her fail in a small, safe way to learn a big lesson."

Carole is a mother of two in the Atlanta area.[7] She refers to the electronic notification system her local schools use to alert parents to their kids' poor grades as "fail mail," and she outright ignores it. Instead, she expects her kids to tell her if there is a problem at school before she hears it from anyone else. When it came time for her children to apply to college, she resisted what was for her a very strong urge to review their applications. She still thought it was valuable for an adult to look over the essays and give some feedback. "I asked them to find an adult they trusted (and who I approved of) to review their essays, and I was able to trust that their applications would reflect who they were so they would get accepted where they would be successful." During his freshman year in college her son ran into big trouble in one class and called home to tell Carole and her husband about it. "He told us he'd already spoken to the teacher, his coach, his adviser, and his dean before he called us. I knew then that he'd be okay in the world. It was my proudest moment."

PARENTS WHO PUT SPORTS AND OTHER EXTRACURRICULAR ACTIVITIES INTO PERSPECTIVE

Palo Alto parent Brian knows many moms and dads whose whole focus is their children.[8] "If that's how you build your social life, self-esteem, or self-worth, then when your kids are gone and married, or at college, what happens to you?" Instead of leading this "child-centric" life, Brian and his wife lead what they call a "family-centric" life based on this simple philosophy: "We don't focus on the kids as the primary reason for being."

This means Brian isn't interested in what he calls the "child sports industrial complex," through which whatever the child is interested in becomes the dominant aspect of that family's home life. "Our middle daughter would love to play club soccer," he says, "but we're not going to give her that opportunity, not because she couldn't do it—she probably could—but because three practices and a game every week and traveling around for all of it eats away at the family. So she's in regular old AYSO [American Youth Soccer Organization], which practices once a week and has one game locally. And that's what she'll do until she's old enough to travel to and from these activities herself."

With their lives not scheduled to the hilt with activities, Brian's kids have time on the weekends to be home and *do nothing*, "which some of my friends find obscene," Brian adds. "My girls go outside and play, build forts, and make videos. They spend hours singing and dancing and moving around. They watch TV together. We take walks, they read, they play, they do their homework. Meanwhile, my friends' kids were at this practice or with this tutor or this private coach."

Carmen is a mother in Ann Arbor, Michigan, the college town in which the prestigious University of Michigan is situated, where it's not uncommon for young kids to get up at 6:00 a.m. to be driven an hour each way to a skating rink; they end up half an hour late to school each day, in pursuit of elite athletic competition.[9] Of this all-or-nothing approach to kid sports and activities, Carmen asks, "Does the child want this or does the parent want it for the child? Is getting to the Olympics or to Harvard the only reason for doing all of this? What if the kid *doesn't* make it to those extreme heights, which so few will? Will all of that sacrifice still have been worth it?"

Thinking of her ten-year-old daughter, Carmen says, "She wants a lot of downtime at home. She wants to do art, and play, and it doesn't work with this kid when she's pushed to do too many activities. That's something I am careful about when we're signing her up for things. Maybe Rec & Ed soccer is better than travel soccer. Or with choir—maybe the citywide choral group she auditioned for and got into turns out not to be right because of its demanding practice schedule, and a chance to sing with a lower-key group is in fact the better choice for her."

In a community like Carmen's, if a kid isn't involved in playing a sport or an instrument early on, it can wreck their chances of being able to do anything along those lines further down the road—or so people say—and parents can fear making the "wrong" decision. Carmen says, "I like to talk to parents of older kids and check out what's *really* true. There are a lot of myths about the high school—about how competitive it is to get into soccer or orchestra and how you have to do this and that in order to have a chance at it. But all along I've been an information seeker, asking, 'What's the real deal?' For example, the freshman soccer team welcomes all freshmen as long as there's room. The illusion that if you aren't on the travel soccer team you can't play in high school goes out the door. Same with orchestra. You might not be as good as those other kids, but you can still do it and enjoy it. It's amazing how prevalent those myths are that parents pass on as advice to each other. Do I want to be around those people? Are they good and healthy for my kids to be around? That kind of pressure and intensity is so counter to our family values."

PARENTS WHO LOVE AND SUPPORT THE KID THEY'VE GOT

Kristen is a mother of two in Ann Arbor, Michigan, where her older child is a sophomore at a public magnet high school.[10] He is intellectually gifted and, except for struggling with executive function skills, as a child he found academics to be quite easy. But when he started high school, and academics became something to work at, he wasn't particularly driven to do so. Kristen and her husband (both of whom have advanced degrees from prestigious universities) were anguished, certain that if their son just applied himself he could get into highly selective colleges that would "open the world" to him. Their son doesn't have a specific passion yet, but Kristen and her husband felt he could be anything he wanted to be, and that it was a shame for him to "waste those gifts," and they wanted him to "keep those doors open." They also sensed it was time to begin removing the scaffolding and support they'd been providing that had helped him stay on task and get his work done, yet they could see that he might not succeed without that support.

"My initial thinking was my kid is brilliant and can do whatever he wants, and he's so young—how does he know that getting a C in class isn't something he won't regret later?" But as the nightly chore of keeping her son on task for homework began to take its toll on family nerves and harmony, Kristen realized, "We are all miserable all the time because we're constantly pushing him and trying to control him." She sought advice from parents of kids with similar temperaments—gifted and challenged—and found great comfort in the book *The Gift of an Ordinary Day: A Mother's*

Memoir, by author, editor, and memoirist Katrina Kenison.[11] And Kristen's greatest insight may have arisen in response to the words of successful adults in her own community who are doing work they find stimulating and satisfying and whose own path contained twists and turns. "I talked to person after person whose path was not straight. Who didn't have straight As in high school. Who went to a college I've never heard of. Who flunked out their freshman year. The biggest realization for me was our relationship with our son doesn't begin once he ends high school and we've 'gotten through this'; our relationship with him is *now*—but every success doesn't have to *happen* now."

Whereas Kristen once felt she was abdicating her responsibility as a parent by not pushing her son, now she sees that a different way to be a responsible parent is to let him "crash on his own" before college. "People told me that often, for kids like him, if we scaffold or control so much through high school and then he crashes in college, what good will that do? Better to have it happen in high school. Going to summer school is not the end of the world. Being in high school a year longer is not the end of the world.

"Professionals have repeated to me over and over, 'Even if he crashes really hard it's still recoverable.' That's where I had to really open my mind. This is who my kid really is. Maybe he will go to a prestigious college, maybe he won't; maybe he'll go to a prestigious grad school instead. I don't know when he'll hit his own stride. I can't make that timeline for him. It was incredibly freeing to come to the realization that I don't have to control things—to hold those doors open for him. College isn't going to determine what you do with your life. He doesn't have to go to a prestigious college to do something amazing with his life. And he might never be rich, famous, or tops in his field, and that's okay, too."

Christine is a mother of four in Mill Valley, California, an upper-middle-class community located in Marin County just north of San Francisco, where "people start talking about college choice in preschool."[12] When Christine's eldest—a child who was always strong in school but never really loved it—was in eighth grade he told his parents, "I am not interested in being stressed out for the next four years, to go to college and be stressed out for another four years, to graduate and get a job I really don't like." As her son said this, many of her friends' children were applying to private high schools and making plans for that kind of stressful—if prestigious—high school experience to which her son alluded, but Christine and her husband realized they didn't want that for their son and instead supported him in figuring out what he wanted to do as an alternative. Their son chose to begin high school at the local public school—Tamalpais High. By the end of freshman year he realized he wanted to get outside of what he called the Marin County "bubble." His plan for sophomore year entailed many things, none of which could be called traditional schooling: he worked in Kenya at a tuition-free school for girls while taking classes online via National University Virtual High School, and then returned to the United States for a summer stint at the International Center of Photography in New York City, where he lived with extended family. Says his mother, Christine, "It was difficult to let him go and it was a risk to forgo the traditional track. But we let go and trusted these experiences would serve his developing personhood far more than his sophomore year academic life in our hometown. He handled everything on his own during that year."

Although it was obvious to Christine and her husband that their son had thrived and grown while away, his decision to leave traditional schooling was not without its consequences. When he reenrolled at Tamalpais High for his junior year, for example, he was not allowed to enroll in some AP courses because he hadn't been a student there the year prior. "For many, that's a risk not worth taking," says Christine. But Christine—and, more important, her son—were willing to take the risk. "We supported his decisions because we feel that if he was given independence and the opportunity to pursue experiences that were outside the norm, he might be able to find out more about who he is and who he is becoming, and make better choices about life, colleges, and jobs from that position. I really trust that supporting him in these ways is contributing to his ability to become who he wants to be."

Maurice is a minister and historian who lives in Oakland, California, and is the father of a grown daughter.[13] When his daughter was very young people recognized her gifts and talents and urged Maurice to have her tested and get her into a competitive preschool, and start preparing her for the Ivy League. But Maurice and Meshelle wanted to let their daughter emerge rather than to manufacture her. "I think a critical part of parenting is knowing where you end and where your child begins. Nonanxious observation is so important. Wonder is the reward. Her needs, I learned, were, and still are, markedly different from my own. She flourishes in environments that

would drive me to distraction and would wither in the very places I flour-
ish. What has been most surprising is how much she says she learns from
me that has very little to do with my intentional direction at all."

PARENTS WHO FIND A COMMUNITY THAT SUPPORTS
THEIR CHILD-RAISING VALUES

Rani, a San Francisco mother of two, was raised on the Stanford campus
and is a physician with degrees from two elite schools.[14] When she and
her husband had kids, they decided to stay in the city and put their kids
in the public schools, while many of their friends relocated to the suburbs.
"In choosing the public school system in San Francisco, we've surrounded ourselves with families who largely do not overparent, which has
allowed us to buck the overparenting tendencies in ourselves. We feel
excited to let our fifth-grade daughter ride the public bus along predetermined routes alone, and to let her and her fourth-grade brother walk
alone a few blocks to the corner butcher. They are excited to do these things,
and are so ready."

Some parents feel the need to take a semester or year's break from their
home community in order to lessen the stress or refocus on what really matters. Jeff Gamble, cofounder of the very popular Palo Alto summer camp
called Jefunira, did just that in 2014 when he and his wife, Terri, moved
their three kids (aged eight, eleven, and thirteen) to Bali, Indonesia, for one
year.[15] In Bali, Jeff and Terri's kids walked alone or with friends the seven-
to-ten-minute route through the jungle each day to school, through fifty-
foot-tall bamboo, past wild banana and coconut trees, with skinks and
geckos darting across the path, and the sky completely obscured by the can-
opy. "Our children didn't go much further than around the block alone
when we were living in the Bay Area, but here, we're letting them explore
and be more independent. Our two older kids have 'Bali phones' and
they're responsible for communicating to us where they are or if they make
plans; in return they have the freedom to roam the jungle with their bud-
dies, as well as the twenty-acre school campus, which includes warungs
(food spots), pools, and a river. They choose what to study—one of our
kids has a class on scuba diving and another is studying bee keeping—and
when to do their homework. We're standing back and letting them succeed or fail and learn from both. This is our attempt to step back from
our overparenting. All three of them are thriving."

Former Palo Altans Maeve Grogan and her husband, Pat, made a similar kind of trek, a six-month trip exploring the world with their two boys.[16] They'd been pushing their boys to complete mountains of homework that ostensibly would lead to admission to selective schools and good careers, but they came to appreciate that what was really going on for them was that they were perhaps detrimentally risk averse and were, overall, having a hard time dealing with uncertainty. This awareness led them to their six-month trek. "We decided to enter into more risk than usual and go down the path of uncertainty," Maeve told me. "We wanted to let our children learn how to make choices and decisions in uncertainty." In addition, they began to reconnect more deeply with their children. "On a personal level we just wanted to get to know our kids. With all the busyness and external obligations, when does the chance for unstructured communication and just hanging out with each other come in?"

By the time Maeve's family's trek was over, the adventure had culminated in the decision to relocate from Palo Alto to a quiet community in southern Oregon where they had family. "Relationships became the priority in our lives rather than the extraneous things. Those fell away. We started to use more of a dialogue around choice instead of 'you should do this.' That was the gift of those six months away. When the schedule is packed, you don't have time to have the dialogue of choice."

The dialogue of choice.

Those of us who are unable to consider anything other than the currently popular overparenting model of child rearing may not be living lives of choice; we may have let the herd choose for us—and for our children.

CONCLUSION

Just as there are many college students caught between conformity and courage, so are many parents struggling to do their best within a system that has lost its mind. But we need to do more than throw up our hands. We cannot continue to go with the flow, however powerful the current is. If we want our kids to turn out differently, we have to raise them differently.[1]

—William Deresiewicz, social critic and author of *Excellent Sheep: The Miseducation of the American Elite and the Way to a Meaningful Life*

In my decade as Stanford's freshman dean I had the honor and privilege of working with thousands of other peoples' eighteen-to-twenty-two-year-old sons and daughters. It was my job, and that of my many colleagues, to support our students in achieving their goals and to inspire them to grow and stretch toward possibilities they hadn't yet heard of or couldn't yet imagine for themselves. This mentoring required careful listening, as well as patience and a willingness to take the long view; the process of a human being unfolding into their adult self can be messy before yielding beautiful results.

Over the years I bore witness as the once relatively distinguishable stages of adolescence and adulthood increasingly blurred. Each year it was harder to convince parents of college students to take a backseat and let their son or daughter be the driver of his or her college experience. And each year more students were grateful for a parent's involvement rather than wanting to try to handle matters on their own. At some point my gut instinct said, *Something's not right. What's to become of us if the next generation doesn't have the wherewithal to be adults?* And this budding concern led me to scrutinize what was happening not just on my campus and on other campuses, but in my own community, in my kids' schools and in my own home. It appeared as if the developmental steps naturally built into childhood—through which children acquired increasing competencies and independence and in so doing separated from the parent and forged their own self—were becoming overridden by safety concerns and in furtherance of obtaining spots on teams, seats in schools, opportunities, and accolades that seemed attainable only with a parent's concerted involvement. Parents shepherding, handholding, and hovering over children well into adulthood became more rule than exception. And anxiety, depression, and other problems with mental health and wellness in adolescents and young adults were on the rise.

I began writing this book from a place of fierce concern for adolescents and young adults—and I ended up with a good deal of concern for parents as well. I began with a belief that "those parents" were the problem, and was humbled to discover the ways in which I was one of "those parents" myself. I began with a desire to shed light on what was wrong, and was inspired by all I learned about how we can turn things around and make things right. As I complete this book and continue to walk my own journey, which includes raising two young humans to adulthood with a partner I love, I've been changed for the better by what I've learned about the harm of overparenting, and hope you have, too.

As parents our dream was to have a child, but we can't forget that our children have the right to dream for themselves. There is much more to each precious, unique child than we can possibly know, and that unique person—that self—is for each young person to discover. We want so badly to help them by shepherding them from milestone to milestone and by shielding them from failure and pain. But overhelping *causes* harm. It can leave young adults without the strengths of skill, will, and character that are needed to know themselves and to craft a life. They must be the authors of themselves as well as the authors of the twenty-first century, a span of time simultaneously more intimate and global, more understood and unpredictable, than we can yet comprehend. The most seemingly intractable environmental and social problems ever faced by humans will confront the next generation. They will be called upon to be hard workers, skilled thinkers, and problem solvers, compassionate and involved citizens, persons of good character, and perhaps even parents themselves. As parents we'll have succeeded if our kids have the wherewithal to be and do these things on their own rather than by counting on us to assist or stand in for them.

Of course, we aren't meant to stand by and do nothing; there is much we can and must do. While our children are still at home with us, we must nourish them, provide a safe and nurturing shelter, love them for who they are, support their interests, and teach them the skills and values that will foster their independence and prepare them to lead a meaningful, fulfilling adult life. We must also take responsibility for our own happiness and well-being and not pin either on our children's accomplishments. If we develop and sustain good relationships with our kids, they will always value our perspective and perhaps even seek it. But as they age we must not be overly invested in having them do what we say. Soon we must pass the mantle of generational leadership to our children, and it would behoove us to do so gracefully, with great confidence that they have what it takes to be the adult in the room when the time for that comes.

Like our kids, we seek advice on many things, including how to raise children. There is much we can learn from researchers, philosophers, clinicians, thought leaders, spiritual leaders, coaches, authors, and fellow parents. But we shouldn't go so far in the direction of seeking answers from others that we overlook the wisdom of our own life experience and of the instincts that live in our own heads and hearts. We know better than anyone else what's going on with our own kids and what life is like in our own homes. There is no one-size-fits-all answer to any facet of parenting and we'll make ourselves crazy if we try to deduce the best practice at every turn. Trust that you have the capacity to make good choices, and figure this parenting thing out largely on your own. Yes, this author of a book on parenting is saying you might want to stop reading so many books on parenting and give yourself a bit more credit—slow down, take a deep breath, look within, hug your partner, and hug your kid: Parenting doesn't have to feel so hard anymore. You've *got* this.

I began speaking publicly in my community about the harm of overparenting while I was still a dean at Stanford, and I remember more than a few uncomfortable moments when a parent in the audience would ask me pointedly, "Aren't the elite schools to blame?" At the time, deep into my role as a university administrator, I wasn't able to see what if any role the colleges and universities played in incentivizing overparenting—let alone see the culpability my questioner was implying. With distance and time, however, I have gained a wider perspective. And while I don't think the Stanfords and Harvards of the world are to blame for a parent's decision to do their kid's homework, spend thousands of dollars for better test scores, or pad a child's "résumé," I do think that the thoughtful leaders at these and similar institutions are best positioned to wrest their reputations from the clutches of brand-elitism, trumped-up selectivity, and relatively inapposite rankings, and to reshape their admission process so as to evaluate an applicant's authentic intellectual capacity and character instead of stoking the narcissism of small differences. The most highly selective colleges would do an enormous service to children and parents and childhood itself if they were able to pull that off. I do hope they'll try.

In the meantime, despite what's wrong with the college admissions system and the many, many other social and cultural factors that are beyond our control as parents, we've got children who need dinner tonight and breakfast tomorrow morning, and a society and world that are depending on us to raise our children well. Join me in doing right by those children by leaving the herd of hoverers, by fostering independence, not dependence, and by supporting them in being who they are rather than telling them who and what to be. Together we can push the parenting pendulum back in the other direction: toward raising adults.

HARVARD LAW SCHOOL CLASS OF 2016
UNDERGRADUATE PROFILES

American University
Amherst College
Arizona State University
Auburn University
Augustana College - SD
Bard College
Baruch College - SUNY
Bates College
Baylor University
Beth Medrash Govoha
Bethel University - MN
Biola University
Boise State University
Boston College
Bowdoin College
Brandeis University
Brigham Young University
Brooklyn College - CUNY
Brown University
Bucknell University

California Polytechnic State University
   - San Luis Obispo
California State University - Los
   Angeles
Carleton College - MN
Carleton University
Carnegie Mellon University
Case Western Reserve University
Centre College
Claremont McKenna College
Clark Atlanta University
Clemson University
Colgate University
Colorado State University
Columbia University - Columbia
   College
Cornell University - NY
Dartmouth College
Dickinson College
Dillard University

Duke University

Eastern Nazarene College

Embry-Riddle Aeronautical University

Emory University

Florida Institute of Technology

Florida State University

Fordham University - Fordham College at Rose Hill

Furman University

George Washington University

Georgetown University

Hamilton College

Harvard University

Hofstra University

Howard University

Hunter College - CUNY

Indiana University - Bloomington

Indiana University - Purdue University, Indianapolis

Johns Hopkins University

Lafayette College - PA

Loyola University - Chicago

Marquette University

Massachusetts Institute of Technology

McGill University

McMaster University

Metropolitan State University

Miami University Oxford

Middlebury College

Morehead State University

Morehouse College

Nebraska Wesleyan University

Ner Israel Rabbinical College

New York University

Northeastern University

Northwestern University

Oakland University

Oberlin College

Ohio State University - Columbus

Oral Roberts University

Oregon State University

Patrick Henry College

Peking University

Pennsylvania State University - University Park

Point Loma Nazarene University

Pomona College

Princeton University

Queens College - CUNY

Queen's University

Reed College

Rice University

Rutgers University School of Arts and Sciences

Saint Louis University

San Francisco State University

Santa Clara University

Sarah Lawrence College - NY

Seattle University

Seoul National University

Smith College

Southern Methodist University

Southwestern University

Spelman College

Stanford University

Stephen F. Austin State University

SUNY at Albany

SUNY at Stony Brook Center

SUNY College at Geneseo

Swarthmore College

Syracuse University

Texas A&M University - College Station

Texas Christian University

Texas Tech University

The University of Texas at Arlington

The University of Texas at Austin

Torah Temimah Talmudical Seminary
Touro College
Trinity University - TX
Truman State University
Tufts University of Arts and Sciences
Tulane University
United States Coast Guard Academy
University of Alabama
University of Arizona
University of Arkansas - Fayetteville
University of British Columbia
University of Calgary
University of California - Berkeley
University of California - Davis
University of California - Irvine
University of California - Los Angeles
University of California - San Diego
University of California - Santa Barbara
University of Chicago
University of Colorado - Boulder
University of Connecticut, Storrs
University of Florida
University of Georgia
University of Illinois - Urbana
University of Kentucky - Lexington
University of Lethridge
University of Maryland - College Park
University of Miami
University of Michigan - Ann Arbor
University of Minnesota - Minneapolis
University of Missouri - Columbia
University of Montana
University of Nebraska - Lincoln

University of North Carolina - Chapel
   Hill
University of Notre Dame
University of Nottingham
University of Oklahoma
University of Pennsylvania
University of Pittsburgh
University of San Diego
University of South Carolina -
   Columbia
University of Southern California
University of Toronto
University of Virginia
University of Washington
University of Waterloo
University of Western Ontario
University of Wisconsin - Madison
VA Polytechnic Institute and State
   University
Vanderbilt University
Vassar College
Villanova University
Washburn University
Washington State University
Washington University
Wesleyan University
Wheaton College - IL
Wheaton College - MA
Williams College
Wofford College
Yale University
Yeshiva University

Top Colleges & Universities Contributing Graduating Seniors to Teach For America's 2013 Teaching Corps

This year **5,900 individuals** joined Teach For America as part of the 2013 corps. Together with the 2012 corps, they make up more than **11,000 corps members** leading high-need classrooms in 48 regions that span 35 states and the District of Columbia.

Seventy-four percent of Teach For America's 2013 corps are graduating seniors from the class of 2013. They represent **more than 800** colleges and universities across the country.* The schools below are ranked by the number of graduates they contributed to the 2013 corps.

LARGE SCHOOLS		10,000 + Undergrads**	
University of Texas at Austin	73	Indiana University-Bloomington	44
University of Southern California	70	Penn State University Park	43
University of California-Berkeley	69	University of Minnesota-Twin Cities	43
University of Michigan-Ann Arbor	67	Arizona State University	42
University of Florida	59	University of Maryland College Park	42
University of North Carolina at Chapel Hill	57	University of Washington-Seattle	42
University of Illinois at Urbana-Champaign	56	University of California-Los Angeles	40
Cornell University	55	University of Georgia	40
University of Virginia	45	The Ohio State University	38
University of Wisconsin-Madison	45	University of Pittsburgh	38

MEDIUM SCHOOLS		3,000-9,999 Undergrads	
Harvard University	45	Howard University	31
Vanderbilt University	45	Princeton University	30
Georgetown University	40	Washington University in St. Louis	30
University of Pennsylvania	40	Yale University	30
George Washington University	37	Boston College	29
Columbia University in the City of New York	35	Emory University	28
Tufts University	35	Tulane University	26
Dartmouth College	33	American University	23
Northwestern University	33	Gonzaga University	23
Brown University	31	Wake Forest University	23

SMALL SCHOOLS		2,999 or Fewer Undergrads	
Spelman College	27	Barnard College	12
Wellesley College	20	Colby College	12
Smith College	16	Franklin & Marshall College	12
Denison University	15	Washington and Lee University	12
College of the Holy Cross	14	Claremont McKenna College	11
DePauw University	14	Colorado College	11
Grinnell College	14	Amherst College	10
Lafayette College	14	Morehouse College	10
Whitman College	14	Mount Holyoke College	10
Williams College	14	Wesleyan University	10

* Data valid as of August 2013 and includes first day of school projections based on historical patterns

** Categories are based on the Carnegie Foundation for the Advancement of Teaching's basic size classification for colleges and universities

NOTES

INTRODUCTION

1. Antonio Machado, "XXIX," in *Border of a Dream: Selected Poems*, trans. Willis Barnstone (Port Townsend, Wash.: Copper Canyon Press, 2003).
2. By way of comparison, the 1980 "Who Shot J.R." episode of the hit drama *Dallas* still stands as the second-highest-rated regular television broadcast in U.S. history, with 41.5 million viewers. The 2015 Oscars awards show had 43 million viewers.
3. Brian Palmer, "Why Did Missing Children Start Showing Up on Milk Cartons?" Slate.com., April 20, 2012. http://www.slate.com/articles/news_and_politics/explainer/2012/04/etan_patz_case_why_did_dairies_put_missing_children_on_their_milk_cartons_.html (accessed on June 15, 2014).
4. Report by the National Commission on Excellence in Education (1983).
5. Denise Pope, *"Doing School": How We Are Creating a Generation of Stressed Out, Materialistic, and Miseducated Students* (New Haven, Conn.: Yale University Press, 2003).
6. *Race to Nowhere.* (Lafayette, Calif.: Reel Link Films, 2010).
7. By 1986 California had created a task force to promote self-esteem across the state.
8. Amanda Ripley, *The Smartest Kids in the World: And How They Got That Way* (New York: Simon & Schuster, 2013).
9. Merriam-Webster dictionary.
10. *Handbook for Public Playground Safety*, U.S. Consumer Product Safety Commission (1981).
11. Foster W. Cline and Jim Fay, *Parenting with Love and Logic: Teaching Children Responsibility* (Colorado Springs, Colo.: Pinon Press, 1990), 23–25.
12. Nancy Gibbs, "The Growing Backlash Against Overparenting," *Time*, November 30, 2009.
13. Judith Warner, *Perfect Madness: Motherhood in the Age of Anxiety* (New York: Riverhead Books, 2005), 87.

14. Julie Lythcott-Haims, "When Did Caring Become Control: Blame Boomers," *Chicago Tribune*, October 16, 2005.
15. A. Bandura, "Self-Efficacy." In V. S. Ramachaudran, ed., *Encyclopedia of Human Behavior*, vol. 4 (New York: Academic Press, 1994), 71–81.

1. KEEPING THEM SAFE AND SOUND

1. Governor's Highway Safety Association, "Child Passenger Safety Laws, June 2014." http://www.ghsa.org/html/stateinfo/laws/childsafety_laws.html (accessed on June 15, 2014).
2. Patricia Somers and Jim Settle, "The Helicopter Parent (Part 2): International Arrivals and Departures," *College and University* 86, no. 2 (2010): 2–9. http://eric.ed.gov/?id=EJ912004.
3. Dan Lewis, "Where Did the Fear of Poisoned Candy Come From?" Smithsonian.com., October 6, 2013. http://www.smithsonianmag.com/not-categorized/where-did-the-fear-of-poisoned-halloween-candy-come-from-822302/ (accessed on June 15, 2014).
4. Diane Divoky, "Missing Tot Estimates Exaggerated," *Lodi News-Sentinel*, February 18, 1986.
5. David Finkelhor, Heather Hammer, and Andrea J. Sedlak, *NISMART: National Incidence Studies of Missing, Abducted, Runaway, and Thrownaway Children*, October 2002. https://www.ncjrs.gov/html/ojjdp/nismart/03/ns5.html (accessed on June 15, 2014).
6. David Finkelhor, "Five Myths About Missing Children," *Washington Post*, May 10, 2013, http://www.washingtonpost.com/opinions/five-myths-about-missing-children/2013/05/10/efee398c-b8b4-11e2-aa9e-a02b765ff0ea_story.html.
7. Ibid.
8. Nicole Neal, "How Dangerous Is Childhood?" *Palm Beach Post*, August 13, 2006.
9. Robert M. Sapolsky, *Why Zebras Don't Get Ulcers: A Guide to Stress, Stress-Related Diseases, and Coping* (New York: W. H. Freeman, 1994).
10. Ibid., 7.
11. Corey Adwar, "Support Grows Online for Mom Who Lost Custody of Daughter After Letting Her Play Alone at a Park," *Business Insider*, July 16, 2014, http://www.businessinsider.com/debra-harrell-arrested-for-allegedly-letting-daughter-play-alone-at-park-2014-7.
12. Kim Brooks, "The Day I Left My Son in the Car," *Salon*, June 3, 2014, http://www.salon.com/2014/06/03/the_day_i_left_my_son_in_the_car/.
13. Lenore Skenazy, "Crime Statistics," http://www.freerangekids.com/crime-statistics/.
14. Lenore Skenazy, *Free-Range Kids: How to Raise Safe, Self-Reliant Children (Without Going Nuts with Worry)* (San Francisco: Jossey-Bass, 2010).
15. Ibid.
16. Brigid Schulte and Donna St. George, "Montgomery County Neglect Inquiry Shines Spotlight on 'Free-Range' Parenting," *Washington Post*, January 17, 2015, http://www.washingtonpost.com/local/education/montgomery-county-neglect-inquiry-shines-spotlight-on-free-range-parenting/2015/01/17/352d4b30-9d99-11e4-bcfb-059ec7a93ddc_story.html.
17. Ross Douthat, "Forcing Every Mom and Dad to Be a Helicopter Parent," *National Post*, July 23, 2014.
18. Emily Lodish, "Global Parenting Habits That Haven't Caught On in the U.S," *npr*

.org, August 12, 2014, http://www.npr.org/blogs/parallels/2014/08/12/339825261 /global-parenting-habits-that-havent-caught-on-in-the-u-s.

19. Author's interview with parent, April 22, 2014.
20. "Legal Age Restrictions for Latchkey Kids," http://www.latchkey-kids.com/latch key-kids-age-limits.htm.
21. Ibid.
22. From the Girl Scout website: Adults provide supervision and guidance for all grade levels. Adults must accompany Girl Scout Daisies, Brownies, and Juniors when they are selling, taking orders for, or delivering products. Adults oversee Girl Scout Cadettes, Seniors, and Ambassadors; they must be aware of how, when, and where the girls are selling products; be on call when girls are participating in product sales and be able to contact girls in a timely manner; be in an automobile in the area; or be present with the girls.
23. Author's interview with Suzanne Lucas, February 14, 2013.
24. See the writings of Alfie Kohn, including *The Myth of the Spoiled Child: Challenging the Conventional Wisdom about Children and Parenting* (Boston, Mass.: Da Capo Lifelong Books, 2014); and http://www.alfiekohn.org/miscellaneous/trophyfury.htm.
25. Amanda Ripley, *The Smartest Kids in the World: And How They Got That Way* (New York: Simon & Schuster, 2013).
26. Hara Estroff Marano, *A Nation of Wimps: The High Cost of Invasive Parenting* (New York: Crown Archetype, 2008).
27. Susan Eva Porter, *Bully Nation: Why America's Approach to Childhood Aggression Is Bad for Everyone* (Oxford: Paragon House, 2014).
28. Author's interview with Olaf "Ole" Jorgenson, February 13, 2014.
29. Pamela Druckerman, *Bringing Up Bébé* (New York: Penguin Press, 2012), 138–42.
30. Author's interview with Suzanne Lucas, February 14, 2013.
31. Wendy Mogel, *The Blessing of a Skinned Knee* (New York: Scribner, 2001).
32. Hanna Rosin, "The Overprotected Kid," *The Atlantic*, April 2014, http://www .theatlantic.com/features/archive/2014/03/hey-parents-leave-those-kids-alone /358631/.
33. Alice G. Walton, "New Playgrounds Are Safe—And That's Why Nobody Uses Them," *The Atlantic*, February 1, 2012, http://www.theatlantic.com/health/archive /2012/02/new-playgrounds-are-safe-and-thats-why-nobody-uses-them/252108/.
34. See the nationally best-selling book: Richard Louv, *Last Child in the Woods: Saving Our Children from Nature-Deficit Disorder* (Chapel Hill, N.C.: Algonquin Books of Chapel Hill, 2005).
35. Kristen A. Copeland et al., "Societal Values and Policies May Curtail Preschool Children's Physical Activity in Child Care Centers," *Pediatrics* 129, no. 2, February 2012, http://pediatrics.aappublications.org/content/early/2012/01/02/peds.2011-2102.full .pdf+html.
36. Author's interview with Tim Barton, May 22, 2014.

2. PROVIDING OPPORTUNITY

1. Malcolm Gladwell, *Outliers: The Story of Success* (New York: Little, Brown, 2007).
2. "Kids Who Specialize in One Sport May Have Higher Injury Risk, Loyola Study Finds," *Loyola University Health System*, May 2, 2011, http://www.loyolamedicine .org/childrenshospital/newswire/news/kids-who-specialize-one-sport-may-have -higher-injury-risk-loyola-study-finds.

3. David Epstein, "Sports Should Be Child's Play," *New York Times*, June 10, 2014, http://www.nytimes.com/2014/06/11/opinion/sports-should-be-childs-play.html.
4. "Why Are There So Many Youth Baseball-Throwing Injuries?" *Beaumont Health System*, June 14, 2013, http://www.beaumont.edu/press/news-stories/2013/6/why -are-there-so-many-youth-baseball-throwing-injuries/.
5. Salynn Boyles, "Sports-Related Concussions on the Rise in Kids," *WebMD*, August 30, 2010, http://www.webmd.com/parenting/news/20100830/sports-related-concus sions-on-the-rise-in-kids.
6. Robert Cantu and Mark Hyman, *Concussions and Our Kids: America's Leading Expert on How to Protect Young Athletes and Keep Sports Safe* (New York: Mariner Books, 2013).
7. Kevin Sack, "The 2000 Campaign: THE FAMILY; Timeouts for a Son's Football Games," *New York Times*, October 22, 2000, http://www.nytimes.com/2000/10/22 /us/the-2000-campaign-the-family-timeouts-for-a-son-s-football-games.html.
8. John Dickerson, "Wait, Am I That Baseball Dad? How Baseball Encourages Bad Parenting—And How You Can Support Your Kids on the Diamond Without Driving Them Crazy," *Slate*, June 19, 2013, http://www.slate.com/articles/sports/sports _nut/2013/06/baseball_parents_how_dads_stress_their_kids_out_during_little _league_games.html.
9. Michael Lewis, "Coach Fitz's Management Theory," *New York Times*, March 28, 2004, http://www.nytimes.com/2004/03/28/magazine/coach-fitz-s-management-theory .html?src=pm&pagewanted=8.
10. Ibid. and Michael Lewis, *Coach: Lessons on the Game of Life* (New York: W. W. Norton, 2005).
11. Author's interview with Amy Young, April 30, 2014.
12. Author's interview with Tom Jacoubowsky, November 4, 2013.
13. Author's interviews with Catharine Jacobsen, May 12 and May 14, 2014.
14. Author's interview with Sidonia "Sid" Dalby, April 21, 2014.
15. William Deresiewicz, *Excellent Sheep: The Miseducation of the American Elite and the Way to a Meaningful Life* (New York: Free Press, 2014).
16. Statement by audience member Chi Ling Chan, at "Excellent Sheep, Revisited," Cemex Auditorium, Stanford University, April 16, 2014.
17. Author's interview with Chi Ling Chan, April 22, 2014.
18. Author's interview with student, August 22, 2014.
19. Author's interview with Phil Gardner, March 26, 2013.

3. BEING THERE FOR THEM

1. Author's conversation with superintendent, February 20 and February 23, 2013.
2. Author's interview with Donne Davis, June 10, 2013.
3. Po Bronson and Ashley Merryman, *NurtureShock: New Thinking About Children* (New York: Twelve, 2009).
4. Author's interview with Steve Thompson, February 22, 2014.
5. Author's interview with Ty Tingley, April 30, 2014.
6. Author's interview with Colonel Leon Robert, June 28, 2013.
7. Names, school types, and geographical locations are fictional to preserve privacy.
8. Author's interview with Tracy-Elizabeth Clay, July 18, 2013.
9. Author's interview with superintendent, January 20, 2014.
10. Author's interview with Colonel Charles "Gus" Stafford, July 2, 2013.

11. Author's interview with Kate Raftery, April 13, 2014.
12. Author's interview with Jonathan, April 22, 2014.
13. Author's interview with Olaf "Ole" Jorgenson, February 13, 2014.
14. Author's interview with Colonel Charles "Gus" Stafford, July 2, 2013.
15. Michael Gerson, "Saying Goodbye to My Child, the Youngster," *New York Times*, August 19, 2013, http://www.washingtonpost.com/opinions/michael-gerson-saying -goodbye-to-my-child-the-youngster/2013/08/19/6337802e-08dd-11e3-8974 -f97ab3b3c677_story.html.

4. SUCCUMBING TO THE COLLEGE ADMISSIONS ARMS RACE

1. Author's interview with northern Virginia parents, April 22, 2014.
2. Author's interview with Holley, April 22, 2014.
3. Author's interview with Ellen Nodelman, January 22, 2014.
4. Author's interview with Hillary Coustan, May 22, 2014.
5. Author's interview with Sharon Ofek, April 24, 2014.
6. Author's interview with superintendent, February 20 and 23, 2013.
7. Author's interview with superintendent, January 20, 2014.
8. Author's interview with Beth Gagnon, March 28, 2014.
9. Ira Glass interview with Rich Clark, "504: How I Got into College," *This American Life*, September 6, 2013.
10. Ruth Starkman, "Private College Admissions Consultants: Does Your Child Need One?" *Huffington Post*, July 22, 2013, http://www.huffingtonpost.com/ruth-starkman /private-college-admissions-consulting_b_3625632.html.
11. "Obama Getting Emotionally Ready for Malia's College Departure," *CBSNews.com*, July 28, 2014, http://www.cbsnews.com/news/obama-getting-emotionally-ready-for -malias-college-departure/.
12. Derek Thompson, "Who's Had the Worst Recession: Boomers, Millennials, or Gen-Xers?" *The Atlantic*, September 13, 2011, http://www.theatlantic.com/business /archive/2011/09/whos-had-the-worst-recession-boomers-millennials-or-gen-xers /245056/.
13. Mike Konczal, "What Conclusions Can You Draw On Increases in Unemployment by Age and Education?" *Rortybomb.wordpress.com*, October 20, 2010, http://rorty bomb.wordpress.com/2010/10/20/what-conclusions-can-you-draw-on-increases -in-unemployment-by-age-and-education/.
14. Thompson, "Who's Had the Worst Recession."
15. Catherine Rampel, "Data Reveal a Rise in College Degrees Among Americans," *New York Times*, June 12, 2013, http://www.nytimes.com/2013/06/13/education/a -sharp-rise-in-americans-with-college-degrees.html?pagewanted=all&_r=0.
16. Pew Research Center's Social & Demographics Trends, "Millennials in Adulthood: Detached from Institutions, Networked with Friends," March 7, 2014, http://www .pewsocialtrends.org/2014/03/07/millennials-in-adulthood/.
17. Collegiate Employment Research Institute, "Parent Involvement in the College Recruiting Process: To What Extent?" Research Brief 2-2007, http://ceri.msu.edu /publications/pdf/ceri2-07.pdf.
18. Author's interview with Phil Garner, March 26, 2014. For more information, see also Phil Garner's "Parental Involvement in the College Recruitment Process: To What Extent?" Collegiate Employment Research Institute, Research Brief 2-2007, Michigan State University. http://ceri.msu.edu/publications/pdf/ceri2-07.pdf.

19. CERI White Paper: *Parent Involvement in the College Recruiting Process: To What Extent?* Research Brief 2-2007. http://ceri.msu.edu/publications/pdf/ceri2-07 .pdf.

5. TO WHAT END?

1. Katie Roiphe, *In Praise of Messy Lives* (New York: Dial Press, 2012), 193–94.
2. Jon Grinspan, "The Wild Children of Yesteryear," *New York Times,* May 31, 2014, http://www.nytimes.com/2014/06/01/opinion/sunday/the-wild-children-of-yes teryear.html?module=Search&mabReward=relbias%3Ar%2C%7B%222%22%3A %22RI%3A16%22%7D&_r=0.

6. OUR KIDS LACK BASIC LIFE SKILLS

1. Jim Hancock, *Raising Adults: Getting Kids Ready for the Real World* (Colorado Springs, Colo.: Navpress Publishing Group, 1999).
2. Robin Marantz Henig, "What Is It About 20-Somethings?" *New York Times,* August 18, 2010, http://www.nytimes.com/2010/08/22/magazine/22Adulthood-t.html?_r=0.
3. Larry J. Nelson, Laura M. Padilla-Walker, Jason S. Carroll, Stephanie D. Madsen, Carolyn McNamara Barry, and Sarah Badger, " 'If You Want Me to Treat You Like an Adult, Start Acting Like One!' Comparing the Criteria That Emerging Adults and Their Parents Have for Adulthood," *Journal of Family Psychology* 21, no. 4 (December 2007): 665–74.
4. Author's interview with Beth Gagnon, March 28, 2014.
5. Author's interview with physician, April 14, 2014.
6. Author's interview with Todd Burger, April 8, 2014.
7. Terry Castle, "Don't Pick Up: Why Kids Need to Separate from Their Parents," *Chronicle of Higher Education,* May 6, 2012.
8. Robert Krulwich, "Successful Children Who Lost a Parent—Why Are There So Many of Them?" *npr.org,* October 16, 2013, http://www.npr.org/blogs/krulwich/2013/10/15 /234737083/successful-children-who-lost-a-parent-why-are-there-so-many-of-them.
9. Ibid.
10. Terry Castle, "Don't Pick Up."
11. See Pew Research Center Social & Demographics Trends Project, "Forty Years After Woodstock, a Gentler Generation Gap," August 12, 2009. http://pewsocialtrends.org /pubs/739/woodstock-gentler-generation-gap-music-by-age.
12. Arthur Levine and Diane R. Dean, *Generation on a Tightrope: A Portrait of Today's College Student* (San Francisco: Jossey-Bass, 2012).
13. Ibid.
14. Ira Levin, *The Stepford Wives* (New York: Random House, 1972).

7. THEY'VE BEEN PSYCHOLOGICALLY HARMED

1. Author's interview with Charlie Gofen, April 9, 2014.
2. "College Students' Mental Health Is a Growing Concern, Survey Finds," *Monitor on Psychology* 44 (6), June 2013, http://www.apa.org/monitor/2013/06/college-students .aspx.
3. American College Health Association, *National College Health Assessment II: Reference Group Undergraduates Executive Summary,* Hanover, Md., Spring 2013.

4. James Wood, "Parental Intrusiveness and Children's Separation Anxiety in a Clinical Sample," *Child Psychiatry & Human Development* 37, no. 1 (Fall 2006): 73–87.

5. Patricia Somers and Jim Settle, "The Helicopter Parent: Research Toward a Typology," *College and University* 86, no. 1 (Summer 2010): 18–24, 26–27.

6. Rachael Rettner, "'Helicopter' Parents Have Neurotic Kids," *NBCNews*, June 3, 2010, http://www.nbcnews.com/id/37493795/ns/health-childrens_health/t/helicopter-parents-have-neurotic-kids/#.VAJMg2RdXyc.

7. T. LeMoyne and T. Buchanan, "Does 'Hovering' Matter? Helicopter Parenting and Its Effect on Well-Being," *Sociological Spectrum* 31, no. 4 (June 9, 2011): 399–418.

8. L. M. Padilla-Walker and L. J. Nelson, "Black Hawk Down? Establishing Helicopter Parenting as a Distinct Construct from Other Forms of Parental Control During Emerging Adulthood," *Journal of Adolescence* 35, no. 5 (October 2012): 1177–90.

9. H. Schiffrin et al., "Helping or Hovering? The Effects of Helicopter Parenting on College Students' Well-Being," *Journal of Child and Family Studies* 23 (2014): 548–57.

10. Jane E. Barker et al., "Less-Structured Time in Children's Daily Lives Predicts Self-Directed Executive Functioning," *Frontiers in Psychology* 5 (2014): 593, http://journal.frontiersin.org/Journal/10.3389/fpsyg.2014.00593/full.

11. *Emery-Weiner Drug, Alcohol, and Risky Behavior Report*, Survey, Beit T'Shuvah, Los Angeles, January 2013.

12. Author's interview with Harriet Rossetto, April 2, 2014.

13. Author's interview with clinician, April 1, 2014.

14. Madeline Levine, *The Price of Privilege: How Parental Pressure and Material Advantage Are Creating a Generation of Disconnected and Unhappy Kids* (New York: HarperCollins, 2006). Also see Madeline Levine, *Teach Your Children Well: Why Values and Coping Skills Matter More Than Grades, Trophies, or "Fat Envelopes"* (New York: HarperPerennial, 2013).

15. Madeline Levine, "Parenting for Authentic Success," talk at Henry M. Gunn High School, Palo Alto, California, January 29, 2014.

16. Madeline Levine, *Teach Your Children Well: Parenting for Authentic Success* (New York: HarperCollins, 2012).

17. Madeline Levine, *The Price of Privilege*. Also see Schiffrin et al., "Helping or Hovering?"

18. Amy Chua, *Battle Hymn of the Tiger Mother* (New York: Penguin Press, 2011).

19. Author's interview with Frank Wu, May 30, 2014. Also see Frank Wu's "Everything My Asian Immigrant Parents Taught Me Turns Out to Be Wrong," *Huffington Post*, April 28, 2014. http://www.huffingtonpost.com/frank-h-wu/everything-my-asian-immig_b_5227102.html.

20. Desiree Baolian Qin et al., "Parent-Child Relations and Psychological Adjustment Among High-Achieving Chinese and European American Adolescents," *Journal of Adolescence* 35, no. 4 (August 2012): 863–73.

21. *Race to Nowhere*. Lafayette, Calif.: Reel Link Films, 2010.

22. William Deresiewicz, *Excellent Sheep: The Miseducation of the American Elite and the Way to a Meaningful Life* (New York: Free Press, 2014), p. 16.

8. THEY'RE BECOMING "STUDY DRUG" ADDICTS

1. "Attention-Deficit/Hyperactivity Disorder (ADHD)," *cdc.gov*, 2014, http://www.cdc.gov/ncbddd/adhd/data.html.

2. Victoria Clayton, "Seeking Straight A's, Parents Push for Pills. Pediatricians Report Increasing Requests for 'Academic Doping,'" Growing Up Healthy, NBCNews.com,

September 7, 2006. http://www.nbcnews.com/id/14590058/ns/health-childrens
_health/t/seeking-straight-parents-push-pills/#.U-al8vm-2wc.

3. Author's interview with parent, October 30, 2014.

4. The Partnership at Drugfree.org, "2012 Partnership Attitude Tracking Study. Sponsored by MetLife Foundation, Teens and Parents," April 23, 2013. http://www.drugfree.org/wp-content/uploads/2013/04/PATS-2012-FULL-REPORT2.pdf.

5. American College Health Association, *National College Health Assessment II: Undergraduate Students Reference Group Executive Summary*, Hanover, Md., Spring 2013.

6. Arthur Levine and Diane R. Dean, *Generation on a Tightrope: A Portrait of Today's College Student* (San Francisco: Jossey-Bass, 2012).

7. Nancy Shute, "Neurologists Warn Against ADHD Drugs to Help Kids Study," *Your Health*, NPR, March 14, 2013. http://www.npr.org/blogs/health/2013/03/13/174193454/neurologists-warn-against-adhd-drugs-to-help-kids-study.

8. Ibid.

9. James L. Kent, "Adderall: America's Favorite Amphetamine," *hightimes.com*, May 9, 2013, http://www.hightimes.com/read/adderall-americas-favorite-amphetamine.

10. Author's interview with student, April 28, 2014.

9. WE'RE HURTING THEIR JOB PROSPECTS

1. Sarah LeTrent, "How Helicopter Parenting Can Ruin Kids' Job Prospects," *CNN Parents*, July 2, 2013. http://www.cnn.com/2013/07/02/living/cnn-parents-helicopter-parenting-job-search/index.html.

2. David Dobbs, "The Science of Success," *The Atlantic*, December 2009. http://www.theatlantic.com/magazine/print/2009/12/the-science-of-success/307761/.

3. Self-described "youthologist" Vanessa Van Petten, "10 Qualities of Teacup Parenting: Is Your Kid Too Fragile?" RadicalParenting.com, June 19, 2008. http://www.radicalparenting.com/2008/06/19/10-qualities-of-teacup-parenting-is-your-kid-too-fragile/.

4. J. Bradley-Geist and J. Olson-Buchanan, "Helicopter Parents: An Examination of the Correlates of Overparenting of College Students," *Education and Training* 56, no. 4 (2014): 314–28.

5. Find *Evil HR Lady* at http://evilhrlady.org; Suzanne Lucas's articles | Inc.com Suzanne Lucas's articles CBS MoneyWatch.

6. Author's interview with Suzanne Lucas, February 14, 2014.

7. Suzanne Lucas, "Why My Child Will Be Your Child's Boss," June 21, 2012, http://www.cbsnews.com/news/why-my-child-will-be-your-childs-boss/.

8. Author's interview with Lora Mitchell, March 27, 2013.

9. Author's interview with Carol Konicki, March 27, 2013.

10. Author's interview with Hope Hardison, February 7, 2014.

11. Author's interview with Tracy-Elizabeth Clay, July 18, 2013.

12. Author's interview with Eric Scroggins, February 24, 2014.

13. Author's interview with Tracy-Elizabeth Clay, July 18, 2013.

14. Lisa Needham, "Millennials, Your Boss Should Not Call Your Mommy to Talk About Your Job," *HappyNiceTimePeople.com*, April 15, 2014, http://happynicetimepeople.com/millennials-boss-call-mommy-talk-job/.

15. Vince Molinaro, "Do Millennials Really Want Their Bosses to Call Their Parents?" *Harvard Business Review*, April 14, 2014, http://blogs.hbr.org/2014/04/do-millennials-really-want-their-bosses-to-call-their-parents/.

16. Author's conversation with Nancy Altobello, March 6, 2014.

10. OVERPARENTING STRESSES US OUT, TOO

1. Jennifer Senior, "For Parents, Happiness Is a Very High Bar," TED2014, March 2014. http://www.ted.com/talks/jennifer_senior_for_parents_happiness_is_a_very _high_bar. Also by Senior, *All Joy and No Fun: The Paradox of Modern Parenting* (New York: Ecco, 2014).

2. R. F. Baumeister, *Meanings of Life* (New York: Guilford Press, 1991).

3. J. M. Pascoe, A. Stolfi, and M. B. Ormond, "Correlates of Mothers' Persistent Depressive Symptoms: A National Study," *Journal of Pediatric Health Care* 20, no. 4 (2006): 261–69.

4. Shawn Bean, "Xanax Makes Me a Better Mom," *Parenting.com*, (undated) http:// www.parenting.com/article/xanax.

5. "Cancel That Violin Class: Helicopter Moms and Dads Will Not Harm Their Kids if They Relax a Bit," *Economist*, July 26, 2014, http://www.economist.com/news /united-states/21608793-helicopter-moms-and-dads-will-not-harm-their-kids-if -they-relax-bit-cancel-violin.

6. Jordana K. Bayer et al., "Parent Influences on Early Childhood Internalizing Difficulties," *Journal of Applied Developmental Psychology* 27, no. 6 (2006): 542–59. Also see M. M. Weissman et al., "Offspring of Depressed Parents: 20 Years Later," *American Journal of Psychiatry* 163, no. 6 (July 2006): 1001–8.

7. Senior, "For Parents, Happiness Is a Very High Bar." Also by Senior, *All Joy and No Fun.*

8. Markella B. Rutherford, *Supervision Required: Private Freedoms and Public Constraints for Parents and Children* (New Brunswick, N.J.: Rutgers University Press, 2011).

9. Kathryn M. Rizzo, Holly H. Schiffrin, and Miriam Liss, "Insight into the Parenthood Paradox: Mental Health Outcomes of Intensive Mothering," *Journal of Child and Family Studies* 27, no. 5 (July 2013): 14–20.

10. Bonnie Rochman, "Mother Is Best? Why 'Intensive Parenting' Makes Moms More Depressed." *Time*, August 7, 2012, http://healthland.time.com/2012/08/07/mother -is-best-why-intensive-parenting-makes-moms-more-depressed/.

11. Annette Lareau, *Unequal Childhoods: Class, Race, and Family Life* (Berkeley: University of California Press, 2003).

12. Judith Warner, *Perfect Madness: Motherhood in the Age of Anxiety* (New York: Riverhead Books, 2005).

13. Author's interview with Beth Gagnon, March 28, 2014.

14. Author's interview with Stacy Budin, June 16, 2014.

15. Author's interview with parent, August 22, 2014.

16. Author's interview with parent, January 23, 2014.

17. Author's interview with parent, May 23, 2014.

18. Pamela Druckerman, *Bringing Up Bébé* (New York: Penguin Press, 2012), p. 144.

19. Ayelet Waldman, *Bad Mother: A Chronicle of Maternal Crimes, Minor Calamities, and Occasional Moments of Grace* (New York: Doubleday, 2009).

20. Author's interview with Ayelet Waldman, March 26, 2014.

21. Senior, "For Parents, Happiness Is a Very High Bar."

22. Author's interview with group of parents in Dallas, Texas, April 23, 2014.

23. Author's interview with parent, January 13, 2014.

24. Author's interview with Seattle parents, May 12, 2014.

25. Author's interview with Maurina, January 23, 2014.

26. Author's interview with group of parents in Dallas, Texas, April 23, 2014.

27. Ibid.
28. Ibid.
29. Ibid.
30. Judith Warner, *Perfect Madness*.
31. Author's interview with parent, May 24, 2014.
32. Author's interview with Stacy Budin, June 16, 2014.

11. THE COLLEGE ADMISSION PROCESS IS BROKEN

1. "How U.S. News Calculated the 2015 Best Colleges Rankings," *U.S. News & World Report*, September 8, 2014, http://www.usnews.com/education/best-colleges/articles/2014/09/08/how-us-news-calculated-the-2015-best-colleges-rankings.
2. "Mort Zuckerman Abruptly Ends Interview About U.S. News College Rankings," *MediaBistro.com*, May 22, 2007, http://www.mediabistro.com/fishbowlny/mort-zuckerman-abruptly-ends-interview-about-u-s-news-college-rankings_b5056.
3. Author's conversation with Stanford dean of admission and financial aid Richard Shaw, June 26, 2014.
4. Author's interview with Sidonia "Sid" Dalby, April 21, 2014.
5. William Deresiewicz, *Excellent Sheep: The Miseducation of the American Elite and the Way to a Meaningful Life* (New York: Free Press, 2014), p. 242.
6. Catherine Rampel, "Data Reveal a Rise in College Degrees Among Americans," *New York Times*, June 12, 2013, http://www.nytimes.com/2013/06/13/education/a-sharp-rise-in-americans-with-college-degrees.html?pagewanted=all&_r=0.
7. Though recently some colleges have been found to have manipulated these data so as to improve their ranking.
8. Deresiewicz, *Excellent Sheep*, 191.
9. Author's interview with Blaike Young, April 22, 2014.
10. Nona Willis Aronowitz, "Does the New SAT Spell Doom for the Test Prep Industry?" March 6, 2014, http://www.nbcnews.com/news/education/does-new-sat-spell-doom-test-prep-industry-n45936.
11. Author's interview with Barbara Cronan, March 10 and April 28, 2014.
12. Author's conversation with Ayelet Waldman, March 26, 2014.
13. Author's interview with Lloyd Thacker, March 5, 2014.
14. Michele Tolela Myers, "The Cost of Bucking College Rankings," *The Washington Post*, March 11, 2007, http://www.washingtonpost.com/wp-dyn/content/article/2007/03/09/AR2007030901836.html.
15. In 2013 Sarah Lawrence College became SAT-optional and was once again included in the *U.S. News* rankings.
16. Lloyd Thacker, *College Unranked: Ending the College Admissions Frenzy* (Cambridge, Mass.: Harvard University Press, 2005).
17. "U.S. News College Rankings Debated," *PBS Newshour*, August 20, 2007, http://www.pbs.org/newshour/bb/education-july-dec07-rankings_08-20/.
18. The swimsuit issue traditionally sells more than 1 million copies on newsstands (about ten to fifteen times as much as regular *SI*). http://www.businessinsider.com/business-facts-about-the-sports-illustrated-swimsuit-issue-2013-2.
19. Author's interview with Robert Sternberg, April 1, 2014.
20. R. J. Sternberg and the Rainbow Project Collaborators, "The Rainbow Project: Enhancing the SAT Through Assessments of Analytical, Practical and Creative Skills," *Intelligence* 34, no. 4 (2006): 321–50.

21. Author's interview with Larry Momo, March 3, 2014.
22. Deresiewicz, *Excellent Sheep*, 241.

12. THE CASE FOR ANOTHER WAY

1. Jeffrey Jensen Arnett and Elizabeth Fishel, *Getting to 30: A Parent's Guide to the 20-Something Years* (New York: Workman Publishing, 2014).
2. Albert Bandura, "Self-efficacy: Toward a Unifying Theory of Behavioral Change," *Psychological Review* 84 (1977): 191–215.
3. "Self-Efficacy in Children," *AboutKidsHealth*, August 30, 2012, http://www.about kidshealth.ca/En/HealthAZ/FamilyandPeerRelations/life-skills/Pages/Self-efficacy -children.aspx.
4. See William Damon, Foreword, in Richard Lerner and Laurence Steinberg, eds., *Handbook of Adolescent Psychology* (Hoboken, N.J.: John Wiley, 2004).
5. Author's interview with William Damon, October 2, 2014.
6. This information is gleaned from Dan H. Hockenbury and Sandra E. Hockenbury, *Psychology*, 6th ed. (New York: Worth Publishers, 2012); Amanda Ripley, *The Smartest Kids in the World: And How They Got That Way* (New York: Simon & Schuster, 2013); Joe Brewster, Michele Stephenson, and Hilary Beard, *Promises Kept: Raising Black Boys to Succeed in School and in Life* (New York: Spiegel & Grau, 2014); and Jelani Mandara, "An Empirically Derived Parenting Typology," paper presented at the Achievement Gap Initiative Conference, Harvard University, Cambridge, Mass., June 29, 2011.
7. Amanda Ripley, *The Smartest Kids in the World: And How They Got That Way* (New York: Simon & Schuster, 2013): 112.
8. Citing Mandara, "An Empirically Derived Parenting Typology" (paper presented at the Achievement Gap Initiative Conference, Harvard University, Cambridge, Mass., June 29, 2011).
9. Amy Chua, *Battle Hymn of the Tiger Mother* (New York: Penguin Press, 2011), 63.

13. GIVE THEM UNSTRUCTURED TIME

1. Hillary R. Clinton, "An Idyllic Childhood," in *The Games We Played: A Celebration of Childhood and Imagination*, ed. Steven A. Cohen, 161–65 (New York: Simon & Schuster, 2001).
2. Howard P. Chudacoff, *Children at Play: An American History* (New York: New York University Press, 2007).
3. Ibid., 223.
4. Peter Gray, "The Decline of Play and the Rise of Psychopathology in Children and Adolescents," *American Journal of Play* 3, no. 4 (Spring 2011): 443–63.
5. Susie Mesure, quoting Boston College psychologist and author of *Free to Learn*, Peter Gray. http://www.independent.co.uk/life-style/health-and-families/features/when -we-stop-children-taking-risks-do-we-stunt-their-emotional-growth-9422057 .html.
6. UN General Assembly, *Convention on the Rights of the Child*, November 20, 1989. United Nations, Treaty Series, vol. 1577, Article 31.
7. Hanna Rosin, "The Overprotected Kid," *The Atlantic*, April 2014, http://www.the atlantic.com/features/archive/2014/03/hey-parents-leave-those-kids-alone/358631/.
8. Michael Lanza, *Playborhood: Turn Your Neighborhood into a Place for Play* (Menlo Park, Calif.: Free Play Press, 2012).

9. Author's interview with Michael Lanza, July 31, 2013.
10. Peter Sims, "The Montessori Mafia," *The Wall Street Journal*, April 5, 2011, http://blogs.wsj.com/ideas-market/2011/04/05/the-montessori-mafia/.
11. Jay Mathews, "Montessori, Now 100, Goes Mainstream," *Washington Post*, January 2, 2007. http://www.washingtonpost.com/wp-dyn/content/article/2007/01/01/AR2007010100742.html.
12. Johan Nylander, "The Rise of Alternative Education in China," *CNN World: On China*, March 26, 2014. http://www.cnn.com/2014/03/26/world/asia/china-alternative-education/.
13. Yong Zhao, "Be Careful What You Wish For," *Education Week*, October 3, 2013, http://blogs.edweek.org/edweek/international_perspectives/2013/10/be_careful_what_you_wish_for.html?cmp=SOC-SHR-TW.
14. See Mihaly Csikszentmihalyi, "Flow, the Secret to Happiness," TED2004, February 2004. http://www.ted.com/talks/mihaly_csikszentmihalyi_on_flow.
15. "Mihaly Csikszentmihalyi: Motivating People to Learn," *Edutopia*, April 11, 2002, http://www.edutopia.org/mihaly-csikszentmihalyi-motivating-people-learn.
16. Nancy S. Cotton, "Childhood Play as an Analog to Adult Capacity to Work," *Child Psychiatry and Human Development* 14, no. 3 (Spring 1984): 135–44.
17. Stuart Brown, "Play Is More Than Just Fun," TED, May 2008. http://www.ted.com/talks/stuart_brown_says_play_is_more_than_fun_it_s_vital.
18. Judy Woodruff's interview with Hanna Rosin, "Should Parents Let Their Kids Take More Risks?" *PBS Newshour*, May 9, 2014. http://www.pbs.org/newshour/bb/parents-let-kids-take-risks/.

14. TEACH LIFE SKILLS

1. Author's interview with David McCullough, Jr., January 28, 2014.
2. Martin Seligman, *Authentic Happiness: Using the New Positive Psychology to Realize Your Potential for Lasting Fulfillment* (New York: Free Press, 2002).
3. Author's interviews with Harriett Rossetto, Doug Rosen, Adam Mindel, April 2014.
4. Author's interview with student, April 14, 2014.
5. Suniya Luthar, "The Problem with Rich Kids," *Psychology Today*, November 5, 2013, http://www.psychologytoday.com/articles/201310/the-problem-rich-kids.
6. Author's interview with Stacey Ashlund, May 6, 2014.
7. Lindsay Hutton, "I Did It All by Myself! An Age-by-Age Guide to Teaching Your Child Life Skills," *FamilyEducation.com* (undated). http://life.familyeducation.com/slideshow/independence/71434.html?page=1.
8. Author's interview with Adam Mindel, April 25, 2014.
9. Lenore Skenazy, *Free Range Kids: How to Raise Safe, Self-Reliant Children (Without Going Nuts with Worry)* (San Francisco: Jossey-Bass, 2010).
10. Author's interview with Jenny Ryan, Kristen Gracia, and David Ackerman, June 12, 2014.
11. Author's interview with student, April 14, 2014.

15. TEACH THEM HOW TO THINK

1. William Deresiewicz, *Excellent Sheep: The Miseducation of the American Elite and the Way to a Meaningful Life* (New York: Free Press, 2014).

2. Daniel Pink, *Drive: The Surprising Truth About What Motivates Us* (New York: Riverhead Books, 2009).

3. "The Art of Redesigning Instruction," *The Foundation for Critical Thinking* (undated), http://www.criticalthinking.org/pages/the-art-of-redesigning-instruction/520.

4. Amanda Ripley, *The Smartest Kids in the World: And How They Got That Way* (New York: Simon & Schuster, 2013).

5. "Study: Most College Students Lack Skills," *USA Today*, January 19, 2006, http://usatoday30.usatoday.com/news/education/2006-01-19-college-tasks_x.htm.

6. Denise Pope, *"Doing School": How We Are Creating a Generation of Stressed Out, Materialistic, and Miseducated Students* (New Haven, Conn.: Yale University Press, 2003).

7. M. Galloway, J. Connor, and D. Pope, "Nonacademic Effects of Homework in Privileged, High-Performing High Schools," *Journal of Experimental Education* 81, no. 4 (2013); http://www.challengesuccess.org/Portals/0/Docs/ChallengeSuccess-Homework-WhitePaper.pdf; http://www.washingtonpost.com/blogs/answer-sheet/wp/2014/03/13/homework-hurts-high-achieving-students-study-says/; http://www.washingtonpost.com/local/education/does-high-school-stress-have-to-be-a-bad-thing/2014/04/26/a824534c-cc00-11e3-93eb-6c0037dde2ad_story.html; http://time.com/41981/six-ways-to-end-the-tyranny-of-homework/; http://parenting.blogs.nytimes.com/2014/03/12/homeworks-emotional-toll-on-students-and-families/?_php=true&_type=blogs&_r=0.

8. Randye Hoder, "Six Ways to End the Tyranny of Homework," *Time*, March 28, 2014, http://time.com/41981/six-ways-to-end-the-tyranny-of-homework/.

9. Valerie Strauss, "Homework: An Unnecessary Evil? . . . Surprising Findings from New Research," *The Washington Post*, November 26, 2012, http://www.washingtonpost.com/blogs/answer-sheet/wp/2012/11/26/homework-an-unnecessary-evil-surprising-findings-from-new-research/.

10. "The Art of Redesigning Instruction," *The Foundation for Critical Thinking* (undated), http://www.criticalthinking.org/pages/the-art-of-redesigning-instruction/520.

11. Jennifer Fox, *Your Child's Strengths: A Guide for Parents and Teachers* (New York: Viking Adult, 2008).

12. Author interview with Jeff Brenzel, May 12, 2014.

13. Author interview with John Barton, September 23, 2014.

14. Carol Dweck, *Mindset: The New Psychology of Success* (New York: Ballantine Books, 2006).

15. Carol Dweck, "How Can You Change from a Fixed Mindset to a Growth Mindset?" *Mindset Online* (undated). http://mindsetonline.com/changeyourmindset/firststeps/.

16. Ibid.

17. Amanda Ripley, *The Smartest Kids in the World*, 198.

16. PREPARE THEM FOR HARD WORK

1. Author's interview with Stephen Parkhurst, February 25, 2014.

2. "Millennials: We Suck and We're Sorry," http://www.youtube.com/watch?v=M4IjTUxZORE.

3. "The PreparedU Project: An In-Depth Look at Millennial Preparedness for Today's Workforce," Bentley University, January 29, 2014. https://www.bentley.edu/files/prepared/1.29.2013_BentleyU_Whitepaper_Shareable.pdf.

4. For example, see Susan Tordella, *Raising Able: How Chores Nurture Grit and Self-Discipline in Children* (CreateSpace Independent Publishing Platform, 2012).

5. Dava Sobel, "Work Habits in Childhood Found to Predict Adult Well-Being," *New York Times*, November 10, 1981. http://www.nytimes.com/1981/11/10/science/work-habits-in-childhood-found-to-predict-adult-well-being.html.

6. Edward M. Hallowell, *The Childhood Roots of Adult Happiness: Five Steps to Help Kids Create and Sustain Lifetime Joy* (New York: Ballantine Books, 2002).

7. The findings of this 2008 study directed by Dr. Sandra Hofferth, of the Maryland Population Research Center at the University of Maryland, were featured in Sue Shellenbarger, "On the Virtues of Making Your Children Do the Dishes," *Wall Street Journal*, August 27, 2008. http://online.wsj.com/news/articles/SB121978677837474177.

8. Ibid.

9. Markella B. Rutherford, *Adult Supervision Required: Private Freedoms and Public Constraints for Parents and Children* (New Brunswick, N.J.: Rutgers University Press, 2011), pp. 337–53.

10. Annette Lareau, *Unequal Childhoods: Class, Race, and Family Life* (Berkeley: University of California Press, 2003).

11. Talk given at Challenge Success conference *Success by Design: Is it Possible?*, September 26, 2014.

12. Patricia Smith, "Pitch In! Getting Your Kids to Help with Chores," *Education.com*, March 5, 2009, http://www.education.com/magazine/article/Pitch_Getting_Your _Kids_Help/; Esther Davidowitz, "Get Kids to Pitch In," *Parenting.com* 2012, http:// www.parenting.com/article/get-kids-to-pitch-in; Annie Stuart, "Divide and Conquer Household Chores," *WebMD.com* (undated), http://www.webmd.com/parenting /features/chores-for-children.

13. Author's interview with Stephen Parkhurst, February 25, 2014.

14. Author's interview with Alexa Gulliford, May 22 and May 30, 2014.

15. Author's interview with employee, February 4, 2014.

17. LET THEM CHART THEIR OWN PATH

1. Author's interview with Sebastian Thrun, May 16, 2014.

2. William Damon, *The Path to Purpose: Helping Our Children Find Their Calling in Life* (New York: Free Press, 2008), 131.

3. Adam Smiley Poswolsky, *The Quarter-life Breakthrough* (San Francisco: 20s & 30s Press, 2014).

4. Author's interview with Rick Wartzman, June 3, 2014.

5. Rick Wartzman, "Some Words of Wisdom from Peter Drucker to My Daughter," *Time*, May 7, 2014. http://time.com/89695/some-words-of-wisdom-from-peter -drucker-to-my-daughter/.

6. Author's interview with Sebastian Thrun, May 16, 2014.

7. Author's interview with Jennifer Ayer Sandell, May 29, 2014.

8. Author's interview with Michele, January 23, 2014.

9. Author's interview with Holley, April 22, 2014.

10. William Damon, *The Path to Purpose*, 131.

11. Author's interview with Sebastian Thrun, May 16, 2014.

12. Author's interview with Adam Smiley Poswolsky, October 15, 2014.

13. William Damon, *The Path to Purpose*, 130.

14. Author's interview with lawyer, June 2, 2014.
15. William Deresiewicz, *Excellent Sheep: The Miseducation of the American Elite and the Way to a Meaningful Life* (New York: Free Press, 2014), pp. 121–22.

18. NORMALIZE STRUGGLE

1. Brené Brown, *Daring Greatly: How the Courage to Be Vulnerable Transforms the Way We Live, Love, Parent, and Lead* (New York: Gotham Books, 2012).
2. The Resilience Project, http://resilience.stanford.edu.
3. Sir Ken Robinson, "How Schools Kill Creativity," TED2006, http://www.ted.com/talks/ken_robinson_says_schools_kill_creativity.
4. Author's interview with Colonel Leon Robert, June 28, 2013.
5. Author's interview with Harriet Rossetto, April 2, 2014.
6. Author's interview with Phil Gardner, March 26, 2013.
7. Author's interview with Eric Scroggins, February 24, 2014.
8. Author's interview with Stephen Parkhurst, February 25, 2014.
9. Author's interview with Colonel Leon Robert, June 28, 2013.
10. William Deresiewicz, *Excellent Sheep: The Miseducation of the American Elite and the Way to a Meaningful Life* (New York: Free Press, 2014), p. 113.
11. Author's interview with James Willcox, May 22, 2014.
12. Carol Dweck, *Mindset: The New Psychology of Success* (New York: Ballantine Books, 2006); see also Dweck, http://mindsetonline.com/changeyourmindset/firststeps/.
13. Brené Brown, *The Gifts of Imperfection: Let Go of Who You Think You're Supposed to Be and Embrace Who You Are* (Center City, Minn.: Hazelden, 2010); Brené Brown, *Daring Greatly: How the Courage to be Vulnerable Transforms the Way We Live, Love, Parent, and Lead* (New York: Gotham Books, 2012).
14. Brené Brown, "The Power of Vulnerability," TEDxHouston, June 2010, http://www.ted.com/talks/brene_brown_on_vulnerability?language=en.
15. Angela Duckworth et al., "Grit: Perseverance and Passion for Long-Term Goals," *Journal of Personality and Social Psychology* 92, no. 6 (2007): 1087–1101.
16. Tim Elmore, *Generation iY: Our Last Chance to Save Their Future* (Atlanta: Poet Gardener Publishing, 2010).
17. Kenneth R. Ginsburg, *A Parent's Guide to Building Resilience in Children and Teens: Giving Your Child Roots and Wings* (Elk Grove Village, Ill.: American Academy of Pediatrics, 2011).
18. Jessica Lahey, *The Gift of Failure: How the Best Parents Learn to Let Go So Their Children Can Succeed* (New York: Harper, 2015).
19. M. W. Anderson and T. D. Johanson, *GIST: The Essence of Raising Life-Ready Kids* (Eden Prairie, GISTWorks, LLC, 2013).
20. Wendy Mogel, *The Blessing of a B Minus* (New York: Scribner, 2010).
21. Author's interview with Eric Scroggins, February 24, 2014.
22. Paul Tough, *How Children Succeed: Grit, Curiosity, and the Hidden Power of Character* (Boston, Mass.: Houghton Mifflin Harcourt, 2012).
23. Motoko Rich, "As Apprentices in the Classroom, Teachers Learn What Works," *New York Times*, October 10, 2014. http://www.nytimes.com/2014/10/11/us/as-apprentices-in-classroom-teachers-learn-what-works.html?module=Search&mabReward=relbias%3Aw%2C%7B%221%22%3A%22RI%3A8%22%7D&_r=0.

24. Rena Stone, Talk presented at annual fundraiser for Aspire Public Schools, San Francisco, California, May 20, 2014.
25. Author's interview with James Willcox, May 22, 2014.

19. HAVE A WIDER MIND-SET ABOUT COLLEGES

1. Author's interview with William Rivera, April 22, 2014.
2. Mitchell L. Stevens, *Creating a Class: College Admissions and the Education of Elites* (Cambridge, Mass.: Harvard University Press, 2007).
3. Barry Schwartz, *The Paradox of Choice: Why More Is Less* (New York: HarperPerennial, 2005).
4. Author's interview with Larry Momo, March 3, 2014.
5. Kayla Webley, "As College Applications Rise, So Does Indecision," *Time*, May 1, 2013, http://nation.time.com/2013/05/01/as-college-applications-rise-so-does -indecision/.
6. Author's interview with judge, May 12, 2014.
7. Dan Edmonds, "College Admissions: The Myth of Higher Selectivity," *Time*, March 20, 2013, http://ideas.time.com/2013/03/20/college-admissions-the-myth-of-higher -selectivity/.
8. Stacy Berg Dale and Alan B. Krueger, "Estimating the Payoff to Attending a More Selective College: An Application of Selection on Observables and Unobservables," *The National Bureau of Economic Research*, August 1999, http://www.nber.org/papers /w7322.
9. Gregg Easterbrook, "Who Needs Harvard?" *The Brookings Institution,* October 2004, http://www.brookings.edu/research/articles/2004/10/education-easterbrook.
10. William Deresiewicz, *Excellent Sheep: The Miseducation of the American Elite and the Way to a Meaningful Life* (New York: Free Press, 2014), p. 196.
11. Author's interview with Lou Adler, June 3, 2014.
12. Malcolm Gladwell, *David and Goliath: Underdogs, Misfits and the Art of Battling Giants* (New York: Little, Brown & Co., 2013).
13. The President and Fellows of Harvard College, "Undergraduate Colleges," *Harvard Law School* (undated), http://www.law.harvard.edu/prospective/jd/apply/undergrads .html.
14. Thomas L. Friedman, "How to Get a Job at Google," *New York Times,* February 22, 2014, http://www.nytimes.com/2014/02/23/opinion/sunday/friedman-how-to-get-a -job-at-google.html?_r=1.
15. Loren Pope, *Colleges That Change Lives: 40 Schools That Will Change the Way You Think About Colleges* (New York: Penguin, 2012).
16. Loren Pope, *Looking Beyond the Ivy Leagues: Finding the College That's Right for You* (New York: Penguin, 1990).
17. Author's interview with Christina Allen, May 23, 2014.
18. The National Center for Fair and Open Testing, "Colleges and Universities That Do Not Use SAT/ACT Scores for Admitting Substantial Numbers of Students into Bachelor Degree Programs," http://www.fairtest.org/university/optional.
19. Ranked 110th by *U.S. News.*
20. Ranked 38th by *U.S. News.*
21. Rebecca Schuman, "Bard's Better Admissions Application," *Slate,* June 6, 2014, http://www.slate.com/articles/life/education/2014/06/the_bard_admissions_exam _four_essays_no_common_application.html.

22. Ibid.

23. Ibid.

24. Author's interview with Lee Coffin, June 6, 2014.

25. Author's conversation with Tufts provost David Harris, April 24, 2014.

20. LISTEN TO THEM

1. Author's interview with Maeve Grogan, February 5, 2014.

2. Author's interview with Maurina, January 23, 2014.

3. The American Psychological Association, http://www.apa.org/helpcenter/commu
nication-parents.aspx.

4. Author's interview with Brandon, June 7, 2014.

5. Randye Hoder, *Why I Let My Daughter Get a "Useless" College Degree*, http://ideas
.time.com/2014/01/16/why-i-let-my-daughter-get-a-useless-college-degree/.

6. Author's interview with Randye Hoder and Emma, May 29, 2014.

7. Author's interview with student, May 29, 2014.

21. RECLAIM YOUR SELF

1. Author's interview with Catharine Jacobsen, May 14, 2014.

2. Annette Lareau, *Unequal Childhoods: Class, Race, and Family Life* (Berkeley,
Calif.: University of California Press, 2003).

3. Shawn Bean, "Xanax Makes Me a Better Mom," http://www.parenting.com/article
/xanax.

4. American Psychological Association, "APA Survey Raises Concern About Health
Impact of Stress on Children and Families," November 9, 2010, http://www.apa.org
/news/press/releases/2010/11/stress-in-america.aspx.

5. Christine Carter, *The Sweet: Spot: How to Find Your Groove at Home and Work* (New
York: Ballantine Books, 2015).

6. Brigid Schulte, *Overwhelmed: Work, Love, and Play When No One Has the Time*
(New York: Sarah Crichton Books, 2014).

7. Barbara Sher and Barbara Smith, *I Could Do Anything if I Only Knew What It Was:
How to Discover What You Really Want and How to Get It* (New York: Delacorte
Press, 1994); Eckhart Tolle, *A New Earth: Awakening to Your Life's Purpose* (an Oprah
selection), (New York: Penguin, 2005).

8. George Vaillant, *Triumphs of Experience: The Men of the Harvard Grant Study*
(Cambridge, Mass.: Belknap Press, 2012). See also http://positivepsychologynews.com
/news/george-vaillant/200907163163.

9. Christine Carter, *Raising Happiness: 10 Simple Steps for More Joyful Kids and Happier
Parents* (New York: Ballantine Books, 2010).

10. Carter, *The Sweet Spot.*

11. Author's interview with student, April 14, 2014.

12. Author's interview with mother, May 14, 2014.

22. BE THE PARENT YOU WANT TO BE

1. Brian Morton, "Falser Words Were Never Spoken," *New York Times*, August 29,
2011, http://www.nytimes.com/2011/08/30/opinion/falser-words-were-never-spoken
.html?_r=0.

2. Christine Carter, *The Sweet Spot: How to Find Your Groove at Home and Work* (New York: Ballentine Books, 2015).

3. Carter, *The Sweet Spot*, quoting Brené Brown.

4. Author's interview with parent, February 19 and October 27, 2014.

5. Author's interview with Maurina, January 23, 2014.

6. Author's interview with Lisa, November 13, 2014.

7. Author's interview with Carole, November 13, 2014.

8. Author's interview with parent, February 19 and October 27, 2014.

9. Author's interview with parent, November 20, 2014.

10. Author's interview with Kristen, November 14, 19, and 20, 2014.

11. Katrina Kenison, *The Gift of an Ordinary Day: A Mother's Memoir* (New York: Springboard Press, 2009).

12. Author's interview with Christine, November 13, 2014.

13. Author's interview with Maurice, November 14, 2014.

14. Author's interview with Rani, November 13, 2014.

15. Author's interview with Jeff Gamble, November 13 and 21, and December 5, 2014.

16. Author's interview with Maeve Grogan, February 5, 2014.

CONCLUSION

1. William Deresiewicz, *Excellent Sheep: The Miseducation of the American Elite and the Way to a Meaningful Life* (New York: Free Press, 2014), 58.

BIBLIOGRAPHY

Adwar, Corey. "Support Grows Online for Mom Who Lost Custody of Daughter After Letting Her Play Alone at a Park." *Business Insider,* July 16, 2014. http://www.businessinsider.com/debra-harrell-arrested-for-allegedly-letting-daughter-play-alone-at-park-2014-7.

The Alumni Factor, http://www.alumnifactor.com.

The American Psychological Association. "APA Survey Raises Concern About Health Impact of Stress on Children and Families." November 9, 2010. http://www.apa.org/news/press/releases/2010/11/stress-in-america.aspx.

The American Psychological Association, http://www.apa.org/helpcenter/communication-parents.aspx.

"The Art of Redesigning Instruction," *The Foundation for Critical Thinking.* http://www.criticalthinking.org/pages/the-art-of-redesigning-instruction/520.

Anderson, Michael W., and Timothy D. Johanson. *Gist: The Essence of Raising Life-Ready Kids* (Eden Prairie, Minn.: GISTWorks, LLC, 2013).

"Attention-Deficit/Hyperactivity Disorder (ADHD)," *cdc.gov* (Atlanta, Ga.: Centers for Disease Control and Prevention, 2014). http://www.cdc.gov/ncbddd/adhd/data.html.

Bandura, Albert. "Self-Efficacy: Toward a Unifying Theory of Behavioral Change," *Psychological Review* 84 (1977): 191–215.

———. "Self-Efficacy," *Encyclopedia of Human Behavior* 4 (New York: Academic Press, 1994).

Barker, Jane E., et al. "Less-Structured Time in Children's Daily Lives Predicts Self-Directed Executive Functioning," *Frontiers in Psychology* 5:593 (2014). http://journal.frontiersin.org/Journal/10.3389/fpsyg.2014.00593/full.

Baumeister, R. F. *Meanings of Life* (New York: Guilford, 1991).

Bayer, Jordana K., et. al., "Parent Influences on Early Childhood Internalizing Difficulties," *Journal of Applied Developmental Psychology* 27.6 (2006): 542–59.

Bean, Shawn. "Xanax Makes Me a Better Mom." *Parenting.com* (undated). http://www.parenting.com/article/xanax.

Boyles, Salynn. "Sports-Related Concussions on the Rise in Kids," (New York: WebMD, August 30, 2010.) http://www.webmd.com/parenting/news/20100830/sports-related -concussions-on-the-rise-in-kids.

Bradley-Geist, J., and J. Olson-Buchanan. "Helicopter Parents: An Examination of the Correlates of Over-parenting of College Students." *Education & Training*, 56 (4), (2014).

Brewster, Joe, Michele Stephenson, and Hilary Beard. *Promises Kept: Raising Black Boys to Succeed in School and in Life* (New York: Spiegel & Grau, 2014).

Brooks, Kim. "The Day I Left My Son in the Car." *Salon*, June 3, 2014.

Bronson, Po. "How Not to Talk to Your Kids: The Inverse Power of Praise," New York, August 3, 2007. http://nymag.com/news/features/27840/.

Bronson, Po, and Ashley Merryman. *NurtureShock: New Thinking About Children* (New York: Twelve, 2009).

Brown, Brené. *Daring Greatly: How the Courage to Be Vulnerable Transforms the Way We Live, Love, Parent and Lead* (New York: Gotham Books, 2012).

———. *The Gifts of Imperfection: Let Go of Who You Think You're Supposed to Be and Embrace Who You Are* (Center City, Minn.: Hazelden, 2010).

Brown, Brené. "The Power of Vulnerability," TEDxHouston, June 2010. http://www.ted .com/talks/brene_brown_on_vulnerability?language=en.

Brown, Stuart. "Play Is More Than Just Fun." TED, May 2008. http://www.ted.com/talks /stuart_brown_says_play_is_more_than_fun_it_s_vital.

Buckingham, Marcus. *Now, Discover Your Strengths* (New York: Free Press, 2001).

"Cancel That Violin Class: Helicopter Moms and Dads Will Not Harm Their Kids if They Relax a Bit," *Economist*, July 26, 2014. http://www.economist.com/news/united -states/21608793-helicopter-moms-and-dads-will-not-harm-their-kids-if-they -relax-bit-cancel-violin.

Cantu, Robert, and Mark Hyman. *Concussions and Our Kids: America's Leading Expert on How to Protect Young Athletes and Keep Sports Safe* (Boston: Houghton Mifflin Harcourt, 2012).

Carter, Christine. *Raising Happiness: 10 Simple Steps for More Joyful Kids and Happier Parents* (New York: Ballantine Books, 2010).

———. *The Sweet Spot: How to Find Your Groove at Home and Work* (New York: Ballantine Books, 2015).

Castle, Terry. "Don't Pick Up: Why Kids Need to Separate from Their Parents," *The Chronicle of Higher Education*, May 6, 2012.

Challenge Success (www.challengesuccess.org).

"Changing the Conversation About Homework from Quantity and Achievement to Quality and Engagement" (Stanford, Calif.: Challenge Success, 2012). http://www .challengesuccess.org/Portals/0/Docs/ChallengeSuccess-Homework-WhitePaper .pdf.

Chua, Amy. *Battle Hymn of the Tiger Mother* (New York: Penguin Press, 2011).

Chudacoff, Howard P. *Children at Play: An American History* (New York: New York University Press, 2007).

Clayton, Victoria. "Seeking Straight A's, Parents Push for Pills. Pediatricians Report Increasing Requests for 'Academic Doping.'" *NBCNews.com*, September 7, 2006. http://www.nbcnews.com/id/14590058/ns/health-childrens_health/t/seeking -straight-parents-push-pills/#.U-al8vm-2wc.

Cline, Foster W., and Jim Fay. *Parenting with Love and Logic: Teaching Children Responsibility* (Colorado Springs: Pinon Press, 1990): 23–25.

Clinton, Hillary R. "An Idyllic Childhood," in *The Games We Played: A Celebration of Childhood and Imagination*, ed. Steven A. Cohen (New York: Simon & Schuster, 2001): 161–65.

College Board. "Big Future." http://www.bigfuture.collegeboard.org.

Colleges That Change Lives, http://www.ctcl.org.

"College Students' Mental Health Is a Growing Concern, Survey Finds," *Monitor on Psychology* 44 (6) (Washington, D.C.: American Psychological Association, June 2013). http://www.apa.org/monitor/2013/06/college-students.aspx.

Collegiate Employment Research Institute, http://www.ceri.msu.edu.

Collegiate Employment Research Institute, "Parent Involvement in the College Recruiting Process: To What Extent?" Research Brief 2-2007. http://ceri.msu.edu /publications/pdf/ceri2-07.pdf.

Copeland, Kristen A., et al. "Societal Values and Policies May Curtail Preschool Children's Physical Activity in Child Care Centers," *Pediatrics* 129 (2) (Elk Grove Village, Ill.: American Academy of Pediatrics, February 2012). http://pediatrics.aappublications .org/content/early/2012/01/02/peds.2011-2102.full.pdf+html.

Cotton, Nancy S. "Childhood Play As an Analog to Adult Capacity to Work, Child Psychiatry and Human Development." *Human Sciences Press*, Vol. 14 (3) (Spring 1984).

Csikszentmihalyi, Mihaly. *Flow: The Psychology of Optimal Experience* (New York: Harper & Row, 1990).

———. "Flow, the Secret to Happiness." TED2004. February 2004. http://www.ted.com /talks/mihaly_csikszentmihalyi_on_flow.

Dale, Stacy Berg, and Alan B. Krueger. "Estimating the Payoff to Attending a More Selective College: An Application of Selection on Observables and Unobservables." *The National Bureau of Economic Research* (August 1999). http://www.nber.org/papers /w7322.

Damon, William. *The Path to Purpose: Helping Our Children Find Their Calling in Life* (New York: Free Press, 2008).

———. Foreword, in Richard Lerner and Laurence Steinberg, eds., *Handbook of Adolescent Psychology* (New York: John Wiley & Sons, 2004).

Davidowitz, Esther. "Get Kids to Pitch In," *Parenting. http://www.parenting.com/print /388207.*

Dell'Antonia, K. J. "Homework's Emotional Toll on Students and Families," *New York Times*, March 12, 2014. http://parenting.blogs.nytimes.com/2014/03/12/homeworks -emotional-toll-on-students-and-families/?_php=true&_type=blogs&_r=0.

Deresiewicz, William. *Excellent Sheep: The Miseducation of the American Elite and the Way to a Meaningful Life* (New York: Free Press, 2014).

Dickerson, John. "Wait, Am I That Baseball Dad? How Baseball Encourages Bad Parenting—And How You Can Support Your Kids on the Diamond Without Driving Them Crazy." *Slate*, June 19, 2013. http://www.slate.com/articles/sports/sports_nut /2013/06/baseball_parents_how_dads_stress_their_kids_out_during_little_league _games.html.

Divoky, Diane. "Missing Tot Estimates Exaggerated," *Lodi News-Sentinel*, February 18, 1986.

Dobbs, David. "The Science of Success." *The Atlantic*, December 2009. http://www .theatlantic.com/magazine/print/2009/12/the-science-of-success/307761/.

Douthat, Ross. "The Parent Trap." *New York Times*, July 19, 2014.

Druckerman, Pamela. *Bringing Up Bébé: One American Mother Discovers the Wisdom of French Parenting* (New York: Penguin Press, 2012).

Duckworth, Angela, et al. "Grit: Perseverance and Passion for Long-Term Goals." *Journal of Personality and Social Psychology* 92, no. 6 (2007): 1087–1101.

Dweck, Carol. "How Can You Change from a Fixed Mindset to a Growth Mindset?" *Mindset Online.* http://mindsetonline.com/changeyourmindset/firststeps/.

——. *Mindset: The New Psychology of Success* (New York: Random House, 2006).

Easterbrook, Gregg. "Who Needs Harvard?" *The Brookings Institution,* October 2004. http://www.brookings.edu/research/articles/2004/10/education-easterbrook

Edmonds, Dan. "College Admissions: The Myth of Higher Selectivity," *Time,* March 20, 2013. http://ideas.time.com/2013/03/20/college-admissions-the-myth-of -higher-selectivity/.

Ekins, Emily. "UPDATED/Poll: 68 Percent of Americans Don't Think Nine-Year-Olds Should Play at the Park Unsupervised." *Reason-Rupe Poll,* August 19, 2014. http: //reason.com/poll/2014/08/19/august-2014-reason-rupe-national-survey.

Elmore, Tim. *Artificial Maturity: Helping Kids Meet the Challenge of Becoming Authentic Adults* (San Francisco: Jossey-Bass, 2012).

——. *Generation iY: Our Last Chance to Save Their Future* (Troy, Mich.: Poet Gardener, 2010).

"Emery-Weiner Drug, Alcohol, and Risky Behavior Report" (Los Angeles: Beit T'Shuvah, January 2013).

Epstein, David. "Sports Should Be Child's Play." *New York Times,* June 10, 2014. http: //www.nytimes.com/2014/06/11/opinion/sports-should-be-childs-play.html.

FairTest: The National Center for Fair and Open Testing, http://www.fairtest.org/.

Finkelhor, David. "Five Myths About Missing Children." *Washington Post,* May 10, 2013. http://www.washingtonpost.com/opinions/five-myths-about-missing-children/2013 /05/10/efee398c-b8b4-11e2-aa9e-a02b765ff0ea_story.html.

Finkelhor, David, Heather Hammer, and Andrea J. Sedlak. "Second National Incidence Studies of Missing, Abducted, Runaway, and Thrownaway Children" (Washington, D.C.: U.S. Dept. of Justice, Office of Justice Programs, Office of Juvenile Justice and Delinquency Prevention, 2002).

The Foundation for Critical Thinking, http://www.criticalthinking.org.

Fox, Jennifer. *Your Child's Strengths: A Guide for Parents and Teachers* (New York: Viking Adult, 2008).

Frederickson, Barbara. *Positivity: Groundbreaking Research Reveals How to Embrace the Hidden Strength of Positive Emotions, Overcome Negativity, and Thrive* (New York: Harmony, 2009).

Friedman, Thomas L. "How to Get a Job at Google," *New York Times,* February 22, 2014. http://www.nytimes.com/2014/02/23/opinion/sunday/friedman-how-to-get-a-job-at -google.html?_r=1.

Galloway, M., J. Connor, and D. Pope, "Nonacademic Effects of Homework in Privileged, High-Performing High Schools." *Journal of Experimental Education* 81 (4) (2013).

Gallup Strengths Center, http://www.gallupstrengthscenter.com.

Gerson, Michael. "Saying Goodbye to My Child, the Youngster," *New York Times,* August 19, 2013. http://www.washingtonpost.com/opinions/michael-gerson-saying -goodbye-to-my-child-the-youngster/2013/08/19/6337802e-08dd-11e3-8974 -f97ab3b3c677_story.html.

Gibbs, Nancy. "The Growing Backlash Against Overparenting," *Time,* November 30, 2009.

Ginsburg, Kenneth R. *A Parent's Guide to Building Resilience in Children and Teens:*

Giving Your Child Roots and Wings (Elk Grove Village, Ill.: American Academy of Pediatrics, 2011).

Girl Scouts. "Cookie/Council-Sponsored Product Sale: Safety Activity Checkpoints." May 2, 2011. http://www.girlscouts.org/program/gs_cookies/pdf/2012_cookie _product_sale_safety_activity_checkpoints.pdf.

Gladwell, Malcolm. *David and Goliath: Underdogs, Misfits and the Art of Battling Giants* (New York: Little, Brown & Company, 2013).

———. *Outliers: The Story of Success* (New York: Little, Brown & Company, 2007).

Glass, Ira. "How I Got into College" (interview with Rich Clark). *This American Life* 504, September 6, 2013. http://www.thisamericanlife.org/radio-archives/episode /504/how-i-got-into-college.

Gray, Peter. "The Decline of Play and the Rise of Psychopathology in Children and Adolescents." *American Journal of Play*, Vol. 3, No. 4 (2011).

Grinspan, Jon. "The Wild Children of Yesteryear," *New York Times*, May 31, 2014. http: //www.nytimes.com/2014/06/01/opinion/sunday/the-wild-children-of-yesteryear .html?module=Search&mabReward=relbias%3Ar%2C%7B%222%22%3A%22RI% 3A16%22%7D&_r=0.

Hallowell, Edward M. *The Childhood Roots of Adult Happiness: Five Steps to Help Kids Create and Sustain Lifetime Joy* (New York: Ballantine Books, 2002).

Hancock, Jim. *Raising Adults: Getting Kids Ready for the Real World* (Carol Stream, Ill.: Navpress Publishing Group, 1999).

Handbook for Public Playground Safety, U.S. Consumer Product Safety Commission (1981).

Henig, Robin Marantz. "What Is It About 20-Somethings?" *New York Times*, August 18, 2010. http://www.nytimes.com/2010/08/22/magazine/22Adulthood-t.html?_r=0.

Hockenbury, Dan H., and Sandra E. Hockenbury, *Psychology* (New York: Worth Publishers, 6th ed., 2012).

Hoder, Randye. "Six Ways to End the Tyranny of Homework," *Time*, March 28, 2014. http://time.com/41981/six-ways-to-end-the-tyranny-of-homework/.

———. *Why I Let My Daughter Get a Useless College Degree*. http://ideas.time.com/2014 /01/16/why-i-let-my-daughter-get-a-useless-college-degree/.

"How U.S. News Calculated the 2015 Best Colleges Rankings," *U.S. News & World Report*, September 8, 2014. http://www.usnews.com/education/best-colleges/articles /2014/09/08/how-us-news-calculated-the-2015-best-colleges-rankings.

Hutton, Lindsay. "I Did It All by Myself! An Age-by-Age Guide to Teaching Your Child Life Skills," *FamilyEducation.com*. http://life.familyeducation.com/slideshow /independence/71434.html?page=1.

Kenison, Katrina. *The Gift of an Ordinary Day: A Mother's Memoir* (New York: Springboard Press, 2009).

Kent, James L. "Adderall: America's Favorite Amphetamine," *hightimes.com*, May 9, 2013. http://www.hightimes.com/read/adderall-americas-favorite-amphetamine.

"Kids Who Specialize in One Sport May Have Higher Injury Risk, Loyola Study Finds." (Maywood, Ill.: Loyola University Health System, May 2, 2011). http://www .loyolamedicine.org/childrenshospital/newswire/news/kids-who-specialize-one -sport-may-have-higher-injury-risk-loyola-study-finds.

Konczal, Mike. "What Conclusions Can You Draw on Increases in Unemployment by Age and Education?" *Rortybomb.wordpress.com*, October 20, 2010. http://rortybomb .wordpress.com/2010/10/20/what-conclusions-can-you-draw-on-increases-in -unemployment-by-age-and-education/.

Krulwich, Robert. "Successful Children Who Lost a Parent—Why Are There So Many of Them?" *npr.org*, October 16, 2013. http://www.npr.org/blogs/krulwich/2013/10/15 /234737083/successful-children-who-lost-a-parent-why-are-there-so-many-of-them.

Lahey, Jessica. *The Gift of Failure: How the Best Parents Learn to Let Go So Their Children Can Succeed* (New York: HarperCollins, 2015).

Lanza, Michael. *Playborhood: Turn Your Neighborhood into a Place for Play* (Menlo Park, Calif.: Free Play Press, 2012).

Lareau, Annette. *Unequal Childhoods: Class, Race, and Family Life* (Berkeley, Calif.: University of California Press, 2003).

"Legal Age Restrictions for Latchkey Kids." http://www.latchkey-kids.com/latchkey -kids-age-limits.htm.

LeMoyne, T., and T. Buchanan. "Does "Hovering" Matter? Helicopter Parenting and Its Effect on Well-Being." *Sociological Spectrum*, Vol. 31, Issue 4 (2011).

LeTrent, Sarah. "How Helicopter Parenting Can Ruin Kids' Job Prospects." *CNN.com*. July 2, 2013. http://www.cnn.com/2013/07/02/living/cnn-parents-helicopter-parenting -job-search/index.html.

Levin, Ira. *The Stepford Wives* (New York: Random House, 1972).

Levine, Arthur, and Diane R. Dean. *Generation on a Tightrope: A Portrait of Today's College Student* (San Francisco: Jossey-Bass, 2012).

Levine, Madeline. *The Price of Privilege: How Parental Pressure and Material Advantage Are Creating a Generation of Disconnected and Unhappy Kids* (New York: Harper-Collins, 2006).

———. *Teach Your Children Well: Parenting for Authentic Success* (New York: Harper-Collins, 2012).

Lewis, Dan. "Where Did the Fear of Poisoned Candy Come From?" *Smithsonian.com*. October 6, 2013. http://www.smithsonianmag.com/not-categorized/where-did-the -fear-of-poisoned-halloween-candy-come-from-822302/.

Lewis, Michael. "Coach Fitz's Management Theory," *New York Times*, March 28, 2004. http://www.nytimes.com/2004/03/28/magazine/coach-fitz-s-management-theory .html?src=pm&pagewanted=8.

———. *Coach: Lessons on the Game of Life* (New York: Norton, 2005).

LinkedIn University Rankings, http://www.linkedin.com.

Lodish, Emily. "Global Parenting Habits That Haven't Caught on in the U.S." *npr.org*, August 12, 2014. http://www.npr.org/blogs/parallels/2014/08/12/339825261/global -parenting-habits-that-havent-caught-on-in-the-u-s.

Louv, Richard. *Last Child in the Woods: Saving Our Children from Nature-Deficit Disorder* (Chapel Hill, N.C.: Algonquin Books of Chapel Hill, 2005).

Lucas, Suzanne. *EvilHRLady.org*.

———. "Why My Child Will Be Your Child's Boss." http://www.cbsnews.com/news /why-my-child-will-be-your-childs-boss/.

Luthar, Suniya. "The Problem with Rich Kids." *Psychology Today*, November 5, 2013. http://www.psychologytoday.com/articles/201310/the-problem-rich-kids.

Lythcott-Haims, Julie. "When Did Caring Become Control? Blame Boomers," *Chicago Tribune*, October 16, 2005.

Machado, Antonio. "XXIX." In *Border of a Dream: Selected Poems*, translated by Willis Barnstone, Port Townsend, WA: Copper Canyon Press, 2003.

Mandara, Jelani. "An Empirically Derived Parenting Typology" (paper presented at the Achievement Gap Initiative Conference, Harvard University, Cambridge, Mass., June 29, 2011).

Marano, Hara Estroff. *A Nation of Wimps: The High Cost of Invasive Parenting* (New York: Broadway Books, 2008).

Mathews, Jay. "Does High School Stress Have to Be a Bad Thing?" *Washington Post*, April 27, 2014. http://www.washingtonpost.com/local/education/does-high-school-stress-have-to-be-a-bad-thing/2014/04/26/a824534c-cc00-11e3-93eb-6c0037dde2ad_story.html.

———. "Montessori, Now 100, Goes Mainstream," *Washington Post*, January 2, 2007. http://www.washingtonpost.com/wp-dyn/content/article/2007/01/01/AR2007010100742.html.

McCullough, Jr., David. *You Are Not Special: And Other Encouragements* (New York: Ecco, 2014).

Mesure, Susie. "When We Stop Children Taking Risks, Do We Stunt Their Emotional Growth?" *The Independent*, May 25, 2014. http://www.independent.co.uk/life-style/health-and-families/features/when-we-stop-children-taking-risks-do-we-stunt-their-emotional-growth-9422057.html.

"Mihaly Csíkszentmihályi: Motivating People to Learn," *Edutopia*, April 11, 2002. http://www.edutopia.org/mihaly-csikszentmihalyi-motivating-people-learn.

Mogel, Wendy. *The Blessing of a B Minus: Using Jewish Teachings to Raise Resilient Teenagers* (New York: Scribner, 2010).

———. *The Blessing of a Skinned Knee: Using Jewish Teachings to Raise Self-Reliant Children* (New York: Scribner, 2001).

———. "Success by Design: Is It Possible?" Talk presented at the annual conference of Challenge Success, Stanford, California, September 26, 2014.

Molinaro, Vince. "Do Millennials Really Want Their Bosses to Call Their Parents?" *Harvard Business Review*, April 14, 2014. http://blogs.hbr.org/2014/04/do-millennials-really-want-their-bosses-to-call-their-parents/.

Morton, Brian. "Falser Words Were Never Spoken," *New York Times*, August 29, 2011. http://www.nytimes.com/2011/08/30/opinion/falser-words-were-never-spoken.html?_r=0.

"Mort Zuckerman Abruptly Ends Interview About U.S. News College Rankings," *MediaBistro.com*, May 22, 2007. http://www.mediabistro.com/fishbowlny/mort-zuckerman-abruptly-ends-interview-about-u-s-news-college-rankings_b5056.

Myers-Briggs Type Indicator http://www.myersbriggs.org.

Myers, Michele Tolela. "The Cost of Bucking College Rankings," *Washington Post*, March 11, 2007. http://www.washingtonpost.com/wp-dyn/content/article/2007/03/09/AR2007030901836.html.

"National College Health Assessment II: Reference Group Undergraduates Executive Summary" (Hanover, Md.: American College Health Association, Spring 2013).

National Commission on Excellence in Education. "A Nation at Risk: The Imperative for Educational Reform: a Report to the Nation and the Secretary of Education, United States Department of Education" (Washington D.C., 1983).

Neal, Nicole. "How Dangerous Is Childhood?" *Palm Beach Post*, August 13, 2006.

Needham, Lisa. "Millennials, Your Boss Should Not Call Your Mommy to Talk About Your Job," *HappyNiceTimePeople.com*, April 15, 2014. http://happynicetimepeople.com/millennials-boss-call-mommy-talk-job/.

Nelson, Larry J., et al. "'If you want me to treat you like an adult, start acting like one!' Comparing the criteria that emerging adults and their parents have for adulthood." *Journal of Family Psychology* 21, no. 4 (December 2007).

Nylander, Johan. "The Rise of Alternative Education in China." *CNN World: On China*.

March 26, 2014. http://www.cnn.com/2014/03/26/world/asia/china-alternative -education/.

"Obama Getting Emotionally Ready for Malia's College Departure," *CBSNews.com*, July 28, 2014. http://www.cbsnews.com/news/obama-getting-emotionally-ready -for-malias-college-departure/.

Padilla-Walker, L. M., and L. J. Nelson. "Black Hawk Down? Establishing Helicopter Parenting as a Distinct Construct from Other Forms of Parental Control During Emerging Adulthood." *Journal of Adolescence* 35 (2012): 1177–90.

Palmer, Brian. "Why Did Missing Children Start Showing Up on Milk Cartons?" *Slate .com.* April 20, 2012. http://www.slate.com/articles/news_and_politics/explainer /2012/04/etan_patz_case_why_did_dairies_put_missing_children_on_their _milk_cartons_.html.

Parkhurst, Stephen. "Millennials: We Suck and We're Sorry," http://www.youtube.com /watch?v=M4IjTUxZORE.

The Partnership for a Drug-Free America at Drugfree.org. "2012 Partnership Attitude Tracking Study. Sponsored by MetLife Foundation, Teens and Parents." *Drugfree .org*, April 23, 2013. http://www.drugfree.org/wp-content/uploads/2013/04/PATS -2012-FULL-REPORT2.pdf.

Pascoe, J. M., A. Stolfi, and M. B. Ormond. "Correlates of Mothers' Persistent Depressive Symptoms: A National Study." *Journal of Pediatric Health Care* 20 (4) (2006): 261–69.

Pew Research Center's Social & Demographics Trends. "Forty Years after Woodstock, A Gentler Generation Gap." August 12, 2009. http://www.pewsocialtrends.org /2009/08/12/forty-years-after-woodstockbra-gentler-generation-gap/.

———. "Millennials in Adulthood: Detached from Institutions, Networked with Friends." March 7, 2014. http://www.pewsocialtrends.org/2014/03/07/millennials -in-adulthood/.

Pink, Daniel. *Drive: The Surprising Truth About What Motivates Us* (New York: Riverhead Books, 2009).

Pope, Denise Clark. *"Doing School": How We're Creating a Generation of Stressed-Out, Materialistic, and Miseducated Students* (New Haven, Conn.: Yale University Press, 2001).

Pope, Denise, and Maureen Brown. *Overloaded and Underprepared: Strategies for Stronger Schools and Healthy, Successful Kids* (San Francisco: Jossey-Bass, 2015).

Pope, Loren. *Colleges That Change Lives: 40 Schools That Will Change the Way You Think About Colleges* (New York: Penguin, 2012).

———. *Looking Beyond the Ivy League: Finding the College That's Right for You* (New York: Penguin, 1996).

Porter, Susan Eva. *Bully Nation: Why America's Approach to Childhood Aggression Is Bad for Everyone* (St. Paul, Minn.: Paragon House, 2013).

Poswolsky, Adam Smiley. *The Quarter-life Breakthrough* (San Francisco: 20s & 30s Press, 2014).

The PreparedU Project: An In-Depth Look at Millennial Preparedness for Today's Workforce," Bentley University, January 29, 2014. https://www.bentley.edu/files /prepared/1.29.2013_BentleyU_Whitepaper_Shareable.pdf.

Qin, Desiree Baolian, et al. "Parent-Child Relations and Psychological Adjustment Among High-Achieving Chinese and European American Adolescents," *Journal of Adolescence*, 35, no. 4 (August 2012): 863–73.

Race to Nowhere, director Vicki Abeles (Lafayette, Calif.: Reel Link Films, 2010).

Rampel, Catherine. "Data Reveal a Rise in College Degrees Among Americans," *New York Times*, June 12, 2013. http://www.nytimes.com/2013/06/13/education/a-sharp-rise-in-americans-with-college-degrees.html?pagewanted=all&_r=0.

The Resilience Project, http://resilience.stanford.edu.

Rettner, Rachael. "'Helicopter' Parents Have Neurotic Kids," *NBCNews*, June 3, 2010. http://www.nbcnews.com/id/37493795/ns/health-childrens_health/t/helicopter-parents-have-neurotic-kids/#.VAJMg2RdXyc.

Rich, Motoko. "As Apprentices in the Classroom, Teachers Learn What Works," *New York Times*, October 10, 2014. http://www.nytimes.com/2014/10/11/us/as-apprentices-in-classroom-teachers-learn-what-works.html?module=Search&mabReward=rel bias%3Aw%2C%7B%221%22%3A%22RI%3A8%22%7D&_r=0.

Ripley, Amanda. *The Smartest Kids in the World: And How They Got That Way* (New York: Simon & Schuster, 2013).

Rizzo, Kathryn M., Holly H. Schiffrin, and Miriam Liss, "Insight into the Parenthood Paradox: Mental Health Outcomes of Intensive Mothering." *Journal of Child and Family Studies* (5), July 22, 2013.

Robinson, Sir Ken. "How Schools Kill Creativity," TED2006. http://www.ted.com/talks/ken_robinson_says_schools_kill_creativity.

Rochman, Bonnie. "Mother Is Best? Why 'Intensive Parenting' Makes Moms More Depressed," *Time*, August 7, 2012. http://healthland.time.com/2012/08/07/mother-is-best-why-intensive-parenting-makes-moms-more-depressed/

Roiphe, Katie. *In Praise of Messy Lives* (New York: The Dial Press, 2012).

Rosenfeld, Alvin, and Nicole Wise. *The Over-Scheduled Child: Avoiding the Hyper-Parenting Trap* (New York: St. Martin's Griffin, 2000).

Rosin, Hanna. "The Overprotected Kid," *The Atlantic*, April 2014. http://www.theatlantic.com/features/archive/2014/03/hey-parents-leave-those-kids-alone/358631/.

Rutherford, Markella B. *Adult Supervision Required: Private Freedoms and Public Constraints for Parents and Children* (New Brunswick, N.J.: Rutgers University Press, 2011).

———. "Children's Autonomy and Responsibility: An Analysis of Childrearing Advice." *Qualitative Sociology*, Volume 32, Issue 4 (December 2009): 337–53.

Sack, Kevin. "The 2000 Campaign: THE FAMILY; Timeouts for a Son's Football Games," *New York Times*, October 22, 2000. http://www.nytimes.com/2000/10/22/us/the-2000-campaign-the-family-timeouts-for-a-son-s-football-games.html.

Sapolsky, Robert M. *Why Zebras Don't Get Ulcers: A Guide to Stress, Stress-Related Diseases, and Coping* (New York: W. H. Freeman & Co., 1995).

Schiffrin, H., et al., "Helping or Hovering? The Effects of Helicopter Parenting on College Students' Well-Being." *Journal of Child and Family Studies* (2013).

Schulte, Brigid. *Overwhelmed: Work, Love, and Play When No One Has the Time* (New York: Sarah Crichton Books, 2014).

Schuman, Rebecca. "Bard's Better Admissions Application," *Slate*, June 6, 2014. http://www.slate.com/articles/life/education/2014/06/the_bard_admissions_exam_four_essays_no_common_application.html.

Schwartz, Barry. *The Paradox of Choice: Why More Is Less* (New York: Ecco, 2003).

"Self-Efficacy in Children," *AboutKidsHealth* (Toronto, Canada: The Hospital for Sick Children, August 30, 2012).

Seligman, Martin. *Authentic Happiness: Using the New Positive Psychology to Realize Your Potential for Lasting Fulfillment* (New York: Free Press, 2002).

Senior, Jennifer. *All Joy and No Fun: The Paradox of Modern Parenting* (New York: Ecco, 2014).
———. "For Parents, Happiness Is a Very High Bar." TED2014, March 2014. http://www .ted.com/talks/jennifer_senior_for_parents_happiness_is_a_very_high_bar.
Shellenbarger, Sue. "On the Virtues of Making Your Children Do the Dishes." *Wall Street Journal*, August 27, 2008, http://online.wsj.com/news/articles/SB121978677837474177.
Sher, Barbara, and Barbara Smith. *I Could Do Anything if I Only Knew What It Was: How to Discover What You Really Want and How to Get It* (New York: Delacorte Press, 1994).
"Should Parents Let their Kids Take More Risks?" *PBS Newshour*. May 9, 2014. http: //www.pbs.org/newshour/bb/parents-let-kids-take-risks/.
Shute, Nancy. "Neurologists Warn Against ADHD Drugs to Help Kids Study." *Your Health*. *NPR*. org. March 14, 2013. http://www.npr.org/blogs/health/2013/03/13 /174193454/neurologists-warn-against-adhd-drugs-to-help-kids-study.
Sims, Peter. "The Montessori Mafia," *Wall Street Journal*, April 5, 2011. http://blogs.wsj .com/ideas-market/2011/04/05/the-montessori-mafia/.
Skenazy, Lenore. "Crime Statistics." http://www.freerangekids.com/crime-statistics/.
———. *Free Range Kids: How to Raise Safe, Self-Reliant Children (Without Going Nuts with Worry)*. (San Francisco: Jossey-Bass, 2009).
Smith, Patricia. "Pitch In! Getting Your Kids to Help with Chores," *Education.com*, March 5, 2009. http://www.education.com/magazine/article/Pitch_Getting_Your _Kids_Help/.
Sobel, Dava. "Work Habits in Childhood Found to Predict Adult Well-Being." *New York Times*, November 10, 1981. http://www.nytimes.com/1981/11/10/science/work -habits-in-childhood-found-to-predict-adult-well-being.html.
Somers, Patricia, and Jim Settle. "The Helicopter Parent (Part 2): International Arrivals and Departures." *College and University* 86, No. 2 (2010).
———. "The Helicopter Parent: Research Toward a Typology." *College and University* 86, no. 1 (2010).
Spector, Dina. "The Sports Illustrated Swimsuit Issue: A $1 Billion Empire," *Business Insider*, February 12, 2013. http://www.businessinsider.com/business-facts-about -the-sports-illustrated-swimsuit-issue-2013-2.
Starkman, Ruth. "Private College Admissions Consultants: Does Your Child Need One?" *Huffington Post*, July 22, 2013. http://www.huffingtonpost.com/ruth-starkman /private-college-admissions-consulting_b_3625632.html.
Sternberg, R. J., & The Rainbow Project Collaborators. "The Rainbow Project: Enhancing the SAT through assessments of analytical, practical and creative skills." *Intelligence* 34 (4) (2006).
Stevens, Mitchell L. *Creating a Class: College Admissions and the Education of Elites* (Cambridge, Mass.: Harvard University Press, 2007).
Stone, Rena. Talk presented at annual fundraiser for Aspire Public Schools, San Francisco, California, May 20, 2014.
Strauss, Valerie. "Homework: An Unnecessary Evil? . . . Surprising Findings from New Research," *Washington Post*, November 26, 2012. http://www.washingtonpost.com /blogs/answer-sheet/wp/2012/11/26/homework-an-unnecessary-evil-surprising -findings-from-new-research/.
———. "Homework Hurts High-Achieving Students, Study Says," *Washington Post*, March 13, 2014. http://www.washingtonpost.com/blogs/answer-sheet/wp/2014/03 /13/homework-hurts-high-achieving-students-study-says/.

StrengthsFinder https://www.gallupstrengthscenter.com/.

Stuart, Annie. "Divide and Conquer Household Chores," *WebMD*, http://www.webmd.com/parenting/features/chores-for-children.

"Study: Most College Students Lack Skills," *USA Today*, January 19, 2006. http://usatoday30.usatoday.com/news/education/2006-01-19-college-tasks_x.htm.

Thacker, Lloyd. *College Unranked: Ending the College Admissions Frenzy* (Cambridge, Mass.: Harvard University Press, 2005).

Thompson, Derek. "Who's Had the Worst Recession: Boomers, Millennials, or Gen-Xers?" *The Atlantic*, September 13, 2011. http://www.theatlantic.com/business/archive/2011/09/whos-had-the-worst-recession-boomers-millennials-or-gen-xers/245056/.

Tolle, Eckhart. *A New Earth: Awakening to Your Life's Purpose* (an Oprah Selection). (New York: Penguin, 2005).

Tordella, Susan. *Raising Able: How Chores Nurture Grit and Self-Discipline in Children* (CreateSpace Independent Publishing Platform. (Boston, Mass.: Tordella, 2012).

Tough, Paul. *How Children Succeed: Grit, Curiosity, and the Hidden Power of Character* (Boston, Mass.: Houghton Mifflin Harcourt, 2012).

UN General Assembly, Convention on the Rights of the Child. November 20, 1989. United Nations, Treaty Series, Vol. 1577, Article 31.

Vaillant, George. *Triumphs of Experience: The Men of the Harvard Grant Study* (Cambridge, Mass.: Belknap Press, 2012).

Van Petten, Vanessa. "10 Qualities of Teacup Parenting: Is Your Kid Too Fragile?" *RadicalParenting.com*. June 19, 2008. http://www.radicalparenting.com/2008/06/19/10-qualities-of-teacup-parenting-is-your-kid-too-fragile/.

Waldman, Ayelet. *Bad Mother: A Chronicle of Maternal Crimes, Minor Calamities, and Occasional Moments of Grace* (New York: Doubleday, 2009).

Walton, Alice G. "New Playgrounds Are Safe—And That's Why Nobody Uses Them," February 1, 2012. http://www.theatlantic.com/health/archive/2012/02/new-playgrounds-are-safe-and-thats-why-nobody-uses-them/252108/.

Warner, Judith. *Perfect Madness: Motherhood in the Age of Anxiety* (New York: Riverhead Books, 2005).

Wartzman, Rick. "Some Words of Wisdom from Peter Drucker to My Daughter," *Time*, May 7, 2014. http://time.com/89695/some-words-of-wisdom-from-peter-drucker-to-my-daughter/.

Webley, Kayla. "As College Applications Rise, So Does Indecision." *Time*, May 1, 2013. http://nation.time.com/2013/05/01/as-college-applications-rise-so-does-indecision/.

Weissman, M. M., et al., "Offspring of Depressed Parents: 20 Years Later," *The American Journal of Psychiatry*" 163 (6) (July 2006): 1001–8.

"Why Are There So Many Youth Baseball-Throwing Injuries?" (Royal Oak, Mich.: Beaumont Health System, June 14, 2013). http://www.beaumont.edu/press/news-stories/2013/6/why-are-there-so-many-youth-baseball-throwing-injuries/.

Wood, James. "Parental Intrusiveness and Children's Separation Anxiety in a Clinical Sample," *Child Psychiatry & Human Development* 37 (1) (Fall 2006): 73–87.

Wu, Frank. "Everything My Asian Immigrant Parents Taught Me Turns Out to Be Wrong." *Huffington Post*, April 28, 2014. http://www.huffingtonpost.com/frank-h-wu/everything-my-asian-immig_b_5227102.html.

Zhao, Yong. "Be Careful What You Wish For," *Education Week*, October 3, 2013. http://blogs.edweek.org/edweek/international_perspectives/2013/10/be_careful_what_you_wish_for.html?cmp=SOC-SHR-TW.

ACKNOWLEDGMENTS

Writing this book has been a personal journey—part quest, part adventure, part dream—supported by numerous humans who accompanied me, shone a light for me, or moved obstacles out of my path, without whom the book would not exist.

Thanks to the strangers and friends who believed in the concept and pushed and pulled me toward conceptualizing it, creating it, and completing it. To the *Chicago Tribune* for publishing my first piece on overparenting in 2005. To Challenge Success cofounders Denise Pope, Madeline Levine, and Jim Lobdell for providing early platforms for me to speak on my perspective. To author Daniel Pink, who in 2010 heard me talk about the harm of overparenting at a Challenge Success event and encouraged me to move from the short form of essays and speeches to writing a book. To Denise Pope and Madeline Levine again for encouraging me to write. To my former history professor and Stanford colleague Jack Rakove, who in 2012 stopped me while walking the Dish and offered to introduce me to his agent, Donald Lamm. To Donald Lamm, for mentoring me through the process of writing a book proposal, and in particular for that day in Summer 2013 when I was ready to hang up the proposal after numerous rejections, for saying "I'm going to pretend I didn't hear that." To my former Stanford colleague Rob Reich for introducing me to Bill Deresiewicz, and to author Natalie Baszile. To Natalie Baszile for introducing me to her agent

Kimberly Witherspoon. To Kimberly Witherspoon and Allison Hunter at InkWell Management for preparing the proposal for auction, and for their thoughtful omnipresence since. To Barbara Jones, Maggie Richards, and Pat Eisemann at Henry Holt and Company for sharing my vision of what was possible. And to Barbara Jones again for kind and close shepherding through the writing and revisions process, and for masterful editing.

Thanks to the people who helped me write the book. To my research team: Khushboo Bansal, Anne Evered, Leigh Marshall, Katey Mulfinger, and Kyra Vargas, led by the intrepid Amanda Wilson Bergado, who made sure I had what I needed and who managed an ever-growing number of details. To Cynthia Chen for inspiring me about her concept of Zen Parenting at the TED conference in 2012 and for keeping me focused philosophically. To my friend Megan Maxwell for finding each new relevant article before I'd even woken up. To my instructors at California College of the Arts in whose courses I workshopped the proposal and manuscript: Judith Serin, Dodie Bellamy, Caroline Goodwin, and Faith Adiele, and to Tom Barbash, Donna de la Perrière, and Gloria Frym for taking me under their wing and pushing me forward again. To Faith's 2014 creative nonfiction workshop: Jennifer Goldsmith, Zane Hawley, Felicia Hayes, Analee Lapreziosa, Candice Meierdick, Alyssa Montantes, Nelson Rivera, and Patrick Newson for great feedback. To Danna Breen for her cottage in Portola Valley, which became my impromptu writer's retreat in Spring 2014. To Enerspace Palo Alto for providing a place to revise in Summer and Fall 2014. To the Maybell Way Writer's Collective for your feedback and encouragement. To Carole Sams Hoemeke (Atlanta), Mia Jackson (Dallas), Justina Chen (Seattle), and Tara Koslov (northern Virginia) for hosting focus groups in their homes, and to the over 150 interviewees nationwide—millennials, parents, educators, employers, mentors, psychologists, researchers, authors, and writers—whose perspective illuminated and strengthened my own.

Thanks to the tens of thousands of Stanford undergraduates who made deaning the best job ever, who forced me to care about this topic, and who continue to inspire me with their stories of personal growth and their efforts to lead meaningful and fulfilling lives.

Thanks to the family and friends who provided moral support: My mother, Jean Lythcott, my in-laws Judith Haims, Bruce Haims, and Judy Jackson, my sister-in-law Emily Jackson, my aunt Wendy Haims Handler, and the family clan of Lythcotts, Haimses, Jacksons, Snookes, Forresters,

Williams, Averys, McDaniels, Wests, Scors, Handlers, Benders, and Kleins. To my children, Sawyer George and Avery Mia, for putting up with a very absent mother, for letting me tell their stories, and for accepting that no parent is perfect. To my father, George, whose memory has never been stronger, and my brother, Stephen, for showing me how to live a meaningful life in too short a time. To Jessica Armstrong, Koren Bakkegard, Jo Boaler, Susie Brubaker-Cole, Wendy Cook, Deb Gruenfeld, Laura Harrison, Diane Hunter, Brandon Jackson, Stuart Kaplan, Kathleen Long, Jody Nyberg, Victoria Osman, Stacy Parson, Jazmin Quill, Nicole Sanchez, Luke Taylor, Nora Toomey, Miranda Tuttle, and Elaine Wilhelm, for their friendship and support during this period. To my coach and friend Maryellen Myers for walking beside me through this stage of my life. And finally, to my beloved life partner, Dan Lythcott-Haims, for loving me no matter what, for believing in every dream I've ever had, for holding our family life together while I was writing, and for making me long to be home.

INDEX

ABOUT THE AUTHOR

Julie Lythcott-Haims served as dean of freshmen and undergraduate advising at Stanford University, where she received the Dinkelspiel Award for her contributions to the undergraduate experience. She holds a BA from Stanford University, a JD from Harvard Law School, and an MFA in writing from California College of the Arts. She is a member of the San Francisco Writers' Grotto, and resides in the Bay Area with her husband, their two teenagers, and her mother.

howtoraiseanadult.com
@raiseanadult
facebook.com/HowToRaiseAnAdult

1. For better or worse, eighteen is not the magical age at which a child becomes an adult; adulthood is more than just a number. So what *does* it mean to be an adult? On page 145, Lythcott-Haims offers a response to this question with the help of Professor William Damon, who states that "an adult social role is one that is intrinsically not about *you*."
Do you agree or disagree with this definition? How would you define adulthood?

2. As Lythcott-Haims discusses in her introduction, parenting styles, values, and methodologies in the United States have changed through the years and between generations. Does (or will) your parenting style differ from that of your own parents? In your lifetime, have you noticed a broader shift in the ways we, as a culture, think about and practice parenting?

Discussion Questions

3. In the twenty-first century, technology influences nearly every facet of our lives, including the ways in which we parent. On page 14, Lythcott-Haims presents the following examples of how technology has affected parent–child relationships: "Take, for example, the mother of a Beverly Hills high schooler who insisted her son text her hourly on his way to and from a beach outing with friends.... Or the Stanford parent who contacted the university to say he thought his daughter was missing because he hadn't heard from her in over a day." How does technology play a role in the way you parent (or plan to parent)? Is the ability to be in constant contact a blessing or a curse?

4. As parents, it pains us to see our kids get hurt, or fail, or face any variety of disappointment. But Lythcott-Haims argues that the experience of failure is key to building resilience in children and young adults. To what extent, and in what ways, is failure a necessary crucible for growth? At what point, if any, should parents intervene to prevent struggle?

5. Developmental psychologists generally agree that there are four types of parenting: authoritative, permissive/indulgent, neglectful, and authoritarian. These types are diagrammed on a Cartesian chart on page 146. If your parenting style were a plot point on this chart, where do you think it would fall? Has its position changed over time?

St. Martin's
Griffin

6. There are numerous examples throughout *How to Raise an Adult* of parents who become exceedingly involved in their children's schoolwork and responsibilities—sometimes through college and even beyond, into their children's professional careers. Is it ever appropriate or acceptable for parents to assist their children with schoolwork? College applications? The job search?

7. On pages 81 to 83, Lythcott-Haims proposes a checklist of life skills that any self-sufficient eighteen-year-old should be able to exhibit. Do you agree with the contents of this list? Are there skills or behaviors that you think should be added to or removed from the list?

8. On pages 166 to 174, Lythcott-Haims describes a four-step strategy for teaching life skills: 1) first we do it *for* you, 2) then we do it *with* you, 3) then we *watch you* do it, and 4) then *you do it* completely *independently*. She acknowledges that the third and fourth steps are often the most difficult for parents to carry out, and require an enormous leap of faith. In your experience, why is it hard for parents to stand back? What are the fears and hopes involved, and how can a parent mitigate them?

9. When Lythcott-Haims talks with high school students about the "checklisted childhood," and the mental health problems that can result from it, the students ask her to pass along requests to their parents, such as: 1) "Please stop comparing me to my sibling/peers"; 2) "Don't say 'Just do your best,' then when I come up short say I could have done better"; 3) "Please stop worrying about every little thing"; and 4) "I know you're just trying to help, but please let me handle it." To what extent is it possible for parents to encourage effort and achievement without harming their child's development of autonomy, risking their children's mental health, and/or fueling the "brand-name brouhaha," as Lythcott-Haims calls it on page 248?

10. As discussed in Part 4 of the book, overparenting not only negatively affects our children, but also often places undue strain on parents themselves. How does your parenting style affect your stress levels and your sense of self?